CHILE

Political Economy of Urban Development

Harvard Studies in International Development

Reforming Economic Systems in Developing Countries
edited by Dwight H. Perkins and Michael Roemer, 1991

Markets in Developing Countries: Parallel, Fragmented, and Black
edited by Michael Roemer and Christine Jones, 1991*

Progress with Profits: The Development of Rural Banking in Indonesia
Richard Patten and Jay K. Rosengard, 1991*

Green Markets: The Economics of Sustainable Development
Theodore Panayotou, 1993*

The Challenge of Reform in Indochina
edited by Börje Ljunggren, 1993

Asia and Africa: Legacies and Opportunities in Development
edited by David L. Lindauer and Michael Roemer, 1994*

Macroeconomic Policy and Adjustment in Korea, 1970–1990
Stephan Haggard, Richard N. Cooper, Susan M. Collins, Choongsoo Kim, and Sung-Tae Ro, 1994

Building Private Pension Systems: A Handbook
Yves Guérard and Glenn Jenkins*

Green Taxes and Incentive Policies: An International Perspective (Sector Study Number 11)
Glenn Jenkins and Ranjit Lamech*

Framing Questions, Constructing Answers: Linking Research with Education Policy for Developing Countries
Noel F. McGinn and Allison M. Borden, 1995

Industrialization and the State: The Korean Heavy and Chemical Industry Drive
Joseph J. Stern, Ji-Hong Kim, Dwight H. Perkins, and Jung-Ho Yoo, 1995

Moving to Market: Restructuring Transport in the Former Soviet Union
John S. Strong and John R. Meyer, 1996

Economic Recovery in The Gambia: Insights for Adjustment in Sub-Saharan Africa
edited by Malcolm McPherson and Steven Radelet, 1996

The Strains of Economic Growth: Labor Unrest and Social Dissatisfaction in Korea
David L. Lindauer, Jong-Gie Kim, Joung-Woo Lee, Hy-Spo Lim, Jae-Young Son, and Ezra F. Vogel, 1997

Between a Swamp and a Hard Place: Developmental Challenges in Remote Rural Africa
David C. Cole and Richard Huntington, 1997

Getting Good Government: Capacity Building in the Public Sectors of Developing Countries
edited by Merilee S. Grindle, 1997

Assisting Development in a Changing World: The Harvard Institute for International Development, 1980–1995
edited by Dwight H. Perkins, Richard Pagett, Michael Roemer, Donald R. Snodgrass, and Joseph J. Stern, 1997

Environment and Development in a Resource-Rich Economy: Malaysia under the New Economic Policy
Jeffrey R. Vincent, Rozali Mohamed Ali, and Associates, 1997

The New Missionaries: Memoirs of a Foreign Adviser in Less-Developed Countries
Richard D. Mallon, 2000

Development Encounters: Sites of Participation and Knowledge
edited by Pauline Peters, 2000

Economic Development in Central America: Volume I—Growth and Internationalization
edited by Felipe Larraín B., 2001

Environment for Growth in Central America: Environmental Management for Sustainability and Competitiveness
edited by Theodore Panayotou, 2001

Legal Reform in Central America: Dispute Resolution and Property Systems
Martha A. Field and William W. Fisher III, 2001

---

*published jointly by the International Center for Economic Growth

CHILE

Political Economy of Urban Development

Edited by

Edward L. Glaeser and John R. Meyer

John F. Kennedy School of Government
HARVARD UNIVERSITY
CAMBRIDGE, MASSACHUSETTS

DISTRIBUTED BY HARVARD UNIVERSITY PRESS

Published by the John F. Kennedy School of Government

Distributed by Harvard University Press

Editorial Management: Gillian Charters
Cover Design: Schafer/LaCasse Design
Text Design and Production: Northeastern Graphic Services, Inc.

CIP data available from the Library of Congress

ISBN: 0-674-00256-3

Printed in the United States of America

Contents

Acknowledgements

The inspiration, and much of the funding, for this project came from Forestal Valparaiso, an international conglomerate with interests in urban development in Chile. The leaders of Forestal (and its parent banking group, Cruz Blanca or Cruzat Group) have had long-term concerns about how to eliminate distortions that cause over-development of certain geographic areas while other regions lay, perhaps inefficiently, underdeveloped. The basic question they sought to answer was: How does a society design an optimal policy for urban development?

Forestal's involvement was further fostered by a continuing interest in Chile and a desire to develop better economic policies wherever possible. For example, the Cruzat Group had earlier played an important role in researching Chile's widely acclaimed and copied pension reforms. Their interests also were fostered by the purely academic interests of its management. Juan Braun Llora, the Forestal senior economist who was the direct liaison with the research project, received his Ph.D. at Harvard in 1993, writing on internal migration and economic growth. Juan Braun Llora contributed a great deal of his own ideas and knowledge to the project. Much of the early focus came from conversations between Professor Glaeser and Braun Llora at Harvard. Juan Braun, president of Forestal Valparaiso, had also been a doctoral student at Harvard. Manuel Cruzar (CEO of Cruz Blanca) has had a long-term interest in urban policy and economics and received doctorates from both Harvard and the University of Chicago. All three of these men contributed materially to the intellectual as well as to the financial well being of this project. The unusually academic focus of this privately funded project owes much to the unusually academic nature of these three businessmen.

The first stage of the project involved a report (written by Glaeser) on the basic microeconomics of urban development, an essay that touched on all of the topics that appear as separate chapters in this book. Chapter 2 is largely a condensed version of that first report. Glaeser's goal in that first phase essay was to present in one place the microeconomics of designing more efficient urban policies.

To give more substance and tangibility to the concepts developed during the first phase; a second phase was launched to study the specifics of urban development in Chile. After much discussion, this second phase was organized around specific sectors of urban policy concern: the environment, transportation, housing, infrastructure, and social policies (mainly welfare and education). Specialists in each of these topics were recruited to report on the Chilean experience in each of these sectors. Also, as part of the second phase, all the principal researchers involved in the project made at least one trip to Chile. These were filled with interviews and explorations into the availability and content of data sources. The goals were to get an impressionistic sense of the economic institutions at work in Chile and to acquire needed data. Preparing these data involved not only the authors (and their research assistants) but also members of Forestal Valpaiso and the government of Chile. Specific assistance is acknowledged independently in each chapter, but the project owes an overall debt of gratitude to Anna Maria Sanchez at Forestal Valparaiso, who contributed a great deal of time and enthusiasm. She provided much of the coordination and intelligence needed to transmit data from Chilean sources to researchers' offices at American universities.

Phase two of the project was carried out under the auspices of the Harvard Institute for International Development (HIID). The director of HIID at that time was Professor Dwight Perkins. His help in organizing and initiating the project was indispensable and is gratefully acknowledged. Douglas Keare, then the director of urban studies at HIID, contributed both intellectually and organizationally to the effort.

Several people have contributed at a staff level. Among those helping with the research effort are Alberto Ades and Ana Maria Pavez.

Finally, there is always one staff person who makes sure all the pieces are brought together. In this case it was Paula Holmes Carr, who not only provided vital help but also remained cheerful throughout.

John R. Meyer
Edward L. Glaeser

1

Urban Development: The Benefits and Costs of Agglomeration

JOHN R. MEYER AND EDWARD L. GLAESER[1]

Introduction

Cities are important and becoming ever more so. The World Bank, in a policy paper on "Urban Policy and Economic Development: An Agenda for the 1990s" has stated the case as follows:[2]

> Rapid demographic growth will add 600 million people to cities and towns in developing countries during the 1990s, about two-thirds of their expected total population increase. Of the world's twenty-one megacities, which will expand to have more than ten million people, seventeen will be in developing countries. With urban economic activities making up an increasing share of GDP in all countries, the productivity of the urban economy will heavily influence economic growth.

The importance of cities is not limited to the developing world. In developed or industrialized countries a higher percentage of people live in cities than in the developing world, roughly 75% versus 50%. Moreover, while cities in the industrialized world are not growing as rapidly as those in developing countries, they were no longer in decline in the last decade of the twentieth century as they were earlier in that century. As the *Economist* has observed:[3]

> The populations of the west's largest cities, in long-term decline for half a century, stopped falling in the 1980s and are now starting to rise again. The populations of London and Paris both dropped by nearly 20% in the 1970s. Yet in the

1. With considerable assistance from all the contributors to this volume, particularly Denise DiPasquale and Joan Cummings.

2. International Bank for Reconstruction and Development; Washington, D.C., 1991.

3. *Survey of Cities* (London: July 29, 1995).

1980s that of Paris leveled out, that of London recovered from 6.7 million in 1981 to around 7 million in 1991.

Even in the U.S., where suburban flight and urban deconcentration have been most marked, urban populations have at least stabilized, and in many instances grown.

All this suggests that the political economy of urban development is a matter of legitimate policy concern all over the world; better understanding of what makes cities grow or decline would be helpful. The ultimate goal, as the World Bank pointed out, would be a better understanding of how to improve the productivity of urban areas and their contribution to overall economic growth. While the study of one medium-sized urban area (Santiago) in one rapidly developing country (Chile) obviously cannot answer all of these questions, it can at least make a beginning. Furthermore, few, if any, major urban areas have received as much intensive attention and analysis as Santiago, or experienced more demographic growth and change.

In 1992, Chile had a population of 13,231,803, according to the Chilean census. Chile's population grew nearly 50% from 1970 to 1992, with most of the growth between 1970 and 1982. Average annual growth slowed from 2.3% during that period to 1.7% in the following decade. The 50% increase represented over 4 million new inhabitants; still, Chile's growth figures are slightly lower than figures for many other South American countries.[4]

Chile is divided administratively into thirteen regions. Metropolitana (R.M.), de Valparaiso (V), and del Bio-bio (VIII) are by far the largest regions (containing Chile's three main cities Santiago, Valparaiso, and Concepcion, respectively). In 1992, together they accounted for over 62% of the country's population, with R.M. having 39%. The regional share of the country's population has remained relatively constant since 1970, during South America's significant population growth. While the R.M. grew at a rate slightly faster than average, it did not grow as fast as several other regions, particularly the smaller regions of Tarapaca (I) in the north, which nearly doubled in size, and Aisen (XI) in the south.

Employment growth in Chile has been more dramatic than population growth. While the country's population grew nearly 17% from 1982 to 1992, its employment grew over 42% from 1984 to 1992. Regions I, V, and the R.M. had the largest employment growth. The official unemployment rates reveal a remarkable improvement in the employment scenario countrywide. The offi-

4. For example, from 1965 to 1980, Peru's average annual population growth rate was 2.8%, Bolivia's was 2.5% and Brazil's was 2.4%. In the following period, 1980–1989, Peru's growth rate fell to 2.3%, Bolivia's went to 2.7%, and Brazil's was 2.2% (World Bank 1992, Table 26).

cial national unemployment rate dropped from 19.4% in 1982 to 5.3% by 1989.[5] This dramatic improvement was realized across all regions.

Chile has quite a high level of urbanization, even in comparison to other developing countries. In 1990, 36% of the country's population lived in Santiago (World Bank 1992). By 1992, the World Bank listed Chile's urbanization level at 86%, sixth among the fifty-two nations in the survey (Singapore, Hong Kong, Israel, the U.K. and the Netherlands came in higher).[6]

An intellectual underpinning for studying the political economy of urban development can be supplied by the basic theorems of welfare economics. These imply, and strongly argue, that independent agents free to make market-driven decisions generally will arrive at an optimal *economic* outcome. Of course, this optimal economic outcome may or may not be construed as optimal in other dimensions, say social or political.

The bulk of this book is devoted to understanding (1) why the conditions of the real world sometimes deviate from the conditions needed to guarantee that free markets create first-best or optimal economic outcomes; and (2) how government involvement can help reduce, but also create, distortions in real-world urban development. Specifically, problems that are either inherent in a market economy or created by government policy are examined to determine what causes undesirable patterns of urban development and to ask what society can do to fix those problems. The focus is on the particular problems of urban and regional development, and especially on those forces causing a misallocation of resources across geographic space.

As discussed at length in Chapter 2, externalities (e.g., pollution or congestion) arising as an unintended by-product of economic activity are major forms of spatial distortions that would exist in a market economy (even without the presence of government). Externalities are a problem for free markets because they involve situations in which one agent's decisions influence another agent's satisfactions or productivity (e.g., an industry produces smog that makes it harder for all to breathe).

But beyond externalities, and present even in well-functioning market economies, are litanies of government-created problems that also can distort urban development patterns. These government-created spatial distortions can include everything from higher tax levels (without higher service levels) being associated with a particular region, to limited availability of govern-

5. The 19.4% unemployment rate is considered an understatement of actual unemployment because the government provided two large employment programs, PEM and POJH, from 1975 to 1988. For example, if workers under these programs are counted as unemployed in 1982, the unemployment rate was 26.4%.

6. World Bank, 1993.

ment services in regions that would happily pay for more such services, to mispricing of basic government-provided goods.

Chapter 2 also investigates some possible solutions to these problems. For example, the usual solutions suggested for externalities, taxing polluters and contracting between affected parties, are discussed at length. Also addressed are ways to solve the problems created by government-induced distortions. Chapter 2 thus provides a very general set of terms and ideas for use throughout the remaining chapters. By contrast, the remaining chapters mainly focus on *particular* aspects of urban development as experienced in one particular country, Chile. An attempt is made to survey the considerations that might condition urban development, ranging from pollution to infrastructure to various public services. The particular selection of topics, of course, reflects Santiago's particular configuration of problems and concerns.

Chapter 3, authored by Matthew Kahn (Tufts University) and Suzi Kerr (Motu Economic Research, New Zealand) is devoted to determining the actual monetary damages created by different pollution sources in Chile, with particular emphasis on air pollution. Kahn and Kerr produce projections of future pollution costs for Santiago that are higher than most predecessor estimates. Only part of the increase comes from projected increases in pollution levels (that occur in spite of toughened regulations). A large part is also a consequence of projected increases in Chilean income (thus causing, for example, higher costs from lost work days).

Santiago's air quality is particularly vulnerable because of its location in a mountain valley. Activities and policies that would cause fairly minor damage in some cities can be nearly catastrophic in Santiago. In addition, Chile as a whole, and Santiago in particular, may be entering an extended period of rapid economic growth. This poses dangers in terms of rapid changes in transport patterns, housing development, and industrial production that could be irreversible. Growth also provides an excellent opportunity to alter incentives to avoid polluting activities at a time when changes would be relatively painless and could have significant benefits in the future. For example, the health damages from a given level of air pollution reflect the amount of exposure suffered by people particularly sensitive or vulnerable to such pollution, e.g. asthmatics, the elderly, and others with breathing problems. If people do not know the nature and severity of the pollution problem, they cannot take proper actions to protect themselves. If people had better information (were fully aware of the level of risk they faced on different days in different areas) and were aware of the possible measures they could take to protect themselves, the overall damage from pollution could be reduced. Various policies are therefore proposed by Kahn and Kerr for better informing people about the damage of pollution.

Externalities also result in pollution costs that are higher in Santiago than is socially optimal. The externalities largely arise because people do not bear the full costs of their actions. Correctly pricing activities that cause pollution not only would be economically efficient but also would put the cost of controlling pollution on the people who cause pollution and have the power to remedy it.

In Chapter 4, Amrita G. Daniere (University of Toronto) and José A. Gomez-Ibanez (Harvard University) assess how the provision of water, sewage, solid waste disposal, and telecommunications services might influence urban development patterns in Chile. They conjecture that these services might distort the location decisions of Chilean households and businesses in two ways. First, *access* to these services may be restricted or limited in certain areas; for example, new water or telephone connections may not be available at any price to land developers at some locations because the water and telephone agencies lack the capacity or resources. Second, the *prices* charged for these services may not reflect the true costs of providing them at certain locations.

Analyses by Daniere and Gomez-Ibanez suggest that water and sewage provision in Chile are more likely to cause locational distortions than solid waste disposal or telecommunications. In particular, water and sewage services are probably underpriced by about US $70 per household per year in the Santiago metropolitan area (because of the health problems caused by the failure to provide sewage treatment of water subsequently used to irrigate crops) and by US $20 to US $40 per household per year in cities of the extreme north and south (due to the failure to charge the full costs of supplying water). Although charges for solid waste disposal are typically far below social costs throughout Chile, the subsidy probably amounts to only about US $12 to US $14 per household per year in most Chilean cities. Local telephone charges are probably slightly above cost in larger urban areas and below costs in rural areas, but the degree of overcharge or subsidy is difficult to determine. The effect of the rural telephone subsidy also has been partially offset, at least until recently, by limited access to new lines in rural areas. Moreover, emerging technologies and intensifying competition are likely to further reduce any location distortions caused by telephone service.

In Chapter 5, John F. Kain (Harvard University and the University of Texas, Dallas) and Zhi Liu (World Bank) begin by observing that pre-1970 regulations of intercity and urban transportation reduced Chilean incomes and growth rates. They found it much more difficult to be certain about the impacts of these policies on the location of economic activity within Chile, but offer the guarded opinion that these regulations disadvantaged outlying regions more than the nation's urban centers, particularly Santiago.

Kain's and Liu's analyses also suggest that the Chilean Government has under-invested in roads, both intercity and urban. The net effect of this under-investment may have been to encourage more growth in the country's large metropolitan areas, and especially its largest, Santiago, than would otherwise have occurred. The effects on national income and growth, moreover, are quite clear-cut: under-investment in roads almost certainly has acted as a drag on the nation's competitiveness and its internal development. The analysis also suggests that between 1970 and 1980 the government spent too much to subsidize state-owned railways and the government-owned intercity bus company. The nation's welfare would have been improved if these funds had been used for other public purposes with a higher rate of return (including the improvement of the nation's highway system).

The government's investment in Santiago's metro also has some fairly unambiguous implications for Chile's regional development pattern. Because the entire capital costs for the first metro lines were paid by the central government, the net impact on regional economic activity of building the metro was almost certainly to encourage the growth of employment, income, and population in Santiago and to slow growth in other regions.

The impact of the metro on the spatial arrangement of activity within Greater Santiago was to create higher residential dispersal and lower residential densities. In addition, the metro may have encouraged many office activities (that might have otherwise remained in the central area) to relocate at a series of office sub-centers located along the first metro line. The metro facilitated a dispersal of central area functions by providing fast and reliable connections to government offices and private firms in the old center.

Kain's and Liu's analyses also confirm the results of other studies concerning the strong link between per capita or household income and private vehicle ownership and use. Assuming that Chilean incomes continue to grow, rapid increases in car ownership and use are almost certain. Kain and Liu find, like Kahn and Kerr, that without fees for road and street use that reflect the long-run social costs of providing additional capacity, this increased car ownership and use will cause serious problems, including congestion and pollution. Rising congestion, in turn, will increase average trip times and the per trip cost of providing road-based public transport services.

There are essentially two approaches to trying to prevent congestion from degrading public transport speeds and reliability. The first, which is practiced in varying degrees in cities throughout the world, uses a variety of physical restrictions on private car use to protect public transport from growing automobile-induced congestion. At best, these various administrative and physical restraints are usually less than fully efficient; that is, second best in an economic sense.

Congestion pricing is (at least in concept) a far preferable and potentially "first best" or fully efficient approach. At least two congestion-pricing schemes deserve close attention. The first is a simple cordon-pricing scheme, where a cordon around the central business district is demarcated, and a special fee is charged for entry. A scheme such as this has been operating in Singapore since the 1970s. The second would be a sophisticated electronic road pricing system that would allow pricing to be applied over a much wider area and would allow prices to be varied by facility, location, and time of day.

Experience in many parts of the world suggests that serious congestion in the core of large cities tends to accentuate population and employment decentralization. Thus, a failure to deal effectively with congestion could result in a more extended and lower density metropolitan region than would occur if congestion pricing were introduced to achieve more optimal use of urban streets and roads. In general, congestion is a hugely inefficient way of allocating street space. Implementation of congestion pricing could reduce the cost of trip making for most highway users and make an urban region more attractive to households and businesses.

In Chapter 6, Jean Cummings and Denise DiPasquale[7] explore the spatial implications of housing policy in Chile. The Chilean Government intervenes extensively in the housing market. While virtually all residential construction is carried out by the private sector, about 42% of residential construction in the 1980s and 1990s had direct public subsidy. If mortgage subsidies and other indirect subsidies are considered, the government is involved in an even larger portion of the housing market. All government programs focus exclusively on homeownership, which has resulted in Chilean cities typically having a home ownership level of over 80%, one of the highest in the world.

Cummings and DiPasquale evaluate two types of distortions: interregional and intraregional. For the interregional, they examine the extent to which government policy influences the location decisions of households among the thirteen official regions of the country. For the distribution of publicly subsidized units and expenditures on these units, the interregional spatial distortions seem to be quite small. To the extent that there are distortions, more resources tend to be allocated to remote areas of the country, at the extreme north and south, than to urban areas. In fact, this might be quite intentional, motivated by political and national security considerations. Regional disparities are more apparent in the distribution of housing vouchers; specifically, the Santiago region received a notably higher share of both vouchers and voucher expenditures than would be expected from its share of

7. The authors conducted this research at Harvard University and are now at City Research, a Boston consulting group.

the country's population or from governmental estimates of regional housing deficits.

Serious intraregional spatial distortions are generated, however, mainly by government housing policies within Greater Santiago. As in many countries, subsidized housing in Santiago is often located on the fringes of the city where land is cheapest. Generally, housing policymakers consider only the construction and land costs when siting subsidized housing. But these are not the total costs of locating the poor at fringe locations. Other costs can be quite significant, including those for commuting, infrastructure, congestion, and pollution.

Cummings and DiPasquale attempt to quantify some of these other costs. Specifically, they present rough estimates of what the magnitude of these other costs must be in order to justify the higher land costs associated with more central locations for subsidized units. They find that in many cases recognition of these other costs would make more central locations viable. This suggests, in turn, that the selection criteria for siting subsidized housing should consider total costs rather than just land and construction costs. Furthermore, government should consider moving away from very large projects at the periphery to smaller, scattered, and more centrally located sites for publicly subsidized construction.

Cummings and DiPasquale also suggest that the exclusive focus of government programs on homeownership should be reconsidered. This focus results in relatively large subsidies being provided to some households with others receiving none. In addition, the emphasis on homeownership may limit household mobility, since moving costs are usually considered to be higher for owners than for renters.

In Chapter 7, Edward Glaeser (Harvard University) examines the spatial distortions created by social welfare programs and how to structure political institutions to eliminate these distortions. Specifically, he addresses those externalities that are created by the government providing at varied locations (1) different levels of social welfare programs and (2) inappropriate levels of government services. The role of social welfare programs in creating spatial distortions is obvious both in the United States and across the less developed world. In the United States, for example, spatial distortions can arise when central cities vote redistributive programs that then induce the wealthy to migrate to politically independent suburbs. In the less developed world, countries (such as Chile in the 1960s) often provide increased social welfare programs (such as health or education) in the capital city. As a result, the poor of the country migrate to the capital. These spatial distortions can have strongly adverse repercussions.

The major empirical findings in Chapter 7 are that while social welfare programs may have created large spatial distortions in Chile in the past, they do not seem to do so today. Primary schooling, secondary schooling, and health expenditures all seem essentially space neutral in Chile. There is some evidence that university-level education creates a spatial distortion favoring Santiago, but if the universities in the capital are truly centers of excellence, and therefore more productive than universities elsewhere in Chile, this allocation may be efficient. In short, while government transfers may have fueled Santiago's rise in the 1960s or earlier, subsequent reforms have eliminated most of the spatial distortions that once existed in those programs.

Chile, nevertheless, has shown a remarkably slow development of small cities for a country with its rate of economic development. A simple comparison with similar economies elsewhere reveals that Chile seems to have a major problem creating new smaller cities. This failure of urban entrepreneurship may be the result of the centralization of authority within Santiago. New locations do not have the latitude to provide the services needed and therefore do not encourage growth. This lack of liberty or free opportunity at the local level seems to be one of the primary spatial distortions now operating in Chile.

In order to look at this phenomenon more rigorously, a comparison was made of the formation of new cities in Chile and California. The state of California has had less economic growth (starting from a higher base) than Chile over the past twenty years. Its population has grown slightly more in percentage terms. However, in many respects the two areas are at least geographically comparable. They also represent extremes in local government. California is a highly decentralized environment where small cites have an easy time incorporating themselves and funding future growth.

Tables 1-1 and 1-2 show the growth of new cities in California and Chile between 1970 and 1990. The cutoff point for cities in each area was 100,000 inhabitants. *Comuna* was used as the definition of city for Chile, except for Santiago, which was counted as a single city. In 1990 Chile had twelve cities with more than 100,000 inhabitants. California had twenty such cities. Between 1970 and 1990 Chile acquired eight more cities with more than 100,000 inhabitants. This number might seem large, except that over the same period California acquired more than twenty more cities with over 100,000 inhabitants. California had a spectacular rise in the production of new communities; Chile was stagnant. While this evidence does not illustrate any direct social costs of the Chilean system, it does show that the way local government is treated, and the amount of freedom it is allowed may make a great deal of difference to the development of new cities.

In sum, a prima facie case can be made that areas of Chile remain undeveloped because of difficulties in organizing new communities. Customarily,

Table 1-1. Growth of New Cities in California, 1970–1990

Year	Number of cities
1970	20
1980	26
1990	44

Notes: A city is defined as a place with a population of 100,000 or more. In 1970, East Los Angeles and Los Angeles are considered one city.
Source: U.S. County and City Data Book, 1972
U.S. County and City Data Book, 1988
U.S. County and City Data Book, 1994

communities grow because of entrepreneurship on the part of citizens (or firms) or on the part of local governments who try to lure citizens away from pre-existing population centers. Chapter 8 discusses the theoretical issues involved in decentralization and in the creation of healthy, vibrant local authorities.

Of course, spatial distortions coming from the availability and financing of redistributional programs often have political roots. Under the U.S. Constitution, small localities have the authority to redistribute wealth between their citizens. Consequently, once a particular interest group in a community has acquired political power, it will often vote high levels of redistribution that benefit its particular group and, in the process, cause spatial distortions. Similarly, in less than perfectly stable political communities, agents living near the centers of power can acquire exceptional political influence because their unhappiness might threaten the security of the nation's leaders. To quell that unhappiness, wealth is given to the residents of the capital city and spatial distortions occur.

In general, proper public policies will not persist (or will not be implemented adequately) unless the political institutions are designed to provide politicians with the right incentives to implement those policies. Designing the right response to problems in urban development does not just mean

Table 1-2. Growth of New Cities in Chile, 1970–1990

Year	Number of cities
1970	12
1980	13
1990	20

Source: U.N. Demographic Yearbook, 1976
U.N. Demographic Yearbook, 1980
U.N. Demographic Yearbook, 1991

identifying the right amount to tax one city versus another. It also means defining the right division of authority and responsibility between local and national authorities and determining the right ways to set the incentives for local and national government officials. Chapter 8 outlines some basic concepts for thinking about these questions.

The primary recommendation is that transfers should be space neutral. Localities may be effective at determining the right level of government services, but they may also respond to local electoral pressure too easily and therefore not provide the right level of redistribution of wealth. In addition, concerns about equality are the primary reason for income redistribution, which suggest that income equality should be measured across the nation as a whole and not across the *comuna* or local region.

The goals of this study are to provide more insights on both the Chilean case and urban development internationally. Much of the impetus for a particular interest in Santiago is that it is an example of the striking concentration of a country's population in a single city. As already noted, 36% of Chile's population was concentrated in Santiago by 1990. In South America generally, six out of eleven countries have more than 25% of their population living in a single city. The remaining five all have between 12% and 17% of their population in their largest city.[8]

This level of concentration is not necessarily inefficient. There are many good reasons why agents come together in a single city. Still, an interest in concentration is stimulated because (1) this level of concentration is surprisingly common; (2) such levels are a relatively new feature of the urban landscape of the world; and (3) the roots of this concentration seem often to lie in forces beyond the pursuit of economic efficiency.

Intriguingly, and by contrast, the population of European nations (and also European North America as well, Canada and the United States) is rarely concentrated in a single city. Rome, at its height, was no more than 2% of the empire's population.[9] London never reached more than 11% of England's population before the twentieth century; Paris had an even lower share of the French population. By contrast, when Buenos Aires rose to prominence at the turn of the twentieth century, it had 20% of Argentina's population and was the largest city in the Americas south of the Hudson at that time.

The connection between urban concentration and the rise of urbanization in newly industrialized countries suggests still another reason why urban concentration is a naturally interesting topic for policy analysis. In many

8. Ades and Glaeser, 1995.
9. Ibid.

countries the population seems to congregate in a single city for non-economic reasons. Ades and Glaeser (1995) assemble a large amount of data that suggests that while economic forces do play a sizable role in supporting urban growth, political forces also play an important part in creating the most concentrated countries.

If urban concentration has political, not economic, roots then it is more likely that this concentration is inefficient. For example, if a large amount of the populace lives in the capital city because political expression is difficult or impossible in the hinterland, then we are more likely to believe that this concentration is sub optimal and merits a strong policy response. By contrast, if concentration were the outcome of economic forces creating positive rewards from urban concentration, then it may be more dangerous to tamper with the status quo. Cities may have formed for political reasons, but if they remained relatively large because of efficiency considerations, then anti-concentration policies could have large social costs.

Therefore, one goal of this study is to provide a framework for analyzing the efficiency of urban concentration. Evidence on the political roots of urban size is interesting, but hardly enough to establish proper public policy. This study strives to provide a framework for asking if an urban structure is efficient and, if the answer is no, then suggesting how to design an urban development policy to reduce inefficiencies.

References

Ades, Alberto F; Glaeser, Edward L. (1995) "Trade and Circuses: Explaining Urban Giants" 1995. *The Quarterly Journal of Economics.* Vol. 110 (1). (February). p 195–227.

The Economist. 1995. *Survey of Cities. The Economist*: London. (July 29).

International Bank for Reconstruction and Development. 1991. "Urban Policy and Economic Development: An Agenda for the 1990s." World Bank Working Paper. World Bank: Washington, DC.

World Bank. 1992. World Development Indicators.

World Bank. 1993. World Development Indicators.

2

Market and Policy Failures in Urban Development

EDWARD L. GLAESER

The economic approach to urban development does not ask: "Is the central city too big?" Rather, economists ask: "What factors distort people's decisions about where to live?" Admittedly the second question is less likely to grab attention. But the question's modesty makes it answerable and within the reach of the economist and the policy maker. We also know, thanks to a basic theorem of welfare economics, that if we eliminate the distortions, the city size that will result will be the "right" size for society.[1]

In short, once distortions have been corrected, then the free market works fairly well.[2] The policy presumption of this approach always will be in favor of free decisions made without government interference. In the case of urban development, a presumption for private initiative means assuming that when individuals make their own decisions about where to live, those decisions will be good ones both for themselves and for society. Only when private costs differ from social costs might individuals make the wrong decisions.[3] The ultimate goal of urban public policy, therefore, should be to bring those social costs closer to private costs; and when this is impossible, the goal should be to use other policy instruments to encourage better decisions.

Social costs may not equal private costs for several reasons. Some of these deviations may be inherent in almost any economy. For example, the largest sets of fundamental distortions are known as externalities. Externalities exist

1. Specifically, this statement is the Second Welfare theorem, which is explained below.

2. A fuller explanation is the Second Welfare theorem, which is explained below.

3. We are incorporating all social benefits into the costs function, so we would say that social costs of pollution clean up may be much lower than the private costs because the social costs include all of the social benefits. We are particularly interested in marginal social costs.

when an individual takes an action that affects others who are not involved in the decision-making process and the individual does not take into account the effect he is having on those others. Examples include pollution (where a polluter affects the whole community) or congestion (where each new driver slows traffic for everyone else). Other related private sector problems include public goods (which are a form of externality) where, when a good is provided, everyone benefits at no added cost (the most obvious example being military protection).

Another set of private distortions can occur when there are large fixed costs to production or other technologies that lead to increasing returns. Unfortunately, the history of government ownership and intervention to correct for the existence of increasing returns suggests that the solutions to this problem commonly have been more problematic than the problem itself. Government itself often can create distortions. Examples of government-induced distortions can be arranged into three groups: (1) governments charge either too much or too little for a particular service or a particular right; (2) governments provide the wrong level of service; and (3) governments are inefficient and provide the correct level of service incorrectly. Examples of the first type of distortion range from free government utilities or water to location-based taxes that are not connected to the social cost of living in different locations. The second type of distortion occurs when utilities are only provided in one area of the country even though citizens, or potential citizens, of another area would like the service and are willing to pay for that service. The third type of distortion is the simplest but possibly the most important. All these distortions create different types of suboptimal behavior. Charging below cost for electricity encourages too much electricity usage. Income- based taxation induces people to work less. Providing public services primarily in a central city disproportionately draws population to that city.

Not all governmentally induced distortions are avoidable. Income tax induces people to earn less income but concerns for equity may make it necessary for the rich to pay more taxes per person than the poor. Some services are just too difficult to provide in such a way that prices exactly reflect costs. In those cases, we either may have to live with the distortion or try to limit its effect in other ways.

Cities and Pareto Optimality

The standard criterion in almost all of economics (because it avoids value judgments about who is more or less important to serve in society) is Pareto optimality. For a situation to be Pareto optimal, it must be true that no one's situation can be improved without causing someone else harm. Obviously, the Pareto criterion is not all-inclusive. Policymakers might have other concerns. For example, Pareto optimality does not consider equity issues that might matter to some observers. Pareto optimality has nothing to say about human rights concerns. To the extent that economists address such concerns, they discuss them by such terms as "moral goals."

When society is not optimal in the Pareto sense, everyone can be made better off (or at least not worse off) by a policy improvement. The basic condition required for Pareto optimality is that when agents make decisions they set:

MARGINAL BENEFIT = MARGINAL SOCIAL COST

This equality just says that for choices to be optimal, the marginal benefit an agent receives from consuming a good (or from moving to a city or from polluting a river) is equal to the marginal cost that society pays for his or her action.

Economic thought relies critically on a series of theorems proven in the 1950s by Arrow, Debreu, and McKenzie. The most important of these for our purposes is the Second Welfare theorem that tells us that the free market will produce Pareto optimal outcomes if certain conditions also exist. The most important of these conditions are that (1) no externalities exist and (2) production sets are convex. Nonconvexity, generally, just means that producer returns are always constant or diminishing. When a producer can make 0 widgets for $0 and 1000 widgets for $1000, but not 500 widgets for $500, then a nonconvexity occurs. Fixed costs cause problems for free markets because marginal cost pricing (which is a requirement for efficiency) leads to firms losing money (since they don't cover their fixed costs).

When an agent's consumption or production decisions affects his neighbors (positively or negatively), externalities exist and this welfare theorem no longer holds. Similarly, when production sets are nonconvex, which might be because of the presence of fixed costs in production, the welfare theorem is also violated and the free market will not necessarily lead to a social optimum. The goal of public policy should be to create a system in which externalities are eliminated as cheaply and efficiently as possible, so that everyone bears the social costs of their actions. Similarly, solutions should be sought for the nonconvexities problems without resorting, if at all possible, to the failed practices of government ownership and extreme regulation. Since our focus is explicitly spatial, we are interested in discovering when location decisions of firms or workers are wrong and in suggesting how these decisions can be corrected.

Externalities, Pollution, and Congestion

To make our discussion of pollution externalities more tangible, consider a manufacturer of steel who faces a fixed world price for steel. Following usual economic reasoning we know that the steel producer will produce to the point where his marginal cost of steel is equal to the price he receives on the world market.

However, if steel production creates smoke that creates some kind of physical damage (disease, unpleasantness, etc.) to the surrounding area, then the true social cost will be higher that the actual costs faced by the producer. The producer will be creating steel to the point where the price equals the marginal private costs, while he should be producing only to the point where the price equals the much higher marginal social costs. Therefore, too much steel is produced at that location, resulting in too much pollution.

Pollution is an externality with a spatial dimension. Generally, the costs of pollution are local not global (with some exceptions, e.g. global warming, see Kahn, 1994). As a result, the location decisions of firms may create uneconomic levels of pollution, even if the firms produce the same amount of pollution no matter where they locate.

To illustrate, imagine that our steel producer either can locate in densely populated Santiago or in sparsely populated Patagonia. The producer will trade off the private advantages of Santiago (proximity to distribution centers, consumers, and intermediate goods suppliers) with the private advantages of Patagonia (cheap land). No consideration of the costs of pollution will enter into his private calculations.

However, the costs of pollution are likely to be very different in Santiago from Patagonia. First, Santiago suffers from thermal inversion and pollution tends to build up in the city. Second, Santiago has an already high existing level of pollutants and there is some evidence of an increasing marginal cost of pollution, i.e. the costs of each added unit of pollution rise with the total level of pollution. Third, Santiago is densely populated and its larger population leads to greater social costs from pollution, i.e. more people are exposed to polluted air.

Because of the differences in pollution costs between Santiago and Patagonia, society might benefit if the steel producer chooses Patagonia as his location. However, he will not take those social benefits into account in his location decision. The presence of pollution externalities that differ across space can lead to locational distortions, including overly large cities (see Tolley, 1974 and Chapter 3).

Of course, pollution is only one form of negative externality. In the urban context, externalities originating from congestion are even more ubiquitous.

The problem of congestion occurs because each new person coming to a city increases the costs (such as travel time) of all the existing residents of that city. This type of congestion externality may operate because of cars crowding roads or workers crowding streets. The negative costs of congestion also may occur because people simply enjoy relatively open spaces and dislike living with too many other people.

Congestion is a very clear spatial externality. The location decision determines the size of the crowds in each space. Returning to the choice between Santiago and Patagonia, there are many reasons why workers may prefer Santiago (such as higher wages), and may weigh those benefits against the benefits of Patagonia (perhaps cheaper housing), but workers will not take into account the congestion costs of their location decision. The greater population of Santiago means that more people may be affected adversely by any additional congestion. By contrast, the addition of one more person to Patagonia may be irrelevant or even pleasant.

Of course, people still pay the costs of these externalities. They wait for hours because of congestion and breath with difficulty because of pollution. In a sense, these costs act as partial checks on the level of spatial distortions. However, substantial market failure can occur because (and this is also true more generally) people making locational decisions generally confront the average costs of an area not the marginal cost created by their presence, and it is marginal cost that counts. Paying the average cost is not enough in many cases. The same basic intuition occurs, with the consequences reversed, when the externalities are positive (e.g. individuals enjoy living near well-educated neighbors). Indeed, the very existence of cities suggests that for many people positive spillovers may be at least as important as negative spillovers.

Network Externalities and Coordination Failures

A particularly important form of externality for locational economics is the network externality (as discussed in Chapters 4, 5, and 7). Examples of this type of externality range from roads to telecommunications to schooling. When networks are expanded, everyone who is currently tied into the network benefits since they can potentially use the extension. These externalities may justify government subsidization of network expansion. These externalities may also require homogenization of facilities (i.e. the same gauge of rail lines or roads of the same strength or the same type of vaccinations or the same type of schooling).

For this type of externality, often the government's only role may be in suggesting a common technology that will serve as a focal point. In other words, if there is a need for a single strength of road for a nationwide network, the government may be able to help the society greatly without excessively intervening. The government can try to insist that roads be built to a single uniform standard and convince all builders to coordinate their activities. This role as coordinator hopefully will involve minor quantities of regulation and emphasize the persuasive role of government rather than its regulatory role. However, it is worth emphasizing that in many cases this role also can be taken by a private firm.

Coordination failures often can occur in situations without network externalities as well. Consider a situation where agents are crammed into a single city and would all like to form a second city. However no agent wants to strike out on his own, unsure of whether others will follow. It is unappealing to be the only person in the new city because the appeal of cities is the presence of other people. There are locational interdependencies across people.

In many countries, these locational interdependencies are used constructively by entrepreneurial governments or developers. The government can help in creating a focal point for the new location so that agents can reasonably expect that any new city will have only one location or, more plausibly, the absence of local government autonomy may mean that no local governments exist that could initiate the process of forming a new city. The presence of these coordination failures does not mean that the government should intervene, but it does mean that other problems due to governmental mistakes may be exacerbated.

Public Goods

Public goods involve goods that can be provided at the same cost for everyone. The concept was formalized by Samuelson (1956), who argued that there are some goods that could provide the same service to one million people as to one person. The classic example is national defense. An army protects a large population from foreign invaders as easily as a small population. Technically a public good must be both nonrival (i.e. one individual's use of the good does not lessen the amount of the good available to others) and non-excludable (i.e. everyone living in the relevant area enjoys the benefits).

The combination of nonrivalry and nonexcludability makes private provision of these services extremely difficult. Imagine a private contractor trying to provide military protection. People would be very unwilling to pay for military protection since their payments are simultaneously protecting everyone else. Individuals would rather enjoy a "free ride," and let others pay.

Local public goods are services that meet the above definition and provide benefits only to residents of a small locality. It is possible that police work is a local public good. If a police car is in the neighborhood, it deters crime for all the citizens living in the neighborhood. However, even police services have rival and excludable elements. If someone lives in a block patrolled by a cop, that person automatically receives protection. But when one block is patrolled, it limits the police presence available elsewhere. In this manner, police protection has elements that are rival. Police protection is also excludable on a "beat" level. A whole block can be excluded from protection even if, given a level of protection on a block, an individual must receive the same amount of protection. In reality, many goods (like police) fall between being a pure public good and a pure private good (that is completely rival and completely excludable).

Furthermore, while police protection may be a local public good, schooling, health, or sanitation are clearly not public goods. These goods are all rival—spending $100 to educate one child, means having $100 less to spend educating another. They are also excludable. It is easy to deny citizens access to schools, hospitals, and water. So while the public goods explanation is important, it is not relevant for all services.

There are, though, at least two reasons why local public goods may create spatial distortions. First, local public goods are generally charged at something akin to their average cost. So if the total cost of a local public good is one million pesos and the city has 100,000 persons, then each person must pay 10 pesos in taxes to pay for this local public good. Each new migrant to the city must pay 10 pesos in taxes to pay for this good and everyone else's taxes go down infinitesimally. However, the new resident has not actually increased costs to the city at all. After all, there is no less of the good provided to everyone else and they all benefit from the lower taxes. As a result, the new migrant creates social benefits when he pays these taxes. In this case, from an efficiency standpoint, there will be too few residents of the community. There are ways of solving this problem (e.g. local public goods are paid for by the whole nation), but these solutions are generally much worse than the problem because unless residents pay for their own goods, they will make poor choices about which goods to purchase. In general, it makes sense to be aware of the possible spatial distortions created by public goods but not necessarily to attempt to fix these distortions.

Additionally, spatial distortions occur because some local public goods are relatively under-provided. For example, policing is a local public good that is almost always provided publicly. However, there are often differences in the level of policing across space that come from differences in choices made by governments, and these choices often are not dictated by efficiency considerations.

Increasing Returns

Where increasing returns occur, marginal costs are below average, and marginal cost pricing (the only statistically efficient form of pricing) will not allow firms or governments to make profits or break even on their projects. However, if firms or governments charge more than marginal cost, there is a distortion where too little of the good is produced and consumed.

Situations with increasing returns are often referred to as natural monopolies, where productive efficiency requires that supply be provided by a single large firm rather than by many small producers. However, a single firm operating without competitors will tend to produce too little and charge too much (again violating the optimality condition). Therefore, single firm production often seems to justify regulation (to avoid monopoly prices) and subsidization since efficient pricing occurs at marginal cost that will be below average cost (see Marshall, 1890). In theory, the public interest then will be served by the government setting prices equal to marginal costs so as to maximize the total social welfare.

Decisions to subsidize an industry or government service so that pricing can occur below average costs must be adopted warily. Subsidization can eliminate the discipline created by the need to make profits or break even; government-owned firms have a long history of masking losses due to inefficiency by claiming that the losses are a result of efficiently pricing at below average costs. Pricing below average costs also requires cross-subsidization that will, in turn, require taxation that almost always brings social costs of its own. Finally, when investment decisions are being made, government cross-subsidization may well distort initial investment decisions. These factors suggest that below-average cost pricing may be dangerous at best.

Several possible spatial distortions also are commonly associated with increasing returns. As with local public goods, when the government either regulates or nationalizes industries because of increasing returns, the possibility for spatial distortions abounds. When increasing returns exist so that marginal costs are below average costs, and when consumers are charged the average costs (which they may be if firms are to break even, or if governments are not to run a deficit), then too few people will choose to locate where they can use the good. For example, consider a government water purification plant where local taxes pay for the huge fixed costs. Migrants who consider coming to this city will note that their taxes include the full average cost of the plant. Of course, the social cost of their migration is only the marginal cost of producing the water that they will use. Since that marginal cost is below the average cost they will not migrate when efficiency suggests that they should migrate. Spatial distortions are thus created by the absence of marginal cost pricing. This type of issue arises in particular in Chapter 4 when discussing public infrastructure.

Government-Induced Distortions

Among the most common market failures created by government is simple mispricing. These distortions are of three types: (1) situations where the governments should charge the marginal social cost for a service but does not; (2) situations in which the government has decided for other policy reasons not to charge the marginal social cost of a service; and (3) situations in which the government has unwittingly charged more than the marginal social cost for a service.

The connection of mispricing to spatial distortions is quite straightforward. Most government services are tied to a specific location. Locations often differ in their access to water, policing, education, or many other services. Mispricing means that when people make locational decisions they will either pay too much or too little for living in a particular area. So, for example, consider a desert region where the government pumps in water but does not charge for this expensive public service. Migrants to this desert will not internalize the costs that their migration imposes on the government and will tend to over-migrate to this area.

In general, politically powerful groups or areas may be able to force governments to provide them with underpriced services. Ades and Glaeser (1995) argue that it is just this that has created the huge concentrations of population in the capital cities of many developing countries.

Another form of mispricing that leads regularly to spatial distortions is the mispricing of transport costs. Since locating close together is a direct substitute for transportation between firms or between consumers and firms, it follows that when the price of transportation is too low, economic actors will not locate efficiently. For example, the extremely high gas taxes in Europe may be responsible for overconcentration of individuals in urban areas where they have access to public transportation. Correctly pricing transportation is particularly important for generating the right distribution of producers and consumers across space.

Locational distortions also may come from governments simply not providing the right level of services for a community. Private suppliers have advantages over governments in determining the right level of supply. Through the price mechanism, private suppliers receive quick signals about how much consumers are willing to pay, i.e., how much demand there is for a particular good. In addition, private suppliers lose money, and potentially even go bankrupt, if they consistently misgauge the amount of demand.

Frequently, citizens will claim that the government is providing too little of a service when what they mean is that the government is providing less of the service than they would like, given that the service is free. In economic terms, underproduction means that too little of the service is being provided relative to the demand for that service when the demanders are being charged the service's social cost. Again, the socially optimal level of a government service is being provided when the government provides the service to the point where the marginal benefit derived by consumers is equal to the marginal social cost of that service.

Governments, unfortunately, have consistently displayed an inability to assess consumer demand properly. Production in the former Soviet Union frequently resulted in too many undesired goods and insufficient goods that the populace actually wanted. In less extreme cases, governments throughout the world lack clear, consistent signals about what goods consumers actually want and how much consumers are willing to pay for those goods.

For locational decisions, the goal is not only to serve the current populace of a locality but also to provide the services that will be desired by future populations or by potential future generations. Private producers have enough problems gauging potential future demand; for public producers with less or no contact with the market and therefore less information, the problems in determining the right level of government services can be almost insurmountable.

An extreme form of government misprovision occurs when a government-supplied good is only being produced in one location. Agents will then move to the location where production occurs and will desert the other areas unless they can induce an increase in service production in those other areas. An obvious spatial distortion thus occurs. Furthermore the point about transportation's intimate connection with location again applies: in general, when transportation is over or undersupplied, populations will be too loosely or densely located. Agents will move apart to take advantage of overly abundant transportation or move together to make up for absent transportation infrastructure.

A particular form of this problem may occur when the government chooses to locate its activities in particular areas due to nonefficiency related criteria. Locating a military base or a state-sponsored university in some area may be politically expedient but still quite inefficient. This problem can be exacerbated if the base or the university generates large quantities of other related businesses that follow the government's "lead" to this particular location.

Solutions for Externalities

Standard theories of externalities suggest ways for the government to induce socially optimal location behavior. Without government intervention economic actors will set:

MARGINAL PRIVATE BENEFIT = MARGINAL PRIVATE COST.

However, when

MARGINAL PRIVATE COST + EXTERNALITY = MARGINAL SOCIAL COST,

the external effect causes a deviation between the benefits that agents receive when they make a choice and the costs that society bears from that choice. The most natural response to this perceived deviation is simply to impose a tax equal to the external effect so that agents set:

MARGINAL BENEFIT = MARGINAL PRIVATE COST + TAX,

where the tax has been set so that

TAX = MARGINAL SOCIAL COST – MARGINAL PRIVATE COST.

The key to optimal spatial policy is for this tax to differ across space so that firms pay costs that are proportional to area-specific pollution differences between marginal social and private costs.

Taxes are only one way to make people internalize the costs of their actions. For example, if the government issues quotas for pollution and makes those quotas tradable, then firms will face the choice of selling (or buying) a quota to pollute or not to pollute. Since the quotas are tradable, firms can either keep the quotas or sell them or buy more. In any case, the act of pollution imposes costs on the firm. By issuing the right number of quotas, the market price of the quota can be set so it is the same as the social cost of pollution. Quotas also can be auctioned off by a government that wants to receive revenues from the quotas. Of course, in order to be effective spatially, quotas that grant pollution rights must have an explicit spatial aspect to them. In other words, quotas must grant a right to pollute within a narrow geographic area. Unfortunately, this also narrows the market for these tradable quotas.

Perhaps the most intriguing economic idea about annihilating market failures is the Coase theorem. This argument (which won its creator a Nobel prize in 1991) steps back from the ornate theory of market failures and asks: Why can't the free market handle this problem? More precisely, Coase put together a series of conditions under which externalities (or market failures more generally) will be handled by the market. This reasoning led to his theorem that when (1) property rights are well established and (2) costs of bargaining and transactions are low, then the market outcome will be efficient. Moreover, the same outcome will occur, no matter to whom property rights are assigned, as long as there are no "income effects." The argument is essentially that the agents who are hurt by an externality will bribe the externality producer not to pollute and the amount of the bribe will exactly equal the social damage of the externality.

Coase's theorem is critical to thinking about when the free market can solve externalities. The first condition, the establishment of property rights, means that it must be obvious who owns what. For example, in the case of the air in the atmosphere, property rights are not well established because no individual or group of individuals has legal possession of the air. By contrast, in the case of privately owned land that is being polluted by a neighbor's dumping of hazardous waste nearby, property rights are clear. The second condition, low transaction costs, does not hold for externalities such as pollution or congestion where the damaged parties are extremely numerous. In these cases, the transactions costs seem enormous and it is hard to believe that the Coase theorem will lead to an efficient allocation of individuals over space.

Nevertheless, the Coase theorem offers a guide to policy. The Coasian method for solving the problems of externalities is to improve the definition of property rights and to lower transaction costs. Both of these steps are essentially legal or institutional reforms and are absolutely necessary for the market to function robustly without government intervention.

Solution to Government-Created Distortions

One way of eliminating or reducing problems due to governmental mispricing is privatization. Since private profits depend on efficiency, private firms have much stronger incentives to be efficient. Private firms frequently have better information about demand conditions and the costs of production. Private firms also are less likely to follow political motives and more likely to concentrate on efficient provision of the relevant service. Private firms are frequently better at adapting to new conditions. At the same time, there are sometimes costs to using private firms, especially in areas that feature externalities, increasing returns, or a "moral" dimension.

Still another method of improving governmental performance is decentralizing authority. The advantage of localization is that localities can compete for taxpayers. In a sense, the difference between localized control and centralized control is almost the same as the difference between a monopoly and a competitive industry.

Tiebout (1956) developed a model in which the quality and amount of government service would be decided at the local level by voters who would then pay with local property taxes for the service. Tiebout argued that under these assumptions there would be an efficient amount of each service provided in each community. Individuals unhappy with the amount of the service being provided in their community would move—in Tiebout's words they would "vote with their feet." In this manner the mobility of individuals can be used so that people face a menu of quantities and qualities of public service rather than set levels. Then, through migration across jurisdictions, each individual will obtain the amount of public service that they want. In this manner local government efficiency can be created.

However, localizing authority can lead to more heterogeneity across local governments and that can create, as well as eliminate, spatial distortions. For example, if one locality has a terrible government that has somehow managed to retain power, then businesses and people will leave that area. The bad government creates a distortion that moves people away. In a sense, it is efficient for them to leave the area because the bad government is similar to having a natural disaster and efficiency suggests that people should leave blighted areas. However, in another sense, in the absence of the artificial institution of government the area would still be populated and the distortion is inefficient. Ideally, localization should increase competition and efficiency and the likelihood of voters getting the right level of government services, so that spatial distortions will be reduced, not exacerbated, by localization of authority.

Conclusion

This chapter has dwelt on the theory of spatial distortions. It is impossible to tell if locations are too big or too small in the abstract. Alternatively, the economist asks if there are spatial distortions, i.e. forces that warp the location decision, such as externalities, government policy errors, public goods, and increasing returns. All of these will be discussed further in the following chapters. Various solutions for these problems (Pigovian taxes, tradable quotas, well-defined property rights, users fees, etc.) also will be explored, reappearing in various guises in the pages to come.

References

Ades, Alberto F; Glaeser, Edward L. 1995. "Trade and Circuses: Explaining Urban Giants." *The Quarterly Journal of Economics.* Vol. 110 (1). (February). p. 195–227.

Arrow, Kenneth and Tibor Scitovsky. 1969. *Readings in Welfare Economics.* London: Allen and Unwin.

Coase, Ronald H. 1988. *The Firm, the Market and the Law.* Chicago: University of Chicago Press.

Kahn, Matthew E. 1994. Growing Car Ownership in LDCs: The Impact on the Environment and Trade. *Columbia Journal of World Business.* Vol. 29 (4). (Winter) p. 12–19.

Marshall, Alfred. 1890. *Principles of Economics.* London: Macmillan.

Samuelson, Paul. 1956. "Social Indifference Curves." *Quarterly Journal of Economics.*

Tiebout, C. 1958. "A Pure Theory of Local Expenditures." *Journal of Political Economy* 64:416–424.

Tolley, G. 1974. "The Welfare Economics of City Bigness." *Journal of Urban Economics* 1.

3

The Causes and Consequences of Air Pollution in Santiago[1]

SUZI C. KERR AND MATTHEW E. KAHN

Santiago, like many other major cities in developing countries, has a serious air pollution problem. Recent health-based studies have quantified the per-capita costs of air pollution (Ostro 1994, Ostro et al. 1996). Research has not quantified the marginal pollution effects of development on the local populace.

Population migration does not simply redirect pollution damage from other cities to Santiago. The reduction in pollution damage to the city a migrant exits is generally less than the damage caused by Santiago's growth due to the capital's geography, population size, and its relatively high initial pollution levels.

A person moving to Santiago perceives high pollution levels but is unlikely to internalize the externality that her choices further degrade the local environment and raise total health costs. This chapter presents a methodology for quantifying the social marginal environmental costs of Santiago's growth and discusses numerous incentive policies to encourage citizens to face the social costs of their actions.

To further analyze the Santiago air pollution externality, this chapter begins by outlining Santiago's air pollution levels in the early 1990s and the sources of that pollution. To translate ambient air pollution levels into average cost estimates, we borrow health impact estimates from the epidemiology

1. We would like to thank Ricardo Katz, Juan Escudero, and Ana Maria Pavez for their help in our research in Chile. For scientific assistance, we thank Professor Daniel Jacob, Professor Bill Clark, Professor Douglas Dockery, David Maré, and Fiona Murray at Harvard University and Professor Greg MacRae at MIT. We thank the other members of the HIID project for helpful feedback. Any errors and omissions that remain are our responsibility.

literature to predict the excess morbidity and mortality caused by Santiago pollution. Given estimates of the average cost per capita caused by pollution, we sketch a framework for estimating the social marginal cost of economic growth within Santiago. The rest of the chapter addresses ways to design and implement policies to internalize the externality and thus move Santiago closer to an optimal level of air pollution.

Air Quality in Santiago—Background

Air quality is well recognized as a significant problem in Santiago. Table 3-1 compares the standards for various pollutants (both Chilean standards and US. Environmental Protection Agency standards) with the evidence that is available on Santiago's ambient air quality. Pollution patterns are discussed in detail in Préndez (1993).

The Chilean standard for PM10 (particulate matter with a diameter of less than 10 microns) is an annual arithmetic mean of 50 µg / m3 (micrograms per meter cubed).[2] The four central monitoring stations[3] all significantly exceeded this in every year between 1989–1992. The 24-hour standard is 150 $\mu g/m^3$. In 1989, at one of the four monitoring stations in central Santiago, 21% of yearly readings exceeded this. It was exceeded 28% of the time in 1990, 25% in 1991, and 34% in 1992. The total suspended particulate (TSP) standard also is seriously exceeded in every year. Santiago has a serious particulates problem.

The problem does not seem to be worsening over time. Data from the early 1990s shows a significant trend. Because the inversion layer tends to be lower in winter, particulate levels are much higher during the winter months. Particulates are higher when the temperature is higher (controlling for month) and when the wind and rainfall are lower. The lack of a trend across years suggests that, within Santiago, particulates per unit of economic activity must have fallen, because economic activity has continued to increase.

In addition to a high particulate level, Santiago also suffers high ozone levels. Table 3-2 documents Santiago's monthly mean ozone concentrations.

Unfortunately, Santiago ozone data are not directly comparable with the

2. The PM10 data come from the MACAM monitoring network and all the data were supplied by the Comisión de Descontaminación Metropolitana.

3. The four monitoring stations used are those with continuous monitoring equipment operating efficiently. They are all located in Santiago's center city.

Table 3-1. *Actual Air Quality in Santiago Compared to Standards*

Pollutant	Chilean Standard	Actual Air Quality by Year 1989	1990	1991	1992
TSP	75	227	218.3	209.8	
PM10	50	113.7	119.8	112.5	113.26
SO2	80	24.1	16	12.3	
NO2	100	43	51	43.8	
CO	9ppm (8hrs)	7	7.5	7	7

TSP is total suspended particulates. It is measured in micrograms per cubic meter and the standard is an annual geometric mean. PM10 is a subset of smaller particulate matter with a diameter less than 10 microns. PM10 is reported as an annual arithmetic mean. SO_2 is sulfur dioxide and its units are micrograms per cubic meter. It is reported as an annual arithmetic mean. NO_2 is nitrogen dioxide and its units are micrograms per meter cubed. CO is carbon monoxide and its units are measured in parts per million. Unfortunately, the data for CO is measured as the average of the monthly maximum reading and thus is not directly comparable to the standard.

U.S Clean Air Act ozone standard. In the United States, ozone levels are judged as not complying with Clean Air Act standards if the second highest yearly reading exceeds .12 parts per million. The monthly mean data presented in Table 3-2 are not directly comparable to this ozone standard, since that standard is based on an earlier statistic. To facilitate a comparison of Santiago's and U.S ozone levels, we borrow from a study by Henderson (1996). Using U.S. daily ozone data from 1977,1982, and 1987, Henderson constructs each monitoring station's average annual reading. Graphing the distribution

Table 3-2. *Ozone Monthly Mean[a]—hourly measure in 1992*

Month	Ozone (ppm)
January	.077
February	.068
March	.091
April	.073
May	.047
June	.038
July	.018
August	.037
September	.088
October	.082
November	.072
December	.680

[a]Data from Préndez 1993 p 134–136

of these annual means, he finds that the mode of this U.S distribution is only .03 parts per million. Since average monthly ozone in Santiago in 1990 was .063, Santiago's mean annual ozone level would place it at the 99th percentile of the U.S. mean annual ozone distribution. This comparison suggests that Santiago has very high ozone levels.

With respect to other air pollutants, NO_2 and SO_2 were both below the standard until 1991 (Table 3-1) but these measures may not be reliable. Carbon monoxide seems to be below the standard but again the data reported in Table 3-1 are averages of maximums, which may conceal some excesses of CO standards.

In summary, Santiago currently has a serious particulate problem and probably also exceeds acceptable (e.g. U.S.) ozone standards.[4] Given that Chile's economy has grown by over 5% annually during the past several years, and that cars are a major contributor to ambient ozone levels, there is reason to be concerned that Santiago's ozone problem will worsen over time.

A Sectoral Decomposition of Pollution Sources

Table 3-3 shows which sectors contribute most to Santiago's pollution levels.

Transport and related emissions play a key role in the production of NOx and VOCs, which are the precursors of ozone, contributing 85% and 69% respectively, but a lesser role in emissions of PM10 (small particles), contributing only 11%. This may understate their impact on ambient PM10.[5] The major contributor of PM10 is road dust. The composition of emissions particles from transport is different from those from road dust. PM10 created by transport tends to have a longer lifetime in the atmosphere. Unpaved roads tend to be on the periphery. There is very little evidence or information about road dust and the effectiveness of policies to address it.[6] It is interesting to note that buses, which are considered to be major sources of particulate emissions, are not a very important contributor to PM10 emissions. Starting in 1987, the United States Environmental Protection Agency switched from a particulate to a PM10 standard. This decision was based on health studies suggesting that

---

4. Ostro et al. (1996) report that in Santiago the ICAP Air Pollution Index was violated one hundred days in 1990, sixty-nine in 1991 and eighty-four in 1992 with extreme violations (above five times the standard) on seven days each in 1990 and 1991, and three days in 1992.

5. For a discussion of the composition of particulates in Santiago see Prendez (1993).

6. Eskeland (1994) p. 97

Table 3-3 *Santiago Emissions Inventory: Percentage Contributions*

Type of Emissions	*PM10*	*NO_x*	*VOCs*
Source			
Mobile Sources			
Cars	1.6	46.4	58.7
Taxis	.1	3.6	4.6
Buses	.3	20.1	2.9
Trucks	1.6	15.3	2.9
Subtotal	10.6	85.4	69.0
Point Sources			
Industrial processes	2.4	2.3	.04
Industrial boilers	10.8	10.3	.90
Heating boilers	1.4	.8	.05
Bakeries	.6	.2	.06
Subtotal	15.2	13.6	1.0
Group Sources			
Street dust	68.3	.2	
Residential wood burning	5.9	.8	
Subtotal	74.2	1.0	30.0[7]
Total	100.0	100.0	100.0

This table is derived from Table 3-3 p. 96 Eskeland (1994).

PM10 was a more serious health threat. While buses may be a major contributor to larger particulates, if such particles do not create large health problems then the externality caused by polluting buses may be lower than previously thought.

In contrast to transport, manufacturing plays a very small role in ozone formation (14% of NOx and 1% of VOCs), contributing 15% of PM10.[8] In 1988, 25.3% of Greater Santiago's employment was in the manufacturing sector, 7.9% in construction, 57.7% in services and 7.3% in transport, communications, and public utilities. In 1970, 28.1% of employment was in manufacturing, 6.5% in construction, 56.4% in services and 7.1% in transport. From 1960 to 1988, manufacturing's share declined from 31.6% to 25.3%. Given that Santiago's population has been growing, the share numbers suggest that the absolute level of manufacturing has grown over time, even as the sector's relative share declined.

7. This includes 14% that comes from evaporative losses from cars.

8. Because of the relative importance of transport and the paucity of information on road dust, also because point sources have been discussed elsewhere (O'Ryan, 1996), we focus on transport-related emissions in our later discussion of future externalities and policies.

Per-Capita Health Costs of Pollution in Santiago

Estimates of the per-capita costs of air pollution levels are necessary to gauge the economic magnitude of Santiago's air pollution problem. A two-step methodology is followed. In the first step, we translate particulate and ozone levels (see Tables 3-1 and 3-2) into "excess" morbidity and mortality in Santiago. In the second step, this increased morbidity and mortality is translated into a dollar cost estimate using estimates of Santiago citizens' value of time and value of life.

Epidemiological research has focused on how the health of citizens in developing countries is affected by air pollution. In a Chilean study completed by Ostro et al. (1996), they conclude that an extra ten units of PM10 above the U.S Clean Air Act Standard translates into a 1% increase in the population's mortality rate. Based on this estimate, and assuming that Santiago had a baseline mortality rate of 5.7 per thousand and a population of approximately 5.06 million, there were 1990 excess deaths due to Santiago's PM10 level.[9]

Exposure to particulates increases individual mortality and morbidity risk. To quantify the morbidity costs of particulates, we use evidence from a series of studies carried out in the Utah Valley, which is an area suffering winter episodes of high particulate pollution but low ozone, sulfur dioxide, and nitric oxide concentrations. Thus, with these data, it is possible to consider the effects of particulates alone. The studies showed that hospital admissions of children doubled in winters when the US PM10 standard was violated (Pope 1989, 1991). Acute morbidity leads to respiratory-related restricted activity days (RRADs) and work loss days (WLDs). It also leads to visits to emergency rooms, minor respiratory disease, and children's chronic cough.[10] Based on 1990 PM10 levels in Santiago, we predict that, on average, citizens in Santiago suffer 2.4 restricted activity days (RRAD) per year.

Santiago's ozone's morbidity costs can be calculated using estimates of the health consequences from Ostro's (1994) excellent review of the health/pollution literature. Ostro reports that a one part per hundred million reduction in average ozone levels lowers respiratory hospital admissions (RHA) per 100,000 people by 7.7 and lowers asthmatic symptoms by .68 per asthmatic. In addition, the level of respiratory symptoms per person fall by .55 and minor restrictions in activity per-capita fall by .34.The data reported in Table

---

9. The baseline mortality rate assumes that air pollution did not exceed the United States regulatory standard.

10. The dose response curve is drawn from work by Ostro (1987) and Chestnut and Rowe (1988).

3-2 indicate that Santiago's monthly ozone levels rarely average less than .07 parts per million. If sickness rates are a linear function of ozone, then Ostro's estimates can be used to estimate the health gains of eliminating Santiago's ozone problems. Given this assumption, eliminating all ozone would reduce respiratory hospital admissions by 2,724 per year for a metropolitan area with a population of 5.06 million people. While the ozone estimates suggest sizable health gains from ozone reductions, it is not straightforward to translate asthmatic symptoms, minor restrictions in activity, and hospital admissions into dollar losses.

Our cost estimates focus on particulates. To estimate the dollar health costs of air pollution, we combine the morbidity and mortality estimates of air pollution with estimates of individual value of time. To be conservative in our estimates, we use GNP per capita per day divided by two as our cost of experiencing a RRAD. To present one mortality cost estimate, we assume that individuals who die would have lived for twelve more years, and value this lost time at annual GNP per capita ($2070 in 1990).[11] We discount this by 5%, which leads to a one-time cost of $20,417 per excess death.[12]

Table 3-4 summarizes estimates of the dollar health cost of particulates in Santiago as being $14.72 per capita in 1990. This cost represented .71% of GNP per capita in 1990.[13] This estimate is predicated on very conservative estimates and a very low value of life.

Our cost estimates must be interpreted with caution for several reasons.[14] We know little about the Santiago population's investment in self-protection by such devices as staying inside on high pollution days.[15] The costs and bene-

11. Unfortunately, we do not have data on the average age at death for people who died from pollution exposure. Ideally, we would want to estimate a Chilean life expectancy model as a function of personal income and health habits and pollution exposure. Such a model would allow an estimate of the counter-factual of how much longer a Santiago citizen would expect to live if pollution were lower.

12. Ostro et al. (1996) use $45,000 per life in their health cost calculations. This larger number is generated by valuing a lost year at per-capita earnings not at per-capita GNP. Our cost per lost year of life is conservative relative to U.S compensating differential studies estimates of roughly four million dollars per life saved (Viscusi 1993). Braun (1990) presents another set of Santiago air pollution cost estimates.

13. It is important to note that recent World Bank publications indicate that our estimate of $2,070 may sharply underestimate Chile's GNP per capita in 1990.

14. The epidemiology literature relies on episodes of high particulate levels to estimate mortality but one high pollution episode is likely to kill the sickest people in the society. Thus, from observing the impact of a single high pollution episode, a researcher cannot answer the counter-factual: if another high pollution episode occurred, how many people would die? Clearly, the first episode's death rates provide an upper bound on mortality rate estimates.

15. A good reference that discusses issues of exposure in Mexico City is Fernández-Bremauntz (1993).

Table 3-4 Estimates of Particulate Costs in Santiago (1990 US $)

Pollutant Particulates	*1990*
Morbidity $ Per Capita	6.69
Mortality $ Per Capita	8.03
Total $ Cost Per Capita	14.72
Total $ Cost/GNP Per Capita	.71%
Total $ Cost	$74.48 m.

fits of this investment should be incorporated into the air pollution estimates. Our cost estimates only address health costs and ignore all other margins.[16] While the results in Table 3-4 and the estimated ozone health impacts must be interpreted cautiously, even our extremely conservative estimates indicate that air pollution in Santiago has serious cost consequences.

Economic Growth and Santiago's Pollution Externality

While it is important to document the average health costs caused by air pollution, such average costs do not provide information about the *marginal* environmental externality caused by the growth of Santiago's population and of its economy. Since Santiago is the largest city in Chile, people who move there are leaving a smaller city. Migration does not lead to a pollution "zero sum" game. When a person migrates to Santiago from another part of Chile, the pollution cost increase in Santiago is likely to be greater than the pollution cost reduction in the original location. Given Santiago's initial pollution levels, its geography, and its population size, additional population growth generally has larger pollution ramifications than if a citizen had moved to another Chilean city.

The marginal impact of migration on Santiago's environment depends on a migrant's choices relative to the average city incumbent. If the typical migrant is identical to the average person in the city, perhaps because their income and family structure are similar, then it is reasonable to assume that emissions will simply be scaled up per capita. Thus, if Santiago's population grows by 10%, emissions then would grow by 10%. Assuming that ambient pollution rises proportionately with emissions, pollution will rise proportionately with population growth. To illustrate with an externality calcula-

16. In addition to health benefits, reducing air pollution yields benefits for recreation, visibility, and ecology as well as reductions in damage to materials and agricultural productivity (Margulis 1992).

tion, we simply divide Santiago's 1990 PM10 level of 119 by its population stock of 5.06 million people. This yields the average person's contribution to the pollution level. Adding an extra person to this economy would scale up pollution by .0000235 units. To calculate the marginal health impact of this pollution increase we use the same particulate health data sources as used in the average health cost calculations. In Table 3-3, we reported that exposure to 119 micrograms per cubic meter of PM10 caused $14.72 dollars of health damage per capita. Including the new migrant, PM10 levels would now be 119.0000235. This slight increase in particulates will lead to an even larger percentage increase in per capita morbidity and mortality risk because the higher the initial pollution level, the more one's health is susceptible to pollution. Using the health estimates we reported above, we recalculate per-capita health costs caused by this higher level of pollution. Since pollution affects all citizens in Santiago, we multiply this incremental health damage by the size of the entire Santiago population. This calculation indicates that, given our assumptions, adding an extra "average" person to Santiago's population generates a particulate externality of $25.39. It is important to note that this represents an (upper bound) on the environmental costs of population migration because this migrant's origin is now less polluted. If the migrant's origin was a nonmetropolitan area, the environmental gains to that area are zero. Even if the migrant's origin were another Chilean city, the differences in Santiago's geography and population size relative to that of other cities implies that its environmental costs dwarf any environmental gains to the origin city.

It is useful to repeat the steps we follow to estimate the pollution externality. Population growth increases the emissions base that increases particulate levels. Given that the health production functions are nonlinear with respect to pollution, each individual's health is slightly worse due to the increased pollution. The externality caused by migration is the total costs imposed on other Santiago citizens not internalized by the migrant. This social marginal cost is calculated by adding up each individual's health damage caused by the additional pollution. Thus, this pollution externality is larger if there are more people in the city. The externality also would be larger if a person's health were very sensitive to small changes in pollution levels. Given that the externality's size depends on how much people are willing to pay not to be sick or be exposed to a higher probability of death, the externality will be larger if people place a greater value on such health costs. This is likely to be the case as per capita income grows because people are willing to pay more to preserve their health.

Under the assumption that the new migrant is identical to the average Santiago incumbent, and under the assumption that the mortality and morbidity estimates discussed above for PM10 are valid for the entire population, we predict that the aggregate of all Santiago citizens willing to pay to avoid the particulates caused by one more migrant is $25.39. To make a more precise prediction about the size of the externality would first require better estimates of the value of life and the ambient effects of ozone. In addition, it would require individual level data. With micro data, one could estimate which households (as indicated by demographic attributes such as age, education, and income) produce the greatest emissions levels as a byproduct of location and consumption choices. Such households would impose the greatest social costs on Santiago. For example, if new migrants are more likely to be younger, then they may make more transport demands than the older Santiago incumbents. This relative transport usage intensity could be incorporated in calculating the additional externality caused by growth. Future work also could take into account where the new migrant is likely to live in Santiago, where the new migrant will work, and what mode of commuting will be used.

Future work also could incorporate population differences in health outcomes with respect to population exposure. We are treating all Santiago citizens as if they had the same health production functions. Older people, children, people with pre-existing respiratory conditions, and smokers may be more susceptible to high pollution levels. A more disaggregated approach would allow for population health heterogeneity with respect to the marginal increase in sickness caused by pollution. A given increase in pollution would reduce each subgroup's health. To calculate the social reduction in health, one would add up each group's health loss weighted by its share of the population.

While migration to Santiago is probably the leading example of an activity where the social environmental costs would exceed the private costs, there are other spatial externalities that need to be examined. In the Appendix, we present a second externality scenario where we study the impact of locational choice within Santiago. The intuition is that a citizen who chooses to live on the outskirts of the city will impose higher environmental costs than a citizen who chooses to live near the center. If the citizen does not internalize these social costs, then this individual's private optimal choice will not match the social optimal choice. In particular, such citizens will live further from the center of the city than if the full costs of locational choice were internalized. This simulation is relevant for the discussion of optimal housing policy discussed in chapter 6.[17] It is important to note that this simulation assumes that

17. The simulation requires numerous assumptions including how many people ride in each bus, what are average vehicle emissions per mile of driving, how many fewer total miles would be driven if people live closer to the center of the city, and assumptions concerning the morbidity and mortality costs of particulate exposure. Given all of our assumptions, we find that moving one person one mile away from Santiago's Central Business District imposes an environmental social cost of 35 cents.

all Santiago citizens work in the Central Business District. If employment moves to the suburbs, this would reduce the commuting externality.

In sketching how to quantify the social externality of increased population, we have assumed that ambient pollution is a linear function of increases in the emissions base. While this is an acceptable assumption for predicting PM10, it would be especially troublesome for predicting how city growth impacts ambient ozone levels. A nonlinear relationship exists between ozone smog and VOC and NOx emissions. The relationship between emissions and air quality is largely a matter of the structure of the air shed and thus a scientific relationship. Emissions levels do not solely determine an area's actual air quality (Ulriksen 1993).[18]

Future modeling efforts should focus on calculating the marginal impact of migration on the emissions base and its subsequent impact on air quality and health. Allowing for richer models of pollution's impact on a heterogeneous population's health and allowing people to differ with respect to the value they put on health would generate a more realistic estimate of the social costs of pollution.

Implications for Policy

The previous sections have documented that Santiago has a serious particulate and ozone problem. It investigated each sector's contribution to this problem, presented estimates of the average cost of pollution, and sketched the information needed to estimate the marginal pollution externality of increased activity within Santiago. We have not addressed which policies should be enacted to combat local pollution.[19] To answer that question would involve a cost analysis of every potential policy to address pollution. This would need to be followed by the choice of an optimal set of policies. The optimal level of abatement would equate the marginal cost of the policies to the marginal benefit of each pollution abatement activity.

In reality we cannot easily estimate the costs of potential policies, especially in developing countries. Instead of attempting to do that, we take the size of the externality as an indication that some policies need to be implemented.

Ideally, every actor faces marginal incentives to change behavior and these

18. Santiago has poor ventilation and a serious inversion layer. The air shed is about 100 km from north to south and 60 km from east to west. This means that any emissions in this area will affect overall air quality. There is an opening in the air shed along the road toward San Antonio so that these areas also suffer from Santiago's pollution. (Interview with Professor Greg MacRae of MIT, 1994).

incentives relate directly to the damage caused. This leads to the least cost way of abating pollution. Over time each actor also has appropriate incentives to invest in ways of reducing pollution at least cost, to carry out research to improve abatement technology, and to experiment with different approaches.

At least eight characteristics of instruments need to be considered when choosing the optimal set of policy responses to an externality such as pollution. The first consideration is the potential effect the policy will have on air quality, assuming it works as intended. The second is the unintended side effects of the policy. The third characteristic is the ease of monitoring and enforcing the policy and, connected to this, the public perception and acceptance of the regulation. The fourth relevant characteristic is the political viability and distributional implications of the regulation. The fifth is the cost effectiveness of the instrument both in a static sense and in terms of its effect on research, development, and diffusion of new technology. A sixth is that instruments are affected differently by various forms of uncertainty. As seventh, some instruments yield revenue for government and this may sometimes be considered important. Finally, the form of regulatory instrument chosen today may have implications for options in the future. Some instruments are easier to adjust to changing circumstances.

An important side effect of environmental regulation is that it can introduce unintended consequences. For example, the current policy requiring catalytic converters on all new cars is as costly to residents of small towns such as Puerto Montt as it is to residents of Santiago. However the Puerto Montt residents derive little or no benefit from the policy. The incentive to move to Santiago is reinforced. If we could implement optimal policies that only affected activity within Santiago, these policies would limit pollution in Santiago and simultaneously reduce any perverse incentives to move there.[20]

A regulation is only effective in improving the environment if it can be enforced. The ability to enforce depends on what needs to be monitored and on the monitoring equipment and resources available. Ideally, emissions should be regulated. If it is possible to do this, an economic instrument is best. However, in many situations, particularly in developing countries, monitoring emissions is infeasible due to the expense or the lack of institutional capability.

19. Eskeland (1994) attempts to do a cost benefit analysis for a limited group of policies.

20. Studying the impact of new vehicle regulation in the United States, Gruenspecht (1982) finds evidence of a capital substitution effect such that drivers keep their older (nonregulated) vehicles longer than they would have in the absence of the new capital regulation. In a developing country such as Chile such cross-elasticities may be even larger.

Different regulatory instruments have different distributional implications. These can be important for political and equity reasons. Politically, a regulation will not be passed if strong interests are opposed to it. Similarly, even if the regulation is imposed, strong opposition can hinder its implementation. Unless the implementing agency has very strong monitoring and enforcement powers they may be incapable of making the regulation effective. From an equity point of view it may be perceived as unfair for such groups as the urban poor to bear a high share of the cost of pollution control.

The people who really do bear the costs of regulation are those who find it very costly to change their behavior. A gasoline tax would affect taxi drivers, people who own cars and require them to commute because of where they live and work, and small business people who need cars and are unable to raise their prices because they would lose customers.

Cost effectiveness is a critical aspect of policies. If regulation is cheap, the pollution level can be reduced further at the same time as achieving other societal goals. This is particularly important for a developing country where government and private resources are limited and environmental protection may come at the expense of necessities such as food, housing, and health for some citizens. Here economic instruments have definite advantages over direct controls both in the short run and the long run.[21]

One commonly suggested policy for achieving such optimality is a system of tradeable permits for engaging in polluting activities. The efficiency of cost minimization in a tradeable permits system depends on good enforcement and the efficiency of trading the permits. If trading is restricted or high transactions costs exist, or if some firms use the permits as a strategic instrument to gain market power, the final distribution of permits may not be efficient. This means that the design of the market is important. Tradeable permits should only be used where the industry is such that firms cannot gain market power and firms will find it easy to trade permits when needed. The importance of the spatial distribution of pollution also may make economic instruments less valuable. O'Ryan (1996) suggests that an optimally designed ambient permit system could reduce costs of abatement in Santiago considerably relative to command and control. However, he finds that a nonambient emissions trading program may not be more cost effective because of the higher level of control required to achieve ambient standards.

With perfect information, no uncertainty, and no transactions costs, taxes, permits, and direct controls can all achieve the same environmental objective at the same cost. Where uncertainty exists, as Weitzman (1974) shows, the op-

21. For a discussion of the use of economic instruments in the United States see Hahn and Stavins (1992).

timal instrument depends on the form of uncertainty and the elasticities of the marginal benefits and marginal costs of controlling pollution. If costs of pollution are very sensitive to changes in pollution levels while costs of control are fairly constant, it is better to control the quantity of pollution using a quota or tradeable permits system than to control the price through a tax. In contrast, if costs of control are very sensitive because, for example, technology is inflexible in the short run, (while damage does not rise sharply with respect to pollution levels,) it is better to control the price of pollution through a tax. Then, when costs of control turn out to be much higher than expected, firms are not bankrupted by extremely severe regulations.

In developing countries tax collection systems are frequently poorly developed. The cost of raising revenue for government can be very high both in terms of administrative costs and economic distortions. Thus an environmental regulation that can raise revenue at the same time as dealing with a social issue may be very valuable. A tax clearly raises revenue in a direct way. A permit system can raise revenue if the permits are auctioned rather than being "grandfathered" to existing polluters. The potential for revenue gains is a significant advantage of auctions. Auctions are preferred if no driving political need exists to pay off polluters and thereby facilitate the introduction and operation of the permit system. In contrast, direct controls yield no revenue.

Developing countries are, by definition, in a period of rapid change. The optimal level and form of regulation will change as their incomes grow, their institutional capacity expands, and their preferences change. Some forms of regulation are more flexible both in terms of the administrative structures that support them and the political vested interests they create. A direct control system can create a large bureaucracy that can then oppose a movement toward economic instruments. Also direct controls cannot smoothly be made more stringent. Additional controls on emissions often require additional instruments rather than more stringent applications of the existing ones. In contrast, a tax is completely flexible, at least in theory, though the politics of adjusting taxes can be difficult. A tradeable permit market will automatically increase stringency as the economy grows because it limits total emissions. However, creating property rights may encourage people with vested interests to demand compensation if the number of permits is reduced. The flexibility of different instruments will depend on the specific institutional and political structure in which they are created.

Above all, if environmental legislation is to be implemented and enforced in the way the policy makers intend, the organization implementing the policy must not have objectives that conflict with this role. For instance, it may be inappropriate for the Ministry of Transport to have an environmental enforcement role when its primary interests lie in developing the transportation sector. The balance between the profitability of the transportation sector and environmental protection should be made by government, acting as a representative of society as a whole. It should not be made by people in, or intimately involved with, a particular industry. If organizations have conflicting objectives they often cannot perform either appropriately.

For environmental legislation to be effective it must be clearly understood and unambiguous. In most countries, including Chile, environmental legislation has developed piecemeal and in many cases different laws are inconsistent or duplicate each other. Excessive numbers of inconsistent laws can make it impossible to enforce any policy. Laws need to be simplified so they can be clearly understood. Lines of accountability and responsibility for enforcing laws must be clear.

One issue especially relevant to Chile and many other rapidly developing countries is whether they should implement environmental policies now or wait until their resources are greater and their level of concern about the environment is higher. This issue is particularly relevant to ozone, which is not currently seen as such a critical problem. The key reason to regulate early is that capital decisions are being made in the absence of regulation. These capital decisions can be very costly if not impossible to reverse. Relatively low-cost regulations now could lead to significant cost savings in the future. For example, as Santiago develops, the city structure is being determined—the location of employment, residential areas, major transportation routes, public services etc. These have major implications for transportation patterns in the future. As Chile grows, many people and firms are moving toward Santiago. These decisions may be costly to reverse, particularly if they imply less infrastructure and institutional development in other regions. Individuals are investing in private cars and changing their lifestyles. Experience in the United States suggests that these lifestyle changes may be very difficult to alter. Both among consumers and among firms, vested interests are being created. These will support the structure of the city and society that is being developed in the absence of appropriate regulation. Therefore the benefits from even a low level of regulation rather than none could be disproportionate because of effects on long-term costs and decisions.

One possible reason to defer regulation is that an option value related to waiting for improved institutions or technology might exist. If a policy forces the adoption of a specific technology when an improved alternative is expected to be available soon, this may be inefficient even though some environmental gains are achieved immediately. Similarly, designing policies that are implementable with existing institutions may foreclose future regulatory options because of the costs of changing from one regulatory system to another.

Policy responses seem needed at two basic levels. The first level calls for individual regulatory instruments. A wide range of instruments is available for internalizing the costs of pollution and mitigating its impacts. More than one instrument can, and almost certainly should, be used.

The second response is at the overall institutional level. The institutions that design and implement policy are critical to its effectiveness. These institutions have three main roles. The first is to collect and analyze information. The second is to design appropriate policies in terms of stringency and cost effectiveness. The third is to monitor and enforce the implementation of these policies.

Given the current state of development in Chile, and the high level of uncertainty on the appropriate level of pollution control, it is appropriate to focus on policies with the following characteristics: (1) inexpensive, (2) enforceable, and (3) devoid of irreversible changes in the economic structure that will make future pollution control expensive. To select and develop these policies, it would be helpful if Chile had an environmental policy agency with good resources and information and a high level of access to political power. To provide effective enforcement, the implementation of policies needs to be located in socially accountable agencies with no conflicting objectives.

In terms of specific instruments, a tax on gasoline sold in the Santiago metropolitan area would be a cost-effective instrument that is closely related to emissions. It is easily enforced and falls primarily on consumers with private cars who tend to have higher incomes. The tax should have several effects. It could reduce the current use of private cars, discourage car purchase, and encourage people to make housing and employment decisions that reduce their need to commute. Developers might respond to these pressures by building communities where services are accessible without use of a car. On the margin these are low-cost changes because they are largely affecting and improving the economics of new capital decisions.

The current standards requiring all new cars to have catalytic converters are effective, easy to monitor, and mostly affect high-income residents. These standards need to be backed up with a system of emissions testing for new cars to ensure that the catalytic converters are working properly and that the cars are well maintained. Another policy that would indirectly reduce emissions from new cars with catalytic converters would be to tax leaded gasoline at a higher level than unleaded. This would not only reduce lead in the atmosphere but would discourage the use of leaded gasoline in new cars. Leaded gasoline destroys catalytic converters and makes them ineffective at controlling ozone precursors. These regulations could be funded by an increased registration tax on cars in Santiago or through the gasoline tax.

To conclude this policy discussion, transport emissions can be reduced through the adoption of a tax on gasoline and a higher tax on leaded gasoline sold in the Santiago metropolitan area. Road paving would clearly play an important role in reducing particulate emissions. Another environmental policy goal would be to form effective regulatory institutions, facilitating experimentation by consumers and firms in ways to reduce pollution activities, and minimizing irreversible externalities created by capital investments. Policies should be adopted that do not limit future options that may emerge as knowledge about the appropriate level of regulation and the most effective forms evolves.

Conclusion

Air quality is an important health input that affects a city's quality of life. Due to its geography and its high level of economic activity, Santiago features high particulate and ozone levels that are leading to high levels of average health costs. This chapter has presented a methodology for quantifying the marginal environmental costs of economic development and has proposed policies for addressing the spatial distortion.

An important question is whether the pollution externality will grow over time. The size of the pollution externality depends on several factors, such as the extra emissions that are created by a marginal increase in economic activity. In addition, the population's susceptibility to pollution also matters in determining the environmental costs of growth. A population with more children and more senior citizens will be at greater risk from a given level of pollution. For a given increase in pollution-caused health problems, the population's value of time and value of life are key parameters in determining individual willingness to pay to avoid pollution exposure. Finally, since pollution is a public bad, the total size of the population is an important determinant in calculating the total size of the externality.

Predicting the likely trends in each of these components is a challenging assignment. Emissions per capita may rise or fall as per-capita income grows. Emission levels per capita might rise as individuals choose to consume more resources, such as increased travel. Conversely, per-capita emissions might fall as richer people choose to utilize new capital vintages that are less polluting. In addition, new technologies may sharply reduce emissions per unit of economic activity. It is likely that willingness to pay for air quality will increase over time as per-capita income grows and as the population ages. Such forecasts of the future environmental degradation are needed to form expectations about the expected benefits of enacting costly environmental regulation.

References

Becker, Gary. 1968. "Crime and Punishment: an Economic Approach." *Journal of Political Economy.*

Braun, Juan. 1990. *Politica Regional y Urbana en Chile* Pontificia Universidad Catolica de Chile, Instituto de Economia, Documento de Trabajo No. 126 (September).

Centro Latinoamericano de Demografía (CELADE) 1993. *La Poblacion del Gran Santiago: Tendencias, Perspectivas y Consecuencias.*

Chestnut, L.G. and Rowe, R.D. 1988 *Ambient Particulate Matter and Ozone Benefit Analysis for Denver* RCG/Hagler, Bailly, Inc. Prepared for the U.S. Environmental Protection Agency, Boulder, CO.

Coase, Ronald. 1960. "The Problem of Social Cost." *The Journal of Law and Economics.*

Cummings and DiPasquale, D. and Cummings, J. 2001. "The Spatial Implications of Housing Policy in Chile"; Chapter 6.

Eskeland, Gunnar S. "The Net Benefits of an Air Pollution Control Scenario for Santiago" Chapter III *Chile, Managing Environmental Problems: Economic Analysis of Selected Issues.* World Bank, Environment and Urban Development Division Report No. 13061-CH.

Goodstein, Eban. 1995. *Economics and the Environment.* Englewood Cliffs, NJ: Prentice Hall.

Gruenspecht, H. 1982. "Differentiated Regulation: The Case of Auto Emissions Standards." *American Economic Review,* 2, 329–332.

Hahn, Robert W., and Robert N. Stavins. 1992. "Economic Incentives for Environmental Protection: Integrating Theory and Practice." *American Economic Review,* vol. 82, no.2, (May) p. 464.

Henderson, Vernon. 1996. "The Effect of Air Quality Regulation" *American Economic Review.* (September) p. 789–813.

Kain, J and Zhi Liu. 2001. "Efficiency and Locational Consequences of Government Transport Policies and Spending in Chile." Chapter 5.

Kerr, S.C. 1993. *The Operation of Tradeable Rights Markets: Empirical Evidence from the United States Lead Phasedown.* Paper presented at the Air and Waste Management Association meeting "New Partnerships: Economic Incentives for Environmental Management" Rochester, New York. (November).

Kerr, Suzi and David Maré. "Efficient Regulation through Tradeable Permit Markets: The United States Lead Phasedown" Department of Agricultural and Resource Economics, University of Maryland at College Park, Working Paper 96-06.

Office of Air Quality Planning and Standards. *Review of the National Ambient Air Quality Standards for Particulate Matter: Assessment of Scientific and Technical Information* U.S. Environmental Protection Agency. 1982. EPA-450/5-82-001.

Office of Air Quality Planning and Standards. *Review of the National Ambient Air Quality Standards for Particulate Matter: Updated Assessment of Scientific and Technical Information: Addendum to the 1982 OAQPS Staff Paper* U.S. Environmental Protection Agency. 1986. EPA-450/5-86-012.

Office of Air Quality Planning and Standards. *Review of the National Ambient Air Quality Standards for Ozone: Assessment of Scientific and Technical Information* U.S. Environmental Protection Agency. 1989. EPA-450/2-92-001.

O'Ryan, Raùl E. "Cost-Effective Policies to Improve Urban Air Quality in Santiago, Chile." 1996. *Journal of Environmental Economics and Management* 31(3). (November).

Ostro. Bart. "Estimating the Health Effects of Air Pollutants." 1994. The World Bank; Policy Research Working Paper #1301. (May).

Ostro, B.D. 1987. "Air Pollution and Morbidity Revisited: A Specification Test." *Journal of Environmental Economics and Management* vol 14: pp 87–98

Ostro, Bart, Jose Miguel Sanchez, Carlos Aranda and Gunnar S. Eskeland. 1996. "Air Pollution and Mortality: Results from a Study of Santiago, Chile." *Journal of Exposure Analysis and Environmental Epidemiology* vol. 6, No. 1.

Parry, Ian W. H. 1995. "Pollution Taxes and Revenue Recycling." *Journal of Environmental Economics and Management* 29: pp: s64–s77.

Pope, C.A. 1989. "Respiratory Disease Associated with Community Air Pollution and a Steel Mill, Utah Valley." *American Journal of Public Health* no. 79: pp 623–628

Pope, C.A. "Respiratory Hospital Admissions associated with PM10 pollution in Utah, Salt Lake, and Cache Valleys." 1991. *Arch. Environmental Health* no. 46: pp 90–97

Portney, P.R. and Mullahy, J. 1989. "Urban Air Quality and Acute Respiratory Illness." *Journal of Urban Economics*, vol. 20: pp 21–38

Portney, Paul and John Mullahy. 1990. "Urban Air Quality and Chronic Respiratory Disease." *Regional Science Journal of Urban Economics*, vol. 20: pp. 407–418.

Préndez, M. 1993. "Características de los Contaminantes Atmosféricos" in *Characterísticas de los Contaminantes Atmosféricos in Contaminación Atmosférica de Santiago: Estado Actual y Soluciones.* eds. H.L. Sandoval, M.B. Préndez and P.U. Ulriksen. Universidad de Chile, Comisión de Descontaminación Metropolitana and Banco Santander. Pp 109–187

Sandoval, H. 1993. Emisiones de Contaminantes a la Atmosfera in *Characteristicas de los Contaminantes Atmosféricos in Contaminación Atmosférica de Santiago: Estado Actual y Soluciones.* eds. H.L. Sandoval, M.B.

Préndez and P.U. Ulriksen Universidad de Chile, Comisión de Descontaminación Metropolitana and Banco Santander.

Selden, Thomas and Daqing Song. 1994. "Environmental Quality and Development: Is There a Kuznets Curve for Air Pollution Emissions?" *Journal of Environmental Economics and Management* 27: pp 147–162.

Servicio de Salud del Ambiente Region Metropolitana. 1991. *Informe de contaminación Atmosférica*

Stavins, Robert. N. "Transaction Costs and Tradeable Permit Markets." 1995. *Journal of Environmental Economics and Management.*

Stiglitz Joseph E. 1988. *Economics of the Public Sector* 2nd Edition. New York: Norton .

Tietenberg, Tom. 1996. *Environmental and Natural Resource Economics.* 4th edition. Harper Collins College Publishers, New York.

Ulriksen, Pablo U. "Factores Meteorologicos de la Contaminación Atmosférica de Santiago." in *Contaminación Atmosférica de Santiago: Estado Actual y Soluciones,* eds. H.L. Sandoval, M.B. Préndez, P.U. Ulriksen; 1993. Universidad de Chile, Comisión de Descontaminación Metropolitana, Banco Santander.

Weitzman, M.L. 1974. "Prices vs. Quantities." *Review of Economic Studies.* no. 41.

Wichmann, H.E. Mueller, W., Allhoff, P. et al. 1989. "Health Effects during a smog episode in West Germany in 1985." *Environmental Health Perspectives,* 79: pp 89–99

World Bank. 1994. "Chile: Managing Environmental Problems: Economic Analysis of Selected Issues" Country Operations Division, Country Department IV, Latin America and the Caribbean Regional Office, Final Report.

Viscusi, Kip. 1993. "The Value of Risk to Life and Health" *Journal of Economic Literature,* (December): pp. 1912–1946.

APPENDIX A: TIME TRENDS IN SANTIAGO'S PARTICULATE LEVELS

Dependent Variable: The log of monitoring site A's daily particulate reading between 1990 and 1993

Independent Variable	*beta (t-stat)*
Time trend	–0.001
	(–0.51)
Rain	–0.023
	(–4.6)
Wind	–0.14
	(–2.2)
Temperature	0.03
	(5.7)
March	0.47
	(2.2)
April	0.64
	(3.0)
May	1.06
	(5.2)
June	1.39
	(6.3)
July	1.37
	(6.5)
August	0.94
	(4.2)
September	0.48
	(2.3)
October	0.27
	(1.2)
November	0.14
	(0.66)
December	0.07
	(0.33)
Constant	4.89
	(1.66)
Observations /R2	331 0.52

Note: the omitted category is February. Temperature is measured in Celcius. Wind is a dummy variable that equals one if the wind was not zero at the monitoring station that day. Rain is measured in cubic milliliters. The mean of the dependent variable is 4.71.

APPENDIX B: THE POLLUTION EXTERNALITY CAUSED BY EXTRA COMMUTING

In addition to estimating the social costs if an extra migrant moves to Santiago, we estimate the externality if a household is relocated so that the bus commute is one minute shorter in each direction. We assume 500 trips per year. We assume that if people want to travel less on buses, the total distance traveled in buses will fall by the same amount. Fewer people/miles of commuting implies fewer bus/miles and lower transport emissions.

To estimate this relationship requires an assumption about how many people ride on each bus. We also needed to make assumptions about the emissions of the average bus on the road. This was calculated by taking the particulate emissions base and multiplying it by the bus share of total emissions and then dividing by the total number of buses in Santiago. This yields the annual particulate emissions per bus. All of our calculations are available on request. The weakest assumption in this externality scenario is the link between transport and ozone production and these numbers should be considered only as rough estimates.

Policy Simulation of Marginal Damage Caused By Longer Commute in 1990$

Pollutant	*Commute*
Particulates	
Morbidity $ Per Capita	.053
Mortality $ Per Capita	.121
Ozone	
Morbidity $ Per Capita	.176
Total Externality ($)	.350

Our calculation indicates that policies that move the Santiago population away from the central business district impose environmental costs. The relevance of this calculation for housing policy is more fully discussed in Chapter 6.

4

Environmental and Communications Infrastructure in Chile

AMRITA G. DANIERE AND JOSE A. GOMEZ-IBANEZ*

Introduction

Water, sewage, solid waste, and telecommunications traditionally have been provided by public agencies in Chile and, with the exception of telecommunications, the government role is still preponderant. Telecommunications services are provided by recently privatized, but regulated, firms that are moving quickly to improve their services and adjust prices to reflect costs more accurately. Water and wastewater services are provided by regional state enterprises that also are beginning to improve services and to charge more for them. Solid waste collection and disposal is legally a municipal government responsibility but is often contracted out to private firms who conduct the work. Solid waste services are currently highly subsidized by the municipalities, a policy that may prove difficult to sustain in the long term.

These public services can distort urban development patterns in two major ways. The first is by restricting or limiting *access*. New water or telephone connections, for example, may not be available to developers at some locations because of a lack of capacity. The second way is if the *prices* charged for those services do not reflect the costs of providing them at certain locations. Of particular concern is whether the ratio of prices charged to costs varies significantly by location or between new developments and old.

To foreshadow the results, our analysis suggests that water and wastewater

* This research was supported by Forestal Valparaíso, S.A. but the opinions expressed are those of the authors and not those of Forestal Valparaíso. The authors would like to thank John Meyer for his extensive comments on earlier drafts of this paper.

services are far more likely to distort urban development patterns than the other sectors studied. Price distortions in the other sectors are quite small or declining either because of recent privatization efforts (in the cases of the electricity and telecommunications industries) or because of the relatively low costs of supplying the service (solid waste disposal). Conversely, distortions within the water and sewage sectors appear to be significant, given the lack of sewage treatment facilities and the relatively high subsidies given to water users in different regions of the country.

Water and Sewer Services

Organization of the Sector

Most urban households and businesses in Chile have both piped water and sewer services, although the sewage is usually deposited in nearby rivers, irrigation canals, or the ocean without treatment.[1] As of early 1994, approximately 93% of these households and businesses are served by thirteen public water and sewer enterprises while 7% are served by four private companies.

The thirteen public enterprises listed in Table 4-1, were originally part of the Corporacion de Fomento de la Produccion (or CORFO), a large state enterprise that provides a variety of public services. In 1990, CORFO's water and sewer operations were divided into thirteen separate companies, one for each of Chile's twelve regions and for metropolitan Santiago. Although these companies are still owned by the national government, the break-up was intended to give their managers more autonomy and responsibility, and to provide incentives for the companies to become financially self supporting from the fees that they charge households and businesses for their services. Many of these firms are still heavily subsidized by CORFO, however, and CORFO exercises substantial control over their investment programs.

The four private firms are concentrated in the Santiago and Valparaíso metropolitan areas but are quite small relative to the two public firms (EMOS and ESVAL) that serve those regions.[2] In the early 1990s, the largest of the private firms, Lo Castillo, purchased two smaller private companies (Manquehue and Los Dominicos) and, by 1994, served approximately 63,500 cli-

1. According to Eugenio Celadon (interviewed on September 3, 1993), at that time only 6% of Chile's wastewater was treated prior to being released back into the country's rivers and/or coastal areas or used for irrigation purposes.

2. The private firms operating in the Metropolitan Region and Region V are larger (in terms of number of clients) than the two smallest public water enterprises operating in Region XI (EMSSA) and Region XII (ESMAG).

Table 4-1. *Performance Indicators for Chile's Public Water Enterprises in 1992*

Region	*Firm Name*	*Revenues (millions of pesos)*	*Production (millions of m^3)*	*Sales (millions of m^3)*	*Clients–Water*	*Clients–Sewer*	*% Coverage Water*	*% Coverage Sewer*	*Investment (millions of pesos)*
I-Tarapac	ESSAT	4,206.9	35.7	21.0	74,217	70,714	98.5	93.1	1,790
II-Antofagasta	ESSAN	5,026.7	34.7	20.4	82,510	64,676	99.7	78.6	2,196
III-Atacama	EMSSAT	1,827.6	22.6	10.0	49,944	39,771	96.0	79.2	371
IV-Coquimbo	ESSCO	3,515.5	29.4	20.9	87,793	67,226	93.4	70.3	2,021
VI-O'Higgens	ESSEL	3,291.0	46.3	24.1	95,563	69,023	95.3	68.4	2,265
VII-Maule	ESSAM	3,428.9	49.5	26.6	107,939	92,419	98.1	89.0	1,617
VIII-Bio Bio	ESSBIO	8,286.0	111.0	69.3	255,518	180,331	96.3	67.9	2,084
IX-La Araucancia	ESSAR	3,369.5	40.1	24.2	102,550	78,554	97.7	73.5	1,944
X-De Los Lagos	ESSAL	3,430.2	44.0	24.8	107,649	77,013	79.0	56.5	1,449
XI-Alsen del Gen. Carlos	EMSSA	534.8	7.5	4.2	13,188	8,225	99.9	64.7	266
IX-Magell. y de la Antart.	ESMAG	1,385.0	18.5	6.1	33,159	31,246	98.1	94.1	779
	Subtotal	38,301.9	439.2	251.7	1,010,030	779,198	94.7	73.1	16,782
Metropolitan Region	EMOS	33,824.0	466.4	335.8	905,177	868,303	100.0	95.0	19,227
V-Valparaiso	ESVAL	10,982.1	143.6	80.6	293,223	232,672	96.1	82.1	3,148
	Subtotal	44,806.1	610.0	416.4	1,100,975	2,773	99.1	92.0	22,375
	Total	83,108.0	1,049.2	668.1	2,208,430	1,880,173	97.2	83.7	39,157

Source: Memoria, CORFO (1993), p.7.

ents in the Santiago area. Two other private firms, Servicommunal and La Leonora, also serve Santiago neighborhoods but are much smaller than Lo Castillo. The fourth private firm, Santo Domingo, serves customers in Region V (Valparaíso).

Both public and private water enterprises have been regulated by the Superintendencia de Servicios Sanitarios since a 1990 reorganization of the water and sewage sector. The Superintendencia is responsible both for monitoring the quality of the drinking water and sewage treatment and for setting the tariffs that the companies can charge for their services. The tariffs are, in theory, set both to approximate marginal costs and to allow the enterprises to be financially self-supporting. To provide incentives for efficiency, the tariffs are based on the marginal costs of hypothetical "model" companies that use the same technologies and serve the same customer bases as the actual companies. Four different activities are considered separately in calculating the model company costs: water production and purification, water distribution, sewage collection, and sewage treatment. Since few companies actually treat the sewage they collect, however, treatment costs currently are not allowed in the tariffs they are permitted to charge. The basic legislation establishing this regulatory system dictates that the water enterprises should receive at least a 7% real return on their investments, although it is unclear whether this rate of return is being achieved or how it is monitored.

The Failure to Treat Sewage[3]

The most serious problem in this sector is that only approximately 6% of Chile's wastewater is adequately treated before disposal. Included in this 6% are a small number of coastal communities with sewage outfalls far enough offshore that no treatment is considered necessary; a section of the city of Antofagasta served by stabilization ponds; and a *comuna* located within the Santiago metropolitan area that has in place a pilot system using oxidization ditches to treat a portion of the wastewater the neighborhood generates.

The most serious and best-documented treatment problems are in the Santiago Metropolitan Region. The region's 5,080,000 or so inhabitants are served by a modern central water supply system that provides piped water to 99% of the homes and piped sewerage to 92% of the houses (see Table 4-1). The total wastewater flow has been estimated at 10 cubic meters per second or 310 million cubic meters a year, almost all of which goes untreated into the Mapocho and Maipo rivers which drain the Metropolitan Region.

---

3. This section relies heavily on CORFO (1993) and Superintendencia de Servicios Sanitarios, Memoria Anual (1993).

These two rivers in turn connect with the Zanjon canal and together serve as the primary sources of irrigation water for about 62,000 hectares of agricultural land immediately adjacent to the urban areas and in the vicinity. Some 22% of the area, or 13,500 hectares, are cultivated with vegetables and salad crops normally eaten uncooked such as tomatoes, lettuce, cabbage, celery, and onions (Shuval, 1993). Since there is essentially no rain during the irrigation season between November and May, the vast majority of the flow in the rivers and the canals is partially diluted or undiluted raw wastewater, almost all of which is directed to agricultural irrigation. Area III relies entirely on wastewater for irrigation.

There is strong circumstantial evidence that both typhoid and cholera, as well as less dangerous enteric diseases, are effectively transmitted in Santiago by vegetable and salad crops irrigated with raw wastewater. This circumstantial evidence includes Santiago's distinctive summer peak of typhoid cases, coinciding with the wastewater irrigation season. Additionally, typhoid fever rates among infants and young children (zero to two years of age), who are normally extremely susceptible to this disease, are unusually low in Santiago, presumably because young children generally do not eat raw salad crops (Shuval 1993).

Thus, untreated sewerage in river and canal waters used for irrigation by the truck farms surrounding the metropolis poses a serious health threat of gastroenteritis, typhoid, diphtheria, and even (in 1991) cholera (Hopkins et al., 1993). Although EMOS (the state water enterprise that serves the Santiago region) recently built a small pilot sewage treatment plant in Santiago, and eventually hopes to treat all of the metropolitan area's sewage, it is clear that it will be many years (possibly decades) before this goal is attained. In the interim, the government is building interceptor sewers along the rivers and canals in the heavily urbanized portions of the metropolis. The interceptor sewers are designed to eventually carry the wastewater to treatment plants, but until the plants are built they will serve only to carry the waste further downstream before depositing it untreated into the river. The interceptors will reduce the odors and unsightliness of the rivers and canals in the built-up areas but will not, without the treatment plants, significantly reduce the level of waste in irrigation waters or the resulting health risks.

There is very little information about the nature of the health and other problems caused by the failure to treat sewage in Chile's other cities. It is known that typhoid levels in the rest of the country, where wastewater is not used for irrigation, show no summer peak and are much lower than in Santiago with a range of some 30–50 cases a year per 100,000 people vs. 100–200 cases per 100,000 people in Santiago; Ferreccio, 1993. Typhoid rates in Santiago have fallen dramatically since 1991 in response to emergency measures taken as a result of the cholera scare in Peru. Typhoid rates in the Santiago Metropolitan Region peaked in 1984 at 215 cases per 100,000 people, fell to 110 per 100,000 people in 1986 following the prohibition of cultivation of vegetables normally eaten raw, and plummeted to only 8 per 100,000 in 1992. Since wastewater irrigation is not a problem elsewhere in Chile, it is likely that other urban areas are under little pressure to treat wastewater. It is possible, however, that in the north, where there is less agriculture but little annual rainfall, untreated sewage may be causing health problems by contaminating aquifers used for drinking water supply.

Policy Options and Costs

There are a variety of options for alleviating the problems of untreated sewage in Santiago ranging from treating the sewage so it is safe for irrigation to simply educating the populace to not consume raw vegetables.

The options that do not involve treatment sometimes appear inexpensive, but they often involve hidden costs or are not considered very reliable. For example, the recent strategy of the government is to ban the use of contaminated water for irrigating crops that are eaten raw and to mount public education campaigns to warn residents about the dangers of eating raw vegetables. Although the cost for enforcement and publicity is modest, there are hidden costs in lost agricultural productivity and in inconveniences to households. Although this strategy appears to have reduced typhoid cases in 1992 and 1993, this success is due partly to the appearance of a few cases of cholera in Santiago during the 1991 Peruvian outbreak that helped focus public attention on the health risks of untreated sewage. Enforcement and education are likely to prove to be less effective as the cholera scare fades in the public's memory.

Other options besides treatment are an outright ban on all agricultural production in the area around Santiago or finding new sources of clean water to irrigate the agricultural lands surrounding the metropolis. Both options are probably more costly than treatment, although there is no specific cost. Banning agricultural production would simplify enforcement problems greatly, but these lands are reportedly among the most fertile in Chile and the value of the lost output would be considerable. Bringing enough additional clean water to Santiago to irrigate them could also be prohibitively expensive.

For larger inland cities like Santiago there are two main treatment options: lagoon systems and activated sludge plants. Under the first option, the sewage is held in series of lagoons long enough for most pathogens to die off and for most of the organic material to settle out or be consumed by aerobic bacteria. In an activated sludge plant, the action of aerobic bacteria is accelerated by the use of aerators, beaters, or trickle filters; typically, the effluent is chlorinated just before discharge to kill off pathogens. A lagoon system is inexpensive to operate and build but requires a great deal of land since the effluent often must be held for a week or more before it is clean enough to discharge. An activated sludge plant requires more elaborate tanks and maintenance but saves on land since the effluent is usually discharged in less than a day. Coastal cities also have the option of building outfalls for untreated sewage, although these must be designed so as not to contaminate beaches or fishing grounds. Small inland cities may have the option of relying on in-ground septic systems as long as the water table is not too close to the surface and soil conditions are appropriate.

A study of Santiago's water pollution problems prepared for the World Bank estimates that the present value of capital and operating costs for a lagoon system to serve the entire metropolitan area would be US $574 million in 1994 real dollars which implies an average annual cost of around US $7.75 per inhabitant per year or US $0.08 per cubic meter.[4] These estimates do not include all the land acquisition costs, however, and the consultants recognize that a lagoon system would be impractical for Santiago, given the enormous amount of land that would be required. A system that relied partially on lagoons and partially on conventional plants would cost about 30% more, or about US $10 (1994 dollars) per inhabitant-year (US $0.14 per cubic meter).

Similar figures were estimated in an analysis of model water and sewage company costs for cities of 1,000 to 400,000 inhabitants prepared by the Superintendencia de Servicios Sanitarios for the initial (1990) tariff investigation. These estimates suggest that the annual capital costs of sewage treatment in a city of 400,000 would be approximately US $13.50 per inhabitant in 1994 dollars if the effluent met a standard of 1,000 fecal coliform per 100 milliliters, approximately the level regarded as safe for irrigation, and US $8.35 in 1994 dollars if a lesser standard of 10,000 fecal coliform per 100 milliliters is allowed.[5] Capital costs per inhabitant would be higher for smaller cities, partic-

4. The average annual cost is calculated using a 10% real discount rate (the same rate the study uses to calculate the present value) and a population growing from four million to nine million over the life of the project.

5. Cost estimates are reproduced in Appendix Table A-4. Wastewater that meets the World Health Organization standard of 1,000 fecal coliform per 100 milliliters can be used safely for the irrigation of fruits and vegetables normally eaten raw. A number of internationally sponsored studies have found that the quantifiable health effects of wastewater irrigation (such as significantly higher rates of typhoid and gastroenteritis) are almost exclusively associated with the irrigation of salad crops with untreated wastewater. Treated wastewaters, not even approaching drinking water quality, do not appear to be associated with negative health effects (Shuval et al., 1986). Thus, even a treatment method that reduces the number of fecal coliform to 10,000 per 100 milliliters may be a sufficient to attain significant health benefits, particularly if the water is not used to irrigate salad crops but only other types of agricultural products.

ularly those with fewer than 50,000 inhabitants. These results do not necessarily imply that the larger cities enjoy significant economies in total sewage collection and treatment costs, however, since the savings in unit treatment costs with larger plants may be at least partially offset by the added expense of transporting the sewage longer distances to the central plant.

Treatment Benefits

The World Bank study also examines the benefits associated with wastewater treatment in Santiago. The study focuses on the direct and indirect health costs of typhoid in the region, the benefits associated with avoiding export losses in response to a cholera outbreak, and expanded farm output and reduced consumer expenditures on previously prohibited food crops (World Bank, 1994). According to the World Bank, the direct health costs due to endemic typhoid caused by sewage irrigation of vegetables in the Santiago Metropolitan Region over the period 1985 to 1992 are only US $1.4 million per year (1994 dollars).[6]

In addition, the World Bank attempts to estimate the potential loss to agricultural exports in the event that a cholera outbreak were to occur in the Santiago area. Based on previous experiences in Israel in 1970 and Peru in 1991, agricultural export losses could be as high as 5% of the total value of fruit exports or between US $11 and $16 million in 1994. Additional benefits from wastewater treatment and reuse would accrue to farmers in areas downstream of interceptor discharges since they would be able to cultivate vegetable crops without restriction and return to their pre-1991 level of income. If we assume constant prices, this represents US $6.6 million per year. The World Bank also estimates that consumers (who paid up to 100% more for certain prohibited food crops following the 1991 prohibition) would receive benefits in the form of a rollback in prices amounting to US $4.3 million per year. The total value of all these benefits estimated by the World Bank is approximately US $25 million per year, still significantly below full wastewater treatment costs.

The World Bank study does not consider the direct and indirect health costs of other important diseases besides typhoid and cholera, however, and if these other diseases are considered treatment may be justified economically. In Santiago, the large health gains would probably come from reducing the rates of gastroenteritis, typhoid, and hepatitis.[7] For example, wastewater treatment might prevent several million cases of gastroenteritis in Santiago each year. A study of gastroenteritis in a low-income suburb of Buenos Aires

6. This estimate includes direct treatment costs, productivity costs, and mortality costs.

7. Ferreccio (1993).

reported an average of approximately one case per inhabitant per year with an average of around three days of severe diarrhea per case.[8] Two fairly recent studies of diarrheal infections among young children in a poor peri-urban community in Santiago indicate that this demographic group experienced 2.2 episodes of diarrheal disease per twelve child months of observation.[9] Almost 70% of these children had access to piped water inside their home while all but 3% had access to a toilet. Despite relatively good access to water and sanitation, diarrheal infections, particularly strains that persist in industrialized countries, are quite prevalent among low-income young children in Santiago. In addition, estimates of the economic costs of hepatitis and diarrhea associated with wastewater irrigation subsequently developed by Ferreccio (World Bank, 1994, p.84) suggest that in 1986 typhoid represented only 8.8% of direct health costs while hepatitis represented 3.8% and diarrhea 87.4%.

Some observers dispute the possibility of a significant health improvement from sewage treatment, noting that Santiago's typhoid cases have dropped drastically since the cholera scare of 1991 (Ferreccio, 1993). The drop represents a sharp break from historic patterns and probably reflects precautionary practices including a reduced consumption of local raw vegetables. Santiago residents may well revert to their old habits, however, once the cholera scare is forgotten. Even if they do not, these precautions have social costs if only because they inconvenience Santiago's residents and are likely to affect the quality of their diet.

The benefits of avoiding outbreaks of waterborne diseases or chronic waterborne illnesses are substantial but difficult to estimate. A recent study of an outbreak of giardiasis in the United States revealed three categories of treatment benefits (Harrington et al., 1991). These included morbidity (which can be valued in terms of willingness to pay to avoid an incidence of acute illness and perhaps certain chronic illnesses as well); the averting behavior of an individual (the actions people take to reduce their exposure to environmental contaminants); and the values associated with avoiding future anxiety. The authors of this study argue that averting behavior is particularly important when drinking water contamination is involved, since those affected may go to considerable length to secure uncontaminated water. In Santiago, the problem is contaminated fruits and vegetables rather than drinking water, but the principle is the same. Estimating the benefits associated with less contamination requires a valuation of both how much people actually spend to avert contamination, which can be observed, and total willingness to pay to avoid contamination, which cannot. Unfortunately, estimates of these

8. Grinstein et al. (1989).

9. Levine et al. (1993) and Ferreccio et al. (1991).

benefits are not generally collected in epidemiological surveys made during disease outbreaks or in analyses of the effects of chronic diseases. Given Santiago's rather unique experiences with the effects of wastewater irrigation, it might make a great deal of sense to attempt an analysis of these benefits in the near future.

In any event, it is very plausible that the benefits to Santiago's residents would be at least as large as the $10 to $18 per capita cost of sewage treatment. This seems a reasonable price to pay for avoiding an extra case of severe gastroenteritis per year and for reducing the risk of typhoid. Moreover, sewage treatment in Santiago seems even more likely to be justified, given that some public health officials speculate that Santiago's gastroenteritis rates are higher than one case per inhabitant per year and given that there are other health and aesthetic benefits to be gained. Sewage treatment also may be justified in Chile's other large cities. Although the benefits may be smaller, particularly if the groundwater is not heavily contaminated, the costs also may be lower since treatment facilities can be used that rely entirely on lagoon systems.

Subsidized Water and Sewer Tariffs

Another potential problem is that Chile's water and sewer companies do not charge users the full costs of the water supply and distribution and the sewage collection services they provide. These services are subsidized by the state in several ways and the level of subsidies varies across regions.

Forms of Subsidy

Users are undercharged in at least three ways. In the first place, some of the water enterprises still operate at a financial loss even though, by law, they are supposed to be self-supporting.[10] Prices are supposed to be set so that enterprises receive at least marginal costs plus a 7% rate of return but this does not actually occur in practice.

Each water enterprise or firm is required to conduct its own marginal cost pricing study every five years to serve as the basis for setting prices in the industry. The firm then negotiates its rates with the Superintendencia de Servicios Sanitarios based on the study, and if the enterprise and the Superintendencia cannot agree on the tariff an independent arbitrator decides. The tariffs or prices charged by the thirteen firms are to be adjusted according to the results of new cost studies as soon as they are completed. The original marginal cost

10. See Appendix A for more information regarding the financial performance of public water enterprises in Chile.

studies, conducted in 1990, provided cost projections for fifteen years but, as of 1994, these results were already somewhat outdated. The original studies estimated two different sets of prices for each type of firm: *vigentes*, the prices the firms are allowed to charge in the immediate term, and *metas* the estimated marginal costs and the long term target for the firm's prices.

In February 1993, water tariffs were generally 20% below the target (or *meta*) level, although tariffs charged by a few public and private water enterprises were close to the *meta* level. The official explanation is that the consumers need time to adjust to rapid increases in prices (which have been substantial in some cases) but that by the end of the 1990s all *vigentes* will be set equal to the *metas*, i.e., self-financing marginal cost prices. Some skeptics inside and outside the government believe, however, that consumers in Regions I through III, XI, and XII probably will never be forced to pay the marginal cost of their water. They argue that the legislature will be very reluctant to require some of the poorest regions of the country to pay for expensive water since water is widely regarded as a basic necessity.

The problem is illustrated in Table 4-2, which presents the average tariff paid per cubic meter of water in different parts of the country. Water companies in the extreme geographic regions, particularly in Regions I through III, charge more per cubic meter of potable water than water enterprises in the central areas but they recover a smaller percentage of the marginal costs (or *meta*) The only major exception to this pattern is in Region V, the heavily populated region immediately to the south of the Metropolitan Region which is served by the public enterprise named ESVAL, where *vigentes* currently being charged also appear to be substantially lower than marginal costs.[11]

The second way in which consumers are undercharged is through the government's policy of requiring a discounted tariff to small consumers. Since 1991, water enterprises have been required to give a 50% discount on the first ten cubic meters of water per month to households which consume less than twenty cubic meters of water in that month. According to the director of CORFO, approximately 80% of all consumers now use less than twenty cubic meters of water a month whereas most of the households receiving piped water used about forty cubic meters a month before the introduction of this subsidy program.[12] The subsidies are paid by each municipality to the appropriate water enterprises and, as such, are reflected as income in the financial accounts of these firms.

11. Additional information regarding marginal costs and tariffs is provided in Appendix A.

12. We are not certain how this remarkable drop in consumption was achieved in such a short period of time; however, it certainly appears to warrant further study, given the magnitude of consumer response to this price change.

Table 4-2. *Water Tariffs by Region (pesos per cubic meter)*

Region	*Firm*	*Average Tariffs (February 1993)*	*Average Water Leakage Rates (%)*	*Ratio of Average Tariff to Meta (%)*
I-Tarapac	ESSAT	240	41.2	79.1%
II-Antofagasta	ESSAN	253	41.2	59.3
III-Atacama	EMSSAT	171	55.7	74.3
IV-Coquimbo	ESSCO	162	28.9	91.7
V-Valparaiso	ESVAL	135	43.8	87.8
Metropolitan Region	EMOS	93	28.0	75.8
VI-Lib. B. O'Higgens	ESSEL	111	47.9	92.2
VII-Maule	ESSAM	122	46.3	89.6
VIII-Bio Bio	ESSBIO	112	37.6	83.8
IX-La Araucancia	ESSAR	134	39.6	87.6
X-De Los Lagos	ESSAL	119	43.6	83.2
XI-Alsen del Gen. Carlos	EMSSA	158	n.a.	81.1
XII-Magellen	ESMAG	178	n.a.	86.8

Source: Memoria (CORFO), 1993, p.9 and p.15.

Finally, it is likely that a discrepancy exists between marginal and average costs per cubic meter of water in the current system. A careful study of the consultant's marginal cost report and the financial statements of the water enterprises suggests that even *metas* are currently set to equal average rather than marginal costs, even in the case of water supply. This is problematic because, even in areas of Chile where water is very clean and plentiful, the marginal costs of supplying water are likely to increase over the relevant levels of consumption. Thus, marginal costs per cubic meter of water are probably higher than the average costs, particularly for water supply (as opposed to water distribution or sewage collection) and this cost is not currently included in the water tariffs.

Geographic Variation in the Subsidy

In 1994, the level of subsidy varied considerably among regions primarily because the costs of supplying water vary. Water supply is relatively inexpensive in the center of the country around Santiago and Region V (Valparaíso) because of ready access to protected sources of pure water in the nearby mountains. Additionally, the water table in this area is close to the surface and ground water is thus relatively inexpensive to pump. On the other hand, supplying pure water to cities in the extreme north, such as Antofagasta in Region II, is very expensive because of the lack of rainfall and because the aquifers close to Antofagasta are polluted due to the region's copper mining industry. Potable water must be transported from a great distance, which significantly increases costs. The extreme southern regions of the country also suffer from inaccessible and/or polluted groundwater problems. The extent of the cost variation is

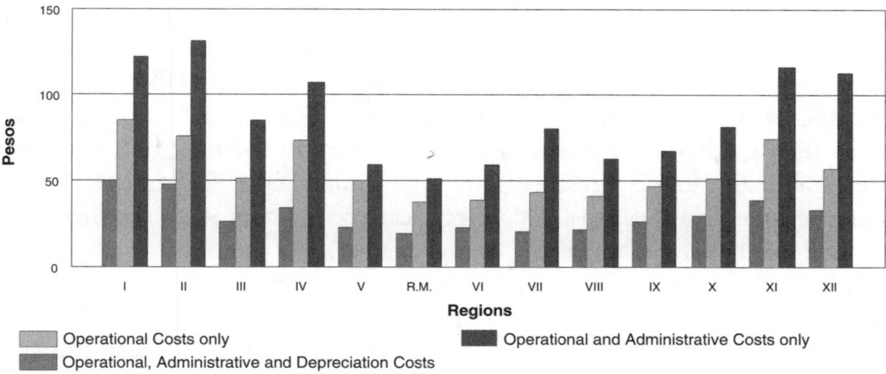

Figure 4-1.

quite large as shown in Figure 4-1 and the appendices. In 1992, for example, the cost of supplying water in Regions I and II, for example, was at least twice that of supplying residents in central areas, while the cost of supplying water to Regions XI and XII was at least 50% more than in the central region.

High rates of water leakage, either from illegal tapping or poorly maintained water pipes, also add to water costs, especially outside Santiago. As Table 4-2 shows, in 1990 leakage rates were much lower in Santiago and Region IV than in the rest of the country. There has been great improvement in the rate of water leakage in Santiago, apparently because of a major upgrading effort completed during the 1980s. As a result, water leakage averages about 28% in Santiago, which compares relatively poorly with best-practice water leakage rates of 15% in most major United States cities.[13] In other parts of Chile, however, leakage rates are even higher and average between 40% and 50%. Firms in the extreme regions are at a severe disadvantage in correcting leakages since they are already losing a great deal of money and thus are hard pressed to finance the investment in upgraded connections, new meters, and other measures needed to correct the problem.

Finally, the costs of providing water in the more extreme regions also may be higher because of their inability to take advantage of economies of scale. By far the largest enterprise in the system is EMOS which is the enterprise serving the Santiago Metropolitan Region. During 1992, the most recent year for which data is available, EMOS provided more than 1,000,000 households with 336,000,000 cubic meters of piped water (approximately eighty-six cubic meters per person) for revenues of 33,824 million pesos. In contrast, other

13. The World Development Report, 1994 estimates that best-practice water delivery rates are 85% in most cities of the industrialized world.

water companies typically supply less than 100,000 customers over a much larger geographic area. International comparative experience suggests that the enterprises that supply water and sanitation services to smaller communities, such as those in Chile's more extreme regions, are at a disadvantage because the fixed costs of building a water purification and distribution system are high relative to the variable costs. In the United States, for example, public water companies appear to achieve significant economies of scale in urban areas of 250,000 people or more.[14]

These cost factors, taken together, result in different levels of subsidies to residents of different regions. The subsidies totaled about $9 (1992 US) per inhabitant-year in Regions I and II, for example, largely because the arid zone's water costs are high and public officials are reluctant to bring tariffs in line.[15] Subsidies in Regions XI and XII were substantially higher, i.e., close to $15, probably because of a combination of high supply costs and small-scale diseconomies accruing to water enterprises. Subsidies averaged less than US $1 (1992 dollars) in the Metropolitan Region and Region V and between 50 cents and US $4 (1992 dollars), primarily depending on the cost of water in other parts of the country.

Access Problems

Connections to the local water distribution and sewage collection system do not always appear to be available in a timely fashion. The evidence is strongest in the Santiago Metropolitan Region, where the four existing private water and sewer companies were formed because real estate developers were unable to get service from the public enterprises in the area.

Land developers established the private water companies in the early 1940s after they were unable to persuade the public water company to build water and sewer lines in newly urbanizing areas outside its service area.[16] The developers decided to supply their clients with water on a private basis for the same rates or tariffs as the public enterprise operating in the region. According to one of the first private companies, Lo Castillo, the regulated price that the private firms are allowed to charge does not cover the full cost of supplying water and sewage services. The companies survive because the land developers transfer income from land sales and construction to the firm on a regular and

14. Superintendencia de Servicios Sanitanios, 1993.

15. This estimate of subsidies accruing to different regions is based on the financial losses of individual enterprises and information on the value of subsidies given to low-income consumers.

16. Alejandro Dussaillant, the executive director of Lo Castillo, interviewed on September 3, 1993.

reliable basis. Lo Castillo has grown gradually from a few hundred customers in 1945 to 7,000 in 1968 to 42,000 in 1983 to more than 65,000 customers in 1994.

An intriguing question is what will happen to these private water firms if land development on the urban fringe slows down or ends. If land appreciation slows in the fringes of Santiago, will the incentive to subsidize these costs end? Only if the private firms are allowed to charge the true marginal costs of water supply, collection (and perhaps treatment), will the water continue to be supplied by private firms. Otherwise, the public sector may well have to step in and provide residents with these services at significant public expense. Nevertheless, the continued growth of Lo Castillo and the emergence of several other money-losing private water enterprises indicate that access to connections in Santiago is still an issue.

This access problem may decline somewhat in the future as the water enterprise reforms, introduced in the early 1990s, increase resources and the capacity for new investments in the water/sewer sector.[17] In theory, the methodology used to set *meta* prices is supposed to guarantee both public and private water enterprises a 7% rate of return on their assets. In fact, however, it is unclear how the rate of return to water enterprises is being monitored and whether many enterprises earn any return at all. The 7% return is calculated on the basis of the expected efficient performance of a model enterprise. Given that few, if any, of the water enterprises function at an optimal efficiency, many firms may make less than 7% and may, thus, be forced to underinvest in capital improvements. Moreover, political pressures probably will keep prices below *meta* targets for some time, particularly in the poorer regions of the country, and thereby impel the affected enterprises to resist improving their services or introducing wastewater treatment.

Spatial Implications

Considering water and wastewater services together, problems of access and subsidy are common throughout Chile but probably especially severe in the large metropolitan areas of Santiago and Valparaíso and in the extreme north and south of the country. In the metropolitan areas, the problem is more wastewater than water. Access to water connections for new developments are apparently limited because water tariffs do not cover costs, but the gap between water tariffs and cost is not that large. The volume of wastewater generated in Santiago and Valparaíso, however, is too great to be disposed of without some type of treatment. Conservatively *low* estimates of treatment costs average

17. See Appendix A for more details.

Table 4-3. *Average Water Tariffs ("Vigentes") In Pesos for Meter Consumers By Region and Group, July 1993*

	Fixed Charges							
Enterprises	*Normal $/mon.*	*Lower $/mon*	*5 m^3/mon. Average $/m3*	*10 m^3/mon. Average $/m^3$*	*15m3/mon. Average $/m^3$*	*20 m3/mon. Average $/m^3$*	*30 m3/mon. Average $/m^3$*	*50 m3/mon. Average $/m^3$*
Emos G1	861	861	286	200	172	157	143	131
G2	854	854	282	197	168	154	140	129
G3	822	822	272	189	162	148	135	124
Esval G1	845	800	287	207	193	186	193	181
G2	941	891	362	263	250	244	257	244
G3	874	825	275	192	176	168	172	160
G4	740	716	242	171	166	149	161	142
Lo Castillo	474	474	196	149	133	125	117	111
Manquehue	405	405	213	173	159	152	148	140
Maipu	730	456	174	129	142	135	139	129
Servicom.	492	415	193	151	149	144	148	139
Region I	852	658	248	192	195	196	228	216
Region II	623	541	223	169	219	244	340	331
Region III	686	456	210	164	171	175	208	198
Region IV	703	516	237	185	178	175	188	178
Region VI	1091	759	252	176	156	147	153	139
Region VII	1069	722	268	196	183	176	191	177
Region VIII	868	605	223	162	149	143	152	140
Region IX	1018	707	273	202	190	184	200	186
Region X	1021	707	286	215	208	204	227	213
Region XI	1262	686	262	194	208	215	279	262
Region XII	771	617	249	187	190	191	221	210
Average	845	639	251	187	185	183	206	194

Source: Informe Mensual de Tarifas al mes de julio, 1993, Superintendencia de Servicios Sanitarios, p. 8.

about $10 per inhabitant-year, which would be the equivalent of an increase of at least US $0.14 per cubic meter in the price charged for water.[18] Thus charging for wastewater treatment probably will increase the cost per cubic meter of water in the cities of Santiago and Valparaíso by at least 50%. Even with such an increase, however, water in the Metropolitan Region would still cost significantly less (135 pesos per cubic meter) than water in the most expensive regions (240 and 253 pesos per cubic meter in Regions I and II, respectively).

In the extreme north and south of the country water is the more serious problem. Water prices are far below costs largely because unit costs are so high. Although sewage usually is not treated, the resulting health problems are probably modest and the treatment options relatively inexpensive. In rural areas and small cities treatment may not be necessary or can be handled using septic systems or lagoon technologies, at least for the foreseeable future. Although the cost of treatment per inhabitant increases as the population being served declines, cities of 20,000 to 100,000 still face sewage treatment costs of only $8 per inhabitant (assuming treatment is necessary). Smaller cities therefore may need to increase the cost per cubic meter of water by only US $0.09 per cubic meter compared to the increase of at least US $0.14 per cubic meter estimated for the Metropolitan Region.[19] Rural areas and smaller cities in the center of the country may have the least water and wastewater subsidy. Water is already priced close to cost and waste treatment, if necessary, is probably significantly less costly than in Santiago.

Recommendations

The spatial distortions in this sector would be reduced if households were charged the full costs of the water they consume and wastewater they generate. This recommendation may be unrealistic and difficult to implement because many policymakers in Chile, as well as in the rest of the world, believe that the price of water should be subsidized, particularly for low-income residents. Unfortunately, the current pricing scheme subsidizes the water consumption of almost all the households in Chile, regardless of their income

---

18. Assuming that the average resident of the Metropolitan Region consumes 78 cubic meters of water per year, the price per cubic meter would need to rise by 10.00/78 or US $0.14. The average price charged per cubic meter in February 1993 was only 93 pesos or US $.25.

19. If we use the prices per cubic meters in effect as of February 1993, we can estimate the costs increases that different regions will incur as a result of wastewater treatment. The tariff per cubic meter in Region III, for example, was 171 pesos in February 1993. If we add the full costs of wastewater treatment to this, i.e., approximately US $0.09 per cubic meter, the total cost per cubic meter in urban areas becomes 206 pesos. This is somewhat more than the price residents of the Metropolitan Region will need to pay for their water, i.e., 135 pesos per cubic meter, if they are charged US $0.14 per cubic meter for wastewater treatment.

level. A more efficient way to subsidize water consumption for poor households is a direct transfer of income or resources from the state to low-income households so that they could afford to purchase an appropriate amount of correctly priced water. A less obvious and compromise solution to some of the pricing problems faced by the public water enterprises might be the refinement of the existing increasing block water pricing system used in Chile, particularly in areas where costs are high. Under a block rate system, consumers would be charged a low rate per cubic meter for the first five or so cubic meters per month. For consumption above the minimum, the price per cubic meter would rise in a step-wise fashion until it was at or above marginal costs of providing water. Block tariffs can assist low-income households because they use less water than high-income households. At the same time, block prices charge heavy water users the true cost of water supply and thus discourage "extravagant" water use and promote water conservation.

Solid Waste Collection and Disposal

Organization of the Sector[20]

Solid waste collection and disposal in Chile are the responsibility of municipal governments, although cities must meet certain national norms or standards set by the National Health Service, an autonomous administrative unit of the Ministry of Health responsible for administering and enforcing the national public health requirements. Since 1994, the law states that waste must be transported in impermeable covered vehicles that remain constantly closed and that the government must ensure that all personnel responsible for collection and transporting garbage be equipped with uniforms, equipment, and showers that adequately protect them from infection. The separation and selection of waste for recycling purposes is to occur only at authorized sites. In addition, the municipality is supposed to select from various methods of approved waste disposal including dumping in sanitary landfills, discharging into the ocean or large lakes, and incineration. Furthermore, as a result of a decree promulgated by the Ministry of the Interior, each municipal government is responsible for keeping its urban zone permanently and entirely clean.

Since 1980, municipalities have been allowed to contract out the collection, transportation, and disposal of solid wastes to private enterprises. The contract between the municipality and the private firm typically specifies frequency and extent of coverage, types of waste to be collected (i.e., residential street waste, street cleaning, industrial services), and sanctions to be imposed in case of fail-

20. This section is drawn primarily from Reiter (1993).

ure to comply with the contract. Some municipalities choose to contract only selected solid waste services, such as collection, while others contract out all aspects of the service including street cleaning, collection, transportation, and disposal. In 1985, 66% of all municipal solid waste in Chile was collected and transported by private companies.[21] By 1994, all but three municipalities in the Santiago area contracted out collection to private firms.

According to statistics compiled in 1988, 98.9% of the urban population (including commercial and industrial enterprises) in Chile receives garbage collection services. Over 370 cities and rural towns have garbage collection services and nearly 94% of these communities collect solid wastes in over 80% of their communities, seven communities cover 50% to 80% of their district and eleven towns cover less than 50% of their district.[22] It is not unusual, however, to find substantial amounts of garbage dumped illegally along main roads that lead to a town or city. The cities generally use their own crews and trucks to collect this trash since the responsibility typically is not included in municipal contracts with private firms.

The Municipal Income Law of 1979 establishes the right and duty of the municipality to charge users for municipal solid waste services but also specifies how the cost and tariffs should be calculated. The cost of the service, for example, is based on the average costs incurred the previous fiscal year by the municipal sanitation department or the private enterprise contracted to carry out the service. These costs are adjusted for inflation and must include personnel costs (salaries of both permanent and temporary employees as well as accident and health insurance), vehicle costs, waste disposal costs, capital costs, contracted services, rental costs (e.g. rental of land) and other costs including that for uniforms and cleaning tools.

Improper Disposal

One of the major problems in Chile's solid waste sector is that approximately 40,000 of the 200,000 tons of solid waste collected in Chile are improperly disposed of. Most of the solid waste is disposed of in sanitary landfills where garbage is covered every day and liners and other precautions are used to reduce the risk of groundwater contamination.[23] But the remainder is disposed of in open dumps that do not meet sanitary standards.

21. Durán de la Fuente, p.13.

22. Ibid., p.19.

23. In a sanitary landfill, solid waste is dumped in a pile and then compacted by a bulldozer. A layer of dirt, between 15 and 20 cm. thick, is added daily to cover the new garbage. The bottom of the landfill is treated or lined with an impermeable coating so that the liquids formed by the fermenting waste do not seep into the groundwater. The direction of surface water is altered to avoid passing near the site. Pipes and vents are installed to collect gases and vent them safely. At the end of its useful life, a final covering of earth (50 to 60 cm. thick) is added to the landfill.

The problem is less serious in the Santiago Metropolitan Region and in the central regions of the country than it is elsewhere, as shown in Table 4-4. In the Santiago area, 95% of all garbage waste in 1990 was properly disposed while the central regions properly disposed of 60 to 80% of their waste. In the extreme north and south of the country, however, there are regions where there are no proper sanitary landfills. According to data from the Ministry of Health, in1994 370 urban areas outside the Santiago area provided collection services, but only 127 disposed of the garbage in sanitary landfills or in other approved methods. This means that 65.7% (or 243) urban areas rely primarily on official open-air dumps to dispose of their garbage. These dumps are often in areas where solid waste is "officially" disposed of by municipalities or their agents and yet is not subject to proper management and control. In many of these dumps, the garbage is not covered with an adequate amount of soil every day and access to the dump is open to *cachureros* (informal sector workers who collect waste materials of economic value). In addition, there is often little or no active management over what is dumped, how it is treated, and what fees are collected. As in much of the rest of the world, Chile also has clandestine dumps that function without any kind of official management or legal status whatsoever.

Some of the social costs associated with improper waste disposal include the contamination of both surface and groundwater due to contact with fermented garbage, the spread of disease through handling disease-carrying ma-

Table 4-4. *Final Disposition of Municipal Solid Waste in Chile by Region (tons and percentage per month for 1990)*

Region	*Population*	*Solid Wastes*		*% Disposed of in Sanitary Landfill*	*Not Disposed of in Sanitary Landfills*	
		tons	*(%)*		*tons*	*(%)*
I	311,521	3,738	1.8	0.0	3,738	100.0
II	384,099	4,609	2.3	91.2	406	8.8
III	180,161	2,162	1.1	0.0	2,162	100.0
IV	307,530	3,690	1.9	0.0	3,690	100.0
V	1,179,878	21,238	10.6	86.0	2,978	14.0
VI	366,021	6,588	3.3	73.9	1,720	26.1
VII	434,378	6,516	3.3	80.9	1,247	19.1
VIII	1,234,643	14,816	7.4	62.5	5,552	37.5
IX	422,651	5,072	2.5	14.2	4,350	85.8
X	510,560	7,658	3.8	26.5	5,680	73.5
XI	49,969	600	0.3	71.2	172	28.8
XII	140,610	2,953	1.5	0.0	2,953	100.0
R.M.	4,830,946	120,291	60.0	95.4	5,528	4.6
Total	10,352,967	199,931	100.0	79.9	40,124	20.1

Source: Durán de la Fuente, p.13.

terial without sanitary precautions, the proliferation of unhealthy bacteria, and frequent fires. A recent engineering study devoted to analyzing the different possible alternatives for treating solid waste in the Metropolitan Region of Santiago assumes that the benefit of disposing garbage properly (i.e., the *valor del servicio*) is $1,810 pesos (US $5) per ton. How this particular team arrived at this figure is unclear particularly since it is very low by world standards which, in general, average between US $10 to $20 a ton.[24] It is likely that their recommendations are based on very conservative estimates of the benefits of proper disposal.

Given that urban areas outside Santiago are less likely to use sanitary landfills, they are also less likely to be charging the marginal or average cost of handling solid waste properly. Residents of Santiago, on the other hand, are asked to pay the average cost of these services because most of their waste is being handled more or less properly. Assuming that residents of Santiago actually pay for solid waste disposal services, the spatial distortions work against the capital (where people are more likely to pay for the garbage they discharge) and towards other, smaller urban areas, which do not charge residents close to the full cost of handling their solid waste.[25]

Inadequate Funding

Not only is solid waste disposed of poorly in many of Chile's urban places but the charges for solid waste services typically are inadequate to cover costs. The standard annual user fee for solid waste services is determined by dividing the total annual cost of the service by the total number of users; users are defined as all the homes registered with the Internal Revenue Service (SNI) (whether or not the household is exempt from property taxes) as well as all businesses that pay commercial licenses. In addition, any user who creates more than 200 liters of garbage daily is charged a special tariff set by the municipality. Commercial users pay their user fee along with the payments for their business licenses while residential users are charged the user fee as part of their property tax payments. The average fee for municipal solid waste ser-

24. Tesam Hartley S.A., p. 12.

25. A caveat to this conclusion is that Lepanto, one of Santiago's primary so-called sanitary landfills, is apparently subject to poor management and functions more or less like an uncontrolled dump. Thus, the amount that Santiago residents and business owners pay for the use of Lepanto is lower than that which corresponds to average proper disposal costs. The other two landfills in Santiago, Cerros de Renca and Lo Errázuriz, are well managed but they were predicted to reach capacity by the end of 1995. The charges at all three landfills ranged from US $1.80 to $4.25 ($600 to $1500 pesos) per ton at the end of 1992. Although cost data are unavailable on a regional basis, it is likely that the costs of proper disposal are similar in other cities and regions of the country. Durán de la Fuente, p.17.

vices in Chile in 1993 was approximately US $1.50 per month, which, again, is quite low by world standards. While we have little information on how user fees vary by urban area or region, we do know that the standard user fee in the city of San Antonio amounted to $8,453 pesos (US $20.60 annually or US $1.72 per month) in 1993.

The primary problem with this system is that many homeowners in Chile's urban areas are exempt from paying property tax and as a result do not pay their solid waste fee either. The most recent data available indicate that 67.7% of all residential properties in Chile are exempt from paying property taxes. Some researchers have claimed that in many of the poorer communities up to 90% of all property is exempt from property taxes.[26] Although municipalities are technically allowed to charge directly for solid waste services, the legality of charging users for these services even if they are exempt from paying property taxes is unclear.

As a result of the property tax exemption, municipal governments, on average, subsidize 70% of the costs of solid waste services. A case study of San Antonio, for example, revealed that fully 15.7% of that city's *entire* budget went to pay for solid waste services over a period of four years.[27] This figure is much higher than the national average because 87% of all households in San Antonio are exempt from paying property tax. Officially, the municipality spent US $355,000 on the provision of solid waste disposal in 1993 through a contract with a private firm, Empresa Blumemberg. The actual cost of the services to the city might have been several thousand dollars more because the city is also responsible for cleaning illegal dumps, which is not provided for under the service contract (Reiter 1993).

The extent to which solid waste use is subsidized varies by region because the regions differ in the proportion of the property base exempt from taxes. The regions that are the least able to recover the costs of providing solid waste services include Regions I, IV, VIII, IX, and XI (see Table 4-5). In Region I, for example, where almost 77% of the homes are exempt from taxes presumably because there are large numbers of low-income households in that region, only17.5% of the cost of municipal solid waste services is covered by user fees. It is likely that urban residents in these regions are less likely to bear the costs of solid waste collection and disposal and, thus, the costs of their decision to live there. Cost recovery is fairly high in cities such as Santiago (33% cost recovery) or Valparaíso (35% cost recovery ratio) where fewer households are exempt from property taxes.

26. Reiter, p. 9.
27. Ibid., p. 18.

Table 4-5. *Cost Recovery for Municipal Solid Waste Service Provision by Region, 1992 (in thousands of pesos)*

Region	*Cost of Service*	*User Fees Collected*	*% of Costs Recovered*
I	555,756	96,957	17.45
II	317,117	112,589	35.50
III	201,454	63,840	31.69
IV	880,218	164,149	18.65
V	2,589,342	914,917	35.33
VI	778,088	228,201	29.33
VII	342,058	119,431	34.92
VIII	2,054,137	462,402	22.51
IX	585,394	109,906	18.77
X	592,539	162,643	27.45
XI	118,885	19,921	16.76
XII	342,692	88,406	27.23
M.R.	8,286,908	2,767,039	33.39
Total	17,626,588	5,310,401	30.13

Source: Reiter, p. 15.

Spatial Implications

Overall, the solid waste system appears to bias residential locations in favor of smaller cities and remote regions and against Santiago and other larger cities in the central regions. This occurs because solid waste is less likely to be disposed of properly in the smaller cities and remote regions, so municipal disposal costs outside the central region probably understate the social disposal costs significantly. Moreover, residents of smaller cities and remote regions are more likely to be exempt from property tax and thus pay, on average, a smaller percentage of municipal collection and disposal costs. In fact, if one ignores the income distribution between regions, one can argue that the patterns of property tax exemptions in Chile are a general source of spatial bias. Residents of large urban areas in the central regions are less likely to be exempt from paying property taxes and are therefore treated unfairly vis-à-vis urban residents in other parts of the country who are rarely required to pay their property taxes.

If we limit the discussion to solid waste disposal, however, the degree of spatial distortion is probably fairly modest largely because the costs of disposal are currently quite low. The average municipal cost of collection and disposal is only around US $20 per household per year, for example, and the average social cost is probably only slightly higher given that only 20% of Chile's garbage is improperly disposed of. A subsidy of at most US $20 per household per year alone probably will not affect residential location.

It is possible that the spatial distortions caused by the solid waste system may become more serious in the future, however. Solid waste disposal costs may increase rapidly in Santiago because of the closing of Santiago's two largest existing sanitary landfills. Capital and operating costs for the new landfills, even using optimistic projections from engineers, will be at least 50% higher. Tesam Hartley S.A. projects that the operational and capital costs of new sanitary landfills will be in the order of $9,560 pesos (or US $23.33) a ton which is more than four times higher than the current collection and disposal costs of garbage in San Miguel.[28]

Recommendations

Although solid waste probably does not cause serious spatial distortions, it is important for environmental and aesthetic reasons that it be properly collected and disposed of. Given that it now costs, on average, only US $20 annually for the service, many more Chileans probably can pay for municipal solid waste services than currently do. If necessary, Chile's municipalities could use some kind of sliding scale of charges, as happens in the case of water. Low-income households could be subsidized by charging other households slightly more than the average cost per ton, or the municipal government could simply subsidize low-income groups directly. For efficiency reasons, the municipalities should begin to require a larger percentage of the population to pay for the solid wastes disposal services they receive.

In addition, it would make a great deal of sense to explore the use of other possible mechanisms for collecting fees. If, in fact, it proves difficult to require a larger portion of households to pay their property taxes, the central government should support efforts to link the fee for solid waste services to an electricity or water bill.[29] Finally, the national government needs to examine the issue of property tax exemption across regions. The current pattern of exemptions seems to favor outlying regions over Santiago and other large centrally located urban areas, as well as allowing a majority of all urban residents to ignore the fiscal implications of their decision to live in a municipality.

---

28. In a recent article from *El Diario*, the Mayor of San Miguel is quoted as saying that his municipality already spends $18 million pesos a month to discharge waste for 85,000 inhabitants at a cost of $1,960 pesos per ton, which he feels is unreasonably high.

29. Rather than adding solid waste charges directly to electricity bills, which the electric company may reject as a threat to its own income, Chile may decide to borrow an idea used with some success in Indonesia. Some municipalities in Indonesia use a "payment point" system, which involves the municipality or its agent setting up a desk adjacent to the electric companies' payment counters. After a customer pays the electric bill, s/he is directed to the next counter to pay the solid waste bill. Signs, leaflets, and prominently displayed official letters from the mayor or other municipal leader urging good citizenship are used to entice payment (Cervero, 1993, p.14).

Telecommunications

Organization of the sector[30]

Since 1990, the telephone industry in Chile has been completely privatized and subject to rate regulation by the Undersecretariate for Telecommunications (SUBTEL), an institution within the Ministry of Transportation and Telecommunications. Approximately 95% of all local telephone service is provided by a single company, the Chilean Telephone Company (CTC), which at one time was owned by the U.S. firm ITT. CTC's coverage is nationwide with the primary exceptions of Regions X and XI, both of which are located in southern Chile. In Region X (Los Lagos) local telephone service is provided by the National Telephone Company of Valdivia, which was established in 1894 and has always been a privately held and managed company (except between 1971 and 1982). Region XI (Aysen) is served by the Coyhaique Telephone Company, a former municipal firm that was privatized in 1982. In addition, there are two relatively small local telephone companies, which compete with CTC for customers in Santiago (the Complejo Manufacturero de Equipos Telefonicos or CEMET) and Viña del Mar (the Manquehue Telephone Company or CTM). Finally, there are several mobile or cellular telephone companies including one—CID-Communicacions Limitada (CIDCOM)—which operates in the provinces of Valparaíso, Cachapoal, and within the Metropolitan Region of Santiago. Other smaller cellular companies, which also operate primarily in the Santiago area, include VTR, CTC, and TELECOM.

Problems with Service Access

Access to telecommunications services has been an important problem for both industry and households. Since 1992, the performance of CTC has improved the situation remarkably. CTC installed over 216,000 lines in 1992, which represents a 13% increase in the total number of lines available to Chileans in 1991 (CTC Memoria, 1992). The severity of the access problems prior to 1992 was reflected by both unequal distribution of telephone lines and the backlog of requests for service across the country.

Distribution of Telecommunication Services

The distribution of CTC telephone lines across the nation clearly favors the Metropolitan Region of Santiago as well as Region XII (Magallenes). For

30. Much of the information in this section was culled from annual reports of the CTC.

the country as a whole, there were, on average, approximately 5.7 lines per 100 inhabitants in 1990.[31] As can be seen in Table 4-6, however, Magallenes and Santiago had 7.5 and 7.8 lines per 100 inhabitants, respectively, while other regions, such as Region VII (del Maule), made do with only 2.4 lines per 100 inhabitants. Similarly, Magallenes and Santiago had, respectively, 12.7 and 10.2 telephones per 100 inhabitants in 1990, compared to only 3.0 and 3.8 telephones per 100 inhabitants in Regions III, VI, and IX that same year.

One potential explanation for the unequal distribution of telephone lines and appliances is the difference in per capita incomes or in business and commercial activity across regions. Santiago may have 61% of all lines, for example, because its residents conduct 60% of the business activity of the country. Santiago households also have higher incomes, and thus are more willing and able to pay for telephone service than residents of other Chilean cities.

Income and business activity differences can probably not, however, account for regional differences in the number of calls placed per line or the number of people on the waiting list for telephone service. Table 4-6 shows, for example, that the average telephone line in Santiago is used to place 85 telephone calls while the average line in Magallenes is used to place 130 calls a month. Telephone lines in Region III or Region IX, which are less populous and poorer, are used to make 483 and 391 calls respectively. Clearly, the telephone lines installed in these latter areas are in use much more frequently than in better supplied areas. This indicates that there may, in fact, be a shortage in the regions where telephone density is lower than average.

Another important aspect of telephone services, particularly for businesses with export aspirations, is access to long-distance and international communication services. This access appears to mirror access to local telephone service, although information on the topic is scarce. Domestic long-distance services are provided exclusively by CTC, while international long distance is provided by ENTEL (National Telecommunications Company) and two other smaller firms, Chilesat and VTR. In general, those regions that are well supplied with telephone lines, such as the Santiago area or Valparaíso, account for a high percentage of the total long-distance calls placed in Chile. Similarly, those regions that have a limited number of telephone lines such as Region III account for a mere 2% of all long-distance calls. Region XII, which has a large number of local lines, however, accounts for even a smaller percentage of long-distance calls, i.e., 1.5%, which is somewhat surprising. Demand for international and long-distance service grew by an average of 17.5%

31. CTC's post-1992 investment program is reflected in the fact that lines increased to 9.8 per 100 people by 1993.

Table 4-6. *Regional Breakdown of Telephone Lines, Telephones and Calls per inhabitant. (1989)*

Region	*Lines in Service*	*Telephones*	*Calls*	*Lines per 100 inhab.*	*Telephones per 100 inhab.*	*Calls per capita*	*Calls per line*
I-Tarapac	19661	30737	4001709	5.58	8.72	11.35	204
II-Antofagasta	17604	27368	6056115	4.56	7.09	15.69	344
III-Atacama	4997	7423	2415685	2.53	3.76	12.24	483
IV-Coquimbo	16438	24924	3855062	3.41	5.17	8.00	235
V-Valparaíso	75790	107511	20733208	5.51	7.82	15.08	274
Metroplitana	403020	531386	34059463	7.77	10.25	6.57*	85
VI-Lib.Gral. B. O'Higgens	19639	26723	6503896	3.04	4.14	10.08	331
VII-Maule	19820	26528	7122218	2.38	3.18	8.54	359
VIII-Bio Bio	43081	69044	12893152	2.59	4.15	7.74	299
IX-La Araucancia	13994	23376	5471428	1.77	2.96	6.93	391
X-De Los Lagos	25987	33704	n.a.	3.16	3.69	n.a.	n.a.
XI-Alsén del General Carlos	3468	3868	n.a.	4.82	4.94	n.a.	n.a.
XII-Magll. y de la Antar	11819	19805	1540516	7.50	12.57	9.78	130
Total	645863	894825	104652000	5.35	7.41	8.67	162

* Figure does not include calls made using other providers of telephone service in the Santiago region.
Source: Anuario Estadistico General del Desarrollo Telefonico (Periodo 1960-1989)
Compañia de Telefonos de Chile, S.A.

between 1985 and 1990 and this trend may continue as the economy expands. What is less clear is if access to these services will continue to be somewhat limited for those who live outside the Santiago Metropolitan Region.

Backlog

Since 1987, all telephone companies have been required by law to provide subscribers with a telephone within two years of a request. In recognition of how difficult this would be for most of the companies, however, SUBTEL established timetables to bring different service areas on line over a period of ten years. Little data are available about how long people have to wait on average for a telephone. It does appear, however, that the absolute number of people waiting for a telephone increased in most regions between 1985 and 1990. Backlogs per capita are fairly evenly distributed across the country, as shown in 4-2. Most regions have around two to three backlog requests per 100 inhabitants, with the principal exception being Region XII, where backlogs reached as high as 4.7 per 100 inhabitants (in 1988). The number of backlogs per 100 inhabitants also increased throughout the 1980s, although it has probably dropped in more recent years.

Backlogs per line are very unequally distributed, however, as shown in Table 4-7. Those regions with the fewest lines per inhabitant also have the largest backlog per existing line. In Region III, for example, the number of people waiting for a telephone line is almost the same as the number who already have lines. In metropolitan Santiago, by contrast, the percentage of people waiting for a line is only one third of the number of existing lines. Of course, it is true that the number of people waiting for lines in Santiago (151,483) is far greater than in any other region. In general, however, Santiago residents are so much better off in terms of telecommunications service that

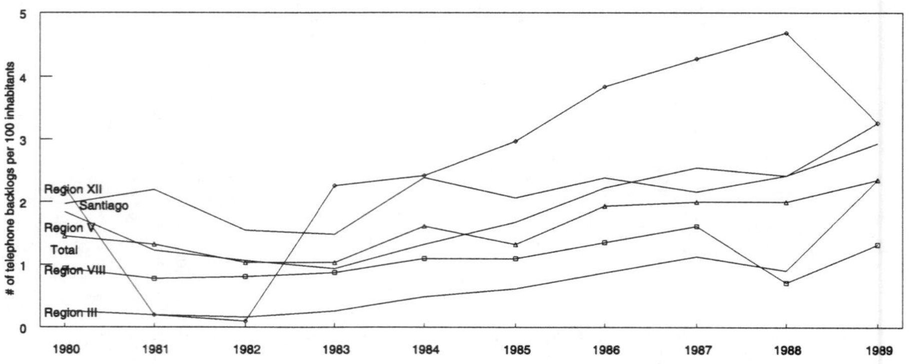

Figure 4-2.

Table 4-7. *Service Backlogs in the Telecommunications Industry by Region (1989)*

Region	*Lines in Service*	*Population*	*Backlog*	*Backlog/Line*	*% of lines Digitized*
I-Tarapac	19661	352634	10722	0.55	31.4
II-Antofagasta	17604	385931	5449	0.31	54.4
III-Atacama	4997	197443	4637	0.93	76.6
IV-Coquimbo	16438	482075	7870	0.48	31.0
V-Valparaíso	75790	1374633	44793	0.59	65.7
Metroplitana	403020	5185034	151483	0.38	50.9
VI-Lib.Gral. B. O'Higgens	19639	645452	10942	0.56	37.5
VII-Maule	19820	833909	11368	0.57	60.7
VIII-Bio Bio	43081	1665532	22083	0.51	51.0
IX-La Araucancia	13994	789271	9530	0.68	30.8
XII-Magll. y de la Antar	11819	157582	5122	0.43	28.4
Total	645863	12069387	283919	0.44	51.1

Source: Anuario Estadistico General del Desarrollo Telefonico (Periodo 1960-1989) Compañia de Telefonos de Chile, S.A. Gerencia Tecnica, Departamento Planificacion

it is clear that their demands are being met more rapidly than those in other areas. Overall, CTC has an unmet need of 283,919 telephone lines, or almost 44% of their existing capacity.

The pattern in Table 4-8 suggests that, at least through the 1980s, CTC was allocating each region about the same number of new lines per inhabitant each year. This meant that the backlog stayed about the same in each region, and that the historical discrepancies in the number of lines per 100 inhabitants was being reduced, although only slowly.

Rate and Cost Structure

The cost structure and rate setting procedures in the telephone industry are complex and thus it is very difficult to determine whether they cause spatial distortions or contribute to the access problems outlined above. The rate-setting procedures were completely overhauled in 1987, when the telephone sector was privatized. Under the new scheme, rates for different areas of the country are intended to reflect the marginal cost of service and to recover the total cost of an efficient company. Regulations were adopted to limit cross subsidies among services where more than one service is provided in a common tariff area.

Rates are established every five years through a decree of the Ministry of Transportation and Communications. During the five-year period for which

Table 4-8. *Telephone Service Rates in Chilean pesos (including taxes) 1990**

Servicio Local Medido:

	North	*Central*	*South*
Monthly Service Charge			
Residential	2,119	2,000	*2,317*
Commercial	3,859	3,717	*3,966*
Combined (R&C)	4,821	*5,165*	5,074
Rate per minute			
Standard	7.882	6.435	*8.360*
Low	3.866	3.374	*4.181*
Evening	0.164	0.164	0.164

Servicio Tariffa Plana: (cost per month)

	Type of Service	*North*	*Central*	*South*
RESIDENTIAL	Automatic	4,241	*4,668*	3,973
	Bateria Central	3,605	*3,967*	3,377
	Magneto	2,968	*3,268*	2,782
COMMERCIAL	Automatic	6,618	*6,832*	6,334
	Bateria Central	5,625	*5,808*	5,384
	Magneto	4,633	*4,783*	4,434
COMBINED (R & C)	Automatic	17,238	*17,949*	16,523
	Bateria Central	14,652	*15,256*	14,044
	Magneto	12,066	*12,564*	11,566

*Italics denote highest charge/tariff for a type of service.
Source: Anuario Estadistico General del Desarrollo Telefonico, Periodo 1960-1989
CTC, Gerencia Tecnica, Departamento Planificacion

specific rates are in effect, companies may automatically readjust their fees in accordance with variations in the prices of inputs as stipulated in the indexation formulas. The procedures for conducting studies and implementing tariff schedules are described in detail in the legislation. In essence, three stages are called for: definition of the bases for the study, realization of the study, and review and implementation of the resulting rate formulas. The first and final stages are conducted by SUBTEL while the second is conducted by the telephone companies, either directly or through specialized consultants. Should differences arise in terms of the definition of the bases for the study or the results of the review process, the opinion of a specialized committee can be requested. In any case, the final decision lies in the hands of government officials.

The tariffs for CTC local telephone service are summarized in Table 4-8. Two basic tariffs are offered. The first, Servicio Local Medido (SLM), includes both a fixed monthly charge plus a charge based on the minutes of use. The second, Tariffa Plana (STP), allows for unlimited local calls for a fixed monthly fee. The charges vary according to geographic area (three different zones) and type of establishment (residential, business, or both). In addition, charges vary by time of day, in the case of the SLM tariff, and by the type of communication system used to handle the call (automatic, *bateria central*, or *magneto*) in the case of the Tariffa Plana.

The CTC tariff structure probably does not closely reflect spatial variations in cost in that the tariff schedule provides for only three different geographic zones for the entire country. The northern zone includes Regions I through IV (Arica, Iquique, Antofagasta, and La Serena), the central zone includes Regions V, VI, and the Metropolitan Region, while the southern zone includes Regions VII, VIII, IX, and XII (Talca, Chillán, Concepción, Los Angeles, and Temuco y Magallanes).

Rates are not always cheaper in the central than in the northern or southern zones despite the economies of scale and traffic density that would lead one to expect telephone services to be less costly in urban than rural regions. The rate for the STP service is actually higher in the central zone, which is particularly puzzling since central zone users make fewer telephone calls per line on average. The SLM rates are lower in the central zone, but only by about 10 to 20% and only about 60% of all residential users in the metropolitan region have the SLM plan available to them since it necessitates a technological modification to the preexisting system. Almost all consumers in the Santiago area who have SLM available choose to use that option. Only 40% of all households outside the central region have the option of using SLM service.

The tariff structure also does not include a charge for either the initial connection of a line to a building or for the initial start of service, both of which may reduce the incentives of the company to resolve backlogs. Customers or businesses are responsible for paying CTC or a private electrician for the cost of installing a line from the CTC pole to their building.

Additional spatial distortions may be introduced by long-distance rates, although it is difficult to tell if this is the case. Discrepancies between costs and rates on long-distance service might have spatial implications, if only because rural regions and small city dwellers use long-distance services more intensively in Chile. Long-distance rates for all areas and types of service are simply based on the distance of the call and the time of day. Rates for long-distance calling via direct dialing range from 28.59 to 97.83 pesos per minute during the day and from 13.22 to 82.45 pesos per minute at night depending on the distance between the two points of communication. Long-distance service using an operator is generally much more expensive, starting with 82.51 pesos per minute for a station-to-station call and going up to 291.21 pesos per minute for a person-to-person call.

Some observers suspect that these long-distance rates favor the long-distance carrier (typically ENTEL) over the local company (typically CTC). ENTEL has sustained profit levels of more than 40% over costs since 1985 compared to profit levels of between 10 and 15% for CTC.

Spatial Distortions and Implications

The telecommunications sector appears to distort spatial decisions in complex and perhaps offsetting ways, although these conclusions are very speculative, given our lack of spatially detailed cost data. On the one hand, residents of remote regions and small cities are disadvantaged in that they have to wait longer to get a line than residents of the central regions or Santiago and they rely more on long-distance services. On the other hand, residents of remote regions and small cities are favored in that they pay about the same local telephone rates as residents of the central region and Santiago even though their costs per subscriber or call are probably higher.

These offsetting distortions may, of course, be related. In particular, the combination of the lack of a connection fee and smaller mark ups on local telephone services in rural and remote regions may account for the telephone company's delay in providing new lines in these areas. In any event, some of these spatial distortions probably will decline over time as the newly privatized telephone industry becomes more efficient and invests in new technologies. Recent evidence suggests that, in fact, the CTC has moved to solve the access problem by increasing the number of lines in service from 646,000 in 1989 to 2,600,000 in 1997. Apparently, the backlog for telephone lines has decreased dramatically and the number of lines in service per 100 inhabitants has increased to 17.8.[32] In addition, CTC is expanding its long-distance capacity by launching a system of satellites and installing fiber optic networks between the principal urban areas of communication, Valparaíso to Santiago and Santiago to Temuco. In terms of cellular communications, CTC has a subsidiary, Telefonia Portatil Celular, which has installed cellular phone service, both automobile and residential, in the Santiago Region and Region V.

Indeed, the newly emerging telephone technologies probably will reduce the cost of communications in general, and in particular, spatial cost differences and, thus, the potential for spatial distortions. Cellular technology, for example, while currently available in the largest urban areas of Chile, probably will spread to smaller urban areas quite quickly (at least as quickly as rising incomes require). In addition, fiber optics and satellites will lower the price of telephone service throughout the country. In short, while the level of spatial distortions, particularly in terms of better access for Santiago residents

32. International Telecommunications Union (ITU) data, 1998.

and businesses, was probably quite severe until 1990 or so, the situation appears to be improving rapidly and all indications are that service will improve even more in the near future.

Recommendations

The recommendations for this sector focus primarily on the improved compilation and analysis of telecommunications data. In particular, public regulatory action should monitor differences in costs, rates, and service quality by region or city size. These analyses should focus on both the costs and revenues of providing different types of services to different areas of the country. CTC, in particular, should be required to present information about which types of lines and regions are receiving subsidized service and what provision of these services costs for different cities and regions within Chile. In other words, the spatial implications of telecommunication services should be made transparent so that the various cost and revenue issues can be debated in an explicit fashion.

In addition, we recommend that the CTC and other providers of telecommunication services consider the introduction of a connection fee related to providing service to individual homes and businesses after a telephone line has been installed. Most other countries use connection fees to cover the marginal costs associated with transferring the line from one individual to another as well as investing in capital improvements to the general system. The lack of a connection fee in Chile may have contributed to the relatively poor performance of CTC prior to 1991.

Conclusions

The table below summarizes our best estimates of the U.S. dollar value of subsidies received by the average urban household in Chile for each of these services discussed here. The estimates of the subsidy for water and sanitation are based on multiplying the subsidy per inhabitant times four (the average size household in Chile). In the case of solid waste services the subsidy was already calculated in terms of household costs, while the telecommunications figure is obtained by simply dividing the costs (net of revenues) of subsidized services in remote regions by the number of clients served.

None of these subsidies is large in absolute dollar amounts, especially given that the average GDP per capita in Chile in 1989 was US $2,770 (Of course, a $10 or $15 per year decrease in income may make a difference to many low-income households.

Table 4-9. Average Household Subsidy per Year for Various Infrastructure Services in Santiago and Elsewhere

Avg. Subsidy p/HH p/year	*Potable Water*	*Waste Water Treatment*	*Solid Waste Services*	*Telecommunications*
Santiago	$2.00	$40.00	$14.00	$0.00
Rest of Chile	$14.00	$20.00	$12.00	$4.00

In spatial terms, there does not appear to be a strong pattern favoring Santiago and other large urban areas except in the provision of wastewater treatment. The lack of wastewater treatment causes substantial problems in the large urban regions yet the residential and commercial polluters who create the problems are not required to pay for its cleanup. Currently, residents of the metropolitan area bear the cost of this decision through ill health, lower productivity, and some inconvenience, i.e., having to purchase or boil drinking water, not being able to eat salad in restaurants, etc. The costs probably are borne more by low-income households who do not have as many options about where to get their drinking water and are less likely to enjoy as good health as high-income households. A system that treats the wastewater and apportions the costs of the treatment on the basis of consumption would be both a more equitable and efficient way of dealing with what is becoming a very unpleasant and unhealthy problem.

The value of subsidies for other types of services, such as drinking water and solid waste provision, do not differ as dramatically as that of wastewater treatment and are much smaller. While the provision of these public services cannot be ignored, they are of relatively less concern than wastewater treatment. The public and private sectors both need to spend some of their resources monitoring both access and price to these services on an urban and regional basis. Only careful analysis and state-of-the-art knowledge about the provision of these types of services will ensure that the urban population of Chile is adequately provided with the necessary conditions of modern life.

The main recommendation of the water and sanitation sector has to do with adjusting prices to reflect marginal costs more accurately. The Chilean Government should provided low-income households in each region with direct subsidies of enough water to live healthily but it should no longer subsidize the consumption of all households without regard to income. A potential solution to this problem a refinement of the current increasing block water tariff, assuming that it is determined that urban households do not commonly share meter connections or otherwise purchase their water indirectly. In addition, we believe that wastewater treatment, particularly in metropolitan Santiago, needs to be initiated as soon as possible. The funding for this program could be user-based with water customers bearing most, if not all, of the treatment costs or, since the availability of potable water may have many external benefits, some financing could be justified from general taxes since better health (fewer epidemics, etc.) would be broadly experienced.

References

CADE-IDEPE, "Estudio para la implementación de un sistema de reciclaje de residuos solidos urbano (domiciliarios) del Gran Santiago con clasificación de origen (executive summary)." 1992. Santiago: Intendency of the Metropolitan Region.

Cervero, Robert, "Organizational Options for Providing Urban Waste Management Services: The Case of Indonesia." 1993. IURD Working Paper 604. Berkeley: University of California at Berkeley.

Compañia de Telefonos de Chile, S.A. 1990. Anuario Estadistico General Del Desarrollo Telefonico: Periodo 1960–1989. Santiago de Chile: Gerencia Tecnica Departamento Planificacion.

CORFO, Memoria de Subgerencia de Empresas de Servicios Sanitarios. 1993. Santiago.

Durán de la Fuente, Hernán, "Políticas para la Gestión Ambientalmente Adecuada de los Residuos: el Caso de los Residuos Solidos Urbanos e Industriales in Chile a Luz de la Experiencia International" 1992. Working Paper No. 10. Santiago: Economic Commission of Latin America and the Caribbean, United Nations.

El Diario, "Cerrada la Primera Etapa en la Licitación de la Basura" 1993. (Monday, October 18) p. 11.

Empresa Metroplitana de Obras Sanitarias S.A. (EMOS), Memoria y Balance Anual 1992, Filial CORFO (Santiago de Chile:1993).

Ferreccio, Catterina, "Estudio de la Salmonella Typhi en Cursos de Agua del Ciudad de Santiago 1983." Unpublished thesis, Master of Public Health, School of Public Health, Faculty of Medicine, University of Chile, Santiago.

Ferreccio, Catterina, Valeria Prado, Alicia Ojeda, Marisol Cayyazo, Paulina Abrego, Linda Guers, and Myron M. Levine, "Epidemiologic Patterns of Acute Diarrhea and Endemic *Shigella* Infections in Children in a Poor Peri-urban Setting in Santiago, Chile," 1991. *American Journal of Epidemiology* 134: 614–627.

Ferreccio, Catterina, "Associaciones Epidemiologicas Entre Contaminacion del Agua y Daño en Salud en la Region Metropolitan de Chile." 1993. Prepared for the World Bank, Urban Development Division (December).

Grinstein, Saul and Gorge Gómez, Jorge Bercovich, Eelma Biscotti, "Epidemiology of Rotavirus Infection and Gastroenteritis in Prespectively Monitored Argentine

Families with Young Children." 1989. *American Journal of Epidemiology* 130: 300–308.

Harrington, Winston, Alan J. Krupnick, and Walter O. Spofford, Jr. 1991. *Economics and Episodic Disease: The Benefits of Preventing a Giardiasis Outbreak*, Washington DC: Resources for the Future.

Hopkins, Robert J., Pablo A.Vial, Catterina Ferreccio, Jimena Ovalle, Priscilla Prado, Viviana Sotomayor, Robert G. Russell, Steven S. Wasserman, and J. Glenn Morris, Jr. 1993. "Seroprevalence of *Helicobacter Pylori* in Chile: Vegetables May Serve as One Route of Transmission," *Journal of Infectious Diseases* 168: 222–226.

International Telecommunications Union website (www.itu.int/ti/).

Katz, Ricardo and Maria Benitez. 1993. "Costos Economicos de Intervenciones para el Control de la Contaminacion Hidrica," prepared by Gestion Ambiental Consultores for The World Bank, Urban Development Division (December).

Lo Castillo, 3 Memoria Anual 1992 (Santiago, Chile: 1993).

Larroulet, Cristián, ed. 1993. *Private Solutions to Public Problems: the Chilean Experience*, Institution Libertad y Desarrollo, The Center for International Private Enterprise (Chile: Editorian Trineo, S.A.).

Levine, Myron M., Catterina Ferreccio, Valeria Prado, Marisol Cayazzo, Paulina Abrego, Juan Martinez, Leonardo Maggi, Mary M. Baldini, Wendy Martin, David Maneval, Bradford Day, Lina Guers, Hermy Lior, Steven S. Wasserman, and James P. Nataro 1993. "Epidemiologic Studies of Escherichia coli Diarrheal Infections in a Low Socioeconomic Level Peri-Urban Community in Santiago, Chile," *American Journal of Epidemiology* 138: 849–869.

Ministerio de Obras Publicas, Servicio Nacional de Obras Sanitarias, Estudio de Tarificacion a Costo Marginal en Agua Potable y Alcantarillado–Informe Final, prepared by INECON and ECONSULT.

Monreal, Julio U. 1992. Identificacion de Metodos y Sistemas para la Disposicion Final de Residuos Solidos Domesticado en Comunidades Urbanas Pequeñas y Rurales Representativas del Territorio Nacional, GESAT Ltda (Chile).

Reiter, Zoe. 1986. "Municipal Solid Waste Provision in Chile: Possibilities for Greater Cost Recovery." Austin, Texas: Sociedad Interamericana de Planificacion.

Shuval, Hillel, A. Adin, B. Fattal, E. Rawitz and P. Yekutiel. 1986. "Wastewater Irrigation in Developing Countries: Health effects and technology solutions," Washington DC: World Bank Technical Paper Number 51. The World Bank.

Shuval, Hillel, Yochanan Wax, Perez Yekutiel and Badri Fattal. 1989. "Transmission of Enteric Disease Associated with Wastewater Irrigation: A Prospective Epidemiological Study." *American Journal of Public Health* 79:850–852 (July).

Shuval, Hillel. 1991. "The Development of Health Guidelines for Wastewater Reclamation." *Water Science Technology* 24: 149–155.

Shuval, Hillel. 1993. "Investigation of Typhoid Fever and Cholera Transmission by Raw Wastewater Irrigation in Santiago, Chile." *Water Science Technology* 27:167–174.

Superintendencia de Servicios Sanitarios, Memoria Anual 1992 (Santiago: 1993).

Superintendencia de Servicios Sanitarios. 1992. Analisis de Resultados Financieros de Empresas Sanitarias y su Relacion con la Empresa Modelo. Chile: Departamento de Tarifas, Seccion Control de Gestion (October).

Superintendencia de Servicios Sanitarios. 1993. Informe Mensual de Tarifas al mes de julio 1993. Chile: Departamento de Tarifas, Seccion Analysis Tarifario (July).

Tesam Hartley S.A. 1992. "Estudio de analisis de esquema de disposicion de residuos solidos municipales (domiciliarios) para el gran santiago y alternativas de tratamiento (executive summary)." Santiago: Intendency of the Metropolitan Region.

Whittington, Dale. 1992. "Possible Adverse Effects of Increasing Block Water Tariffs in Developing Countries." *Economic Development and Cultural Change* 41:75–87.

World Bank. 1994. "Chile—Managing Environmental Problems: Economic Analysis of Selected Issues." Washington DC: Report No. 13061-CH, Environment and Urban Development Division, Country Department 1, Latin America and the Caribbean Region.

World Development Report. 1994: Infrastructure for Development. New York: Published for the World Bank by Oxford University Press.

Appendix A: Financial Analysis of the Water/Sanitation Enterprises

Public Enterprises

A comparison of the relative size of the public water enterprises reveals that EMOS, the water enterprise serving the Region Metropolitana, is several times larger than almost every other water enterprise in Chile. In addition to serving five or six times more customers than the other enterprises, EMOS also invested more than 19,000 million pesos during the course of 1992, or almost half of all investments by the thirteen enterprises. Investment levels of this magnitude are probably justified in that EMOS clients make up 41% of all customers served by CORFO enterprises. On the other hand, some regions of the country appear to have investment levels which are somewhat lower than we might expect given the size of the population to be served. These include regions VII (ESSAM), VIII (ESSBIO) and X (ESSAL).

To discover if these levels of investment do, in fact, make economic sense, it is important to analyze regional data. Looking at some of the other financial data across regions and enterprises, there are some definite cost trends which emerge. The debt/capital ratio of each enterprise, which is presented in Figure A-1, is a good example of the trend in financial data across regions. Although most of the firms, i.e., those operating in Regions I, II, IV, VI, II, VIII, IX, X and XI, have debt ratios of around 20% to 30% of assets, there are a number of exceptions. Region II, in particular, has a debt ratio of almost 64% while the firms operating in the Region Metropolitana in Region

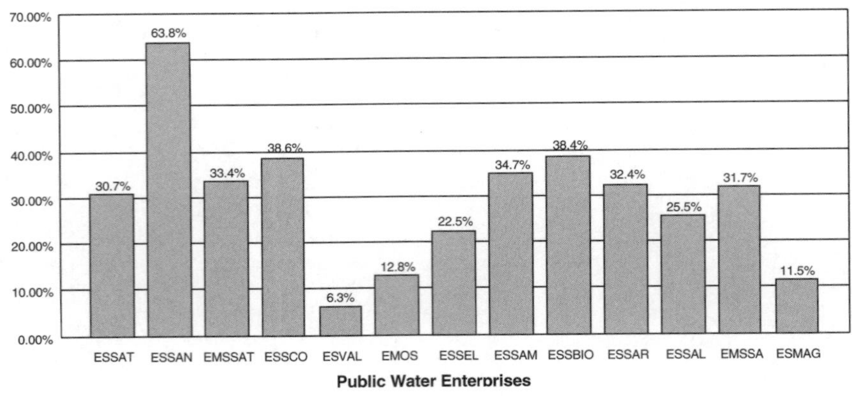

Figure A-1. Water Enterprise Debt/ Capital Ratios
Source: Memoria, CORFO (1993), p. 11.

Table A-1. *Wastewater Treatment Costs Using Lagoon Systems for Different Standards of Cleanliness*

	*Lagoon System I**				*Lagoon System II***			
	1000 Fecal Coliform/100 ml.		*10000 Fecal Coliform/100 ml.*		*10000 Fecal Coliform/100 ml.*		*100000 Fecal Coliform/100 ml.*	
Population	*Total Cost in US $*	*Cost/ Capita*	*Total Cost in US $*	*Cost/ Capita*	*Total Cost in US $*	*Cost/ Capita*	*Total Cost in US $*	*Cost/ Capita*
1,000	101,895	102	86,017	86	86,766	86	67,467	67
5,000	210,586	42	163,932	33	168,739	34	123,229	25
10,000	307,149	31	231,762	23	245,264	25	170,943	17
20,000	449,011	22	339,451	17	382,815	19	248,628	12
30,000	591,098	20	421,329	14	512,510	17	314,327	10
40,000	717,533	18	502,023	13	637,792	16	387,873	10
50,000	856,002	17	580,135	12	763,843	15	444,582	9
60,000	995,291	17	628,188	10	886,488	15	519,537	9
70,000	1,101,566	16	736,868	11	1,015,181	15	571,282	8
80,000	1,247,837	16	825,983	10	1,133,652	14	646,816	8
90,000	1,384,220	15	899,700	10	1,260,618	14	697,658	8
100,000	1,474,169	15	962,336	10	1,387,445	14	774,257	8
200,000	2,770,511	14	1,733,073	9	2,643,266	13	1,431,536	7
300,000	4,067,766	14	2,485,334	8	3,909,908	13	2,075,151	7
400,000	5,364,673	13	3,254,441	8	5,176,364	13	2,730,898	7

Sistema de Lagunas en Serie (Facultativa y de Maduracion)
** Sistema de una Laguna Facultativa
Source: Ministerio de Obras Publicas, A.5.3–24 and A.5.3–25.

V and in Region XII have very low levels of debt, i.e., 12.8%, 6.3% and 11.5%, respectively.

The data in Figures A-2 and A-3, which present information regarding the value of operational revenues vis-à-vis fixed assets and in comparison to operational costs, confirm this result. Operational revenues represent only about 12% of fixed assets in a number of the more remote regions, i.e. Regions I through III and XI and XII, are close to 30% in the Santiago region and are near 20% in Regions V, VI, VIII and IX. Similarly, the ratio of operational costs to operational revenues is highest in the northernmost region (75%) and in Regions XI and XII in the south (90% and 79%) while it is the lowest in the Metropolitan Region (50%). An interesting point that emerges from Figure A3 is that the operational costs of supplying residents in Region II are only 50% of operational revenues but because of the fixed costs associated with transporting water into the region, ESSAN (the firm operating in Region II) is having severe financial trouble.

The financial status of ESSAN, as well as the other enterprises, is further illustrated in Figure A-4 and Table A-2. ESSAN's debt service ratio is close to 50%, by far the highest of any other enterprise. Firms operating in Region III and Region XI also have high debt service ratios while EMOS, ESVAL (Region V) and ESMAG (Region XIII) have very low debt service ratios of 10% or less. The financial statement prepared by each firm, summarized in Table A2, indicates that, even if we exclude nonoperational costs, firms in Regions I, III, VII, X, XI and XII are operating at a loss. If we include nonoperational costs, only five out of the thirteen firms made an accounting profit in 1992. The firms which made a profit are those operating in the central region of the country and include ESVAL, EMOS, ESSEL (Region VI), ESSBIO (Region VIII) and ESSAR (Region IX).

Despite this relatively uninspiring level of financial performance, recent investment levels in water supply and distribution networks have increased across all regions. Table A3, which presents investment data for 1991 and 1992, indicates that most of the investment resources come from the firms themselves, while a small portion of the funds come from the Planning Ministry (MINVU) and the National Development Fund (FNDR). Investment levels grew by 55% during these two years and are expected to continue to grow. The only region which did not see substantial investment in water was Region II, presumably because the debt ratio carried by ESSAN is already so high compared to the other enterprises.

It may be possible, given additional time and data, to derive how much of the investment in each region is being spent on the construction of new services vs. maintenance or rehabilitation, etc. At present, the investment information is quite general in nature and all we know is the name of each project that the funds were spent on and nothing about how actual service is im-

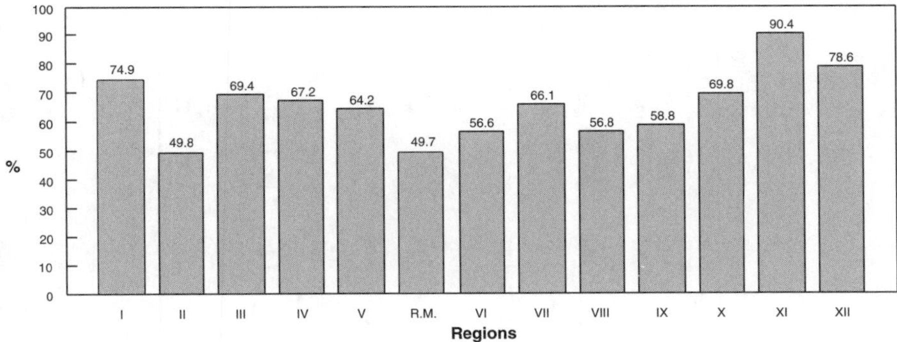

Figure A-2. Operational Revenues as a Percentage of Fixed Assets by Region in 1992
Source: Memoria, CORFO (1993), p. 11.

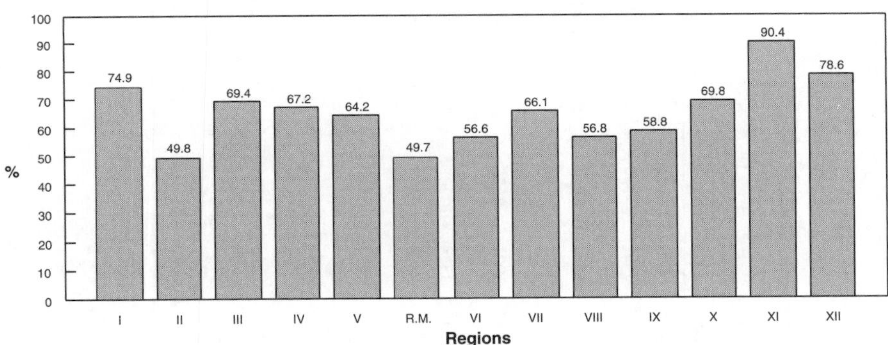

Figure A-3. Operational Costs*/Operational Revenue by Region in 1992
Source: Memoria, CORFO (1993), p. 12.

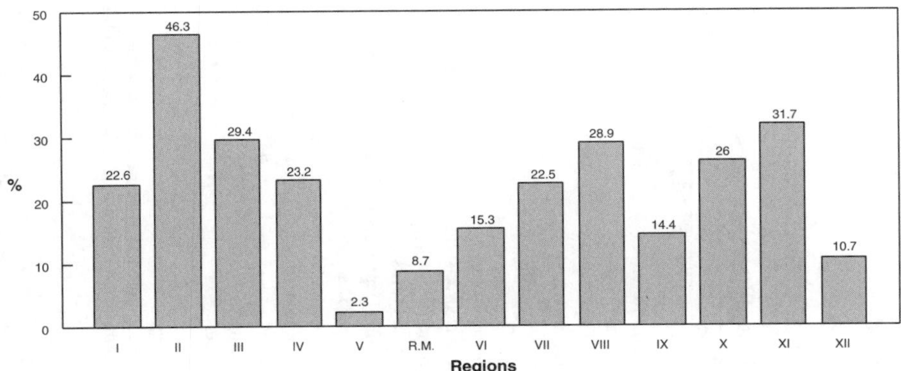

Figure A-4. Debt Service/Operating Revenue by Region in 1992
Source: Memoria, CORFO (1993), p. 14.

Table A-2. *Financial Status of Chile's Public Water Enterprises by Region* 1992*

(Millions of Pesos)

	Essat	*Essan*	*Emssat*	*Essco*	*Esval*	*Emos*	*Essel*	*Essam*	*Essbio*	*Essar*	*Essal*	*Emssa*	*Esma*
Item	I	11	111	IV	V	RM.	VI	VII	VIII	IX	X	XI	XII
Operational Revenues	3908	5223	1633	3193	10557	34798	3195	3271	8146	3195	3164	594	1399
Operational Costs Before Depreciation	**1807**	**1675**	**585**	**1004**	**3322**	**8962**	**1033**	**1040**	**2461**	**1053**	**1286**	**1.293**	**623**
Administration and Overhead Expenditures	**1239**	**970**	**575**	**1159**	**3901**	**8628**	**749**	**1118**	**2176**	**853**	**977**	**270**	**443**
Operational Profits (before Depreciation)	863	2578	473	1030	3334	17208	1413	1113	3510	1290	902	32.	332
Depreciation	**1301**	**1921**	**760**	**989**	**1382**	**6330**	**1002**	**1838**	**2403**	**820**	**1330**	**310**	**1024**
Operational Profits (including Depreciation)	**439**	657	**287**	41	1952	10878	411	**725**	1107	470	**428**	**278**	**692**
Profits before Dep./ Depreciation (%)	66.3	134.2	62.2	104.1	241.3	271.9	141	60.6	146.1	157.3	67.8	10.2	32.5
Non Operational Costs	**542**	**1455**	**252**	**287**	28	294	**258**	**425**	552	**264**	**349**	**146**	**95**
Extraordinary Expenses		**437**											
Total	**981**	**1236**	539	**248**	1980	11172	153	**1150**	1652	206	**777**	**424**	**787**

*Numbers in bold face type are negative values.
Source: Summarized from data in Memoria, CORFO (1993), p.18.

Table A-3. *Investments in Chile's Water and Sanitation Systems by Source and Region 1991 and 1992*

(millions of current pesos)

	1991 Investments				*1992 Investments*			
Firm/Region	*by Firm*	*by MINVU*	*by FNDR*	*Total*	*by Firm*	*by MINVU*	*by FNDR*	*Total*
ESSAT/I	19,203	0	223	1,426	1,790	269	569	2,628
ESSAN/II	2,108	0	750	2,858	2,083	157	643	2,883
EMSSAT/Ill	181	44	178	403	371	279	320	970
ESSCO/IV	11,094	19	499	1,612	2,021	58	1,172	3,251
ESVAL/V	27,463	27	277	2,767	3,148	4	302	3,454
EMOS/RM	11,926	8	1	11,935	19,227	0	0	19,227
ESSEL/VI	1,082	0	144	19226	2,265	110	384	2,759
ESSAM/VII	1,086	0	335	11421	1,617	48	257	1,922
ESSBIO/III	19,530	0	844	21374	2,083	122	458	2,663
ESSAR/IX	19,174	0	236	1,410	1,944	69	279	2,292
ESSAL/X	19,362	1.8	33	1,413	1,449	111	514	2,074
EMSSA/XI	25	0	345	370	266	20	992	1,278
ESMAG/XII	526	0	237	763	779	0	320	1,099
TOTAL	25,760	116	4,102	29,978	39,043	1,247	6,210	46,500
US$ Total	74	0	12	86	108	3	17	128

Exchange Rate: $1U.S. = 349.22 (199 1)
$1U.S. = 362.58 (1992)

Source: Memoria, CORFO (1993), p. 23.

pacted by the type of investment listed. It is worth noting here, however, that the while the data indicate that enterprises which are operating in the central region are making a profit and apparently sustaining a relatively high level of investment there are several problems which all firms share. One is that every firm appears to have a list of customers waiting to be connected to the system and the second is that the costs of treating wastewater from the system is completely absent in the financial data presented thus far.

Private firms

Data on the financial performance of the private firms is presented in Table A4. It appears that there is a fairly wide range in the values of the financial indicators among private companies similar, if not greater in variety, to those of public enterprises. The Lo Castillo firm, however, appears to be closest in terms of financial performance to public enterprises which makes sense given that it serves approximately the same number of clients as ESSAT (Region I) and ESSAN (Region II) among others. Lo Castillo had a debt/capital ratio of 0.49 in 1991 which is comparable to that of ESSAT and other public enterprises although substantially more than that of EMOS and ESVAL (Region V) whose debt/capital ratios were 0.07 in 1991. Several private firms have extremely low debt/capital ratios, including La Leonora and Servicommunal and Manquehue, which had debt/capital ratios between 0.01 and 0.11 in 1991. The firm of Los Dominicos (which at the time of its acquisition by Lo Castillo had some 2,000 customers) had a debt/capital ratio of 1.44 in 1991.

The ratio of operational expenses to operational revenues among private firms are quite similar to those of public firms. The ratio ranges between 1.39 and 0.70 which is well within the range of public enterprises and quite similar to that of EMOS (0.74) and ESVAL (0.90), the public firms operating in Region V and in Gran Santiago. The profitability picture, however, is somewhat better for private firms than is true of public enterprises. In 1991, four out of five of the private firms made an accounting profit compared to only three out of thirteen public enterprises. The two private firms which ran losses, i.e., Manquehue and Santo Domingo, lost only 2.7% and 1.2%, respectively whereas some of the public enterprises lost as much as 7% that year. It is important to note, however, that the public firms that did run an accounting profit according to the Superintendencia de Servicios Sanitarios, were located in Regions V, VI and Gran Santiago where, apparently, supplying water is quite inexpensive relative to other parts of the country.

Table A-4. *Financial Performance of Private Water and Sanitation Firms 1989–1991*

Firm	*Region*	*1989*	*1990*	*1991*
		Liquidity Ratio		
EMOS*	R.M.	3.7	3.8	1.9
Lo Castillo	R.M.	0.6	0.9	1.7
Servicommunal	5.3	5.0	4.9	
R.M.				
Manquehue	R.M.	2.7	1.1	0.5
Los Dominicos	R.M.	11.0	0.3	0.5
La Leonora	R.M.	1.6	0.1	0.5
Sto. Domingo	V	1.1	0.9	2.5
		Debt/Cal2ital Ratio		
EMOS*	R.M.	0.12	0.11	0.07
Lo Castillo	R.M.	0.27	0.33	0.49
Servicommunal	0.14	0.14	0.11	
R.M.				
Manquehue	R.M.	0.02	0.03	0.09
Los Dominicos	R.M.	0.04	1.57	1.44
La Leonora	R.M.	0.00	0.02	0.01
Sto. Domingo	V	0.45	0.35	0.32
		Operational Costs/		
Operational Revenues				
EMOS*	R.M.	0.83	0.74	0.74
Lo Castillo	R.M.	0.99	0.79	0.86
Servicommunal	0.80	0.47	0.70	
R.M.				
Manquehue	R.M.	1.12	1.12	1.39
Los Dominicos	R.M.	1.21	1.08	0.93
La Leonora	R.M.	0.69	1.57	0.82
Sto. Domingo	V	0.92	1.09	0.80
		Profitability Rate**		
EMOS*	R.M.	2.68	4.79	6.58
Lo Castillo	R.M.	3.07	4.66	1.86
Servicommunal	22.74	55.39	23.43	
R.M.				
Manquehue	R.M.	22.82	−0.76	−2.70
Los Dominicos	R.M.	58.71	1.03	1.14
La Leonora	R.M.	−0.85	−3.62	−1.17
Sto.Domingo	V	3.33	−2.71	18.88

*EMOS is the public enterprise serving the metropolitan region of Santiago. It is included for comparison purposes only.
**Tasa de Rentabilidad sobre Activos Propios (Utilidad despúes de Impuesto/Total Activos Propios(%).
Source: Superintendencia de Servicios Sanitarios (1992).

Rate Regulation

The marginal cost study used data from average firms to calculate operating and maintenance expenses. The resulting price is then corrected or modified for each enterprise to account for differences in distance from the source of the water, the density of consumers and the number of consumers. The resulting *meta*, or the marginal cost pricing which the Superintendencia is aiming for, consists of both a fixed and a variable portion and the formula for setting the tariff is written into the existing water regulation law. This apparently is in response to the concerns of water companies who wanted to have the rate-setting formula as transparent a procedure as possible. According to the Superintendente, Eugenio Celedon, there are approximately 300 local water service providers divided into the thirteen regional firms discussed above. Within the thirteen firms, the providers are divided into groups with similar characteristics for the purposes of establishing tariffs. All types of customers, e.g., household, industrial, agricultural, etc., within each group pay the same tariff.

In all, across the thirteen regions, there are 36 different tariffs. On average there are two or three different tariffs per region which take into account differences in distance from the water source, technologies, etc. Each tariff includes all four parts of the costs (production, distribution, collection of wastewater, and treatment of wastewater) and all four parts are generally controlled by the same water enterprise. It is possible that the costs could be separated so that, for example, collection and/or treatment of wastewater might be done by a different firm or enterprise than the firm that provides clean water to the household, although this is not currently the case anywhere in Chile.

Each water enterprise is aware of how much their prices will be allowed to increase over time as they move toward marginal cost pricing and, in addition, knows that *vigentes* change every year due to indexation. The tariffs are indexed to the cost of certain key inputs including electricity and wages. Under the current law, the water enterprises are only allowed to increase the *vigentes* when their costs increase by at least 3%. According to the Superintendencia, this happens on average every two months or so. We have some historical data on water tariffs and it appears that, in some regions, the average tariff charged for a cubic meter of potable water has increased by some 400%. In Region II, for example, tariffs increased from 75 pesos per cubic meter in December 1989 to 110 pesos per cubic meter in December of 1990 to 200 pesos per cubic meter in December 1991 to 253 pesos per cubic meter in February of 1993. The price increase in the Region Metropolitana has been less dramatic with prices increasing from 48 pesos per cubic meter in December of 1989 to 93 pesos in February of 1993.

Tariff data for the public enterprises is presented in Table A5. The data is quite complicated because it includes not only the actual price charged, the *vigentes normal*, but also the price charged to users who qualify for a subsidy from the government *vigentes rebajado*.

Subsidies

According to the director of CORFO, Hernán Herrera, the majority of all the state-owned enterprises charge rates based on long-term marginal costs plus a small profitability factor over capital assets and are, therefore, much closer to a private-sector type of situation than in the past. There are regions of Chile, however, including Regions I, II, III, XI, and XII, where all of the population receives water at a subsidized price because the price of water in those regions is quite high.

There are at least three types of subsidies that are routinely granted to water and sanitation customers in Chile. The first type of subsidy, which is "voluntary" in that the enterprise is not required to provide this subsidy, represents a lower price for water than the normal *vigente*. Only public enterprises can offer their customers this subsidy or discount and, we believe, it is the price that is indicated as the *vigentes rebajado* or lower price per cubic meter of water in Table A5.

In addition, all the water enterprises provide a subsidy to customers who consume less than 20 cubic meters of water a month. All water customers are given a 50% discount on the first 10 cubic meters of water they consume in any given month if their household consumes less than 20 cubic meters of water that month. According to the director of CORFO, approximately 80% of all consumers now use less than 20 cubic meters of water a month whereas, before the introduction of this subsidy program, most of the households receiving piped water used about 40 cubic meters a month. The effects of this subsidy are yet to be analyzed on a spatial basis but we believe that the data we have will allow us to say something definitive about its impact on a regional basis.

The third type of subsidy that is given to consumers is a subsidy directed at poor households that is based on CASEN. As far as we can ascertain, approximately 20% of all consumers in each region pay a subsidized rate for their water. The subsidy is subtracted from their water and sewer bill each month and the subsidy is charged to the municipality in which they reside. The Treasury apparently reimburses the municipality so that the water enterprises do not have to make up the subsidy themselves.

If this is, in fact, the way this particular subsidy works, it has direct spatial

Table A-5. *Prices Charged by Region and Group as of July 15, 1992*

	Region I		*Region II*		*Region III*		*Region IV*		*Region VI*	
	G. I	*G. 2*	*G. 1*	*G. 2*	*G. 1*	*G. 2*	*G. 1*	*G. 2*	*G. 1*	*G .2*
Fixed Price ($/month)										
Water (Normal)	308.0	320.0	253.1	248.4	204.8	182.5	203.0	200.0	438.0	392.0
(Lowered)	201.5	187.0	219.9	193.3	136.4	116.0	149.0	147.0	305.0	272.0
Sewer (Normal)	139.4	141.0	80.5	86.5	52.9	44.8	86.0	78.0	161.0	168.0
(Lowered)	91.2	83.0	69.9	67.3	35.2	28.5	63.0	58.0	112.0	117.0
Customer Service										
(Normal)	274.8	283.0	194.1	191.8	322.8	334.1	307.0	304.0	326.0	320.0
(Lowered)	179.8	166.0	168.6	149.3	215.0	212.4	225.0	223.0	227.0	222.0
Variable Charge $/m3 (not peak season)										
Water (Normal)	129.0	208.1	227.7	244.4	94.3	181.9	92.7	125.6	51.1	71.9
(Lowered)	94.2	116.7	79.4	73.4	74.4	73.3	76.8	99.5	48.0	62.6
Sewer (Normal)	39.8	39.4	42.5	31.8	62.2	42.4	46.5	57.8	48.1	53.7
(Lowered)	21.7	17.4	17.5	14.0	26.4	12.9	36.3	43.0	36.8	39.6
Sewage Treatment*										
(Normal)	47.4	58.2	69.3							
(Subsidized)	25.8	43.4	51.6							
Variable Charge $/m3 (peak Season)**										
Water (Normal)	129.0	205.8	226.1	244.4	91.1	181.1	89.5	122.1	47.8	68.4
(Lowered)	94.2	116.3	79.4	73.4	72.8	73.0	74.4	97.0	45.5	60.1
Sewer (Normal)	39.9	39.4	42.5	31.8	62.2	42.4	48.1	53.7		
(Lowered)	21.7	17.4	17.5	14.0	26.4	12.9	36.8	39.7		
Sewage Treatment*										
(Normal)	47.4	25.8								
(Subsidized)										
Overconsumption										
Surcharge	336.4	510.5	586.0	337.3	219.9	327.4	196.9	310.6	110.2	172.6

*Sewage treatment charge allowed for services at a limited number of localities.
**Peak season defined as the months of December through March.
Source: Superintendencia de Servicios Sanitarios (July 1993), p. 5–9.

Table A-5 (continued) *Prices Charged by Region and Group as of July 15, 1992*

	Region VII			*Region VIII*		*Region IX*			*Region X*	
	G. I	*G. 2*	*G. 3*	*G. 1*	*G. 2*	*G. 1*	*G. 2*	*G. 3*	*G. 1*	*G .2*
Fixed Price ($/month)										
Water (Normal)	400.0	385.0	415.0	333.0	366.0	389.0	439.0	395.0	409.0	341.0
(Lowered)	273.0	266.0	281.0	232.0	250.0	270.0	299.0	273.0	283.0	243.0
Sewer (Normal)	179.0	173.0	199.0118.0	131.0	150.0	146.0	140.0	125.0	108.0	
(Lowered)	122.0	120.0	135.0	83.0	90.0	104.0	100.0	97.0	87.0	77.0
Customer Service	1									
(Normal)	319.0	315.0	319.0	284.0	284.0	325.0	334.0	334.0	331.0	331.0
(Lowered)	217.0	218.0	216.0	198.0	194.0	225.0	228.0	231.0	229.0	236.0
Variable Charge $/m3 (not peak season)										
Water (Normal)	74.2	58.4	72.6	63.7	97.6	81.4	95.1	87.1	83.5	64.1
(Lowered)	61.6	51.3	60.6	52.2	72.9	68.7	78.4	73.5	71.6	58.6
Sewer (Normal)	57.9	45.9	69.1	40.5	54.5	59.0	102.9	79.8	80.1	60.1
(Lowered)	43.3	36.4	50.1	34.1	42.9	42.8	66.6	54.5	51.0	40.8
Sewage Treatment*										
(Normal)	164.4	123.2								
(Subsidized)	106.4	84.1								
Variable Charge $/m3 (peak Season)**										
Water (Normal)	67.8	55.2	67.8	60.5	94.4	78.0	89.7	74.3		
(Lowered)	57.4	49.0	57.4	50.1	71.0	66.4	74.8	64.7		
Sewer (Normal)	40.5	54.5	59.0	102.9	79.8					
(Lowered)	34.1	42.9	42.8	66.6	54.5					
Sewage Treatment*										
(Normal)	164.4	123.2								
(Subsidized)	106.4	84.1								
Overconsumption Surcharge	163.3	122.2	155.8	133.5	227.0	166.1	199.2	173.8		

*Sewage treatment charge allowed for services at a limited number of localities.
**Peak season defined as the months of December through March.
Source: Superintendencia de Servicios Sanitarios (July 1993), p. 5–9.

Table A-5 (continued) *Prices Charged by Region and Group as of July 15, 1992*

	*Region XI**		*Region XII**	
	G. 1	*G. 2*	*G. I*	*G.2*
Fixed Price ($/month)				
Water (Normal)	498.0	478.0	275.0	309.0
(Lowered)	271.0	269.0	220.0	242.0
Sewer (Normal)	180.0	106.0	126.0	109.0
(Lowered)	98.0	60.0	101.0	85.0
Customer Service				
(Normal)	392.0	393.0	253.0	258.0
(Lowered)	213.0	221.0	202.0	202.0
Variable Charge $/m3				
Water (Normal)	104.8	80.1	118.9	85.0
(Lowered)	66.6	60.5	80.9	60.9
Sewer (Normal)	95.6	129.8	46.3	80.6
(Lowered)	39.5	43.2	25.6	32.6
Sewage Treatment*				
(Normal)				
(Subsidized)				

*Regions XI and XII also have a number of clients who do not have meters. Charges to these users are based on the number of faucets in the building and the diameter of the pipe leading into the residence or business. In Region XI, monthly charges for water range from 3,226 pesos for one to three faucets with a pipe of 15 mm. diameter to up to 34,209 pesos for four to ten faucets and a 25 mm. pipe. In Region XII, the charges are as low as 2,070 per month for one to three faucets and a 15 mm. pipe up to 55,328 pesos in buildings with more than 10 faucets connected to a 38 mm. diameter pipe.
Source: Superintendencia de Servicios Sanitarios (July 1993), p. 5–9.

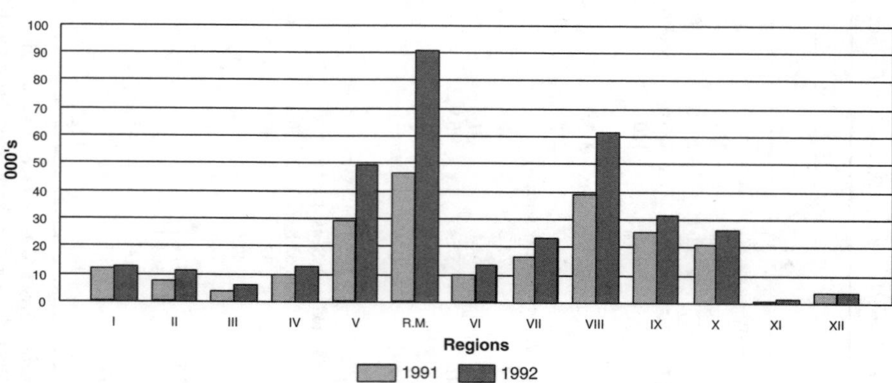

Figure A-5. Number of W&S Subsidies Allocated by Region 1991 and 1992
Note: This subsidy described here refers only subsidies to consumers who consume less than 20 cubic meters a month.
Source: Memoria, CORFO (1993), p. 21.

implications in that it is probably true that the 20% lowest income households in Santiago have much higher incomes than the poorest 20% in the rest of the country. There may be a great many poorer households in the northern regions, in particular, who do not qualify for a low-income subsidy based simply on their location and not on their actual standard of living. We do not, at present, have a great deal of data regarding this issue, however.

As of February 1992, the number of subsidies allotted to various regions followed a somewhat predictable pattern. Figures A-5 and A-6 illustrate that subsidy levels overall are growing dramatically, from 298 million pesos in 1991 to more than 2,256 million pesos in 1992, and that a larger share of the absolute number of subsidies is going to Regions V and VIII as well as to the Region Metropolitana. While the absolute numbers within these three regions have increased more than in other locations, the share of all subsidies going to Regions V, VII and Gran Santiago increased by about 5%. The Santiago area, for example, increased its share of all water subsidies from 25% to 30% during this period.

Figures A-7 and A-8 present information on the peso value of subsidies reaching each region of Chile. According to information presented in Figure A-7, the share of all subsidy money going to the Region Metropolitana is, even after the quite dramatic growth noted above, still only 22%, which is much less than that region's share of all water consumers (41%). The region with the next largest share of subsidy funds is Region V which had subsidies of 15.5% of the total subsidy funding distributed during 1992. Regions which lost shares of subsidy money between 1991 and 1992 include Regions 1, III, VI, IX, X and XII. It is true, however, that all these regions still have a higher share of subsidy money than is warranted if we look only at the number of cli-

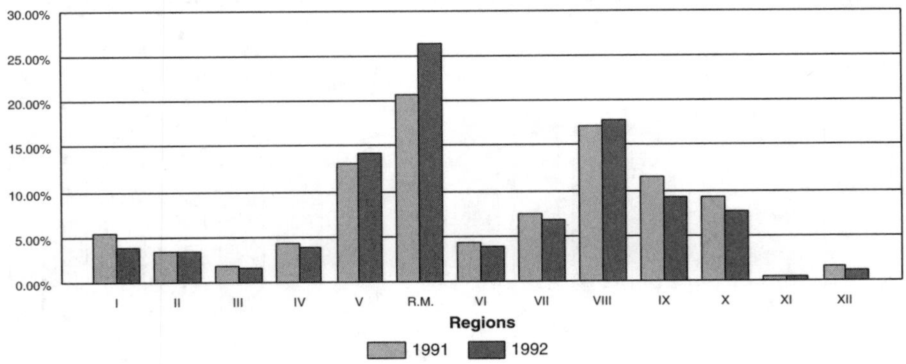

Figure A-6. Share of Subsidy Allotment by Region 1991 and 1992
Note: This subsidy described here refers only subsidies to consumers who consume less than 20 cubic meters a month.
Source: Memoria, CORFO (1993), p. 21.

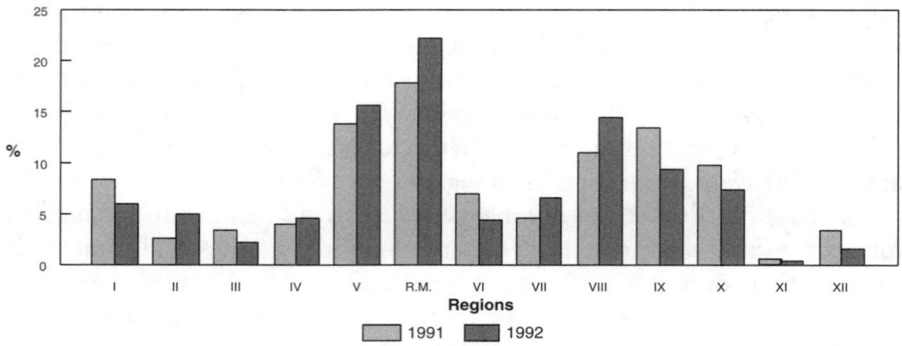

Figure A-7. Share of Water Subsidy Funds by Region 1991 and 1992
Note: This subsidy described here refers only subsidies to consumers who consume less than 20 cubic meters a month.
Source: Memoria, CORFO (1993), p. 21.

ents served by the public water enterprises. The region receiving the smallest share of subsidy funds, for example, is Region XI (0.4%) but this is quite comparable to its share of the nationwide customer base, i.e., 0.5%.

As shown in Figure A-8, the average subsidy per user varies quite a bit across regions. The highest subsidy levels, on average, accrue to Regions I and II where users receive on average 1,257 pesos and 1,599 pesos per month, respectively. Given the relatively high price of water in these regions as well as the low-income levels this is probably justified. Other regions receiving relatively high levels of subsidy per user include Region V (1,222 pesos), Region

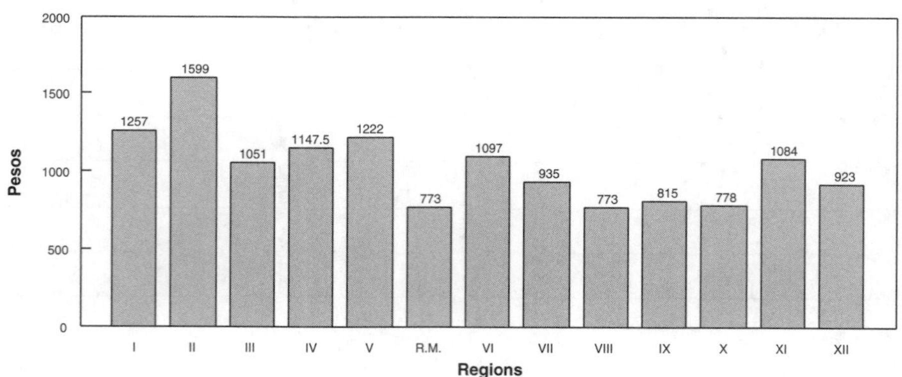

Figure A-8. Average Monthly Subsidy per User by Region 1991 and 1992
Note: This subsidy described here refers only subsidies to consumers who consume less than 20 cubic meters a month.
Source: Memoria, CORFO (1993).

IV (1, 148 pesos), Region XI (10,448 pesos) and Region III (1,051 pesos). The lowest levels of subsidies are received by users in the Region Metropolitana and Region VII where users receive an average of 773 pesos a month.

Overall, there does appear to be a problem with the distribution of water subsidies, at least given the 1992 data. The problem is not within the Region Metropolitana but within Region V. Users in Region V receive a high level of subsidy per user, receive a share of subsidy funding which is higher than their share of the total customer base and, at the same time, face lower prices per cubic meter of water than many other regions. The rationale used to justify this distribution needs to be explored since, at least given the data available, it is difficult to understand on a purely economic basis.

Appendix B

Table B-1 *Property Exemption Rates by Region (1992)*

Region	*Total Properties*	*Properties Exempt*	*% Exempt*
I	74,866	57,524	76.84%
II	67,302	51,883	77.09
III	40,468	31,535	77.93
IV	96,059	73,504	76.52
V	350,577	225,338	64.28
VI	142,207	91,727	64.50
VII	164,800	116,329	70.59
VIII	326,446	239,705	75.75
IX	175,595	136,105	77.51
X	178,378	123,298	69.12
XI	21,058	15,727	74.68
XII	35,040	23,508	67.09
R.M.	1,108,795	692,445	62.45
Total	2,771 ,591	1,878,628	67.78

Source: Reiter, p.22.

Appendix C

Table C-1 *Long Distance Calls By Region and Zone (1989)*

Zone	*Region*	*Operator Assisted*	*Direct Dial*	*% of Total*	*Total*
Arica	I	303,696	1,452,061	1.7	1,755,757
Iquique	I	484,255	1,761,697	2.1	2,245,952
Antofagasta	II	1,709,256	4,346,859	5.8	6,056,115
Copiapó	III	972,091	1,443,594	2.3	2,415,685
La Serena	IV	2,021,450	1,833,612	3.7	3,855,062
Los Andes	V	708,124	3,470,115	4.0	4,178,239
Valparaíso	V	3,564,420	12,990,549	15.8	16,554,969
Santiago	R.M.	6,278,496	27,780,967	32.6	34,059,463
Rancagua	VI	3,308,433	3,195,436	6.2	6,503,869
Talca	VII	2,538,658	4,583,560	6.8	7,122,218
Chillan	VIII	1,109,853	1,646,511	2.6	2,756,364
Concepci6n	VIII	2,931,950	4,817,710	7.4	7,749,660
Los Angeles	VIII	1,331,023	1,056,105	2.3	2,387,128
Temuco	IX	3,236,844	2,234,584	5.2	5,471,428
Magallanes	XII	588,707	951,809	1.5	1,540,516
Total CTC		31,087,256	73,565,169	100.0	104,652,425

Source: Anuario Estadistico General del Desarrollo Telefonico, Periodo 1960–1989
CTC, Gerencia Tecnica, Departamento Planificacion

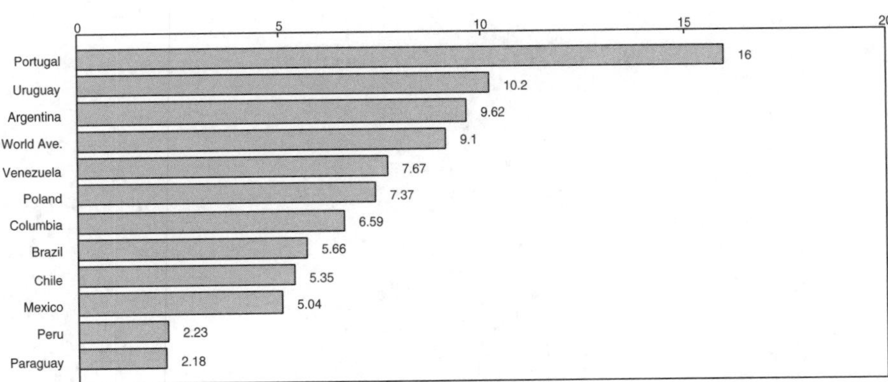

Figure C-1. Telephone Lines in Service per 100 Inhabitants, Selected Countries 1988
Source: Anuario Estadistico General del Desarrollo Telefonico, Periodo 1960–1989 CTC, Gerencia Tecnicia, Departamento Planificacion

5

Efficiency and Locational Consequences of Government Transport Policies and Spending in Chile

JOHN F. KAIN AND ZHI LIU

Introduction

This chapter is concerned with four kinds of questions: (1) To what extent have Chilean government policies and spending for transportation affected the regional distribution of employment and population and the spatial distribution of economic activity within urbanized areas? (2) Have government policies and expenditures for transport been efficient, or would other policies and expenditures have increased the real incomes and welfare of Chileans by more? (3) Has the government made the right investment decisions in the transport sector and what principles should guide future government spending in this sector? and (4) What kinds of policies should be implemented to ensure that existing and future government investments in transport are efficiently used?

In considering these issues, the first important distinction is between the provision of transportation services and the provision of transport infrastructure. In Chile, as in most other countries, transportation services are largely supplied by private companies. The principal exceptions are intercity rail freight and passenger services and urban rail passenger services. On the other hand, in Chile, as in most other countries, governments are nearly monopoly providers of transportation infrastructure.

Simply noting whether or not transportation services are provided by for-profit firms is not enough, however. Transportation industries throughout the world tend to be highly regulated. The demands for regulation reflect concerns that some transportation industries or providers are natural monopolies or have significant monopoly power, and the frequently expressed belief that various transportation services are in some sense more "essential" than those provided by other sectors or industries. The notion that some transportation modes are subject to economies of scale and are thus natural monopolies has made some governments unwilling to permit multiple providers and competition in transportation on the grounds that competition would be wasteful. Realities and attitudes concerning scale economies and natural monopolies have begun to change throughout the world, however, as the emergence of new modes and new technologies have reduced scale economies and eliminated or weakened concerns about the monopoly power of actual and potential providers of transportation infrastructure and services. As a result, governments increasingly have sold government-owned transportation infrastructure and public transportation enterprises to the private sector and reduced the range and severity of regulation.

Until about twenty years ago, intercity and urban transportation providers in Chile were among the most heavily regulated in the world. Starting in the early 1970s, however, the central government completely deregulated intercity and urban bus services, eliminated most subsidies to government owned transport enterprises, and increasingly encouraged private sector participation in investment and operations of ports and airlines. In 1991, the Chilean Government initiated a new form of public/private partnership. Legislation passed during that year permitted concessions to the private sector for the construction, maintenance, and operation of intercity roads, urban roads, airports, and irrigation projects under a BOT (Build, Operate, and Transfer) scheme.

Under Chile's BOT program, private enterprises are allowed to build toll roads and to maintain, manage, and collect tolls for a specified period of time. At the end of the contract period, the road will revert to the government. The acceptance of these private toll road schemes in Chile is made easier by the fact that tolls are already charged for the use of many of the country's major intercity roads. The history of public ownership and operation and of regulation and deregulation in Chile's transport sector will be discussed subsequently for each of the several intercity and urban transport modes. First, however, we describe briefly the major instrumentalities and government organizations that are currently responsible for policymaking and investment in the transportation sector in Chile. The discussion is followed by a brief description of Chile's unusual geography and its climatic extremes, as these have had major impacts on both the nation's settlement pattern and the nature of its transportation system. We follow these observations by a short examination of international and interregional freight and passenger transportation and a more extensive examination of urban transportation. The chapter ends with a discussion of the impacts of government policies and spending on the location of economic activity both among regions and within Santiago, and with our views on what policies should be considered by Chilean policymakers.

Institutional Arrangements

Responsibility for government spending and policy in both intercity and urban transport in Chile is divided among several central government ministries and organizations. Governmental decision making in this sector, as in most other sectors in Chile, is highly centralized. Surprisingly detailed determinations concerning the provision of transport infrastructure and transport policy for distant regions and urban communities are made in Santiago. One of the most striking examples is that urban transportation planning for Valparaiso and Concepcion, the nation's second and third largest metropolitan areas, is done by (SECTRA) (Executive Secretariat of the Interministerial Infrastructure Committee), a central government planning organization located in Santiago.

Chile's Ministry of Transport and Telecommunications (MTT) is nominally the lead agency in establishing transport policy, but the Ministry of Public Works (MOP) and the Ministry of Housing and Urban Development (MINVU) also play important roles. MOP is responsible for the planning and building (using private contractors) of all intercity roads and national roads within urban areas. It also collects road tolls and manages the highly important vehicle weight program. MINVU is responsible for the planning, construction, and maintenance of all urban roads, except those within the municipality of Santiago. The Ministry of Planning and Coordination (MIDEPLAN) makes annual revisions to a rolling three-year plan and determines whether transport investments proposed by MTT, MOP, and MINVU are justified according to its guidelines and whether they conform to the plan's objectives. Not surprisingly, the Ministry of Finance also plays a significant role in setting total spending limits and choosing among proposed investments. Loans from the World Bank and the Inter-American Development Bank, plus various bilateral loans from foreign governments and suppliers have made important contributions to financing investments in transport infrastructure in Chile, and the central government makes extensive use of benefit-cost analyses in choosing its transport investments. As in other countries, however, the actual selection of projects is tempered by a variety of political and distributional concerns.

Two other organizations, the Commission of Planning and Investments in Transport Infrastructure and its secretariat and policy analysis arm, SECTRA, have important roles in the development of overall investment plans for urban transport, and particularly for Santiago. SECTRA has made important contributions to integrating the planning of transport investments in the nation's metropolitan areas. At the same time it appears that SECTRA, like similar agencies in other countries, has had a difficult time influencing the actions of the central government's powerful mainline ministries, which tend to have somewhat separate agendas and have strong independent political bases. The most obvious recent example where SECTRA's findings and views appear to have been overridden, is the government's decision to construct a third line for Santiago's metro system.[1] We know too little about the factors that led the government to proceed with building a third metro line for much comment on the decision. We do note, however, that investment analyses completed by SECTRA suggest that competing investments would have yielded much larger benefits for the same expenditure of resources. We return to this question at a latter point when we discuss estimated rates of return from highway and urban transportation investments.

Santiago's metro is obviously yet another governmental organization that should not be overlooked in discussing the institutional arrangements for providing urban transportation. Built by MOP it was initially operated by a unit of that ministry. Subsequently, the government created a government agency to operate the metro, and it has very recently made further institutional changes that are intended to allow the metro to operate more efficiently.

Chile's Economic Geography

Chile's settlement pattern and the nature of its transportation system have been strongly influenced by its unusual geographic and topographic features, its climatic extremes, and the location and character of natural resources among regions. Chile is a very long and very narrow country. Figure 5-1 iden-

1. One of the Chilean reviewers of this paper took exception to this statement and claimed that "SECTRA didn't oppose the construction of the third metro line," and that "they even demonstrated the return and justification of it." While this may be strictly true of SECTRA's official position, we have the very strong impression that SECTRA and its staff "informally" opposed the decision prior to the time it was made, and that a fair amount of ingenuity was needed to obtain an estimated rate of return for the project that narrowly exceeded the government 12 percent rate of return guideline for public projects. While we were unable to obtain enough information about SECTRA's modeling and evaluation procedures to make an independent assessment of their adequacy, transport specialists in both Chile and abroad who are familiar with the analyses and process believe the final estimates are overly optimistic. This would not be surprising given the experience in other countries (Acevedo and Salazar, 1989; HFA, 1989; Kain, 1990, 1991b, 2001, 1992b, and 1992c; Pickrell, 1989). While it appears SECTRA analysts were unable to persuade Chilean decision makers to implement more cost-effective alternatives, such as the segregated busway proposed for the same corridor discussed at later point in this paper, it does appear that they achieved valuable and important changes in the alignment and design of the third metro line.

Figure 5-1. Map of Chile

tifies the 13 regions that are used in reporting most Chilean regional statistics. Chile is over 4,300 kilometers long but its average width is only 180 kilometers.[2] Chile shares common borders with Peru in the north, with Bolivia in the northeast, and mostly with Argentina on the east. Its territorial claims extend southward to the South Pole.

Data on area, population, employment, and regional products, shown in Table 5-1, illustrate some of the consequences of Chile's geographic and topographic features on its settlement pattern and economic activity by region. The three northernmost and two southernmost regions are very sparsely settled, with population densities of fewer than seven persons per square kilometer. These five regions account for over 66% of the country's land area, but less than 16% of its population. The three northernmost regions have almost no rainfall, while the two southernmost have ample precipitation but their cold and inhospitable climates result in very short growing seasons. As a result of these climatic extremes, nearly all (94.7%) of the residents of these five regions live dispersed. Agriculture, mining, and tourism located in these peripheral regions, however, are important contributors to the national income, and exports depend on good transport facilities. Other legitimate concerns, such as national cohesiveness and real or imagined concerns about national defense, also may create pressures for transport investment in these sparsely settled peripheral regions beyond levels that could be justified by a narrow calculation of user benefits and project costs.

Intercity Freight and Passenger Services

As is true in most market economies, domestic freight transportation in Chile is dominated by road transportation (trucking) which carries about two-thirds of domestic freight (World Bank, 1989b, p. 1). Railways, the second largest supplier, carry about one-fifth, coastal shipping and oil pipelines together carry about one-tenth, and air transport carries less than one percent. Intercity passenger traffic is mainly by bus, although there is some rail service. Chile also has a modest, but critical, pipeline network, which totaled 622 km in 1986. The network was built by the government, but was recently privatized. The pipelines are mainly used to transport gasoline, diesel, and liquefied petroleum gas (LPG). Virtually all (95% in tons and approximately 85% by value) of international trade is sea-borne.

---

2. With a land area totaling 746,767 square kilometers, Chile is the seventh largest Latin American country. It is, moreover, larger than any European country except Russia. Chile's unusual shape, of course, is due to the Andes mountains, which create a nearly absolute barrier along its eastern border.

Table 5-1. *Area and Socio-Economic-Demographic Characteristics by Chilean Region in 1989*

	Area		Population							Regional GDP in 1986 (in 1997 CH$)		Percent of RGDP (1986)		
Region	Total (Sq. Km.)	Regional Share	Total ('000)	Regional Share	Percent Urban	Gross Pop Density	Labor Force ('000)	Employment ('000)	Empl./Pop	Total (mil.)	per Capita	Agriculture	Mining	Manufacturing
I	58,073	7.7	347	2.7	95	6	122	116	33	12,258	3,531	2.3	1.5	35.6
II	125,306	16.6	382	2.9	99	3	133	125	33	20,331	5,318	0.5	51.4	7.3
III	78,268	10.3	197	1.5	93	3	74	71	36	8,046	4,086	4.2	2.3	46.2
IV	39,647	5.2	478	3.7	77	12	154	145	30	8,083	1,692	15.2	8.6	14.2
IX	32,472	4.3	783	6.0	59	24	241	235	30	11,976	1,530	29.7	0.1	16.1
R.M.S	15,782	2.1	5,134	39.6	97	325	1,945	1,827	36	156,291	3,044	3.8	0.7	24.8
V	16,378	2.2	1,367	10.5	92	83	471	447	33	38,457	2,813	6.6	8.5	26.6
VI	15,950	2.1	641	4.9	67	40	230	218	34	22,110	3,448	23.4	32.5	10.1
VII	30,518	4.0	827	6.4	59	27	299	279	34	15,188	1,836	31.2	0.1	13.8
VIII	36,007	4.8	1,657	12.8	78	46	599	567	34	36,394	2,197	14.0	2.3	32.8
X	69,039	9.1	914	7.1	61	13	306	300	33	17,777	1,944	20.2	0.5	17.7
XI	107,153	14.2	79	0.6	82	1	32	31	39	1,725	2,197	17.7	2.0	3.9
XII	132,034	17.5	155	1.2	93	1	68	65	42	10,429	6,715	4.2	38.2	8.9
All	756,626	100.0	12,961	100.0	84	17	4,675	4,425	34	359,065	2,770	9.3	7.8	22.8

Source: Banco Central de Chile, "Indicadores Economicos y Sociales Regionales, 1980–1989."
Notes: (1) Valparaiso is in Region V; Santiago is in Region RMS, and Concepcion is in Region VIII.

Ports and Shipping

Chile's long narrow shape and 5,000 km of coastline affords the country over seventy cargo ports, of which twenty-six are commercial ports involved in international trade. Eleven of these twenty-six general cargo ports are owned by the Chilean Port Authority (Empresas Portuaria de Chile, EMPORCHI), a public enterprise which reports to MTT. The remainder are specialized ports (mainly minerals and petroleum) and privately owned general cargo ports at Lirquen and Corral. Data on regional shares of general and bulk cargo by region and on EMPORCHI's share of both general and bulk cargo in each region are presented in Table 5-2. This table does not provide separate data for greater Santiago, as that city has no port of its own. Two ports, Valparaiso and San Antonio in Region V, serve it.

In common with many parts of the world, ports in Chile were hugely inefficient in the early 1970s. Asecio (1991) reports that in 1973 Chilean ports were so crowded that ships had to pay between US $60,000 and US $80,000 in demurrage. Since 1981, institutional changes have entailed the transferring of all operations (other than wharfage and storage) at publicly owned ports to private stevedoring companies under concession agreements. The efficiency of these ports has improved significantly. As a result, Chile's publicly owned ports have been able to accommodate a huge increase in shipping with little or no physical expansion. In August 1993, officials at MTT claimed that there was adequate port capacity in all parts of the country at that time. They added, however, that a reasonable argument could be made for some port expansion in the south, and that serious planning should begin for expanding and modernizing port facilities in Valparaiso and San Antonio.

In the case of the central region, there is some consensus among neutral experts that the government made a mistake in deciding to split its recent investment in new container port capacity between Valparaiso and San Antonio, rather than concentrating it in San Antonio.[3] The decision to invest in container facilities in both Valparaiso and San Antonio reflects the government's concerns about Valparaiso's declining economic base. The harsh truth is that Valparaiso, which has a proud history and holds great emotional appeal for many Chileans, is a very poor site for a large, modern city. Its picturesque topography and narrow and winding streets have obvious appeal; but

3. Magni (1994), in commenting on an earlier draft of this paper, agreed that port capacity is adequate at the present time, but observed that there could well be shortages in two or three years at some ports and noted that new port facilities are under construction in Quintero. He also argued that the investments in Valparaiso's port consisted of the rehabilitation of facilities that were destroyed, and modernization of the port's container operations. Finally, he stated that "The government is not constructing new facilities in these two ports," and that "The government is willing to let the private sector construct and operate new ports."

Table 5-2. *Regional Shares of Population, GDP, and Total Port Cargo and Emporchi's Shares for General and Bulk Cargo*

Region	*Population Share by Region*	*GDP Share by Region*	*Total General Cargo (tons)*	*Total Bulk Cargo (tons)*	*Regional Shares of Total Port Cargo*		*Emporchi's Share*	
					General	*Bulk*	*General*	*Bulk*
I	2.7%	3.4%	1,088,591	1,743,631	8.6%	5.8%	100.0%	38.8%
II	2.9%	5.7%	1,221,161	3,995,817	9.7%	13.2%	91.9%	16.1%
III	1.5%	2.2%	221,406	4,412,777	1.8%	14.6%	0.0%	0.0%
IV	3.7%	2.3%	220,610	4,440,311	1.7%	14.7%	74.5%	3.0%
V	10.5%	10.7%	5,692,548	7,344,907	45.0%	24.3%	99.5%	26.0%
VIII	12.8%	10.1%	3,225,574	4,487,584	25.5%	14.9%	67.7%	34.8%
X	7.1%	5.0%	357,230	1,023,868	2.8%	3.4%	100.0%	63.3%
XI	0.6%	0.5%	230,221	72,439	1.8%	0.2%	100.0%	100.0%
XII	1.2%	2.9%	390,314	2,670,275	3.1%	8.8%	99.9%	0.0%
Total	100.0%	100.0%	12,647,655	30,191,609	100.0%	100.0%	88.6%	18.7%

Source: Empresa Portuaria de Chile, Memoria, 1992

they are serious impediments to providing the modern transport infrastructure that will increasingly be demanded by Chilean households and businesses. Possibly as a way of reducing the likelihood of similar uneconomic port investments in the future, the Chilean government's current policy is to leave further investments in ports to the private sector. Unless the government changes its policy or provides special incentives, further port expansion presumably will occur at locations where it is justified by market demand.

Chilean Railways

Chile's first railways were built and operated by private firms. The first rail line was opened in 1851 between Caldera and Copiapo. Just over 30 years later in 1884, the government of Chile created the Empresa de los Ferrocarriles del Estado (EFE) and charged it with building, operating, and developing a national railway system for Chile. The current system includes several private railways owned by mining companies, the privately-owned Antofagasta-Bolivia Railway, the small state-owned FERRONOR, and EFE, which owns and operates the bulk of the track.[4] As is also true throughout the western world, railway traffic, of which freight comprises 70%, has been declining in importance during the last two decades as improved roads, larger and more economical trucks, and deregulation have enabled trucks to capture a growing share of the intercity freight market.

According to Asecio (1991, p. 269), between 1960 and 1973 the EFE was "considered a public service and its investments, as well as its operating deficit, were financed by the State." In the early 1970s, as a result of overstaffing and a requirement to operate a number of uneconomical lines, EFE was covering less than half of its total expenditures. The resulting deficits were covered by government subsidies that reached US $123 million in 1974 (Asecio, 1991, p. 273). Starting in 1973, the government required EFE to implement measures that would reduce its deficits and ultimately enable it to become self-sufficient. As a result, the railway phased out many uneconomic services and reduced its workforce from 27,000 in 1970, to 9,000 in 1980, and to 7,000 in 1984. The government also discontinued all subsidies in late 1978 (Asecio, p. 269).

EFE reduced its deficits by implementing a number of technological improvements by contracting out both track and maintenance work to private firms, and by contracting with another private firm for the provision of small

4. Chile currently has about 8,900 km of track in service. About 4,300 km, mainly the railways south and west of Santiago, is broad 1.676 meter gauge, while the rest, mainly in the north, is narrow 1.0 meter gauge. Of the broad gauge lines, 1,900 km (the Santiago-Valparaiso line and part of the Santiago-San Antonio line) are electrified, albeit with different electrical systems, and 700 km (Santiago to the south) are continuously welded.

shipments. In addition, it doubled its tariffs in real terms between 1971 and 1980. As a result of these measures, and the sale of a number of properties that were unrelated to its core rail business, EFE reduced its debt from US $53.1 million in 1974 to US $36.8 million in 1976. Thereafter, EFE's debt again began to grow and reached US $44.4 million in 1978 (Asecio, 1991, p. 269). In 1980 the government took the further step of requiring EFE to take over its debt service, including the amounts resulting from the devaluation of debt denominated in foreign exchange. Asecio (1991, p. 270) describes the subsequent period as "a new era" for EFE "when for the first time, the company began operations without government funding or compensation of any type."

EFE achieved significant increases in system productivity after 1980 and in some years it had no operational deficits. As Asecio (1991, 270) emphasizes in his discussion of this period, EFE also benefited from changes in government policy that gave it greater freedom to set rates, to close unprofitable branch lines, and to discontinue uneconomic services. Tariffs declined by roughly 30% in real terms between 1980 and 1984, unprofitable passenger services were cut back, and profitable heavy cargoes were increased considerably. The Chilean Government, however, continued to require EFE to operate the Arica-La Paz line, serving mainly the La Paz area in Bolivia, at a loss, though it is unclear why EFE should subsidize rail service for Bolivia.

In the 1990s, the government decided to further privatize railway operations. Legislation enacted in August 1992 mandated the separation of the physical network from the provision of services. While the details of these schemes are still evolving, the general idea is that private firms will operate their own trains and be allowed equal access to EFE's existing rail lines. EFE will continue to own and maintain the physical network (tracks and stations), most likely under contract to private firms, as is already the case, and will be paid a usage fee by the private operators. The scheme envisions that these private operators will either own or lease the rolling stock and compete in running these operations. It is expected that the freight services will be sold quickly, but there has been very little interest in the unprofitable passenger services and no current plans for privatizing them. It is expected that EFE will continue to operate these unprivatizable services for the foreseeable future.

Intercity Roads

As the data in Table 5-3 indicate, Chile's road network consisted of nearly 80,000 kilometers in 1989, of which only about 13% were paved. Estimates prepared by MOP analysts in January 1993 indicate that 54% of paved roads are in good condition, 35% are in fair condition, and 11% are in poor condition. Not surprisingly, the condition of unpaved roads is generally poorer: less

Table 5-3. *Road Network, Administrative and Service Classification in December 1989*

Classification	*Concrete*	*Asphalt*	*Total Paved*	*Engineered Gravel*	*Gravel & Earth*	*Total Unpaved*	*Total Roads*
Basic Network	3,211	6,279	9,490	10,643	2,882	13,525	23,015
National Roads	2,087	2,576	4,663	1,292	20	1,312	5,975
Primary Regional Roads	754	2,726	3,480	3,194	567	3,761	7,241
Secondary Regional Roads	370	977	1,347	6,157	2,295	8,452	9,799
Local Network	260	574	834	22,048	33,285	55,333	56,167
Primary Local Roads	154	297	451	11,553	12,223	23,776	24,227
Secondary Local Roads	106	277	383	10,495	21,062	31,557	31,940
Total Network	3,471	6,853	10,324	32,691	36,167	68,858	79,182

Sources: MOP; and World Bank. Staff Appraisal Report, August 23, 1989, p. 23.

than 8% were in good condition, 59% were in fair condition, and 33% were in poor condition. For the entire network the shares are 16% good, 55% fair, and 29% poor (World Bank, 1993a, p. 49).

Chile's road network is divided into a basic network of about 23,000 km of roads, including the previously mentioned national roads, and a local network of about 56,000 km of roads (Table 5-3). The basic network is further subdivided into about 6,000 km of national roads, 7,300 km of primary regional roads, and about 10,000 km of secondary regional roads. Nearly 80% of the national roads, just under half of the primary regional roads, and about 14% of the secondary regional roads are paved. The local network consists of 56,000 km of roads of which just under half are part of the primary local roads network; the rest are classified as secondary local roads. Less than 2% of primary local roads and just over 1% of secondary local roads were paved in 1988. These roads receive only the most rudimentary maintenance.

Route 5, a section of the longitudinal road that runs from the Peruvian border in the north to Quellon on the island of Chiloe in the south, is the backbone of Chile's 6,000 km network of national roads. In addition to Route 5, Chile's national roads include two other major north-south roads—the Austral Road running from Puerto Varas, north of Puerto Montt in Region X, to Villa O'Higgins—and Road 9 from Paso Baguales on the Argentine border north of Torres de Paine to Fuertes Bulnes, south of Punta Arenas.

We have been unable to obtain systematic information on either user tax

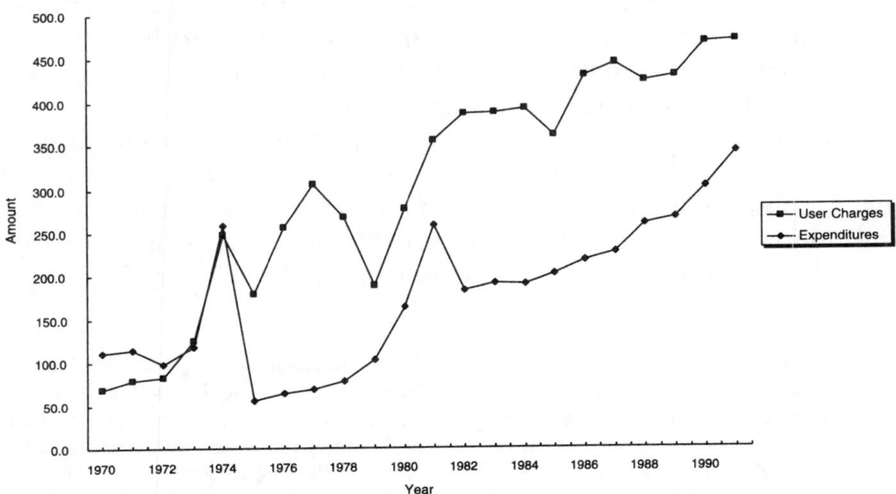

Figure 5-2. Indexes of Real Per-Capita GDP and Per-Capita Vehicle Ownership, Chile 1960–1990

collections or road spending by region or for individual cities and towns within regions. This is less of a disadvantage in terms of assessing the distributional and efficiency implications of road investments than it might at first appear. As the data in Appendix Table A-1 and in Figure 5-2 reveal, aggregate road user charges (fuel taxes, tolls, and vehicle registration fees) have exceeded aggregate road expenditures (maintenance, rehabilitation, and new construction) by substantial margins since 1974. Between 1975 and 1978, road expenditures were only 26 percent of road user charges. While the ratio increased between 1979 and 1991, the average for the entire period was still less than 60%. These figures do not include the relatively small expenditures for urban streets and roads by MINVU and the even smaller maintenance outlays by local governments. While we have no intention of joining the long-standing debate about whether fuel taxes and auto registration fees should be regarded as user charges or discretionary taxes, it is undeniable that in Chile the total sums paid by highway-based vehicles and their users annually far exceed the total sums spent on building and maintaining the roads and streets they use.[5]

More important, the user tax collections and expenditures by region, city, and town are not very meaningful measures of the benefits and costs of road investments to these same places. By its very nature, the national road system serves private cars and trucks between regions, cities, and towns. Neither the amounts paid by the residents and/or businesses located in particular regions or communities nor the amounts spent there are good indicators of the benefits that accrue to the individuals and firms who live, produce goods and services, or pay road user taxes in these specific places. This is less true, however, for urban roads and for public transport investments. It is very hard to argue, for example, that taxpayers or firms located in Antofagasto, or even Valparaiso, benefit in a measurable way from the Santiago metro.

The regional allocation of roads by type of pavement and data on total vehicle and car registrations and kilometers of road per square kilometer, per 100 persons, and per 100 vehicles are shown in Table 5-4. These data reveal the unsurprising facts that the Santiago Metropolitan Region has the fewest kilometers of roads per capita and per vehicle and the highest proportion of

5. This conclusion needs to be qualified by the fact that we do not know much about the details of road user taxes and road expenditures in Chile. For example, neither the taxes collected by local governments nor road expenditures by local government appear in Appendix Table A-1. Similarly, we do not know how the activities of the traffic police are counted. Finally, private land developers provide at least some of the streets in their developments. It is questionable whether these local service roads should be regarded as part of the highway network in any case, but these examples illustrate the need for some caution in interpreting these and similar numbers. We very much doubt, however, that the omitted road taxes and expenditures are large enough to change the overall conclusion.

Table 5-4. *Area, Population, Vehicle Ownership, and Road Characteristics by Region*

			Motor Vehicles		*Motor Vehicles Per 1000 Persons*							*Total Kilometers of Roads*		
Region	*Area (Sq. Km.)*	*Total Population ('000)*	*Total*	*Cars*	*Total*	*Cars*	*Buses*	*Large Trucks*	*Small Trucks*	*Total Roads (Km.)*	*Percent Paved*	*Per Sq. Km.*	*Per 1000 Persons*	*Per 1000 Vehicles*
I	58,073	347	33,935	19,329	97.7	55.7	1.9	7.2	22.2	4,993	16.7	0.09	14.4	147.1
II	125,306	382	35,314	19,690	92.4	51.5	2.5	9.1	22.0	5,142	25.9	0.04	13.4	145.6
III	78,268	197	18,707	9,176	95.0	46.6	1.8	12.1	26.6	6,237	14.8	0.08	31.7	333.4
IV	39,647	478	33,908	16,657	71.0	34.9	1.6	6.7	21.5	5,018	15.8	0.13	10.5	148.0
IX	32,472	783	37,568	18,785	48.0	24.0	1.0	5.0	15.2	12,001	6.5	0.37	15.3	319.4
R.M.S	15,782	5,134	459,900	317,744	89.6	61.9	2.6	4.8	16.3	2,620	41.5	0.17	0.5	5.7
V	16,378	1,367	98,206	63568	71.8	46.5	1.6	4.2	15.7	3,546	34.3	0.22	2.6	36.1
VI	15,950	641	51,623	27,109	80.5	42.3	2.0	7.6	21.9	4,191	13.5	0.26	6.5	81.2
VII	30,518	827	59,076	31,485	71.4	38.1	1.2	7.3	21.2	7,441	8.9	0.24	9.0	126.0
VIII	36,007	1,657	92,473	48,345	55.8	29.2	1.7	6.5	15.8	11,555	10.9	0.32	7.0	125.0
X	69,039	914	53,884	27,431	58.9	30.0	1.1	6.3	17.4	10,846	12.0	0.16	11.9	201.3
XI	107,153	79	2,737	1,170	34.9	14.9	0.5	7.8	9.2	2,422	3.2	0.02	30.9	884.9
XII	132,034	155	24,056	14,524	154.9	93.5	2.4	11.3	38.1	3,262	5.2	0.02	21.0	135.6
All	756,626	12,961	1,001,387	615,013	77.3	47.4	2.0	5.8	17.7	79,274	13.9	0.10	6.1	79.2

Source: Banco Central de Chile, "Indicadores Economicos y Sociales Regionales, 1980–1989."

paved roads. Greater Santiago also has the second highest rates of per-capita passenger car ownership, although its rate of total motor vehicle ownership per capita is only fifth highest among the thirteen regions.

Vehicle Ownership and Per-Capita Income

Plots of indexes of per-capita GDP, per-capita auto, per-capita truck, and per-capita total motor vehicle registrations by year are shown in Figure 5-3. Regressions of per-capita vehicle ownership on per-capita GDP, shown in Table 5-5, exhibit surprisingly low income elasticities of demand. The resulting estimates suggest that per-capita car ownership and per-capita truck ownership in Chile as a whole would be expected to increase by 0.6 percent with each one percent increase in per-capita GDP. The most likely explanations for these rather low income elasticities are the failure of the real per capita income estimates used for the regressions to account correctly for the sometimes exceptional changes in the structure of the Chilean economy, especially given that the equation does not include a number of variables that may have had important influences on levels of auto ownership. Among these omitted variables would be real petrol prices, the retail prices of private cars and other vehicles, and variables measuring the impacts of tariffs and various import restrictions.

Support for the view that omitted variables, and possibly inadequacies of the income measures used, account for the relatively low income elasticities of demand shown in Table 5-5, is provided by estimates obtained for Chile by Braun and Fontaine (1989, p. 7) using time series data for the period 1964–

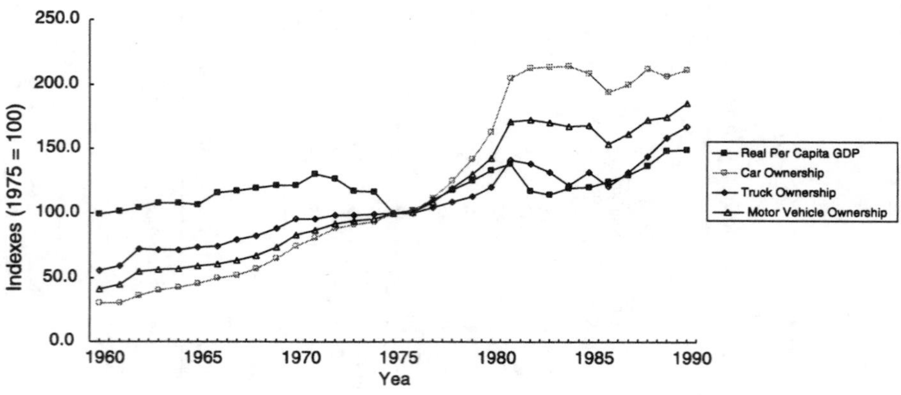

Figure 5-3. Annual Passenger Boardings for the Santiago Metro by Line, 1975–1991

Table 5-5. *Time Series Estimates of Motor Vehicle Ownership Models for Chile, 1960–90*

	AR1 Coefficient Estimate and (Standard Error)					
	Ln Ownership per 1000 Population			*Ln Total Ownership*		
Variable	*Cars EQ (1)*	*Trucks & Vans EQ (2)*	*All vehicles EQ (3)*	*Cars EQ (4)*	*Trucks & Vans EQ (5)*	*All Vehicles EQ (6)*
Constant	−3.21	−3.52	−2.02	−5.76	−3.61	−2.55
	(2.89)	(1.99)	(2.23)	(4.98)	(3.46)	(3.94)
Ln Real Per Capita GDP	0.60	0.60	0.56			
(Lagged one year)	(0.27)	(0.19)	(0.21)			
Ln Real Total GDP				0.92	0.80	0.80
(Lagged one year)				(0.25)	(0.18)	(0.20)
R-Squared	0.92	0.87	0.91	0.95	0.94	0.95
D-W Statistic	1.23	1.96	1.49	1.26	1.95	1.51
RHO	0.99	0.98	0.99	0.99	0.98	0.99

1986. Braun and Fontaine use total vehicle registrations rather than per-capita registrations as the dependent variable, and use aggregate real GNP and an index of the retail price of private cars as explanatory variables. They obtain an income elasticity of demand of 1.7 and a price elasticity of demand of –1.0. Braun and Fontaine (1989) do not present estimates for either trucks or total vehicles. Table 5-5 also includes equations relating total vehicle ownership to real total GDP, which we estimated after we obtained Braun and Fontaine's estimates. An alternative specification, more like the one used by Braun and Fontaine, yields higher income elasticities of demand. The estimate is still smaller than the one obtained by Braun and Fontaine, however.

An income elasticity of demand for automobile ownership (discussed subsequently), obtained using cross section data by *comunas* within the Santiago metropolitan area in 1991, is also somewhat larger than 1.0 and is much closer to the Braun and Fontaine (1989) estimate and to the estimates obtained in various time series studies for individual countries and from cross country data. Table 5-6 presents cross-section regression estimates for auto, truck, and total vehicle ownership per capita obtained using data for fifty-two countries in 1990. The data used for these regressions are shown in Appendix Table A-2. The income elasticities of demand for per capita GNP obtained using these data are 1.58 for passenger cars, 1.15 for commercial vehicles, and 1.44 for total motor vehicles.

Table 5-6 also includes an equation explaining variations in per-capita auto ownership in 1980 among the 60 large metropolitan areas (in forty countries) shown in Appendix Table A-3. This regression, which uses per-capita GDP

Table 5-6. *Estimates of Motor Vehicle Ownership Models for 52 Countries in 1990 and 60 Large Cities in 1980*

	OLS Estimate and (Standard Error)			
	52 Countries			*60 Cities*
Dependent/ Explanatory Variable	*Ln Passenger Cars Per 1000 Persons EQ (1)*	*Ln Commercial Vehicles Per 1000 Persons EQ (2)*	*Ln Total Motor Vehicles Per 1000 Persons EQ (3)*	*Ln Passenger Cars Per 1000 Persons EQ (4)*
Constant	−8.29	−5.92	−6.90	−1.93
	(0.88)	(0.70)	(0.72)	(0.95)
Ln Per Capita GDP	1.58	1.15	1.4	1.02
(Country Level)	(0.10)	(0.08)	(0.08)	(0.08)
Ln Population Density	−0.28	−0.20	−0.24	
(Country Level)	(0.07)	(0.06)	(0.06)	
Ln Population Density				−0.21
(City Level)				(0.07)
R-squared	0.84	0.81	0.87	0.79

and an estimate of the gross population density for the built-up parts of the metropolitan areas as explanatory variables, demonstrates about 81% of the variance in per-capita auto ownership in 1980, even though both the estimates of median household income and metropolitan area density contain significant errors. The income elasticity obtained for this equation, 1.02, is considerably smaller than those obtained in the cross-country regressions. Even though the city density measure is error prone, it is highly significant statistically and is consistent with other results that indicate denser cities have lower levels of auto ownership than less dense cities, presuming per-capita income remains constant.

Predictions of auto and vehicle ownership per thousand persons, obtained from international cross-country regressions, are shown in Appendix Table A-2. For Chile actual levels of commercial vehicles in 1990 (27.2 per 100 persons) exceeded the predicted levels of (23.1 per 100 persons), while the predicted levels of passenger car registrations (25.2 per 100 persons) was smaller than the actual number (53.9 per 100 persons). Total vehicle registrations per capita are also less than the predicted values. These results are consistent with the notion that above average barriers to auto ownership have somewhat restrained the level of auto ownership in Chile. In so far as these barriers will be fewer in the future than in the past, this could lead to a more rapid growth in auto ownership than would be expected, given a particular growth rate in per-capita GNP.

Predictions of auto ownership per thousand persons obtained from the cross-city regressions are shown Appendix Table A-3. Both 1980 and 1990 data are included for Santiago. Each of the other cities appears only once, and the data for them is from 1980. The predicted value of cars per 1000 population for Santiago in 1980 (86 per 1000 persons) is larger than the actual 1980 value (60 per 1000 persons), a result that is consistent with the one obtained for the nation from the cross-country regression. The 1990 prediction for Santiago is also larger than the actual value. Again, not too much weight should be given to these primitive regressions or the predictions obtained from them; there are many important explanatory variables omitted, and the variables used are all measured with substantial error. Nonetheless, the results have some relevance and suggest that the levels of vehicle ownership in Chile are determined by the same fundamental economic variables as in other countries and, in particular, are strongly affected by household and per capita income levels. Additional evidence supporting this proposition is presented in the section on urban transportation.

Intercity Trucking and Buses

Deregulation of intercity road transport in Chile occurred in roughly a four-year period. Trucking companies opposed deregulation when it was first proposed by the government in 1973, and when it became clear the government was committed, the companies requested the continuation of regulated tariffs and routes. The result was a compromise in which the government agreed to provide the operators with a fixed transitional period to adapt to a deregulated environment.

Since 1976, there have been no restrictions on entry, tariffs, and types of services in the trucking industry. Truckers initially were required to register with the Registro Nacional del Transporte Profesional. This Registry, established in 1971, was something of a barrier to entry. Members had to renew their membership annually, and nonmembers were prohibited from operating. The Antimonopoly Commission, however, ruled in 1975 that the Registry was an illegal restraint of trade, and further legislation introduced in 1979 made any compulsory union affiliation illegal.

As a result of deregulation and other measures, the intercity trucking industry expanded considerably. Among these other measures were easy credit policies. It has been estimated that attractive credit terms induced private individuals and firms to purchase an additional 15,000 vehicles for commercial use from 1979 to 1981. The recession and the mid-1982 devaluation caused shipments by truck to plummet, at the same time installment payments doubled. The government response was to have the Bank of Chile (Banco de Chile) reschedule 30% of each debt. Most truckers, however, could not qualify for refinancing because they were insolvent. Those that were eligible, however, typically took advantage of favorable credit terms. By September 1985 some 3,500 debts totaling US $116 million had been rescheduled and an additional 2,000 debts valued at US $74 million were being processed.

The relaxation of import restrictions and tariffs on trucks and buses was another policy implemented during this period. In 1974 a 100 percent import duty was charged on vehicles of under eight tons and a 40% duty was charged on heavier units. Imports of trucks, moreover, were limited to the Pegaso brand. In 1975 the government changed the duty on truck imports to a uniform rate of 80%. In 1977 nearly all import restrictions were lifted, and in 1979 the duty on imported vehicles was reduced to a uniform 10% rate, in line with the overall reduction in import duties enacted at that time. Exceptions were made for light and utilitarian vehicles, which were taxed at 65% and 45% respectively, but a phased rate reduction was implemented for these categories, reaching 10% by 1986.

Consequences of Intercity Bus Deregulation

Intercity bus services also were subject to strict regulation and the State Bus Company (ETC) provided most of them. ETC, which ran a yearly deficit of US $10–15 million, was sold in 1975 to private operators, who provide the same services at a profit.

The deregulation of intercity bus services was complete by 1978 and seems to have been an unqualified success. The number of intercity buses has increased greatly, the quality of services improved, and the fares reduced. The speed and extent of improvement in interurban bus services throughout the country can only be described as remarkable. Before deregulation, for example, the Santiago/Vina/Valparaiso city pairs were served by only two firms; by 1986 these markets were served by twelve firms with modern buses running every fifteen minutes. As a result of these improvements, and due to diversion from the railways, the number of intercity bus passengers increased from 17.4 million in 1970 to 60 million in 1980.

Economic Evaluations of Intercity Road Investments

Chile has relied heavily on the World Bank and, to a lesser extent, on the Inter-American Development Bank and Japan to finance road improvements. The World Bank has been making loans for highway improvements since 1961 and has made at least five major loans to the Chilean Government for road building or maintenance. To obtain these loans, the Ministry of Public

Works (MOP) had to complete economic evaluations that compared the investment costs to the projected benefits from making the proposed improvements. These analyses typically obtain estimates of each project's IRR (Internal Rate of Return), B/C (Benefit/Cost) ratio, and NPV (Net Present Value). The principal benefits identified in these studies are reductions in vehicle operating costs and time savings. Validad, MOP's road building directorate, has made extensive, and apparently effective, use of the World Bank's Highway Design and Maintenance (HDM) model in identifying and assessing proposed road construction projects and in developing a cost-effective maintenance and rehabilitation program for Chile's intercity road network.

The Second Highway Reconstruction Project

The earliest economic evaluations of Chilean road projects we were able to obtain are pre- and post-project evaluations of intercity road projects completed under the World Bank's Second Highway Reconstruction Project between 1984 and 1990. The project was designed to correct serious deterioration of Chile's road network, caused by increased traffic and inadequate maintenance. The most serious deterioration occurred from 1976 to 1980, when MOP apparently diverted road building and maintenance moneys to pay for the completion of the Santiago metro, which cost nearly twice as much to build as had been forecast.

Using the World Bank's Highway Design and Maintenance HDM model, Validad obtained ex post estimated IRRs for a sample of fourteen rehabilitated road sections (totaling 578 km) and for seven bridges and access roads. The mean IRRs obtained in the pre- and post-project assessments of the fourteen road projects were identical, i.e. 34% although the before and after estimates for individual sections varied. Estimates for the individual sections and other details relating to these evaluations are shown in Appendix Table A-4. The mean ex post IRR obtained for the seven bridge and access road projects, however, which was greater than 71% was more than twice the pre-project estimate for the same sample of projects. One of the project's major goals, to increase the level of road maintenance, was amply achieved as maintenance outlays increased from 26% of total Chilean road expenditures for the period 1982 to 1985 to 55% for the period 1986 to 1989.

The Second Road Sector Project

An August 23, 1989, World Bank Staff Appraisal Report provided a description of the Second Road Sector Project. About 60% of the proposed project funds were to be used for periodic and routine maintenance and about 40% for investment, new construction, or the upgrading of existing facilities.

Roughly half of the funding for this US $907 million project was to be provided by the Chilean Government; the remainder was to come from the World Bank (25%), the Inter-American Development Bank (9%), and other cofinancing (19%). Validad's engineers and analysts identified and evaluated projects with projected total direct costs of US $1,013 million (in 1989 dollars) and with a mean projected IRR of 36.5%. The size of Chile's road program from 1990 to 1993, however, was limited by the Chilean Government's concerns about inflation, by IMF conditionality, and by projections of competing government expenditures. According to the appraisal report, the projected total direct cost of the authorized road program for the period 1990 through 1993 was only US $433.8 million; the mean IRR for these projects was 44%. Actual expenditures, however, were larger than anticipated by the World Bank as the government spent about US $200 million per year during this period for urban and interurban roads (Magni, 1994). The projected IRRs for paved road maintenance were about 30% and the IRRs for unpaved roads were even higher. The IRR for maintenance of Chile's 3,470 km of roads with concrete surfaces was in excess of 50% and the IRR from the construction of 156 km of dual carriageways (mostly Route 5) was estimated at 70%. Details related to the pre-project assessment of the authorized road program are shown in Appendix Table A-5.

MOP's 1994–1998 Road Program

MOP/Validad engineers and analysts have completed assessments of projects that are to be included in a World Bank loan to provide partial funding for MOP's US $1,650 million (in 1992 dollars) road maintenance program for 1994–98.[6] As in the case of earlier loans, MOP staff used the World Bank's HDM model to carry out economic evaluations of the proposed program. These analyses indicated that proposed maintenance expenditures would produce mean IRRs of 50% for asphalt paved roads, 54% for concrete roads, and 54% for unpaved roads.[7]

Economic Evaluations of Urban Road and Street Projects

Only limited information is available in Chile about the economic rates of return for new construction and for the maintenance of streets and roads in

6. While we refer to this project as a road maintenance program, it includes relatively modest amounts for road safety (6% of total project cost), for support of BOT schemes (1% of total project cost), and for environmental impact assessment and monitoring (less than 0.1% of total project cost). Road maintenance was to account for about 93% of total project cost.

7. HDM-II cannot be used for cement concrete roads. Thus, the economic analyses for these roads were carried out using a separate model developed for MOP by the University of Chile.

urban areas. The most serious omission is the lack of any information on actual or projected rates of return for road and street projects in the Santiago metropolitan area.[8] There are three actors in this arena: (a) MOP, which has responsibility for national roads within the metropolitan area, including some of the most important projects, such as the Ring Road; (b) the municipality of Santiago, which builds and maintains streets within its jurisdiction; and (c) MINVU, which has primary responsibility for road building and maintenance in the remaining *comunas* in the region. Developers, who are supposed to provide infrastructure, including roads in new development areas, also play a role, but we were unable to obtain much information about the nature or extent of their activities in these areas.

Only about half of Chile's roughly 10,000 km of urban roads and streets are paved; the remainder are gravel or earth roads. As Kahn and Kerr point out in the previous chapter, unpaved roads and streets in Santiago are a major source of air pollution. Maintenance is inadequate and the condition of these unpaved roads is generally poor. The municipality of Santiago is responsible for planning, design, implementation, and maintenance of the streets and road systems within its boundaries (the central area of Greater Santiago). All maintenance and rehabilitation are done by private contractors and are supervised by MINVU's regional organizations.

With the exception of the municipality of Santiago, MINVU is responsible for most of the funding and all of the planning, design, construction, and maintenance of urban street networks throughout the country, including the rest of the thirty-three municipalities that comprise the Santiago metropolitan area. Each municipality, however, is responsible for traffic management, while the national police (*Carabineros de Chile*) enforce traffic regulations.

According to the World Bank (1989a), expenditures for urban street programs for the entire country, which are primarily the responsibility of MINVU, averaged US $12.2 million (1988 dollars) per year between 1984 and 1987. This figure does not include expenditures by MOP for national roads within city boundaries, by developers, by the municipality of Santiago, or by other municipalities. Over the four years from 1985 to 1988, net funds for additional capital outlays and debt service for urban streets and roads have been increasing at a real average annual growth rate of over 22% (World Bank, 1989a, p. 56).

The Urban Streets and Transport Project

Preproject evaluations of projects included in the World Bank's Urban Streets and Transport Project were the only systematic assessments of urban

8. The road network for the Santiago metropolitan area circa 1990 consisted of 91 kms of expressways, 583 kms of arterials, and 257 kms of secondary streets.

road projects available to us. This report was overwhelmingly based on experience with a World Bank loan to MINVU to improve urban road maintenance. The World Bank loan totaled US $75 million for the period 1990 to 1995 and the Republic of Chile provided a matching sum. The project also provided modest funding for traffic management and for public transport (both were about 9% of estimated direct cost).

Eighty-two percent of the planned direct program costs (this excludes a 21% of base cost allowance in the project budget for physical and price contingencies) of the Urban Streets and Transport Project were for a MINVU street maintenance and rehabilitation program in the country's thirteen regions, and a five-year rehabilitation and maintenance program designed to restore the nation's badly deteriorated urban streets to a point where they could be kept in good condition with a cost-effective maintenance program.[9] While the mean IRR obtained for these urban road maintenance projects at 25.4% was less than those obtained for the intercity road projects discussed previously, it was still more than twice the government's 12% target rate of return for government investments.

The pre-project evaluations, moreover, found that the small amounts (about 8% of base costs) that were allocated to a variety of traffic management measures in Greater Santiago, Greater Concepcion, and Greater Valparaiso would yield even higher returns. The mean projected IRR for these projects, which included bus priority lanes in Santiago, Concepcion, and Valparaiso, was 43.7 percent. An even higher IRR was obtained for traffic management projects in Valparaiso (78.7%); the IRRs obtained for traffic management projects in the other two metropolitan areas, though smaller, were still quite large, 38% for Santiago and 49.4 percent for Concepcion. The loan also provided funding for the construction of a pilot at-grade, physically segregated bus/tramway in Santiago and for carrying out assessments of anticipated internal rates of return for three corridors. The results of these evaluations are discussed in the next section, which considers public transport investments.

9. Estimated program requirements and costs for the MINVU program were based on studies by local consultants in three pilot cities. The pilot cities were Iguique (southern zone), Curico (central zone), and Temuco (northern zone). The objective of these studies was to develop prototype street maintenance and rehabilitation programs. For each city, the consultants developed a detailed description and inventory of the primary street network and relevant urban features, completed a diagnosis of problems and an evaluation of alternative solutions, and prepared a five-year investment program. In combination with information obtained independently by consultants for La Serana (north central zone), and in Coyhanque and Punta Arenas (extreme south), these data were used to prepare estimates of the extent and cost of a nationwide urban street investment program.

Regulations implemented during the Pinochet regime required developers to contribute land for urban streets, to build and pave the streets and to deed them to the local government. The same was true for water and other utility connections. If the site they were developing required the provision of facilities for intermediate sites, they received bonds from government that were to be repaid when these closer sites were developed.

Actual and Estimated Rates of Return for Public Transport Investments

Between 1968 and 1987 the Chilean Government spent an estimated US $1,203 million (1993 dollars) to build a two-line, 26 km metro in Santiago. Line 1 was completed on time and according to plan; Line 2, however, took eight years to complete against a projected completion time of four years, and was, moreover, modified to save money (HFA, 1989, 6.26). Following the pattern of metro projects in both developing and developed countries (HFA, 1989; Pickrell, 1989), the actual costs of the Santiago metro exceeded projected costs by 84%.[10]

The estimated US $1,203 million cost of the Santiago metro did not include either the cost of capital during the construction period or any disruption costs. The later must have been quite large. To save on construction costs, MOP completely closed Santiago's principal central area street for most of the five-year construction period. Nor did the estimated capital cost include any allowance for the costs imposed on road users by MOP's decision to under-maintain the nation's roads to pay for the metro. The construction costs reported by the government for Lines 1 and 2 of the Santiago metro are also quite low by world standards, causing some observers to wonder whether MOP may have overlooked some items in preparing its estimate of project cost.[11]

While project planners seriously underestimated the capital cost of Lines 1 and 2 of the Santiago metro, the same cannot be said for their ridership. HFA,

10. When the project was initiated, the Chilean Government expected that French loans would cover 60% of the construction cost of the metro and that the remainder would be paid by grants from the central government. We have no hard information on how the project's large cost overrun was financed. However, it has been suggested that deferred road maintenance and construction may have been part of the solution.

11. In their economic assessment of the Santiago metro, for example, HFA (1989, p. 11.21) observes that "Capital costs were relatively low in Santiago, where it was claimed (emphasis added) that the metro was built and operated more cheaply than any comparable metro in the world."

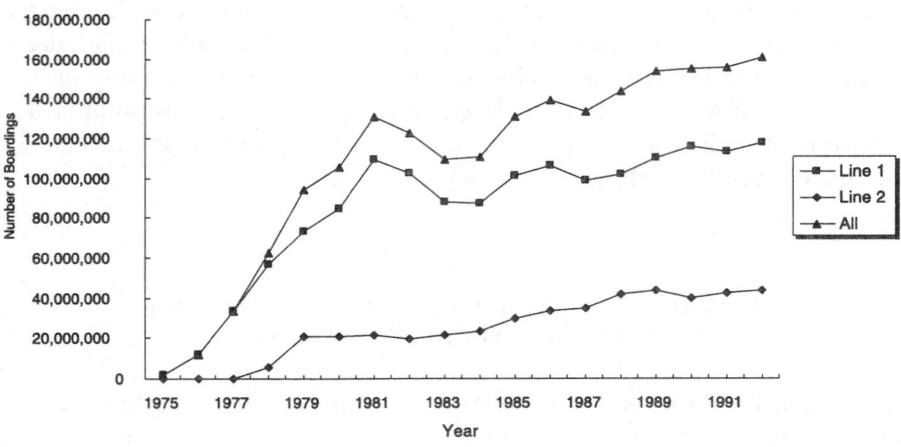

Figure 5-4. Annual Passenger Boardings for the Santiago Metro by Line, 1975–92

(1989, p. 74) reports that while ridership for Lines 1 and 2 was projected at 300 million passenger boardings for the forecast year of 1986; actual ridership for that year was only 139 million boardings or 46% as large as projected. As shown in Figure 5-4, with the exception of 1987 when the number of boardings dipped to 133 million annually, total system ridership has grown slowly. The metro's ridership of 161 million, achieved in 1992, was still only 54% of the 300 million boardings project planners had predicted for that same year. Part of the gains in ridership since 1986 were undoubtedly attributable to the opening of an additional 1.5 km of line and an additional station.[12]

HFA completed a crude ex-post economic evaluation of the Santiago metro as part of their study of metros in developing countries. Using less complete data than they used for similar assessments in a number of other cities, HFA (1989, p. 11.23) analysts obtained an IRR of 13.7 percent for Lines 1 and 2. This result caused them to conclude that the Santiago metro "has enjoyed good management throughout and despite problems with the alignment of

12. Not shown are a series of ridership models for the Santiago metro that are similar to models we have estimated for transit systems in the United States (Kain, 1994; Liu, 1993; Kain and Liu, 1994). For several reasons, particularly the short period of metro operation and the fact that few relevant explanatory variables were available, these equations are less informative than similar models we have estimated for other systems. Nonetheless, they explain a large fraction of the variation in annual system boardings and provide further evidence that Line 2 was much less productive than Line 1. The results suggest that each 1% increase in the length of Line 1 increased system ridership by 0.8%, while each additional kilometer increase in the length Line 2 increased ridership by only 0.07%.

line 2, appears to have achieved a satisfactory return." Of the thirteen metro projects assessed by HFA, they obtain higher estimates only for Cairo (15.6%); Hong Kong (20.8%), Pusan (15.4%), Seoul (16.6%), and Singapore (21.9%.).

In spite of the modest internal rates of return obtained by HFA for Lines 1 and 2 of the Santiago metro, and the fact that prospects for further extensions are probably even less advantageous, the government decided to built a third metro line. Projected capital costs of the third metro line, which roughly follows the alignment envisioned for Line 5 of the original metro plan, were estimated at approximately US $300 million. Figure 5-5, which is a map from the metro's 1992 Annual Report, shows the alignments of Lines 1 and 2 and what is presumably a fairly general indication of the likely alignment of the third metro line.

SECTRA's economic evaluation indicated that it had examined eight options for the third metro line, of which three were apparently given serious consideration (SECTRA, circa 1993). The three alignments are referred to in SECTRA report as Vicuna Mackenna (Alt. 6), Ramon Carnicer (Alt. 7), and Arturo Prat (Alt. 8). All three lines would have connected to Line 1; important differences among the three alternatives were the location of the Line 1 interchange station and how well each would have served the central area without a transfer.

SECTRA, after noting that MIDEPLAN has established a minimum rate of return for public investments of 12%, finds that the Ramon Carnicer alternative would have the lowest direct cost (US $221.8 million) and highest IRR, which it estimated at 14.7. The direct costs and IRRs for the remaining two options are US $226.9 million and 11.4% for Vicuna Mackenna, and US$ 310 million and 10.2 percent for Arturo Prat. SECTRA's forecast of total system ridership in 1996 was 166.7 million per year if none of the alternatives was built, 208.6 million for either the Ramon Carnicer or Vicuna Mackenna alternatives, and 212.6 million for the Arturo Prat alternative.

Projected Rates of Return for Segregated Bus ways

As previously discussed, the Urban Streets and Roadway Project funded by the World Bank and Inter-American Development Bank included financing for the construction of a pilot segregated busway. The intent was to evaluate ten corridors in Santiago and to select the most promising one for a pilot project. This, it was hoped, would demonstrate the feasibility and cost-effectiveness of the kinds of at-grade, segregated busways, that were originally developed in Brazil and that have been implemented, with considerable success, in a growing number of metropolitan areas in developing countries. Kain

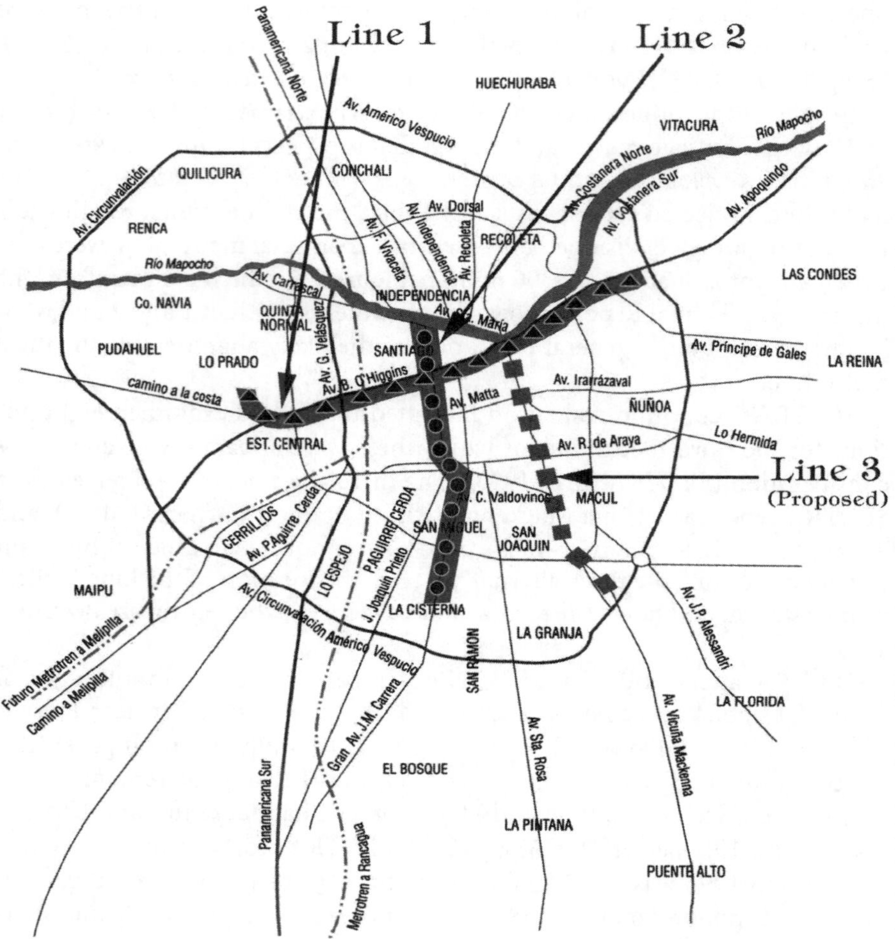

Figure 5-5.

(1991b) and TRRL and TTC (1989 and 1990) review the performance of these projects.

While we were unable to obtain much information about the studies of segregated busways in Santiago, it appears that three projects were selected for preliminary engineering and economic evaluation, Vicuna Mackenna, Ave Grecia, and Ave Independencia (Miquel, 1993). The estimated IRR's on these projects were approximately:

- Vicuna Mackenna 36%
- Ave. Grecia 28%
- Ave. Independencia 18%

The Vicuna Mackenna alternative, with the highest IRR, suffers from having much the same alignment as the proposed metro Line 3. Magni (1994) indicated that the evaluation of Line 3 was done against "other alternatives like bus lines and surface rails." While we have not seen these analyses, it appears that the rates of return calculations for Line 3 were *not* incremental calculations that assumed the completion of a Vicuna Mackenna segregated busway.

Fare Box Recovery Ratios for the Santiago Metro

The ex-post estimates of IRRs for Lines 1 and 2 reported previously, and the preconstruction estimates for Line 3, are very likely modest when compared to the rates that would have been earned by investing the same sums in intercity and urban road improvements or from building segregated bus ways.[13] Nonetheless, Santiago's metro is considered a success story by world standards. It is nearly impossible to find a metro built since the end of World War II anywhere in the world where fares have made any significant contribution to the capital cost of building. Worse yet, it is difficult to find systems in which fares exceed operating costs. Kain (1991b, p. 5-2), for example, found that only two of the six metros operating in Latin America at the time were covering their operating costs through fare revenues, and the HFA (1989, p. 7.13) study of metros in developing countries found that only half of the systems they studied had fare box recovery ratios of 1.0 or greater.

The highest fare box recovery ratios reported by HFA were 2.2 for the Hong Kong metro and 1.8 for the Manila light rail system. The Santiago metro, with a fare box recovery ratio of 1.6, ranked sixth among the ten systems for which HFA was able to obtain total revenue and operating cost data for at least one year. On the low end, HFA found fare box recovery ratios of 0.4 for Calcutta, 0.2 for Porto Alegre, 0.5 for Rio de Janeiro, and 0.6 for Sao Paulo. As the data in Figure 5-6 reveal, the fare box recovery ratio (using either fare revenues or total operating revenues in the numerator) for the Santiago metro has been well in excess of 1.0 since at least 1982. The Santiago metro's relatively high fare box recovery ratios reflect the relatively high pub-

13. For a critique of economic evaluations of rail transit proposals in other situations see Kain (1990, 1992b, 1992c and 2001).

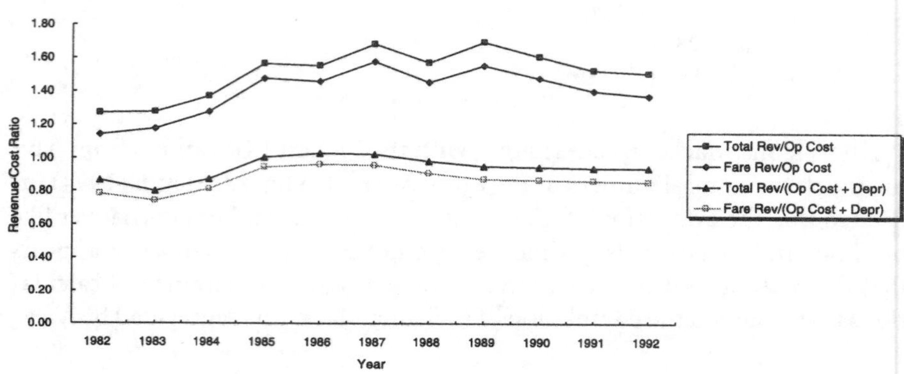

Figure 5-6. Revenue-Cost Ratios by Year, Santiago METRO, 1982–92

lic transport fares in Santiago generally and the metro's relatively low operating costs by world standards.[14]

The downside of the Santiago metro's high fare box recovery ratio is relatively low ridership per km compared to metros that are more heavily subsidized and have lower fare box recovery ratios. Since it appears that the metro's operating surplus is not large enough to allow it to cover the system's capital costs, questions might be raised about a fare policy that results in relatively low ridership levels and presumably smaller benefits to nonmetro users.[15] Of course, the government may not want to add annual operating subsidies to its already heavy capital subsidies for the Santiago metro in order to increase ridership and presumably the time saving and other benefits of nonmetro users. At the same time, the question of how the government should think about the trade-offs between capital and operating subsidies deserves more attention than it has thus far received.[16]

An analysis of the extent and nature of central government capital subsidies to the metro, based on the its annual reports and other sources, indicates

14. Magni (1994) indicates that "projections of the metro enterprise for 1994 indicate that the revenues will cover the operational cost and depreciation, so the surplus is not going to be only a nominal contribution to capital costs."

15. Hohmann (circa 1992, p. 4) observes that "Demand for the subway has reached 18,000 passengers/hour/direction in Line 3, while the system's maximum capacity is in the order of 55,000 passengers/hour/direction." He adds that, "buses and minibuses operating on the main corridor of the city, Alameda B. O'Higgins, which is parallel to the subway, at peak hours move more than 30,000 passengers/hour/direction."

16. This issue is examined in the context of Atlanta, Georgia's (USA) public transport investments and policies in Kain (1997).

that well in excess of 80% of the original capital cost of Lines 1 and 2 may have been an outright government grant. While it appears that the metro is currently paying some debt service, it is difficult to figure the exact amount or to determine the source of funds. The most likely source is unfunded real depreciation of the system.

As the data graphed in the lower part of Figure 5-6 indicate, the ratio of total operating revenues to operating costs plus depreciation for the Santiago metro has exceeded unity in only three of the eleven years from 1982 to 1992. If only fare revenues are used in the numerator, the ratio never exceeds 1.0; the highest value during the eleven-year period was 0.96 in 1986. Depreciation, of course, is an accounting convention and does not imply a cash outlay or actual need, particularly for a relatively new system. This suggests the possibility that the metro has been using depreciation allowances to cover the debt payments for that part of Lines 1 and 2 capital costs that were not covered by a government grant.

We know little about the proposed financing for the third metro line. Since the ratio of operating revenue to operating costs plus depreciation for Line 3 almost certainly will be inferior to those for lines 1 and 2, the data in Figure 5-6 raise the issues of whether building the third metro line will worsen the system's operating ratios and how the likely deficits from operating the new line and its capital costs will be financed.

An Overview of Urban Transportation in Chile

As noted previously, Chile is one of the most highly urbanized countries in the world. Nearly 85% of the nation's 13 million people live in cities, and about 60% of urban residents live in one of the three largest metropolitan areas: the Santiago metropolitan area (4.4 million population), Valparaiso (0.7 million population), and Concepcion (0.6 million population). It goes without saying that the quality and condition of urban streets and roads and the quantity and quality of urban public transport services have major impacts on the welfare of the nation's citizens.

As is true of every other country in the world, the root of Chile's growing urban transportation problem is the failure of governments, who are monopoly providers of urban streets and highways, to charge users appropriate fees for the use of these facilities. As the data previously presented in Figure 5-2 and Table A-1 indicate, vehicle users in Chile pay more road-user charges in the aggregate than governments in Chile spend on building and maintaining roads. Nonetheless, existing road-user charges, that are more or less proportional to miles traveled, do not prevent serious inefficiencies in the use of specific urban roads and streets during periods of heavy demand. There is huge variation in the cost of building and maintaining roads from one place to another, and even larger differences in the cost of increasing the capacity of roads and streets within the developed parts of large cities. In addition, there are huge differences in the demand for urban street space by time of day and location. Uniform prices and large variations in the cost of adding capacity and demand are a recipe for enormous waste and inefficiencies.

The failure of local governments in Chile to charge vehicle users amounts that approximate the long-run social costs of providing urban street space leads to the over-utilization of streets and roads in the congested, built-up parts of Chile's largest cities during peak hours. Congestion, even in these cities, is still not very great by world standards but it is becoming an increasingly serious problem. Congestion in Chile's cities, however, will worsen as household incomes, car ownership, population, and employment continue to grow, unless a fee structure to reflect these costs is adopted.[17]

With the rapid growth of vehicle use of frequently substandard, and increasingly congested, facilities, traffic safety and fatalities are becoming a growing concern. At the present time, traffic accidents are the third leading cause of death in Chile. The *Carabineros de Chile* have produced estimates indicating that the direct and indirect costs of road accidents were at least US $130 million in 1991. Approximately 80% of reported traffic accidents occur on urban streets, which are under the jurisdiction of MINVU, but more than 50% of deaths due to road accidents occur on the national road network, which is MOP's responsibility.

The Demand for Urban Travel and Urban Form

Urban travel is a derived demand that depends largely on the distribution and density of economic activity within urban areas. High-density cities, and metropolitan areas with highly centralized employment patterns, generally have very different patterns of trip making than low-density cities and metropolitan areas with more dispersed employment patterns. Levels of per-capita or household income and vehicle ownership are perhaps even more impor-

17. It cannot be overemphasized that the failure to implement appropriate charges for the use of urban roads and streets is a worldwide problem. There are few examples of direct road pricing, although there are many more instances where regulations and/or physical modifications to road systems mimic the allocations of road space that would be achieved by road pricing. Singapore's cordon pricing scheme is the most widely cited use of money charges to discourage excessive use of central area street space. There are dozens of papers and reports that discuss road pricing. See, for example, Gomez-Ibanez (1992); Hendrickson and Wohl (1982); Hau (1991 and 1992); Kain (1991 and 1993); Keeler and Small (1977); Morrison (1986); Small (1992); Vickery (1969); and Walters (1991).

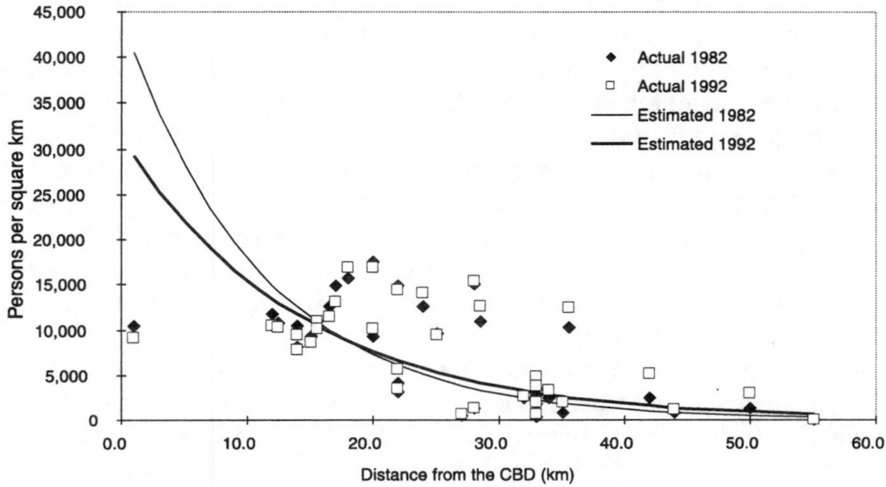

Figure 5-7. Santiago Metropolitan Area Gross Population Density, 1982 and 1992

tant determinants of the extent and nature of urban trip making, and both strongly influence, and are influenced by, the location and density of workplaces and residences.[18]

Figure 5-7 plots 1982 and 1992 gross population densities for Santiago's 34 *comunas* by distance from the center, as well as graphs of fitted negative exponential density functions for both 1982 and 1992.[19] Density functions, which were first used by Colin Clark (1951) and which are widely used by urban economists to provide an economical description of urban spatial structure, have been estimated for large numbers of metropolitan areas throughout the world (Mills 1970; Mills and Tan, 1980; Muth, 1969; Ingram and Caroll, 1981). Because detailed land use data are seldom available, gross population density (population/total km) is usually used to estimate density functions. However, net household density (households/km of residential land) would be much closer to the notion of residential space consumption that appears in the housing cost and travel cost trade-off models that are used by economists to explain the declines in densities with distance from the center (Alonso,

18. Transportation planners have developed complex computer models to replicate and predict urban travel. These models, which are used throughout the world, are derived from land use-transportation models developed in the United States during the 1950s and 1960s. The Chilean variant, ESTRAUS, was developed and is maintained by the Commission de Transport Urbano (CTU, 1990).

19. The 1982 equation is $D(t) = 10.7e^{-0.09t}$ ($R^2 = 0.55$) and the 1992 equation is $D(t) = 10.4e^{-0.07t}$ ($R^2 = 0.45$), where D(t) is density t kilometers from the CBD and e is the base of natural logarithm.

1964; Brueckner, 1987; Solow, 1973). Gross population density functions for Santiago in 1982 and 1992 are similar to those obtained for large numbers of other cities in other parts of the world. Appendix Table A-6 provides density function estimates for Santiago using gross household density, net household density, gross population density, and net population densities as the dependent variable and airline distance, average private mode travel time, and average public mode travel time as explanatory variables.

The density functions for Santiago reported here all assume the negative exponential form, even though experimentation might demonstrate that other functional forms would fit the data better. Use of the negative exponential form, moreover, facilitates comparison to the large number of density functions that have been estimated for other cities throughout the world, including several Latin American cities (Ingram and Caroll, 1981). Net household density provides the best statistical fit for all three accessibility measures. In addition, of the three accessibility measures, distance from the center explains the most variation in density among *comunas.*

The three equations in Table 5-7 interpret net household density as residential space consumption per household. Since greater space consumption (lower residential densities) is presumably a superior good, it would be expected that net household density would decline with income. The elasticities of net household density to income, which range between −0.42 and −0.47 for all the equations, are highly significant statistically. Equations 1 and 2 also include average household size and travel time from the center by either public or private modes. These regressions suggest that net household density is strongly affected by average household size; in other words, larger families strongly prefer lower residential density, holding income constant. The effects of the travel time variables are very similar when taken one at a time, and are nearly three

Table 5-7. *Estimates of Regression Models for Net Household Density, 34 Comunas of the Santiago Metropolitan Area*

	OLS Estimate and (Standard Error)		
Variable	*EQ. 1*	*EQ. 2*	*EQ. 3*
Constant	16.11	16.25	16.33
	(0.97)	(0.95)	(0.96)
Ln Household Income	−0.47	−0.42	−0.43
	(0.07)	(0.07)	(0.07)
Ln Household Size	−2.06	−2.57	−2.23
	(0.77)	(0.60)	(0.76)
Ln Travel Time by Public Mode	−0.77		−0.31
	(0.30)		(0.42)
Ln Travel Time by Private Mode		−0.74	−0.56
		(0.25)	(0.36)
R-squared	0.73	0.74	0.75

times their standard errors. The estimated constant elasticities are −0.77 when travel time from the center by the public mode is used and −0.74 when travel time from the center by the private mode is used. When travel time from the center for both modes are included (Equation 3), multicollinearity increases the standard errors for both, although they are still negative.

Some care should be taken not to overstate the results in Table 5-7. Residential structures and urban infrastructure and development patterns are very durable, and, as a result, household densities change very slowly (see Harrison and Kain, 1974). This suggests the possibility that rather than net household densities changing in response to changes in household income, household size, and accessibility, Equations 1–3 may describe ways of sorting in which households with different incomes and family sizes sort themselves among housing units and communities that differ in terms of lot size and net household density.

As a result of Chile's high levels of urbanization, the rate of growth of population in the Santiago metropolitan area is relatively slow. This growth, moreover, as in most metropolitan areas throughout the developed and less developed world, is occurring at the periphery. Core area populations are generally declining. The population of the Santiago municipality, for example, declined from 233,000 in 1982 to 202,000 in 1992 or by 13.3 percent (Chile, 1992, Census, Junio, 1992). This may be due partly to declining family size, both as a result of lower birth rates and fewer extended families living together. It also may reflect the sorting process referred to above. If this were true, declines in households would be smaller than the declines in population. To some extent, however, the declines also may be a consequence of growing space demands by nonresidential users.[20]

The spatial distribution and density of employment are even more important determinants of trip making and various aspects of urban travel behavior, such as mode choice, than population densities. Figure 5-8, which maps the ratio of employment by *comuna*-of-work to *comuna*-of-residence for employed residents and the original data in Appendix Table A-7, reveal that two *comunas* have more than three jobs for every employed resident, and Santiago, with a employment-to-employed resident ratio of 6.9, has nearly seven jobs for every employed resident.[21] These data reveal further that eight

20. This contention is supported by Magni (1994) who states that "There is a great change of use of the land in the central comunas of Santiago," and that this is " . . . one of the reasons why the population has declined in these sectors," adding that this is a conclusion of a study by the Ministry of Public Works of the central area.

21. The number of work trips made during the period 7:00–8:30 A.M., the measure used in calculating the ratio work trip origins/destinations, is obviously less than total employment. For our purposes, however, this is not a particularly serious problem. Indeed, peak hour work trips, which this measure corresponds to, is probably a better measure to assess travel demand than twenty-four- hour employment by *comuna*.

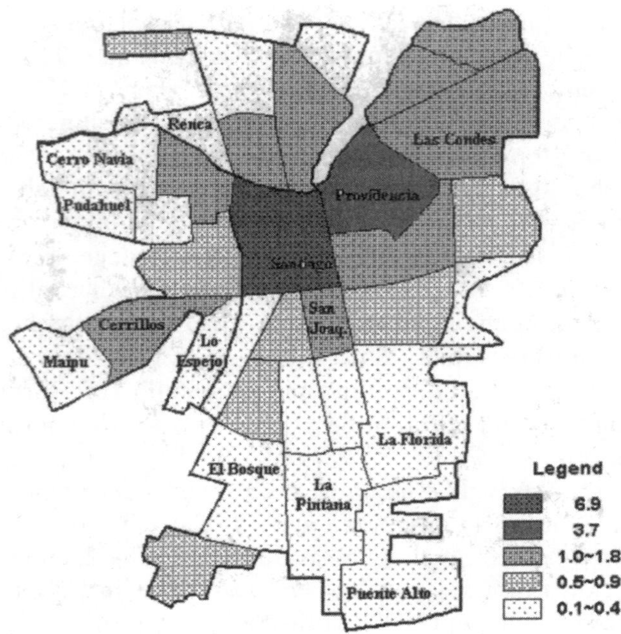

Figure 5-8. Ratio of Jobs to Employed Residents by Communa

comunas are net importers of workers and have more jobs than employed residents, and three more have the same number of jobs as employed residents. The remaining 21 *comunas* have fewer jobs than employed residents and 16 of them have 0.4 or fewer jobs for each of their employed residents. This imbalance between the location of jobs and the resident population is the principal source of demand for travel during peak periods.

Determinants of Vehicle Ownership in the Santiago Metropolitan Area

Auto and vehicle ownership rates in Chile and in the Santiago metropolitan area were relatively low in the early 1990s.[22] As Figure 5-9 indicates, moreover, vehicle ownership per household in Santiago's thirty-four *comunas* is

22. Data supporting this claim are presented in Appendix Table A-2, which contains estimates of auto, commercial vehicle, total vehicle ownership per 1000 persons, per capita income, and other statistics for fifty-two countries and in Appendix Table A-3, which presents similar data for sixty large cities in thirty-nine countries.

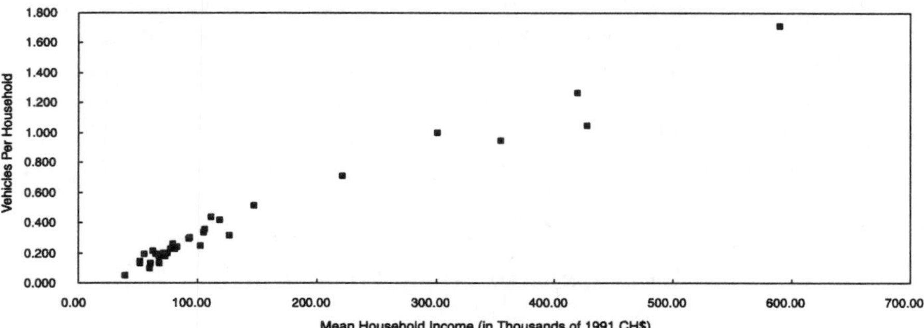

Figure 5-9. Mean Household Income and Vehicles per Household by **Comunas,** ***Santiago, 1992***

strongly related to income per household. The regression equations in Table 5-8 further probe this relationship. All but two of the six equations included in the table explain more than 90% of the variation in the levels of vehicle ownership among *comunas.* The two equations that explain less than 90% of variance use only density measures to explain auto ownership.

The four equations that explain more than 90% of the variance in *comuna* vehicle ownership rates all include household income. Indeed, household income by itself explains 92% of the variation in vehicle ownership rates, a result that strongly supports the results described previously for inter-country

Table 5-8. *Estimates of Household Vehicle Ownership Models for the 34 Comunas of Santiago Metropolitan Area (Dependent Variable: Ln Household Vehicle Ownership)*

	OLS Coefficient Estimate and (Standard Error)					
Variable	*EQ. 1*	*EQ. 2*	*EQ. 3*	*EQ. 4*	*EQ. 5*	*EQ. 6*
Constant	0.51	11.13	11.95	−1.12	0.76	−1.56
	(0.26)	(2.24)	(2.18)	(2.45)	(0.35)	(2.49)
Ln Household	1.11		1.16	1.06	1.11	
Income	(0.06)			(0.09)	(0.07)	(0.11)
Ln Gross House-		−0.72				
hold Density		(0.29)				
Ln Net Household			−0.79	0.13		0.12
Density			(0.27)	(0.15)		(0.15)
Ln Persons				0.22		0.75
Per Household				(0.71)		(0.88)
LN Worktrip					0.06	0.08
D/O Ratio					(0.05)	(0.08)
R-Squared	0.92	0.16	0.21	0.93	0.93	0.93

and large city cross sections. The constant elasticity estimates obtained for income in the four equations all exceed unity and fall in the narrow range 1.06 to 1.16. Somewhat surprisingly, adding the employment/resident labor force ratio, household size, and the net residential density of each *comuna* to the equation has almost no effect on overall explanatory power and only net household density has a coefficient that is much larger than its standard error.

Determinants of Mode Choice

Mode choice data from recently completed origin and destination surveys in the Santiago, Valparaiso, and Concepcion metropolitan areas, shown in Table 5-9, reveal that Chile's low rates of vehicle ownership are associated with low mode splits for private modes and high mode splits for public modes in all three metropolitan areas. No more than one in five daily vehicular person trips were made as an auto driver or auto passenger in any of the three metropolitan areas. Rates of private car use for the three metropolitan areas were 19.7% for Santiago in 1991, 16.4% for Concepcion in 1989, and 20% for Valparaiso in 1986. At the same time, trips made by private transport in the Santiago metropolitan area are increasing very rapidly; from 11.5% in 1977 to 20.8% in the fifteen-year period 1977 to 1991.

The cause of the nearly doubling of the private vehicle share in Santiago between 1971 and 1991 is not hard to identify. Auto registrations nationwide increased from 2.0 per 100 persons in 1977 to 5.6 per 100 persons in 1991, and vehicle ownership in Greater Santiago grew from 6.6 per 100 persons in 1977 to 10.2 per 100 persons in 1991. As discussed previously, the growth of per-capita income during the same period is the primary explanation of the increased level of private car and total vehicle registrations, although changes in relative prices, tariffs, and other import restrictions may have played a role as well.

Table 5-10, which presents additional *comuna* level regressions for Santiago in 1991, further quantifies the relationship between vehicle ownership per household and the shares of total work trips that were made by three modes: (a) all public modes combined, (b) private autos, and (c) the metro.[23] As model P1 indicates, vehicle ownership per household by itself explains

23. SECTRA (circa 1993), Daly and de D. Zortuzar (1990); Jara-Diaz (1991); Jara-Diaz and Videla (1989 and circa 1990); and Jara-Diaz and de Dois Ortuzar (1989) have estimated state-of-the-art disaggregate modal split models with micro data from the 1991 and earlier origin and destination surveys for Santiago. While the much more primitive estimates shown in Table 5-10 should not be viewed as substitutes for these more sophisticated estimates based on far better data, they nonetheless seem broadly consistent with the results obtained from the more

81% of the variation in the share of work trips that are made by public transport. The coefficient, which is a constant elasticity, indicates that the public transit share of work trips declines by 0.41 percent with each 1% increase in vehicle ownership per household. Model P2 reveals that the public transport modal share increases as net population density increases. While the net residential density coefficient has the expected sign, it is not very significant statistically. Similarly, the coefficient of public/private travel times to work for each *comuna* is tiny relative to its standard error. This low statistical significance of the travel time ratio is not surprising. Only a fraction of work trips from each *comuna* are made to the center and the relative travel times for trips to other destinations are likely to be very different from those for trips made to the center. The final equation, Model P3, adds a dummy variable for the seven *comunas* that have one or more metro stops. The results indicate that having a metro stop has little or no effect on the transit modal share, holding constant the effects of density, vehicle ownership, and relative travel times.

Equation A1, which is a regression of the auto share on per-capita vehicle ownership, explains 96% of the variation in the fraction of trips that are made by private cars; the vehicle ownership constant elasticity, moreover, is nearly one (0.98). When the public/private travel time ratio is added (Equation A2), its coefficient has a value of −0.3 and is larger than its standard error; but again this ratio is not a very good measure of relative travel times. The metro dummy in Equation A2 is positive and slightly larger than its standard error; taken at face value, indicates that *comunas* with metro stops have higher levels of private car use, holding constant vehicle ownership per household and relative travel times. The final auto share equation includes household income as an explanatory variable. As the auto ownership equations presented previously make clear, household income is a major determinant of vehicle ownership. Thus, it should come as no surprise that including both variables reduces the size of the coefficient estimate for vehicle ownership, from 0.94~0.98 to 0.71, and reduces its statistical significance. Even so, the coefficient of vehicle ownership in Equation A3 is more than five times its standard error and the coefficient estimate for household income is nearly twice its standard error. The public/private trip time variable is not very significant statistically in Equation A3. The metro dummy is somewhat more significant statistically and again indicates that holding household income and vehicle

sophisticated treatments. They have the further advantage of being more understandable to persons unfamiliar with behavioral choice modeling. Because of their nonlinear character, moreover, the behavioral choice models are difficult to use or interpret without access to the data used in estimating the models. We made a halfhearted effort to obtain the micro data from SECTRA so that we might use these data to estimate similar models, but time limitations and SECTRA's obvious reluctance to provide us with the data dissuaded us from pursuing the matter.

Table 5-9. *Trips by Mode in Major Chilean Cities*

	Total Linked Trips				*Mode Split (Share of Trips)*			
	Santiago		*Concepcion*	*Valparaiso*	*Santiago*		*Concepcion*	*Valparaiso*
Mode	*1977*	*1991*	*1989*	*1986*	*1977*	*1991*	*1989*	*1986*
Motorized Modes								
Automobile	412,537	1,320,787	174,857	158,185	14.4%	19.7%	16.4%	20.0%
Auto Driver	—	—	105,203	95,387	—	—	9.8%	12.1%
Auto Passenger	—	—	69,654	62,798	—	—	6.5%	7.9%
Bus-Taxibus	2,355,929	4,007,251	708,833	553,649	82.2%	59.7%	66.3%	70.0%
Minibus		32,972	—	—		—	3.1%	0.0%
Taxi	—	74,619	4,947	3,110	—	1.1%	0.5%	0.4%
Shared Taxi	—	144,616	51,987	41,704	—	2.2%	4.9%	5.3%
Funicular	—	—	—	5,524	—	—	—	0.7%
Commuter Rail	—	—	—	3,110	—	—	—	0.4%
Metro	96,327	309,246	—	—	3.4%	4.6%	—	—
Auto-Metro	—	14,375	—	—	—	0.2%	—	—
Bus-Metro	—	134,088	—	—	—	2.0%	—	—
Taxi-Metro	—	4,035	—	—	—	0.1%	—	—
Shared Taxi-Metro	—	54,857	—	—	—	0.8%	—	—
Other-Metro	—	17,705	—	—	—	0.3%	—	—
Other	—	626,705	23,351	7,173	—	9.3%	2.2%	0.9%
Company Bus	—	—	53,971	16,344	—	—	5.0%	2.1%
Motorcycle	—	—	17,920	2,612	—	—	1.7%	0.3%

Table 5-9. *Continued*

Total Motorized	2,864,793	6,708,284	1,068,838	791,411	100.0%	100.0%	100.0%	100.0%
Non-Motorized Modes								
Bicycle (en bicicleta)	—	—	—	12,157	—	—	—	—
Walking (a pie)	596,745	1,658,247	805,612	788,671	—	—	—	—
All Modes	3,461,538	8,366,531	1,874,450	1,592,239	—	—	—	—
Alternative Mode Definitions								
Private Transport	412,537	1,395,406	179,804	161,295	11.9%	16.7%	9.6%	10.1%
Public Transport	2,452,256	4,686,173	793,792	603,987	70.8%	56.0%	42.3%	37.9%
Other Motorized	—	626,705	95,242	26,129	0.0%	7.5%	5.1%	1.6%
Bicycle and Walking	596,745	1,658,247	805,612	800,828	17.2%	19.8%	43.0%	50.3%
All	3,461,538	8,366,531	1,874,450	1,592,239	100.0%	100.0%	100.0%	100.0%

Sources: (1) Pontificia Universidad Catolica de Chile, Facultad de Ingenieria (1992), "Encuesta Origen-Destino de Viajes del Gran Santiago, 1991, Informe Final." (2) Universidad Catolica de Chile (1978), "Encuesta de Origen y Destino de Viajes 1977 para el Santiago, Informe Final."
Notes: Bus-Taxibus trips for Valparaiso are for a broader category termed En Locomocion Colectiva.

Table 5-10. *Estimates of Regression Models for Mode Share by 34 Comunas of the Santiago Metropolitan Area, 1991*

	OLS Estimate and (Standard Error)								
	Ln Public Modal Share			*Ln Auto Share*			*Ln Metro Share*		
Variable	*EQ. P1*	*EQ. P2*	*EQ. P3*	*EQ. A1*	*EQ. A2*	*EQ. A3*	*EQ. M1*	*EQ. M2*	*EQ. M3*
Constant	2.02	0.62	0.69	−7.32	−7.05	−7.04	−3.46	−9.61	1.83
		(0.20)	(0.93)	(1.01)		(0.21)	(0.28)	(0.27)	
(0.92)	(3.74)	(2.28)							
Ln Household	−0.41	−0.38	−0.38		0.98	0.94	0.71	−0.002	
Vehicle Ownership	(0.04)	(0.05)	(0.05)		(0.04)	(0.04)	(0.13)	(0.01)	
Ln Net Population	0.13	0.12						0.63	
Density	(0.08)	(0.09)						(0.39)	
Ln Average					0.28				−1.35
Household Income					(0.15)				(0.57)
Ln Travel Time Ratio		−0.02	−0.02		−0.30	−0.29			
Public vs Private Mode	(0.21)	(0.22)		(0.22)	(0.21)				
Ln Bus-Taxibus								−0.54	−2.36
Modal Share								(0.41)	(1.00)
Dummy for Comunas			0.01		0.09	0.12	1.71	1.38	1.08
Served by Metro			(0.07)		(0.07)	(0.07)	(0.31)	(0.36)	(0.39)
R-squared	0.81	0.83	0.83	0.96	0.96	0.96	0.50	0.55	0.58

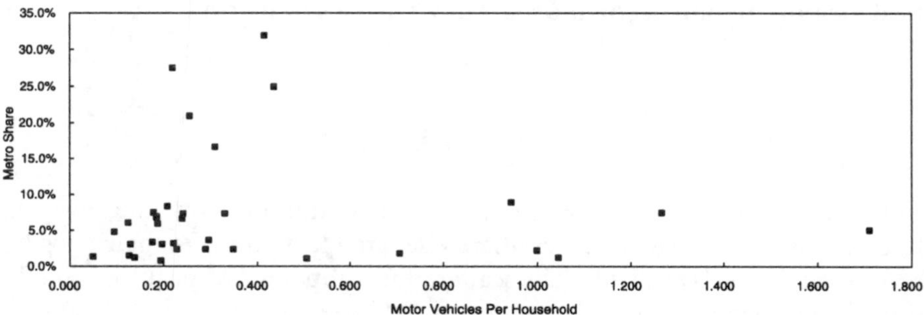

Figure 5-10. Motor Vehicle Ownership and Morning Peak Metro Modal Share Santiago Metropolitan Area, 1991

ownership constant, persons living in *comunas* with a metro station are more likely to commute to work by auto.

Figure 5-10 is a plot of the metro mode share for the thirty-four *comunas* against vehicle ownership per household. These data suggest there is no simple relationship between the metro modal share and vehicle ownership per household. This result is confirmed by a bivariate regression of the natural logarithm of metro modal share on the natural logarithm of *comuna* vehicle ownership per household; the R^2 for this equation is only 0.01 and the coefficient of vehicle ownership per household has a t-statistic of only 0.54. The most striking feature of Figure 5-10, however, is the presence of five upper left outliers: Santiago, Estacion Central, Lo Prado, San Miguel, and La Cisterna, which happen to be *comunas* with one or more metro stations within their boundaries. Equations M1–M3 in Table 5-10 formalize this relationship. The first model, Equation M1 which includes only vehicle ownership per household and a metro dummy, explains 50% of the total variance; the coefficient for vehicle ownership per capita, moreover, is less than one fifth as large as its standard error. Equations M2 and M3, which are richer specifications, include the same explanatory variables except that Equation M2 includes net population density as an explanatory variable and Equation M3 replaces this measure with household income. Equation M3, the more interesting of these two specifications, explains slightly more total variance than Equation M1, which includes only vehicle ownership per household and a metro dummy as explanatory variables. Including average household income and the bus/taxi bus share (as a bus/taxi bus supply proxy) reduces the size of the metro dummy, but the presence of a metro station in a *comuna* nonetheless continues to have a statistically significant impact on the share of work trips by metro.

Public vs. Private Trip Times

Inspection of the plot in Figure 5-11 clearly indicates why auto owning households in Santiago, as everywhere else, are likely to make their trips by private car, if one is available. The scatter plot compares AM peak period trip times by bus between pairs of *comunas* to AM peak period trips by private car between the same *comunas*. In contrast to the *comuna* regressions presented previously, the travel time estimates are for *comuna*-to-*comuna* trips, i.e. i-j pairs. Both the auto and bus times include allowances for access (walking and waiting time). *Comunas* are fairly large and heterogeneous, and the estimated public and private trip times may not fully capture this heterogeneity. The largest potential problem is presumably for public trip times, since within zone access times are likely to vary by more than those for private vehicle trips. If this introduces a bias, the most likely effect is to understate the *comuna* to *comuna* travel times of the public modes somewhat, relative to those by private modes.

The graph of a weighted quadratic regression on peak period auto travel time that explains about two-thirds of the variation in peak period bus travel time is also shown in Figure 5-11. This quadratic regression as well as linear

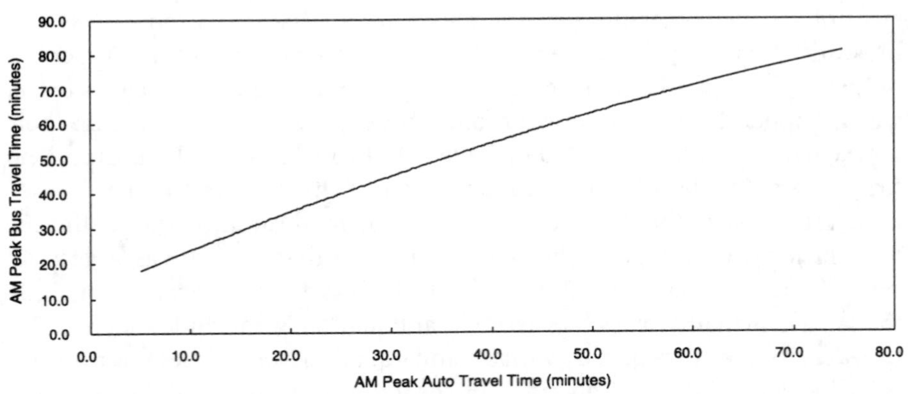

Figure 5-11. Relationship between Bus Travel Time and Auto Travel Time in the 7:00–8:30 A.M. Peak Period for All Commun-to Communa Pairs with Available Data, Santiago Metropolitan Area

Weighted Regression: $BUSPK = 11.93 + 1.22\ AUTOPK - 0.004\ AUTOPK^2$ R-squared = 0.63

and log-log specifications for the peak period and all three specifications for the midday period are presented in Appendix Table A-8. Table 5-11 presents the estimated bus travel times that correspond to particular auto travel times obtained from these equations. For the peak period, estimated bus and taxi bus times are always longer than auto times. In most other cases, *comuna*-to-*comuna* trip times by bus are substantially longer than by auto. Inspection of the estimates of peak period auto and bus trip times in Table 5-11 reveals that bus trip times are roughly fifteen minutes longer than the same trip by auto. Because bus access and waiting times are apparently so much longer than auto access and waiting times, the travel time disadvantage for bus trips appears to be relatively greater for shorter trips. As the data in the lower panel reveals, the expected relationship between bus and auto travel times does not hold for very long trips, i.e. auto trips of over sixty minutes, in off-peak periods.

The regression equations presented in Table 5-12 provide another view of the determinants of journey-to-work travel times. These equations attempt to explain variations in estimated journey-to-work travel times in forty-two of the world's largest cities. These are once again the city data collected by the

Table 5-11. *Travel Time Comparisons for Peak and Off-peak Auto and Bus-Taxibus Modes, Santiago Metropolitan Area*

A. Peak Auto vs. Peak Bus-Taxibus

	Predicted Bus-Taxibus Travel Time (minutes)		
Auto Travel Time (minutes)	*Linear*	*Quadratic*	*Log-Log*
5.0	20.3	17.9	14.7
15.0	30.1	29.3	29.0
30.0	44.8	44.9	44.64
5.0	59.5	58.7	57.46
0.0	74.2	70.7	68.6
75.0	88.9	80.9	78.8

B. Off-Peak Auto vs. Off-Peak Bus-Taxibus

	Predicted Bus-Taxibus Travel Time (minutes)		
Auto Travel Time (minutes)	*Linear*	*Quadratic*	*Log-Log*
5.0	23.5	19.8	18.7
15.0	30.4	30.1	29.7
30.0	40.8	42.1	39.9
45.0	51.1	50.2	47.3
60.0	61.5	**54.1**	**53.4**
75.0	**71.8**	**54.1**	**58.7**

Note: Generated using the weighted travel time regression models shown in Appendix Table C-1.

Table 5-12. OLS Estimates of Regression Models for Journey to Work Travel Time, 42 World Cities, 1990 (Dependent Variable: LN Travel Time)

	OLS Estimate and (Standard Error)			
Variable	*EQ. 1*	*EQ. 2*	*EQ. 3*	*EQ. 4*
Constant	2.05	2.15	1.39	1.48
	(0.96)	(0.98)	(0.96)	(0.98)
LN Population	0.18	0.19	0.17	0.18
	(0.06)	(0.06)	(0.06)	(0.07)
LN Median Income	−0.13	−0.14		
	(0.04)	(0.04)		
LN Cars/1000 Population			−0.07	−0.07
			(0.03)	(0.03)
LN Population Density		−0.05		−0.05
		(0.06)		(0.08)
R-Squared	0.29	0.29	0.26	0.26

World Bank (1993b) as part of its housing indicator study; the data for individual cities are presented in Appendix Table A-9. As in the previously discussed regressions based on these data, the measurement errors are almost certainly very large (especially those for the travel time measure) and the choice of explanatory variables is seriously limited. Nonetheless, the results are interesting. Not surprisingly, they indicate that mean travel times increase with city size; the constant elasticity estimates for metropolitan area size for all four equations cluster in the narrow range 0.17 to 0.19. Holding city size constant, the results indicate that mean trip times decline as either vehicle ownership per household or household incomes increase. Given the strong association between household income and vehicle ownership rates, these results suggest that, as incomes increase, growing fractions of households shift to more expensive but faster private modes (private cars and taxis) from less expensive but slower public transport modes. The substitution of higher cost, higher speed modes, moreover, will normally be associated with increases in trip lengths. It is unfortunate, that the World Bank (1993b) did not collect data on average distances as well as average trip times. Cross-city estimates for United Sates metropolitan areas by Kain (1991a and 1993) indicate that the length of the journey to work in terms of distance increases by about 1% for each 1% increase in trip speed in miles per hour. Kain (1991a and 1993) also found that trip time increased with metropolitan area size.

Some Crude Estimates of Congestion

Figure 5-12 and analyses presented in Appendix A-10 describe crude efforts to use Santiago *comuna*-to-*comuna* trip times for the AM peak and mid-

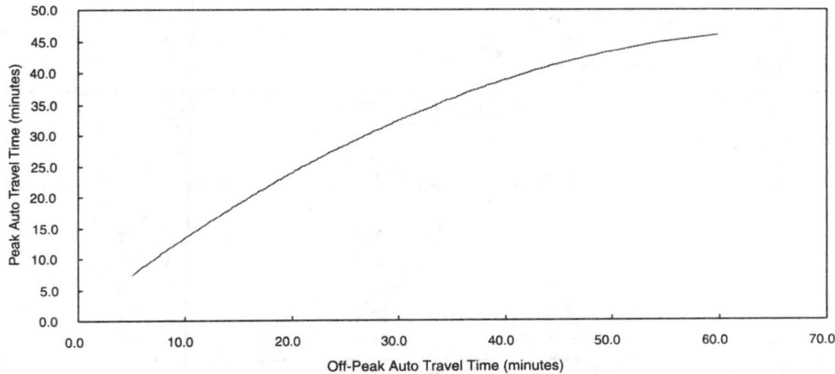

Figure 5-12. Relationship between Peak (7:00–8:30 A.M.) and Off-Peak (10:00–12:00 P.M.) Auto Travel Time for All* Communa-*to*-Communa *Pairs with Available Data, Santiago Metropolitan Area

Weighted Regression: AUTOPK = 0.92 + 1.35 * AUTOOPK – 0.01 * AUTOPK^2 R-squared = 0.61

day period to obtain estimates of the time losses that result from congestion. Taken at face value, these results confirm the view that congestion is not very great, currently. An alternative interpretation would be that there is serious congestion during both the midday period and the AM peak, but congestion during the AM peak is slightly worse. It would be easier to interpret these data if both trip distance and trip time data were available.

As was true of the preceding analysis of *comuna*-to-*comuna* trip times, the results, which are presented in detail in Appendix A-10, are easier to interpret if the estimating equations are used to estimate values of peak period travel times for particular values of off-peak travel times. Situations where the equations predict lower peak period than off-peak trip times are shaded. The estimates in Table 5-13, which summarize the several equations included in Appendix A-10, give very little evidence that midday trip times are substantially shorter than AM peak period trip times, particularly for longer trips. The linear equation, for example, suggests that an auto trip that takes 15 minutes at midday will take 19.2 minutes during the AM peak; if the midday trip is 30 minutes, however, the same trip made during the AM peak is only 0.6 of a minute longer.

All in all, the estimates in Table 5-13 give very little evidence of congestion during the peak period, especially for trips of thirty-five minutes or more duration.[24] It is, of course, possible that congestion in Santiago is highly local-

24. Magni (1994) has suggested that the small differences in congestion between peak and nonpeak hours we obtained may be due to restrictions on vehicle use that prevent one fifth of the vehicle fleet from driving from 7:30 AM to 7:30 PM. While this is an interesting speculation, it puts more faith in our estimates of peak/off-peak speeds than may be justified.

Table 5-13. Travel Time Comparisons for Peak and Off-peak Auto and Bus-Taxibus Modes, Santiago Metropolitan Area

A. Peak Auto vs. Off-Peak Auto

	Predicted Peak Auto Travel Time (minutes)		
Off-Peak Auto Travel Time (minutes)	*Linear*	*Quadratic*	*Log-Log*
5.0	11.6	7.4	8.6
15.0	19.2	19.0	18.5
30.0	30.6	32.5	30.0
45.0	**42.0**	**41.6**	**39.8**
60.0	**53.4**	**46.2**	**48.7**
75.0	**64.8**	**46.2**	**57.0**

B. Peak Bus-Taxibus vs. Off-Peak Bus-Taxibus

	Predicted Peak Bus-Taxibus Travel Time (minutes)		
Off-Peak Bus-Taxibus Travel Time (minutes)	*Linear*	*Quadratic*	*Log-Log*
5.0	16.7	11.2	10.2
15.0	24.2	21.4	21.8
30.0	35.5	35.5	35.2
45.0	46.7	48.0	46.7
60.0	**58.0**	**58.8**	**57.0**
75.0	**69.2**	**68.0**	**66.6**

Note: Generated using the weighted travel time regression models shown in Appendix Table D-1.

ized and affects certain trips, but not others. In particular, some *comuna*-to-*comuna* trips might exhibit congestion, while many other *comuna*-to-*comuna* trips might not. It needs to be emphasized, moreover, that data for *comuna*-to-*comuna* peak and off-peak travel times are far from ideal measures for qualifying the extent of peak period congestion. As we have indicated previously, *comunas* are large and heterogeneous. In addition, trips are made on the highway network and the way in which serious localized congestion affects *comuna*-to-*comuna* trips may be difficult to assess using these data. The analyses only provide some very weak confirmation for the view that congestion is still not very serious in Santiago.

The Provision of Urban Public Transport Services

With the exception of Santiago's metro, all urban public transport and taxi services in Chile are provided by private firms or individuals.[25] The

25. Valparaiso has a private trolley bus system, and the same operator has recently begun to operate a single trolley bus line in Santiago and has a franchise for a second line.

Ministry of Transport and Telecommunications (MTT) is responsible for licensing and supervising public transport operators and, after a period of several years when it placed virtually no restrictions on bus and taxi operations, it began in 1993 to take a more aggressive posture, at least in Santiago. As discussed in greater detail below, MTT has prohibited taxis from picking up passengers at stops on Santiago's principal central area street and has limited the number of buses and taxi buses that may operate within the central area. It achieved this latter result by implementing a central area route-tendering scheme, in which bus operators are required to compete for the right to operate specific routes that serve or pass through the center. Route awards are based on a point system that emphasizes the age and size of vehicles and fares.

Bus ownership remains widely dispersed in Santiago, although the government has been trying to force smaller operators to become part of public companies, which are awarded rights to operate specific routes. Before recent changes in the legal and institutional structure of bus and taxi bus providers in Santiago, the number of bus owners was estimated at between 5,000 and 5,500. Since the fleet consisted of roughly 8,300 vehicles, the mean owner possessed only a little over 1.5 buses. As in other parts of Latin America, individual routes were operated by route associations, with each association providing services for three to five routes. Until 1980, there was a state-owned bus company in Santiago with a fleet of about 1,500 vehicles, of which only about 500 were in daily service. At its point of peak operation, the public bus company carried out less than 7% of all trips.

Shared taxis, which are regular cars that operate over 148 different routes and charge a fare that depends on journey length and other aspects of the trip, have become an important public transport mode in Santiago. The fleet of shared taxis exceeded 4,200 cars in 1989. In addition, there were about 20,000 regular taxis. Together, the shared taxis and regular taxis carried an estimated 500,000 passengers per day. In the past when the number of taxis was strictly controlled, taxi medallions were worth more than the cars themselves. These medallion quotas were eliminated in 1977 and any car built after 1971 could become a taxi. The largest percentage increase in the taxi fleet occurred between 1977 and 1982 when the number of taxis increased from 18,000 to 58,000.

Urban public transport in Chile was strictly regulated until the mid-1970s, when the government eliminated all regulations, allowed private bus operators to set their own fares, and eliminated all entry barriers. Before 1971, restrictions on urban bus and taxi operators had been very extensive. MINTRALTEL (Ministry of Transport and Telecommunications) determined routes, fares, the number of vehicles per route, vehicle types, scheduling, and all other service variables. Starting in 1977, the central government began to deregulate public transport services with the result that Santiago's bus system became one of the least regulated in the world.

Chile's experience with bus deregulation has been widely criticized by Chilean transport analysts, who have argued that the complete elimination of all regulations on urban bus operators had a number of undesirable consequences. Deregulation was followed by a rapid expansion of the bus/taxi bus fleet. Rapid growth of the fleet and the government's failure to charge operators for the use of valuable central area street space, led to a rapid growth in the number of buses operating in the central area and growing bus congestion there. Fernandez (1993, p. 2), comparing real fares and the number of buses and taxi buses operating in Santiago during 1978–1991, concludes that after eleven years of deregulation, "the fleet of public transit vehicles in Santiago had doubled (at the same time reducing the transport capacity per vehicle), the fare had more than doubled in real terms; traffic congestion, pollution, and accidents had increased and the "public opinion at the time had become totally negative in relation to public transport."[26] The data Fernandez relied upon in reaching these conclusions are presented in Appendix Tables A-11 and A-12. On the plus side, he acknowledges that "the geographic coverage of the system grew, and the waiting periods and the walking distances were reduced," and that "an intermediate service was created, mixing public transport and cars, in the form of collective taxis (shared taxis), which in 1991 were able to serve 3% of the daily trips."

In assessing these developments, Fernandez (1993, p. 2) concludes that these outcomes occurred because the operators' cartel fixed fares that guaranteed them high profits. He adds that these high fares "encouraged the incorporation of new operators," and put "additional pressure on the fares." As further evidence of the cartel's market power, Fernandez (1993, p. 11) reports that before re-regulation, the cartel—which couldn't legally prevent the entry of new operators—was, nonetheless, charging new operators an access fee that sometimes reached as much as $3,000 per bus.[27]

Extending his critique of bus deregulation, Fernandez (1993, p. 3) observes

26. Fernandez (1993) states further that "from the start of fares liberalization (1977) until 1985, the value of the bus fares . . . increased 131% in real terms, and that of taxibuses had increased by 75%," and that the combined bus (average capacity of eighty passengers) and taxibus (forty-seven passengers) fleet "increased from 5,440 to 8,500 vehicles, and by 1987 it had grown to 10,300 vehicles," while the demand "was relatively stable at an average of 1,050 million trips per year."

27. As further support for his claims about the role of Santiago's cartel in setting uneconomic fares, Fernandez (1993, p. 3) points out that the large increase in real bus fares that occurred in Santiago in the period following deregulation did not occur in Valparaiso. His explanation is that Valparaiso's private trolley bus company, which was " independent of the cartel," "regulated" fares there.

that the average age of transit vehicles "increased considerably between 1980 and 1988 (from seven to ten years for buses and from five to ten years for taxi buses)." He adds, "by the end of this period there were more than 400 different kinds of vehicles, with different types of engines, framework, designs, etc.," and argues that as a result of changes in engine types and poor maintenance public transport vehicles were the source of 71% of total particulate emissions. Santiago's buses are now much cleaner than they were during the period studied by Fernandez. A discussion of these issues by Kahn and Kerr is included in the previous chapter.

Hohmann (circa 1992, p. 3) reaches similar conclusions, pointing out that, "[I]n recent years the number of buses and minibuses providing services in urban zones has increased considerably."[28] Like Fernandez, he finds that, "[E]xpansion of supply is not an answer to the growth of demand, but a consequence of market distortions wherein a concerted action for fixing prices permits the entrance of a 'surplus' of operators, the existence of which would be economically unsustainable if actual competitive conditions were to prevail."[29] Gomez-Ibanez and Meyer (1993) in evaluating the Santiago experience with bus deregulation, reach conclusions that are similar to those of Fernandez and Hohmann.

Citing a 1986 World Bank study as authority, Hohmann (circa 1992, p. 4) makes the claim that, "[I]f the transport expense is higher than 10% of income for more than 15% of the population, the price of services is discriminatory in respect to low income sectors." Applying this notion to Santiago, he refers to estimates for 1985 that indicate that "more than 30%" of Santiago households in 1980 spent a minimum of 17% of their income on transport; and estimates for 1986 that indicate that 45% of Santiago inhabitants spent 11% or more of their income on urban transport.

---

28. Hohmann (circa 1992, p. 9) also charges that the government encouraged uneconomic expansion of the bus industry in Santiago by providing generous credits (subsidies) for the purchase of buses. "In the eighties the state granted loans for an approximate amount of US $100 million for the purchase of public transport vehicles, thus contributing to the indiscriminate acquisition of more than 4,000 buses and minibuses with almost no administrative or technical conditions." He adds that the government permitted bus owners to renegotiate their debt, "a fact that can be understood as a form of subsidy (again without conditions) to a sector whose development, as was said, was based on free markets."

29. Hohmann joins Fernandez in identifying pollution as one of the most serious social costs of deregulation. He notes that "Motor vehicles, *especially those of public transport*, (emphasis added)are responsible for emitting some of the most important pollutants that accumulate in the city's atmosphere. Hohmann adds that while the number of private cars is approximately thirty-eight times greater than that of public (450,000 and 12,000 vehicles, respectively), buses and minibuses, unlike cars, operate all day long with the result that public transport vehicles account for more than one-fourth of the total number of kilometers by motor vehicles. See Kahn and Kerr (previous chapter) for a critical discussion of these issues.

Data similar to those used by Hohmann and others in assessing the impact of transit fares on poor households in several Latin American cities are shown in Table 5-14. Authors of a 1992 ECLAC (Economic Commission for Latin America and the Caribbean) report containing these data reached many of the same conclusions about Santiago's experience with complete public transport deregulation and private cartelization as Hohmann and Fernandez.[30] Like Fernandez (circa 1992), Hohmann (circa 1992), and Gomez-Ibanez and Meyer (1992), ECLAC concludes that "Santiago's large bus fleet is mainly a direct consequence of deregulation and collusion among operators, which result in high fares and encourage fleet expansion" (ECLAC, 1992, p.15). Observing that the "Advocates of deregulation generally claim that it produces an array of different services at different prices, to cater for all tastes and budgets," they note, "[T]his did not happen in Santiago," adding that "[N]o luxury buses appeared of the kind encouraged by the regulatory authorities in cities such as Bogota, Buenos Aires, or Rio de Janeiro," and that "... there was a proliferation of shared taxis, which were hardly ever seen in Santiago before the introduction of the first deregulation measures" (ECLAC, 1992, p. 87).

Bus fares in Santiago are undeniably higher than in most of the other cities studied. At the same time, ECLAC's presentation of fare data exaggerated the difference. Reported transit fares are very sensitive to the choice of dates. In Latin American countries with high inflation rates, the real value of regulated fares decline rapidly following an upward revision of fares. In the table as originally printed, the fare shown for Santiago, US $0.28, is dramatically higher than all but the fare for Brasilia. The second Santiago fare shown in the table, however, is only slightly higher than the second fare for Sao Paulo and is equal to the second fare for Buenos Aires.[31]

Mexico City's heavily subsidized metro fare more than doubled from US $0.04 in late 1989 to US $0.10. As Kain (1991b) reports, Mexico's government refused to increase metro fares for a period of twelve years. As a result, the fare box recovery ratio for Mexico City's metro reached a low of 4% before the government finally raised fares for the metro and for the public bus system.

---

30. In discussing the relationship between fares and ridership in Santiago, they observe, "In Santiago, increasing real fares resulting from the deregulation policy went hand in hand with the decline in mean bus ridership over the period 1977 to 1988. . . . The inverse correlation coefficient between the annual values of real fares and ridership over the 1977 to 1988 period is 0.97" (ECLAC, 1992, p.15).

31. The second fare entries for several of the cities shown in Table 5-14 were buried in footnotes in the original report. The second fares listed for Sao Paul, Mexico City, and Bogota demonstrate that fares reported less than a year apart in highly inflationary environments can differ by as much as 100%.

Table 5-14. *Bus Fleet Size and Fare- and Service-Level Indication in Various Cities of Latin America (Data for Late 1988)*

City	*Fare Date*	*Estimated Population (millions)*	*Number of Buses in the Fleet*	*Average Fares (US$)*	*50 Fares as % of Minimum Monthly Wage*	*Daily Motorized Trips made by Bus (millions)*	*Percent of Daily Motorized Trips made by Bus*	*Buses per Million Persons*	*Bus-Km per Person per Month*
Sao Paulo									
City	07/89	11.16	9,501	0.12	0.10	N/A	N/A	851	4.66
City	03/90		0.25						
Metro region	Late 89	16.74	12,329	N/A	N/A	8.058	42.8%	736	N/A
Brasilia	Late 89	1.71	1,717	0.32	0.26	0.815	47.9%	1,004	5.59
La Paz/El Alto	Late 89	0.98	1,305	0.16	0.33	N/A	N/A	1,332	3.02
Santiago	Late 89	4.38	10,500	0.28	0.28	2.578	65.0%	2,397	8.40
Lima	Late 89	6.05	7,058	0.07	0.09	4.280	84.3%	1,167	7.39
Havana	Late 89	2.06	2,325	0.03	0.03	3.740	86.1%	1,129	5.51
Mexico	Late 89	12.71	7,729	0.04	0.02	6.800	26.2%	608	2.11
(Fed. District)	Early 91		0.10						
Bogota	Late 89	4.67	14,150	0.10	0.06	5.236	84.0%	3,030	10.63
Quito	Late 89	1.12	2,110	0.05	0.05	1.143	N/A	1,884	8.71
Buenos Aires	Late 89	11.90	14,000	0.15	0.08	9.120	55.0%	1,176	9.79
Buenos Aires	04/91		0.28						

Source: Adapted from the United Nations, "The Impacts of Subsidies, Regulation, and Different Forms of Ownership on the Service Quality and Operational Efficiency of Urban Bus Systems in Latin America," 1992.

Subsidies for Mexico City's metro and public bus company became a nearly intolerable burden on government budgets and Mexican authorities in recent years have been making serious efforts to reduce them and to shift a larger share of Mexico City's public transit services to the private sector.[32]

Route Tendering of Central Area Bus Routes in Santiago

In December 1990, the government passed legislation that gave MTT the power to implement a bus route tendering scheme for Santiago and to take a number of other measures to deal with what was increasingly seen as a growing congestion problem in the central area. In February 1993, the government implemented a policy prohibiting the circulation of shared taxis along Alameda Avenue (Fernandez, 1993, p. 9). This policy was designed to reduce congestion and, perhaps of equal or greater importance, to send a signal to public transit operators that the new central area restraint policies would be fairly applied.

The first attempts to implement route tendering for central area routes was set for April 1991. The affected routes accounted for 85% of the city's buses. The form of the tender was an auction of operating rights for particular routes using central city streets for an initial period of eighteen months. Routes were defined in terms of end points and specific itineraries, as well as required frequencies (Fernandez, 1993, p. 10). A bus operators' boycott of the initial tender succeeded, as only a small number of independent operators bid for routes. Public transport owners also attempted an unsuccessful one-day general strike in early April 1991. The strike received little public support, however, and failed (Fernandez, 1993, p.9). Following a presentation by MTT, the Antimonopoly Preventive Commission found there had been concerted action by the bus operators to avoid the auction, which was understood to be a mechanism to introduce competition into the public transport market. (Fernandez, 1993, p. 10).

Two other decrees implemented in July 1991 set out the characteristics that public transport vehicles must satisfy to operate in the city, established the

32. Given these observations about Mexico City's experience with subsidies, it is worth considering Hohmann's (circa 1992, p. 10) unfavorable comparisons of Santiago bus/taxi bus operations to those in Mexico City. As evidence that there were too many buses in Santiago during the deregulation period, he observes that the average occupancy per bus/taxi bus in Santiago was approximately 400 passengers per day in 1990, or roughly one passenger per km. traveled, as compared to Mexico City in the same year, where the average number of passengers carried per vehicle was 1,600 per day. He adds that only 6% of Mexico City's buses were more than eleven years old as contrasted to an estimate of 47% for Santiago.

National Register of Passenger Transport Services, and required buses and taxi buses to register before they were allowed to serve transit users within the city center. In September 1991, in further response to the bus owners' boycott, MTT barred buses built before 1979 and taxi buses built before 1981 from the central area. This prohibition reduced the number of road-based public transit vehicles that could legally operate within the central area from 10,200 to 7,500. Fernandez (1993) suggests this action had the further effect of splitting the cartel into two competing groups with different interests.

A second attempt at route tendering, announced on October 8, 1991, succeeded. By December 8, 1993 (the final due date for applications), 307 proposals had been received for 255 routes and awards were made for 226; the remaining 29 routes were allocated in a second tender completed a few months later. In addition to the direct transportation goals of reducing bus congestion in the central area and reducing emissions, the designers of the route tendering scheme saw it as a way of creating more effective transportation organizations. Route awards were only made to incorporated companies.

MTT used a point system to choose among competing bids. There were, however, very few multiple bids. Larger numbers of points were given for (1) newer buses, (2) larger buses, (3) for faster methods of toll collection (to reduce the time spent at central area bus stops), (4) for lower fares, and (5) for higher service levels. The number of buses per hour allowed to operate on each route was specified by the scheme's designers, but there were other dimensions of service that could increase the number of points awarded to particular bidders.

Specifications for two of the routes called for trolley buses, and the two trolley bus routes were awarded to a single bidder, Valparaiso's trolley bus operator. Only one of these routes, with twenty-four operational vehicles, was operated in 1993, however, and it has apparently encountered problems. Trolley buses were once an important mode in Santiago, as they were in many other metropolitan areas in Latin American and throughout the world (Kain, 1991b). As in most of these cities, they were replaced by more efficient (lower cost per vehicle and seat mile) motorbuses, and Santiago's last trolley bus line stopped operating around 1975. The renewed interest in trolley buses in Santiago and in many other cities reflects a growing concern about air pollution.

Using the criteria described above, MTT awarded eighteen-month contracts for 284 routes. As a result of the scheme, the number of buses operating in the central area fell from about 7,500 to about 5,200. The vehicles operating under the central area route-tendering scheme, moreover, had an average age of only 3.2 years and charged an average nominal fare of 91.5 Chilean pesos, as contrasted to a pre-tender nominal fare of 100 Chilean pesos (US $0.27). Fernandez (1993, p. 11) reports that the number of buses and taxi buses operating on Alameda Avenue gradually fell from 1,200 buses per hour in March 1990 to 550 buses per hour in 1992.

The central route-tendering scheme was supplemented by a series of complementary government policies, implemented in the early 1990s, that were designed to reduce the number of buses operating in Santiago. According to Fernandez (1993, p. 8), the government made a decision to remove 2,600 buses and taxi buses, and particularly the oldest and most polluting ones, from the streets of Santiago. The most successful of these measures was a purchase and scrapping program in which the government bought 2,600 buses manufactured before 1974 from private operators.

The government also created a registry of public transport vehicles for Santiago and specified that only new vehicles could be added the registry. In addition, it issued a variety of new regulations for both vehicles and services, set up state-controlled inspection shops to carry out safety and other vehicle inspections, and implemented a program of emissions testing that required all public transport vehicles operating in Santiago to be tested every three months in government inspection stations (Fernandez, 1993, p. 9; Kahn and Kerr, previous chapter).

The Congestion Pricing Alternative

Policymakers and the public in Chile are increasingly recognizing the problems caused by the failure to charge vehicle users for valuable street space in dense built-up areas. In August 1991, MTT submitted a fairly general road pricing law to the Parliament that would provide economic disincentives for private car use. The legislature reacted with some caution, asking the government for a more specific proposal and for more information about the likely impacts of congestion pricing. Given the resistance to road pricing throughout the world, the legislature's cautious response is hardly surprising.

Congestion pricing would allocate street space in dense built-up areas to the highest-value and highest productivity users. In comparison to the current policy of arbitrarily limiting the number of buses in the central area, the number of public transport vehicles operating in the central area would be determined by the willingness of bus operators to pay for the use of valuable central area street space. As compared to the current scheme bus operators would have greater incentives to bypass the center and to offer lower fares and more direct services between outlying areas.

The current quantity restrictions on the use of central area streets appear to have induced a greater number of direct *comuna*-to-*comuna* services. Unsuccessful bidders for central area routes provided most of these new services.

Congestion pricing, which would presumably create a significant operating cost differential between buses that used central area streets and were charged a fee and those that were not charged fees because they did not use central area streets would very likely lead to the introduction of more services of this kind. These new services would benefit trip makers who continued to use the central area buses, by reducing bus congestion and increasing bus speeds and reliability. At the same time, users of the new services between suburban origins and destinations would be provided with faster, frequent, and more direct services, and very likely lower fares. The size of these advantages would depend on many considerations, including the equilibrium levels of congestion prices on various facilities. A determination of these questions cannot be made without detailed simulations using a policy-sensitive transportation model. Even then, the quantitative estimates would undoubtedly be uncertain, although the qualitative effects are not.

The reorientation of many transit trips that currently pass through the center but do not begin or end there is only one of the many anticipated benefits from congestion pricing. Buses are relatively efficient users of street space and would presumably be able to outbid most private vehicles for scarce street space. The buses that remain would be able to operate at higher speeds and at greater reliability as a result of the lower levels of congestion that would presumably exist with congestion pricing.[33] Important and largely unanswered questions are the equilibrium speeds that would exist in the currently congested parts of Santiago during peak periods under a congestion-pricing regime, and how these general traffic conditions and speeds would translate into bus speeds .

Whatever the specific congestion prices turned out to be, it is certain that the relative speeds and out-of-pocket costs of road-based transit would improve relative to both private transportation and the metro. The result would be a shift from private to public modes and possibly from metro to bus. The benefits from further additions to the metro system would almost certainly be much smaller than they would be without congestion pricing. The metro's principal advantage is its ability, at considerable cost, to segregate its passengers from road-based congestion, at least for that portion of the trip that is made by metro (25% of all metro trips in 1991 originated by bus or taxi bus, 11% by taxi and shared taxi, 2.7% by auto, and 33% by other road-based modes). If buses were able to operate on uncongested roads and streets, they would generally be able to provide shorter door-to-door travel times than the metro, since they would have a much larger network to use and would nor-

33. The likely impacts of congestion pricing on the supply of public transport services in the United States context are discussed in Kain (1993).

mally be able to provide much more direct trips, with fewer transfers and shorter walking distances.

Summing Up: Spatial Impacts and Policy Recommendations

Transport services in Chile are largely supplied by private firms. The railways and Santiago's metro are the principal exceptions. The fact that private firms supply most transport services, however, does not mean that government policies and actions have had no impact on the spatial distribution of economic activity. Government is a near monopoly provider of transportation infrastructure and, while intercity and urban transport in Chile are currently largely unregulated, before the early 1970s few countries in the world had more extensive transport regulations than Chile. This intense regulation of intercity trucking and bus services increased the costs of passenger travel and of moving goods and services among cities and particularly between interior regions and the ports. There is little doubt that an ill-conceived interest in protecting inefficient state-owned railways and the state-owned intercity bus company from competition was a major reason for these regulations.

One clear effect of these regulations was a reduction in Chilean incomes and growth rates, and Chile is fortunate to be rid of them. It is much more difficult to be certain about their impacts on the location of economic activity within Chile. As we noted previously, however, the regulations on intercity transport modes disadvantaged outlying regions more than the nation's urban centers (Concepcion, Valparaiso, and Santiago), particularly Santiago. The hugely inefficient operation of state-owned ports similarly made Chilean exports less competitive on world markets and thereby both reduced national income and disproportionately disadvantaged regions that were actual or potential producers of export goods. This source of inefficiency was largely eliminated when the central government privatized most operations at state-owned ports.

The fact that governments are monopoly providers of nearly all transportation infrastructure means that their investment decisions strongly affect transport costs, and possibly the levels and distribution of economic activity among regions. If governments provide too few, or inadequate, intercity roads, these deficiencies will increase the costs of shipping goods and services and of moving passengers among cities and regions. In addition, if transportation infrastructure is under-priced, congestion or premature destruction of facilities will similarly result in higher transportation costs, even if the right amount of infrastructure is provided. Worse yet, setting prices below the long-run marginal cost of providing additional capacity may simultaneously lead to situations where more than optimal amounts of infrastructure are provided and, as a result of congestion, the costs of both goods and passenger movements are higher than they need be.

Table 5-15 pulls together the fragmentary data we have been able to assemble on government spending for intercity and urban road and rail investments and associated economic rate of return estimates for these investments. Taken at face value, the rate of return estimates suggest that the government has under-invested in both intercity and urban roads as their returns exceed by large amounts the 12% figure used by the Chilean Government as the minimum rate of return for public sector investments. Since we presume this figure corresponds to estimates of the rates of return on equally risky investments in the private sector, these data provide rather strong evidence that larger investments in roads would have increased Chilean incomes and growth rates.[34]

We are more confident of this conclusion in the case of intercity roads than for urban roads. An unknown share of the expenditures shown for intercity roads in Table 5-15 is for parts of the national road system located within metropolitan areas and an unknown share of this capacity is used by local traffic. While the fraction of national road system mileage in urban areas is quite small, these roads tend to be more expensive than those built outside the cities. Nonetheless, we would be surprised if more than a fourth of the Ministry of Public Work's expenditures were for facilities that primarily benefit urban residents.

The effects of the government's apparent under-investment in intercity roads are qualitatively the same as we previously discussed for regulation. Intercity road-based freight and passenger costs are higher than they would be if the central government had spent more on intercity roads. The impacts on the location of economic activity within Chile are similarly hard to assess, but the net effect of this under-investment may have again worked to the relative advantage of the country's large metropolitan areas, and especially its largest, Santiago. As with the impacts of regulation the effects on national income and growth are more clear-cut than the locational impacts; under-investment

34. A caveat is in order here. These rate of return estimates rely on estimates of the amounts of time saved, reductions in wear and tear for vehicles, fuel savings, and time values that implicitly assume existing facilities are correctly priced and that various market prices are accurate measures of the social costs of the resources used. These assumptions are most suspect when there is serious congestion as a result of under-pricing. For the periods when these rate of return estimates were done, average prices for road use and total user charges (the sum of tolls, fuel taxes, and various vehicle taxes and fees) were substantially higher than the amounts spent on building roads in Chile. This suggests the possibility that, if anything, the estimated internal rates of return for intercity roads may be too low.

in roads almost certainly acts as a drag on the nation's competitiveness and its internal development.

Table 5-15 also includes an estimate of central government railway subsidies for a single year, 1974. While 1974 may be unrepresentative (it clearly is in the case of highways), the magnitude of the subsidy for railways in this single year seems all out of proportion.[35] Dividing the sum of 1970–1990 constant dollar expenditures on roads by 21 yields an upper-bound estimate of the annual expenditures for intercity roads of US $261 million per year in US 1993 dollars. This figure is only 76% of the central government subsidies for the state-owned railways in the same years. Considering only the intercity and road freight movements, intercity roads carried three times as much domestic freight by weight as all Chilean railroads and only a portion of this traffic was carried by the state-owned railways; the ratio by value, of course, is much greater.[36]

While we have no hard data on the level of total spending for roads in Santiago and many other cities, it is difficult to avoid the impression that there was a similar imbalance in road and rail investments in the capital. As Table 5-15 indicates, the central government spent an estimated US $1,203 million to build Lines 1 and 2 of the Santiago metro and is planning to spend another US $330 million for a third metro line. A little bit of arithmetic reveals that the capital outlays for Lines 1 and 2, all of which were paid directly or indirectly by the central government, were equal to 31% of MOP's investments in roads for the entire country during the twenty-one-year period 1970–1990.

We suggested previously that national road expenditures for building or reconstructing roads in the Santiago region were unlikely to have been more than 25% of MOP's total road expenditures. If this surmise is correct, it would imply that the government's investments for roads in Greater Santiago

---

35. While the railroads deficit and central government subsidies in 1974 may be unusually large, we know that spending for roads certainly was. Total spending for roads in 1974, which was US $588 million (in 1993 dollars) was 2.2 times the average annual expenditure for the entire twenty-one-year period 1970–1990. The next highest expenditure was US $344 million in 1970. In addition, Asecio (1993) reports that the railroads experienced large operating deficits for the entire 1960–1973 period, when "... the railroad was considered a public service company and its investments, as well as its operating deficit, were financed by the state." Whatever the total deficits during this period, there seems to be a strong presumption that relatively too little was spent on roads during this period relative to the amounts spent on the railways. As we indicated in our discussion of Chilean railways, the Chilean Government, starting in 1973, required EFE to make strenuous efforts to reduce its operating deficits, with considerable success. While EFE still receives modest subsidies, they are no longer much of a factor.

36. Table 5-15 also includes an estimated US $227 million in subsidies for the state-owned bus company for the period 1970–75. These funds would have been better spent on improvements to Chile's intercity roads.

Table 5-15. *Central Government Expenditures and Rates of Return for Intercity and Urban Road and Rail Investments, Chile Various Years Since 1970*

Item	*Amount Millions US93 $s*	*IRR*	*Revenue Source*
Intercity Roads			
Maintenance (1970–90)	$2,186	44.0%	User Charges
Investment (1970–90)	3,924	34%–70 %	User Charges
Government Subsidies			
Railroad EFE (1974)	345	Prob. Negative	Central Govt.
Govt. Owned Bus Co. (1970–75)	227	Negative	Central Govt.
Urban Roads			
Maintenance (1984–87)	14.6 per yr.	25.4%	Mostly Central Govt.
Investment (1984–87)	N/A	N/A	Mostly Central Govt.
Traffic Engineering	N/A	49%–79%	Mostly Central Govt.
Santiago			
Public Transport			
Metro Lines 1 & 2	1,203	13.7%	Central Govt.
Metro Line	330	14.7%	Central Govt.
Govt. Bus Company (1970–80)	Unknown	Negative	Unknown
Roads			
Maintenance	Unknown	N/A	User Charges/Local
Taxes			
Investment	Unknown	N/A	User Charges
Traffic Engineering	Unknown	38.0%	User Charges
Segregated Busways			
Line 3 Alignment	Unknown	36.0%	NA
Other Alignments	Unknown	18 %–28%	NA

for the entire twenty-one-year period were only 82% as large as the amounts that were spent to complete metro Lines 1 and 2. Even if the movement of goods, which, of course, have no counterpart for the metro, are ignored, daily passenger trips by metro (including the 42% of metro trips that use a highway-based mode for part of the trip) were only 8% of daily person trips in 1991; the other 92% of daily trips use the highways. When metro trips that rely on a highway mode for part of the trip are included, highways modes were used for 95.4% of all daily person trips in Santiago in 1991.

In addition to the disproportionate outlays for rail transit in Santiago, Table 5-15 contains other information that raises questions about the government's previous decision to build Lines 1 and 2, and its more recent decision to build a third metro line. We were unable to obtain any rate of return estimates for specific highway projects in Santiago.[37] Nonetheless, we would be

37. We think it likely, but are not completely certain, that the rates of return for MOP's investments in what we have listed as in intercity roads in Table 5-15 include some segments of national roads located within cities and metropolitan areas. The rates of return for these segments are presumably close to the average rate of return shown for intercity roads in Table 5-15.

very surprised if they were significantly less than the actual or projected rates of return for intercity road projects outside Santiago, which are well in excess of 25%. HFA's (1989) estimated economic rate of return for lines 1 and 2, by contrast, was only 13.7% and the estimated rates of return of the projected US $330 million outlay for the third line is only 14.7%, a figure we suspect is an overestimate.

While it is true that the both HFA's (1989) rate of return estimate for Lines 1 and 2 and SECTRA's (circa 1993) estimate for Line 3 exceed the 12% cutoff for government investments, there is a strong presumption, given the evident capital rationing, that those urban road projects with much higher rates of return should have been built first. An even stronger case exists for having postponed, or perhaps for not even having built, Line 2, since HFA (1989, p. 12.7) analysts indicate Line 2 would not have produced "a satisfactory return . . . if evaluated properly." It should also be emphasized that HFA's rate of return estimates for Lines 1 and 2 of the Santiago metro are highly dependent on the road network assumed for the analysis and on the characteristics of the public transport system assumed for the do-minimum case. If a smaller than optimal road network is assumed for the analysis, the travel time savings from building the metro (the principal benefit from the metro) will be larger than if an optimal network is assumed for the analysis.[38] We think it likely, given the history of under-investment in roads, that a smaller than optimal road network was assumed for both HFA's analyses of Lines 1 and 2 and SECTRA's

38. The simplified models used by HFA in obtaining the 13.7% rate of return estimate for Lines 1 and 2 incorporated with and without metro, base year and evaluation year speeds as inputs and, as noted above, these speeds and the estimated travel time savings from building the metro were the principal benefits. The average trip times for each mode, which, of course, are derived from these speeds were used by HFA (1989, p. 11.14) in their analysis of Lines 1 and 2. These trip times were (a) base year, private modes: 35.2 min. (without), 34.6 min. (with); (b) base year, bus: 41.0 min. (without), 40.5 min. (with); (c) base year, metro: not applicable (without), 27.2 min. (with); (e) evaluation year, private modes: 52.2 min. (without), 36.9 (with); (f) evaluation year, bus: 64.6 min. (without), 33.5 (with); (g) evaluation year, metro: not applicable (without), 32.8 min. (with). It is obvious from the preceding figures that the HFA analysis assumes very large increases in congestion between the base year and the evaluation year and assumes that building the metro would have a substantial impact on bus and private vehicle speeds. It is evident from the large increase in bus travel times between the base and evaluation year, which is largely the result of lower bus speeds, that the HFA analysis assumes very modest, if any, efforts to protect buses from congestion in the "without metro" comparison. The importance of defining appropriate alternatives in evaluations of metro investments and impact of using low-performance all-bus strawmen is demonstrated by Kain (1992a and 1992b) and by Acevedo and Salazar (1989). HFA's forecast metro ridership for Lines 1 and 2, which is 900,000 trips per day in 2010, also seem optimistic. Since the final segment of Line 2 was completed, ridership on Santiago's metro has been growing at about 2.2% per year. If this rate is projected to 2010, a somewhat optimistic assumption given apparent land use trends and growing car ownership, ridership for Lines 1 and 2 in 2010 would be only 689,000 trips per day.

assessment of Line 3, and that, as a result, the rates of return obtained in both analyses are too high.

Still another reason to question the past and proposed allocations of urban transportation investments in Santiago is provided by the estimated economic rates of return shown for segregated bus ways in Table 5-15. Transport planners studied three segregated bus ways for Santiago. One of them, the Vicuna Mackena Bus Way, has almost the same alignment, for at least part of its length, as the third metro line. The estimated rate of return for this competitive bus way is 36 percent or nearly three times the estimate for the third metro line. While we were unable to obtain detailed information about this evaluation, or for that matter the evaluations of the third metro line, the reported estimated rate of return for the bus way is in line with pre-project estimates and ex post evaluations of similar facilities in other cities (Acevedo and Salazar, 1989; Kain, 1991b). On the basis of experience in other countries where such facilities have been implemented, the proposed bus way is likely to carry nearly as many passengers as are projected for the third metro line, at similar door-to-door travel times, and would cost much less to build (Kain, 1991b).

The HFA's (1989) previously mentioned rate of return estimate for Lines 1 and 2 was relative to a do-minimum alternative. More specifically, HFA (1989, p. s.4) analyses assumed no changes in the bus system and a 20% increase in that the corridor's base year highway capacity " . . . reflecting progress in traffic management, driving standards, vehicle performance and road standards." Similarly, while we were unable to obtain information on the precise methods and assumptions SECTRA (circa 1993) used in evaluation of the third metro line, we are certain that the internal rate of return calculation was not an incremental one that assumed the construction of a bus way in the same corridor. As HFA (1989, p. 9.5) analysts indicate, however, the proper procedure would have been to compare the estimated return for the third line to the return for the competing bus way. Thus they observe, "[T]he best procedure is to define a 'do-minimum' future and to evaluate all alternative solutions against the do-minimum. If a metro shows up better than the do-minimum, it will only be recommended if its results also compare favorably with those other lower cost solutions." We could find no indications that SECTRA's assessment included these comparisons.

The government's investment in Santiago's metro also has some fairly unambiguous implications for Chile's regional development pattern. The entire capital costs of Lines 1 and 2 were paid by the central government. Households and businesses in other regions thus contributed to its cost in amounts that would have been roughly proportional to their contributions to total government revenues, although it is hard to discern any direct or indirect benefits to them. The resulting higher taxes paid by taxpayers in other regions, of course, unambiguously reduced the relative attractiveness of these regions. In addition, while the user-benefits to residents and firms in Greater Santiago may have been less than their tax contributions, the metro was nonetheless a major public works project that no doubt created jobs and income for the region's population and businesses. The metro's net impact on regional economic activity was thus most likely a modest stimulus to Santiago and a modest drag on investment, employment, income, and population in other regions.

Turning to the metro's impact on the spatial arrangement of economic activity within Santiago, and assuming that the metro investment did not come at the expense of other urban transport investments for Santiago that might have increased mobility by more, the first impact of building the metro was almost certainly to encourage greater residential dispersal, or what is termed suburbanization in the United States. The metro, however, also significantly increased the passenger capacity serving the central area and reduced travel times to the center from some areas. These decreases in travel times and increases in transport capacity in turn might have increased central area employment.[39] If central area employment grew, this would act as a countervailing influence to the suburbanizing influence of an increase in transport capacity serving the central area. At the same time, it should be clearly understood that improved core accessibility would only increase central area employment if there were a demand for central area locations by employers that was being discouraged by high travel costs between outlying areas and the center.[40]

In the case of Santiago, the completion of Line 1 may have affected the regional distribution of employment in still another, and possibly unanticipated, way. Completion of Line 1 may have encouraged the relocation of many offices from the central area to sub-centers located near Line 1 stations. While we do not have any data on changes in the location of employment within Santiago, the extensive office construction in Providencia and Los Condes provides visual clues of a rapid growth of office and commercial employment at these fast-growing sub-centers. These sub-centers offered nu-

39. An excellent discussion of these questions is provided by Meyer and Gomez-Ibanez (1981, pp. 104–122).

40. While central area locations confer cost and productivity advantages for some activities, high land costs at central locations, and perhaps higher wages, discourage many firms from choosing these locations. Various changes in information and communication technologies may be making central locations less desirable or necessary for many activities that formerly clustered there. A more extensive discussion of these issues is contained in Meyer, Kain and Wohl (1965).

merous advantages over the older central area: (a) lower land values than in the old center, (although this may be changing rapidly); (b) less congestion; (c) possibly lower wages; and (d) locations much closer to Santiago's middle- and high-income residential areas.

By providing a fast and reliable (low travel time variance) connection between these emerging office and commercial sub-centers and the old central area, Line 1 may have made it easier for many firms to relocate to one of these outlying areas or, in the case of new firms, choose entirely new locations outside the old center without seriously compromising their employees' ability to attend meetings and maintain other types of contacts with government offices and private firms still located in the old center. If these impressions are accurate, the completion of metro Line 1 may have carried with it the seeds of its own destruction. By aiding in the creation of a linear office and commercial axis and by making it easier to locate office and commercial activities in areas of lower congestion outside the old center, building Line 1 of the metro may have had the largely unanticipated effect of reducing radial travel within the region and thereby encouraged workers employed in these formerly central area functions to commute to work by bus, shared taxi, taxi, or private car.

The analyses presented in this study also confirm the results of other studies regarding the strong connection between per-capita or household income and private vehicle ownership and use. On the assumption that Chilean incomes continue to grow, rising car ownership and use will be the inevitable result. Without the prompt implementation of policies to charge private vehicle owners fees for road and street use that reflect the long-run social costs of providing additional capacity, growing congestion is inevitable. While the timing will differ, rising car ownership and use eventually will lead to serious and costly congestion in all Chilean cities and metropolitan areas unless some form of congestion pricing is implemented. Since it is likely that Santiago will be the first to experience serious congestion, it makes sense to consider the case for congestion pricing first in Santiago.[41]

The fairly crude analyses presented in this paper support impressions based on limited personal observation that congestion in Santiago is still not

41. During an August 1993 visit to Chile, the senior author of this paper visited Calama. While Calama is a small city, traffic congestion in the downtown area and on the few narrow roads and streets leading into and out of the downtown area during the evening peak period was as bad as any he encountered in Santiago during the same visit. This heavy traffic greatly reduced the environmental and aesthetic quality of what was otherwise a very pleasant and appealing central area and, of course, had seriously adverse effects on the performance of the road-based public transport vehicles serving the resident population. These conditions are certain to become worse as incomes and car ownership continue to grow, with predictable adverse impacts on the quality of life in this and other smaller cities in Chile.

very serious by world standards, a consequence of the fact that car ownership and use are still relatively low. This does not mean that current levels of congestion are costless, however, or should be ignored. Instead, current congestion and its fairly rapid increase should be viewed as an early warning signal, and the government would be well advised to move aggressively to implement policies that would prevent it from reaching unacceptable levels.

The most serious of the several adverse impacts of congestion is clearly its effects on road-based public transport.[42] Buses, taxi buses, company buses, and other high capacity public transport vehicles carried 71.5 percent of Santiago's motorized trips in 1991 and shared taxis carried an additional 2.2%. Rising congestion will increase the average trip times of the users of road-based public transport, increase the variance of trip times, and cause a roughly proportional increase in the per-trip cost.

To appreciate the connection between rising car ownership and the performance of road-based public transport services, it is important to understand the sharply nonlinear nature of street-highway capacity-speed relationships. The nature of this relationship is shown in Figure 5-13. As the volume of travel on a particular segment of roadway begins to approach that segment's capacity, speeds rapidly fall. The curve labeled AVC in Figure 5-13 shows the way trip costs for individual motorists change as vehicle flow increases. The curve MCa, in turn, shows the marginal costs of an additional vehicle where all trips are made by private car, and MCb shows the marginal cost for situations (typical of Santiago), where 70% of trips are made by road-based public transport. As this comparison indicates, the marginal costs from an additional vehicle, for situations where 70% of trips are made by public transport, are much larger than when most or all trips are being made in private cars with perhaps 1.5 persons per car. Under the former situation, adding an addi-

42. Congestion pricing also would reduce trip times for commercial vehicles. These include trucks carrying goods but, perhaps even more important, passenger vehicles and small vans making service calls or other business related trips. High levels of congestion, and the increased travel times and scheduling distortions that are associated with them, significantly increase the cost of producing goods and services. These higher costs reduce the international competitiveness of Chilean firms, increase domestic prices, and/or result in lower wages. Because congestion is still not very great in Chilean cities, these impacts are presumably still fairly small in Chile. In the absence of effective policies, however, these costs can be expected to grow very rapidly in the near future. As we discuss subsequently, if congestion becomes more serious in Santiago than in other metropolitan areas, the relative cost of producing goods and services in Santiago would grow relative to other cities and rural areas, with the effect that Santiago's growth would be adversely affected. Similarly, if congestion is especially serious in the inner parts of Santiago these high levels of congestion will encourage both existing and new firms to chose locations in less congested parts of the region.

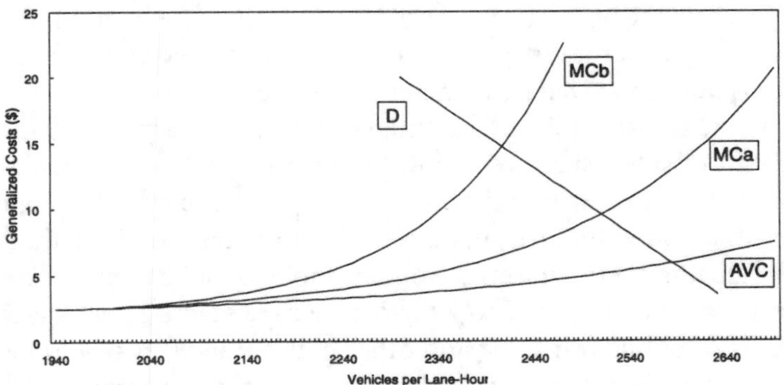

Figure 5-13. ***Marginal Cost Curves for Bus Trips and Auto Trips***

tional vehicle to a heavily used road would impose additional time costs on twenty to thirty times as many persons as when the road is used primarily by persons in private cars.

There are essentially two approaches to trying to prevent congestion from degrading public transport speeds and reliability. The first, practiced in varying degrees in cities throughout the world, employs a variety of physical restrictions on private car use to protect public transport from growing automobile induced congestion. These measures include prohibitions of curb cuts, turning restrictions for cars and trucks using streets that are heavily used by buses, bus-only lanes and streets, and at-grade segregated bus ways. These measures, which are discussed in numerous reports, are useful palliatives, but their effectiveness is limited because they do not address the root problem, the under-pricing of scarce street space (Gomez-Ibanez and Meyer, 1981, pp. 209–218; HFA, 1989; Kain, 1991b, 1992a, Kain and Fauth, 1979; Small, 1977 and 1983a; and TRRL and TTC, 1989 and 1990).

At best, various administrative and traffic engineering or physical restraint measures are second-best ways of protecting road-based public transport from private vehicle-induced congestion. What has come to be called congestion pricing is far preferable. It is likely to be cheaper to implement and administer than the diverse mix of administrative, traffic engineering, and physical restraints on private vehicle use that are employed with varying degrees of success in cities and metropolitan areas throughout the world. Perhaps, most important, however, congestion pricing allows the facilities to be used to their fullest extent, while most physical schemes waste scarce street and highway capacity and create a variety of operational difficulties for public transport services. By charging potential road users according to the fraction of capacity they would use, scarce street space comes to be allocated to those users that value it most and total welfare is thereby increased.

Since public transport vehicles in high density areas carry many more persons per unit of street space required, the operators of these vehicles would easily be able to pay more than all but a few single occupancy vehicle users. At the same time, individual trip makers and commercial vehicles that place a very high value on their trip times would be able to make their journeys during peak hours. As compared to situations where scarce street space is unpriced, users of public transport and other high value users would be able to travel at much higher speeds than they are able to do currently under congested conditions, particularly in the future when congestion would be even worse in the absence of congestion pricing.

The implementation of congestion pricing, by keeping congestion on the streets and roads used by road-based public transport vehicles at low levels, would have a major impact on the performance of bus systems and the relative performance of alternative public transport modes. The implementation of congestion pricing, for example, would reduce the relative attractiveness of rail modes. Much of the attraction of rail transit, and particularly systems that have their own rights of way, is that they are able to avoid congested streets and thereby maintain higher line-haul speeds. As Meyer, Kain, and Wohl (1965), and others have pointed out, however, this advantage of grade-separated rail systems in congested metropolitan areas is offset to some extent by the fact that station or stop spacing is greater on rail than on segregated bus ways or on local bus routes, and that the use of rail transit frequently requires an auto-to-rail or a bus-to-rail transfer. Where congestion is very serious, commuters are often willing to accept the inconvenience of these transfers in order to obtain the benefit of the higher line-haul speeds provided by rail transit. The implementation of congestion pricing, however, would reduce or eliminate congestion on urban streets and arterials and permit significant improvements in bus speeds and reliability. With lower congestion levels, direct buses would be able to provide significantly lower door-to-door travel times in many cases, especially when the disutility attached to transfers is taken into account. If buses were permitted to compete with rail transit for many trips that are currently made by rail, they would very likely be able to supply many of them at lower generalized cost than rail does currently.[43]

A dense network of buses operating on congestion-controlled roads and streets would be better able to serve the dispersed pattern of workplaces and residences that will increasingly mark Chilean cities, than an expanded, radi-

43. See Kain (1993) for a more extensive discussion of these questions.

ally oriented metro network. Such a bus network would have much less of a radial orientation than the present one and would be characterized by many more *comuna*-to-*comuna* services and circumferential routes. Replacing the current central area bus tendering scheme, which arbitrarily limits the number of buses that are permitted to operate in the central area with a congestion pricing scheme that charges both buses and other vehicles for the use of valuable central area street space, would encourage more services of this kind to be offered.

Even if there is agreement about the desirability of requiring vehicle users to pay appropriate amounts for their use of street and roads, many problems remain. The most obvious is what kind of road pricing system should be implemented? This is a complex question and we would not want to offer a definitive answer without much more extensive analysis. Two schemes deserve close attention, however. The first is a simple cordon-pricing scheme, similar to the one that has been operating in Singapore for several years (Gomez-Ibanez and Meyer, 1981, pp. 223–224; Hau, 1992, pp. 44–50; Watson and Holland, 1978). The second is a sophisticated electronic road pricing system that would allow pricing to be applied over a much wider area and would allow prices to be varied by facility, location, and time of day (Hau, 1992). Such a scheme might also allow for higher charges for more polluting vehicles, but it would also be more complex than one that deals only with the pricing of road space and might not be equally feasible under all kinds of technologies.[44]

While there are no examples of a sophisticated electronic road pricing system of this kind to date, there is much to recommend such a system. Until recently such a system would have been prohibitively expensive and there were legitimate questions about the availability and reliability of the required equipment. These obstacles are rapidly being overcome, however. The cost of the required electronic devices is plummeting and the equipment required for such a system is being used in an increasing numbers of applications (Hau, 1992).

---

44. In order to add emission charges to a congestion pricing system it would be necessary to distinguish among vehicles in terms of the amount of emissions per mile they produce. The easiest way to accomplish this would be to use a vehicle identification system that is related to each vehicles emission characteristics. A system of this kind was tested in Hong Kong and it was widely believed it would be implemented (Hau, 1992, pp. 44–50). At the last moment the scheme was rejected, in part because of concerns about privacy. For this reason a smart card with stored value has emerged as the preferred technology for a congestion pricing scheme. Our sense is that the same objectives could be achieved more simply and at much lower costs by introducing a per mile emission tax in conjunction with the vehicle inspection program. A simple program would take odometer reading at each inspection and charge vehicle owners a per mile fee that depended on vehicle characteristics and perhaps the emission rates (as determined by the emission test) at each inspection.

In Santiago, we believe a strong argument can be advanced for replacing the current central area bus-tendering scheme with a cordon-pricing scheme that would charge all users of central area streets a fee that corresponded to the amount of central area street space they used. Such a fee would charge large trucks and large buses more than small trucks and small buses, and charge these smaller commercial vehicles more than taxis and private cars. In contrast to the current scheme, which has apparently reduced central area congestion by reducing the number of buses and taxi buses that are allowed to operate there, a cordon pricing scheme would prevent the future growth of central area congestion, something that will be the inevitable result of growing incomes and car ownership in the absence of restrictions on private vehicle use.

At the same time that the government implements a simple cordon-pricing scheme for the central area, it should also begin to investigate and consider seriously the subsequent implementation of an electronic road pricing scheme for Santiago. As noted, we believe there would be substantial benefits from such a scheme relative to a more primitive central area cordon pricing scheme, and that, if the cost and technology do not favor the implementation of such a scheme in the near future, we are confident that they ultimately will. Indeed, we think it likely that by the time extensive analyses had been completed to devise a cost-effective scheme, any remaining technical obstacles would have been overcome. While it would probably make sense to begin with Santiago, we doubt if the applicability of congestion pricing is limited to it. Parallel studies should be undertaken of the applicability of both simple cordon pricing schemes and more sophisticated electronic schemes for other parts of the country.

Given that congestion in Santiago, and the nation's other large cities, is still relatively modest by world standards, it might be thought that the argument for implementing such a system at the present time is a weak one. We believe just the opposite. Experience elsewhere suggests that implementing congestion pricing is politically difficult and we would be surprised if this were not true in Chile as well. At the same time, the task will only become more difficult as rising incomes lead to increasing levels of per-capita auto ownership and use (Gomez-Ibanez, 1992; Howitt, 1980; Small, 1992).

At the present time, congestion levels are relatively low even in the most congested parts of Santiago during peak periods. As a result, very few private vehicle users who currently use central area streets and roads during peak hours would have to be persuaded to make their trips at different times, to make them to different destinations or by different routes, or to shift to modes that carry more passengers per unit of street space. It is likely, therefore, that modest charges would reduce the levels of vehicle use to their optimal levels. Equally, if not more, important, is the increase in the numbers of persons and voters who would benefit from lower congestion levels both today and in the near future, since 70% of all daily person trips in Santiago in 1991 were made by road-based public transport and all of these users would benefit from policies that reduced current levels of congestion and prevented higher levels of congestion in the future. By waiting, Chilean policymakers will not only run the risk of allowing serious deterioration of public transport services, but will allow the number of private vehicle owners and users who would very likely oppose the implementation of congestion pricing to grow, and the number of public transport users who would receive a clear benefit to decline.

What would be the likely impacts of congestion pricing on the distribution of economic activity both among regions and within those metropolitan areas where congestion pricing turns out to be a feasible and desirable policy? The first problem in answering this question is to specify the alternative and its implications for urban and regional development patterns. As indicated, our analyses of Chilean data and experience, and those from other countries, makes it clear that a failure to implement policies that charge vehicle users appropriate fees for using streets and highways in urban areas will lead to growing congestion, the deterioration of road-based public transport and increases in its cost, and higher trip making costs for the users of private vehicles, both cars and trucks. Half-hearted efforts to protect road-based public transit service from congestion will have some effect, but will not prevent the deterioration of road-based public transport and a large shift to private cars, an outcome that eventually will only make the situation worse and more costly.

While there is no completely convincing quantitative evidence, experience in other parts of the world that have experienced growing congestion suggests that serious congestion in the core parts of large cities tends to accentuate the forces of both population and employment decentralization, and particularly the latter. Thus, we think it likely that a failure to deal frontally with congestion will result in a more dispersed and lower density metropolitan region than would occur if congestion pricing were used to ensure the optimal use of streets and roads. While dispersal will tend to limit the extent of congestion, the cost of producing goods and services and the expenditures of households for passenger transportation will be significantly larger than they would be if appropriate road pricing had been implemented.

Many discussions of congestion pricing have suggested that another result of implementing congestion pricing will be to make the region smaller in population and employment than it otherwise would be. This view is almost certainly wrong. It results from a failure to recognize the impacts of congestion pricing on the supply of transport services, and particularly in large cities, such as Santiago, where a large proportion of trips are made by road-based public transport. Congestion is a hugely inefficient way of allocating street space, and the implementation of congestion pricing would reduce the cost of trip making for most highway users and make the urban region with congestion pricing more attractive than one without for both households and businesses This is particularly true if there were a per-capita rebate of congestion tolls to the residents of the metropolitan area where they were collected.[45]

A tendency exists to confuse the use of congestion tolls to ensure appropriate use of road space with other goals, such as discouraging households and firms from locating in areas where pollution is very great and where the continued growth of employment and population will make the situation worse. As Kahn and Kerr suggest in the previous chapter, these environmental concerns may justify strict emission controls for all vehicles, which will presumably increase the costs of both vehicle ownership and use and perhaps fuel surcharges that reflect the social cost of vehicle emissions. Congestion taxes (everything else equal) would reduce vehicle use and emissions, but this benefit should be regarded as a bonus and distinct from the efficiency gains achieved from otherwise pricing roads efficiently.

References

Acevedo, Jorge and Manuel Salazar. 1989. "Evaluacion del proyecto de construccion de un metro para Bogota," in Ernesto Guhl N. and Alvaro Pachon (eds.), *Transporte masivo en Bogota.* Bogota: Fondo Nacional de Proyectos de Desarrollo (FONDE), Departmento Administrativo de Planeacion Nacional (D.N.P.), and Universidad de los Andes.

Alonso, William. 1964. *Location and Land Use.* Cambridge: Harvard University Press.

Asecio, Jorge. 1991. "Transportation." In Cristian Larroulet (ed.), *The Chilean Experience: Private Solutions to Public Problems.* Santiago: The Center for International Private Enterprise.

Brueckner, Jan K. 1987. "The Structure of Urban Equilibria: A Unified Treatment of the Muth-Mills Model." In E. S. Mills (ed.) *Handbook of Regional and Urban Economics,* Vol. II. Elsevier, Chap. 20: 821–45.

Chile. 1992. "Censo de Poblacion y v de Vivienda, Resultados Preliminares, Region, Provincias y Comunas, XVI, Santiago, Chile, Junio.

Clark, Colin. 1951. "Urban Population Density," *Journal of the Royal Statistical Society,*" Series 114: 490–496.

45. See Kain (1993) for a more extensive discussion of these issues.

CTU (Commission de Transporte Urbano). 1990. "ESTRAUS: Estudio de Evaluacion y Dessollo del Sistema de Transporte Urbano de la Ciudad de Santiago." Santiago.

Daly, A. J. and J. de D. Ortuzar. 1990. "Forecasting and Data Aggregation: Theory and Practice." *Traffic Engineering and Control*, December.

ECLAC (United Nations, The Economic Commission for Latin America and the Caribbean). 1992. "The Impacts of Subsidies, Regulation, and Different Forms of Ownership on the Service Quality and Operational Efficiency of Urban Bus Systems in Latin America," August 7.

Empresa Portuaria de Chile. 1992. *Memoria 1992.*

Fauth, Gary R., et al. 1978. "Central Area Auto Restraint: A Boston Case Study." Report prepared for the U. S Department of Transportation, Urban Mass Transportation Administration, Department of City and Regional Planning, Harvard University, Cambridge, Massachusetts, (December).

Foster, Christopher D. 1974. "The Regressiveness of Congestion Pricing." *International Journal of Transportation Economics*, 1: 133–141.

Gomez-Ibanez, Jose. 1992. "The Political Economy of Highway Tolls and Congestion Pricing." *Transportation Quarterly*, Vol. 46, No. 3, (July): 343–360.

Gomez-Ibanez, Jose and Gary R. Fauth. 1980. "Downtown Auto Restraint Policies: The Costs and Benefits for Boston." *Journal of Transportation Economics and Policy*, 14: 133–153.

Gomez-Ibanez, Jose, and John R. Meyer. 1993. *Going Private: The International Experience with Transport Privatization.* The Brookings Institute, Washington, D.C.

Fernandez, Daniel Koprich. circa 1992. "The Modernization of Santiago's Public Transport: 1990–1992." Commission for the Planning of Investment in Transport Infrastructure, Chile. (forthcoming in *Transport Review*).

Harrison, David, Jr. and John F. Kain. 1974. "Cumulative Urban Growth and Urban Density Functions." *Journal of Urban Economics*, January.

HFA (Halcrow Fox and Associates). 1989. "Study of MASS RAPID TRANSIT in Developing Countries." Report prepared for the United Kingdom, Transport and Road Research Laboratory, The Overseas Unit (June).

Hau, Timothy. 1991. "Economic Fundamentals of Congestion pricing: A Diagrammatic Analysis." Washington, D. C.: The World Bank, Policy Research Working Papers, Transport, WPS-1070.

Hau, Timothy. 1992. "Congestion Charging Mechanisms for Roads: An Evaluation of Current Practice." Washington, D. C.: The World Bank, Policy Research Working Papers, Transport, WPS-1071.

Hendrickson, C., and M. Wohl. 1982. "Efficient Prices for Roadways and Transit Service." *Transportation Quarterly*, 36(3), (July): 433–449.

Hohmann, Claudio. circa 1992. "Implementation of a Road Tendering Scheme for Bus Routes." Ministry of Transport, Chile, mimeo.

Howitt, Arnold M. 1980. "Downtown Auto Restraint Policies: Adopting and Implementing Urban Transport Innovations." *Journal of Transport Economics and Policy* 14: 155–167.

Ingram, Gregory K. and Alan Caroll. 1981. "Symposium On Urbanization and Development: The Spatial Structure of Latin American Cities." *Journal of Urban Economics*, Vol. 9, No. 2 (March): 257–273.

Jara-Diaz, Sergio. 1989. "Income and Taste in Mode Choice Models: Are They Surrogates?" *Transport Research-B*, Vol. 25B, No. 5: 341–350.

Jara-Diaz, Sergio and Juan de Dois Ortuzar. 1991. "Introducing the Expenditure Rate in the Estimation of Mode Choice Models." *Journal of Transport Economics and Policy*, September: 293–308.

Jara-Diaz, Sergio and Jorge Videla. 1989. "Detection of Income Effect in Mode Choice: Theory and Application." *Transport Research-B*, Vol. 23B, No. 6: 393–400.

Jara-Diaz, Sergio and Jorge Videla. circa 1990. "Underestimation of Users' Benefits When Income is Misspecified in Mode Choice Models." Santiago, Universidad de Chile, memo.

Kain, John F. 1981a. "The Impact of Higher Crude Oil Prices on Future Vehicle Ownership." In Roads into the Future. *Proceedings of the IXth IRF World Meeting*, Stockholm, June 1–5.

Kain, John F. 1981b. "Impacts of Higher Petroleum Prices on Transportation Patterns and Urban Development." In Theodore E. Keeler (ed.), *Research in Transportation Economics* Vol. I (JAI Press), pp. 1–27.

Kain, John F. 1990. "Deception in Dallas: Strategic Misrepresentation in the Promotion and Evaluation of Rail Transit." *Journal of the American Planning Association*, Spring 1990, pp. 184–96.

Kain, John F. 1991a. "Trends in Urban Spatial Structure, Demographic Change, Auto and Transit Use, and the Role of Pricing." In U. S Senate Committee on Environment and Public Works, "Demographic Trends and Transportation Demand: Hearing before the Subcommittee on Water Resources, Transportation, and Infrastructure." 102nd Conf., 1st Sess., (February 7).

Kain, John F. 1991b. "A Critical Assessment of Public Transport Investments in Latin America." Report prepared for The Inter-American Development Bank, Washington, D. C (October).

Kain, John F. 1992a. "Increasing the Productivity of the Nation's Urban Transportation Infrastructure: Measures to Increase Transit Use and Carpooling." Report prepared for University Research and Training Program, Federal Transit Administration, (January).

Kain, John F. 1992b. "The Use of Strawmen in the Economic Evaluation of Transport Investments." *American Economic Review*, May 1992.

Kain, John F. 1992c. "Analysis de las Propuestas para el Metro de Bogota." In Enesto Guhl N. and Alvaro Pachon (eds.), *Transporte Masivo en Bogota*, Departamento Nacional de Planeacion and Universidad de los Andes, Fonade, Columbia.

Kain, John F. 1994. " Impacts of Congestion Pricing on Transit and Carpool Demand and Supply." In National Research Council (U. S.), Transport Research Board Commission on Behavioral and Social Sciences and Education. *Curbing Gridlock: Peak-Period Fees To Relieve Traffic Congestion, Vol. 2, Commissioned Papers*, National Academy Press: Washington, D. C., Special Report 242: 502–553.

Kain, John F. 1997. "Cost-Effective Alternatives to Atlanta's Costly Rail Rapid Transit System." *Journal of Transport Economics and Policy*, Vol. XXI, No.1 (January): 25–50.

Kain, John F. 2001. "A Tale of Two Cities: Relationships Between Urban Form, Car Ownership and Use and Implications for Public Policy. *Journal of Transport Economics and Policy*, Vol. 35, Part 1 (January): 31–70.

Kain, John F. and Gary R. Fauth. 1979. "Increasing the Productivity of Urban Expressways: Combining TSM Techniques and Transit Improvements." Report prepared for the U.S. Department of Transportation, Urban Mass Transportation Administration, Department of City and Regional Planning, Harvard University, Cambridge, Massachusetts. Research Report R79-1, (October).

Kain, John F., and Zhi Liu. 1995. "Secrets of Success: How Houston and San Diego Transit Providers Achieved Large Increases in Transit Ridership: Final Report." Prepared for Federal Transit Administration (FTA), U.S. Department of Transportation, May 1995. FTA TX 08-7004.

Keeler, Theodore E. and Kenneth A. Small. 1977. "Optimal Peak Load Pricing, Investment and Service Levels on Urban Expressways." *Journal of Political Economy*, 85: 1–25, Sergio.

Kraus, M. 1981. "Indivisibilities, Economies of Scale, and Optimal Subsidy Policy for Freeways." *Land Economics*, Vol. 55, No. 1 (February): 115–121.

Kraus, M. 1989. "The Welfare Gains from Pricing Road Congestion Using Automatic Vehicle Identification and On-Vehicle Meters." *Journal of Urban Economics*, 25(3): 261–281.

Kulash, Damian J. 1974. "Income-Distributional Consequences of Roadway Pricing." The Urban Institute, Washington, DC, An Urban Institute Paper, 1212–12, (July).

Levinson, Herbert S, *et al.* 1973. "Bus Use of Highways: State of the Art," National Cooperative Highway Research Program Report 143. Washington, DC: Highway Research Board.

Liu, Zhi. 1993. "Determinants of Public Transit Ridership: Analysis of Post World War II Trends and Evaluation of Alternative Transit Networks." Ph.D. Dissertation, Harvard University.

Magni, Alejandro. 1994. "Comments on earlier draft." Ministry of Public Works, Chile.

Metro de Santiago. 1986 and 1990. "Annual Report." Santiago.

Metro Filial Corfo. 1992. "Memoria Anual 1992." Santiago.

Meyer, John R., John F. Kain, and Martin Wohl. 1965. *The Urban Transportation Problem*. Harvard University Press.

Meyer, J., J. Gomez-Ibanez. 1981. *Autos, Transit & Cities*. Harvard University Press, Cambridge.

Mills, Edwin S. 1970. "Urban Density Functions." *Urban Studies*, Vol. 7, No. 1 (February).

Mills, Edwin S. and Jee Peug Tan. 1980. "A Comparison of Urban Population Density Functions in Developed and Developing Countries." *Urban Studies*, Vol. 17, No. 3 (October): 313–21.

Miquel, Sergio. 1993. Telephone discussion with Sergio Miquel, World Bank consultant on urban transport projects in Chile. (202-473-1995).

Morrison, Steven A. 1986. "A Survey of Congestion Pricing." *Transportation Research*–A, vol. 20A, No. 2: 87–97.

Muth, Richard F. 1969. *Cities and Housing*. Chicago: University of Chicago Press, 139–205.

Pickrell, Don H. 1989. "Urban Rail Transit Projects: Forecast versus Actual Ridership and Costs." Transport Systems Center, U. S Department of Transportation, Cambridge, MA, October.

Quarmby, D. 1967. "Choice of Travel Mode for the Journey to Work." *Journal of Transport Economics and Policy*, l (3), (September): 273–3l4.

Richards, Martin. 1992. "Road Pricing: International Experience." In Federal Highway Administration and Federal Transit Administration, "Examining Congestion Pricing: Implementation Issues." Searching for Solutions, A Policy Discussion Series, Number 6, Washington, D.C. (June 10–12).

SECTRA. (Commission de Planificacion de Inversiones en Infraestructura de Transporte, Secretaria Ejecutiva). circa 1993. "Estudio de Alternativas de Trazado para la Line 5 del Metro."

Small, Kenneth. 1977. "Priority Lanes on Urban Radial Expressways." *Transportation Research Record*, No. 637: 8–13.

Small, Kenneth. 1983a. "Bus Priority and Congestion Pricing on Urban Expressways." In Theodore Keeler (ed.), *Research in Transportation Economics*, Vol. 1, JAI Press Inc., Greenwich, Connecticut: 27–74.

Small, Kenneth. 1983b. "The Incidence of Congestion Tolls on Highways." *Journal of Urban Economics*, 13: 90–111.

Small, Kenneth. 1992. "Using the Revenues from Congestion Pricing." paper prepared for the Congestion Pricing Symposium sponsored by the Federal Transit Administration and the Reason Foundation, (May 21).

Smeed, R. 1968. "Traffic Studies and Urban Congestion." *Journal of Transport Economics and Policy*, 2(l), (January): 33–70.

Solow, Robert M. 1973. "On Equilibrium Models of Urban Location." In J.M. Parkin, (ed.), *Essays in Modern Economics*. Longman.

Thomson, J. M. 1967. "An Evaluation of Two Proposals for Traffic Restraint in Central London." *Journal of the Royal Statistical Society*, Ser. A, Vol. 130: 327–377.

TRRL and TTC (Transport and Road Research Laboratory and Traffic and Transport Consultants). 1989. "Study of Bus Priority Schemes for Less Developed Countries: Phase I Report," United Kingdom, Draft (May).

TRRL and TTC (Transport and Road Research Laboratory and Traffic and Transport Consultants). 1990. "Study of Bus Priority Schemes for Less Developed Countries: Phase 3 Report." United Kingdom, Draft (April 14).

Vickery, W. 1969. "Congestion Theory and Transport Investment." *American Economic Review Papers and Proceedings*, 59 (2): 25l–260.

Walters, A. 1961. "The Theory and Measurement of Private and Social Cost of Highway Congestion," *Econometrica*, 29(4), (October): 676–697.

Walters, A. 1968. "The Economics of Road User Charges." World Bank Staff Occasional Paper, No. 5, Johns Hopkins Press, Baltimore.

Watson, Peter L. and Edward P. Holland. 1978. "Relieving Traffic Congestion: The Singapore Area License Scheme." World Bank Staff Working Paper No. 21 (Washington, D.C., The World Bank.

The World Bank. 1989a. "Chile, Urban Streets and Transport Project, Staff Appraisal Report." Washington, D.C., February 9.

World Bank. 1989b. "World Bank. (1989b)." Chile, Second Road Sector Project, Staff Appraisal Report. Washington, D.C., August 23.

The World Bank. 1992. "Chile, Second Highway Reconstruction Project, Project Completion Report. " April 17.

The World Bank. 1993a. "Chile, Third Road Sector Project, Staff Appraisal Report." Washington, D.C., July 15.

The World Bank. 1993b. "The Housing Indicators Program, Volume II: Indicator Tables." Washington, D.C.

APPENDIX TABLES

Table A-1. *Chilean Motor Vehicle Taxes and Road Expenditures by Year (in Millions of Constant 1993 U.S. Dollars, IFS Average Exchange Rate)*

Year	*Fuel Taxes*	*Tolls*	*Vehicle Regular Fees*	*Total Road User Charges*	*Main-tenance*	*Invest-ment*	*Total Road Expenditures*	*Percent Expenditures of RUCs*
1970	186.0	18.7	35.3	240.0	93.2	288.0	390.7	162.8%
1971	196.4	20.9	47.5	264.7	146.2	226.7	385.6	145.7%
1972	196.0	14.2	56.6	266.8	158.7	139.4	315.4	118.2%
1973	310.5	9.4	57.9	377.7	198.7	135.4	358.6	94.9%
1974	647.0	13.9	28.4	689.2	150.1	543.8	717.3	104.1%
1975	419.1	18.5	17.5	455.0	43.8	86.3	140.2	30.8%
1976	571.4	22.4	16.0	609.7	51.9	85.5	151.0	24.8%
1977	609.9	29.2	41.0	680.1	55.7	83.8	151.4	22.3%
1978	488.4	29.3	34.9	552.7	64.1	85.6	160.4	29.0%
1979	269.3	55.9	33.5	358.6	63.9	122.0	195.0	54.4%
1980	381.9	67.1	31.0	480.1	132.5	143.1	285.3	59.4%
1981	452.9	72.3	34.4	559.6	131.9	264.7	407.6	72.8%
1982	475.4	54.2	44.8	574.4	85.6	177.4	271.9	47.3%
1983	458.1	42.3	51.8	552.3	64.8	183.6	272.6	49.4%
1984	444.1	37.7	52.4	534.3	72.0	153.6	258.9	48.5%
1985	405.2	26.8	42.6	474.5	62.7	158.4	265.3	55.9%
1986	480.2	27.5	42.4	550.1	103.8	116.1	277.3	50.4%
1987	483.1	26.9	41.9	551.9	113.8	83.1	281.5	51.0%
1988	393.3	32.0	81.4	506.7	135.4	80.4	310.1	61.2%
1989	367.3	38.2	86.7	492.2	121.0	69.4	304.4	61.8%
1990	389.6	36.6	86.0	512.1	136.2	68.0	330.0	64.4%
1991	373.7	45.2	76.3	495.3	154.9	76.5	360.3	72.7%

Table A-2. *Population, Density, Urbanization, and Vehicle Ownership by Country, 1990*

								Passenger Cars Per 1000 Persons			Commercial Vehicles Per 1000 Persons			Total Motor Vehicles Per 1000 Persons		
Country	Country Population ('000)	Country GNP per Land Area (sq km)	PWT5 GNP per capita (US$)	Country Level of capita (1) (US$)	Country Passenger Urbaniz-ation (%)	Country Commercial Cars ('000)	Vehicles ('000)	Actual	Est. w. Eq(1)	Diff. A − E	Actual	Est. w. Eq(2)	Diff. A–E	Actual	Est. w. Eq(3)	Diff. A–E
Tanzania	25,635	945,087	110	596	33	49	33	1.9	24.0	−0.5	1.3	2.1	−0.8	3.2	4.5	−1.3
Malawi	8,289	118,484	200	569	12	17	19*	2.0	1.7	0.3	2.3	1.6	0.7	4.3	3.4	1.0
Bangla desh	115,594	143,998	210	1,397	16	41	56	0.4	3.6	−3.2	0.5	2.8	−2.3	0.8	6.8	−6.0
Mada- gascar	11,197	587,041	230	779	25	46	47*	4.1	4.0	0.1	4.2	3.1	1.1	8.3	7.2	1.1
Nigeria	108,542	923,768	290	836	35	413	46*	3.8	2.7	1.1	0.4	2.3	−1.9	4.2	5.2	−0.9
India	827,057	3,287,590	350	1,252	27	2,790	3,456	3.4	4.2	−0.8	4.2	3.1	1.0	7.6	7.7	−0.1
Kenya	24,872	580,367	370	1,079	24	136	158	5.5	5.4	0.1	6.4	3.8	2.6	11.8	9.5	2.3
China	1,139,060	9,596,961	370	2,700	56	1,289	3,685	1.1	17.2	−16.1	3.2	8.8	−5.6	4.4	27.9	−23.5
Pakistan	112,049	796,095	380	1,599	32	715	265	6.4	7.2	−0.8	2.4	4.7	−2.3	8.7	12.6	−3.8
Ghana	15,028	238,533	390	894	33	82	42	5.5	3.6	1.9	2.8	2.8	0.0	8.3	6.6	1.7
Indonesia	179,300	1,904,569	570	2,234	31	1,294	1,478	7.2	13.6	−6.4	8.2	7.4	0.8	15.5	22.5	−7.0
Egypt	53,153	1,001,499	600	2,030	47	1,054	380	19.8	13.7	6.1	7.1	7.5	−0.3	27.0	22.5	4.5
Zimbabwe	9,369	390,580	640	1,521	28	283	83	30.2	10.8	19.4	8.9	6.3	2.5	39.1	18.0	21.1
Senegal	7,327	196,722	710	1,263	38	63	36	8.6	7.2	1.4	4.9	4.7	0.2	13.5	12.4	1.2
Philippines	61,480	300,000	730	2,080	43	455	765	7.4	9.8	−2.4	12.4	5.9	6.6	19.8	16.8	3.1
Cote d'Ivoire	11,998	322,463	750	1,224	40	155	90	12.9	6.8	6.1	7.5	4.5	3.0	20.4	11.8	8.6
Morocco	25,061	446,550	950	2,399	48	670	283	26.7	17.6	9.2	11.3	9.0	2.3	38.0	28.2	9.8
Ecuador	10,782	283,561	980	3,184	56	166	207	15.4	30.5	−15.2	19.2	13.5	5.8	34.6	46.6	−12.0
Jordan	3,407	97,740	1,240	3,015	61	172	68	50.5	28.7	21.8	20.0	12.9	7.2	70.5	44.0	26.5
Colombia	32,987	1,138,914	1,260	3,736	70	1,184	489*	35.9	42.3	−6.4	14.8	17.1	−2.3	50.7	62.7	−12.0
Thailand	57,196	513,115	1,420	4,173	23	1,222	976	21.4	34.8	−13.4	17.1	14.7	2.3	38.4	53.1	−14.6
Tunisia	8,180	163,610	1,440	3,278	54	208	224*	25.5	29.6	−4.2	27.4	13.2	14.3	52.9	45.5	7.4

Table A-2. *Continued*

								Passenger Cars Per 1000 Persons			Commercial Vehicles Per 1000 Persons			Total Motor Vehicles Per 1000 Persons		
Country	Country Population ('000)	Country GNP per Land Area (sq km)	PWT5 GNP per capita (US$)	Country Level of capita (1) (US$)	Country Passenger Urbanization (%)	Country Commercial Cars ('000)	Vehicles ('000)	Actual	Est. w. Eq(1)	Diff. A − E	Actual	Est. w. Eq(2)	Diff. A–E	Actual	Est. w. Eq(3)	Diff. A–E
Jamaica	2,420	10,990	1,500	3,177	52	69	28	28.3	18.8	9.5	11.7	9.4	2.3	40.0	30.4	9.6
Turkey	58,687	779,452	1,630	4,401	61	1,650	450	28.1	42.1	−14.0	7.7	17.0	−9.3	35.8	63.0	−27.2
Poland	38,180	312,677	1,690	4,529	62	5,261	1,138	137.8	38.6	99.2	29.8	15.9	13.9	167.6	58.4	109.2
Chile	13,173	756,945	1,940	4,781	86	711	358	53.9	71.8	−17.9	27.2	25.2	2.0	81.1	101.3	−20.2
Algeria	24,961	381,741	2,060	2,810	52	725	480	29.0	21.6	7.4	19.2	10.4	808.0	48.3	34.2	14.1
Malaysia	17,861	329,749	2,320	5,606	43	1,846	407	103.3	67.5	35.8	22.8	24.0	−1.2	126.1	96.7	29.4
Mexico	86,154	1,958,201	2,490	6,319	73	6,893	2,982	80.0	86.3	−6.3	34.6	28.7	5.9	114.6	120.9	−6.3
South Africa	35,282	221,037	2,530	3,719	60	3,600	1,487	102.0	26.3	75.7	42.1	12.0	30.1	144.2	41.2	103.0
Venezuela	19,735	912,050	2,560	6,513	84	1,582	464	80.2	110.1	−29.9	23.5	34.3	−10.8	103.7	150.0	−46.3
Brazil	150,368	8,511,965	2,680	4,588	75	10,598	2,473	70.5	67.0	3.5	16.4	23.9	−7.5	86.9	95.1	−8.2
Hungary	10,553	93,032	2,780	6,359	61	1,945	289	184.3	67.2	117.0	27.3	23.8	3.5	211.6	97.0	114.6
Czechoslovakia	15,662	127,876	3,140	7,335	78	3,242	462	207.0	82.4	124.6	29.5	27.6	1.8	236.5	117.0	119.5
South Korea	64,566	220,277	5,400	8,318	72	2,075	1,308	32.1	79.1	−46.9	20.3	26.7	−6.5	52.4	113.5	−61.1
Greece	10,048	131,990	5,990	7,894	63	1,738	784	172.9	105.5	67.5	78.0	33.1	44.9	251.0	145.9	105.1
Israel	4,659	20,770	10,920	10,098	92	813	163	174.5	115.5	59.0	35.0	35.3	−0.3	209.5	160.1	49.3
Spain	38,959	504,782	11,020	11,653	78	11,996	2,379	307.9	194.0	113.9	61.1	51.7	9.4	369.0	255.0	114.0
Singapore	3,003	618	11,160	13,232	100	287	127	95.5	75.9	19.6	42.3	25.7	16.6	137.8	112.2	25.5

Table A-2. *Continued*

Country	Country Population ('000)	Country GNP per Land Area (sq km)	PWT5 GNP per capita (US$)	Country Level of capita (1) (US$)	Country Passenger Urbaniz-ation (%)	Country Commercial Cars ('000)	Vehicles ('000)	Passenger Cars Per 1000 Persons: Actual	Est. w. Eq(1)	Diff. A − E	Commercial Vehicles Per 1000 Persons: Actual	Est. w. Eq(2)	Diff. A–E	Total Motor Vehicles Per 1000 Persons: Actual	Est. w. Eq(3)	Diff. A–E
Hong Kong	5,801	1,045	11,490	16,822	94	215	132	37.0	106.8	−69.8	22.7	32.9	−10.2	59.8	153.6	−93.8
U.K.	57,237	244,100	16,100	15,374	89	20,807	2,907	363.5	221.2	142.3	50.8	56.6	−5.9	414.3	290.4	123.9
Australia	17,086	7,713,364	17,000	17,144	86	7,442	1,995	435.6	946.0	−510.4	116.8	166.2	−49.5	552.3	1,051.6	−499.3
Netherlands	14,943	40,844	17,320	15,543	89	5,477	590*	366.6	199.2	167.4	39.5	52.4	−12.9	406.1	264.9	141.2
Austria	7,712	83,853	19,060	15,475	58	2,991	648	387.9	289.1	98.8	84.1	69.1	15.0	471.9	367.8	104.2
France	56,440	551,500	19,490	16,681	74	23,550	3,810	417.3	316.0	101.3	67.5	73.7	−6.2	484.8	399.3	85.4
Canada	26,522	9,976,139	20,470	20,694	77	12,622	3,931	475.9	1,210.2	−734.3	148.2	198.8	−50.6	624.1	1,319.7	−695.5
USA	249,975	9,372,614	21,790	21,571	75	143,549	45,105	574.3	685.5	−111.3	180.4	130.3	50.2	754.7	801.3	−46.6
Germany	63,232	248,577	22,320	18,122	84	30,685	1,895	485.3	280.3	205.0	30.0	67.3	−37.3	515.2	360.9	154.4
Norway	4,242	323,895	23,120	15,967	75	1,612	331	380.0	518.9	−138.9	77.9	106.6	−28.7	457.9	617.0	−159.1
Sweden	8,559	449,964	23,660	17,320	84	3,601	658	420.7	532.4	−111.7	76.9	108.5	−31.6	497.5	633.8	−136.3
Japan	123,537	377,801	25,430	17,792	77	34,924	21,571	282.7	254.1	28.6	174.6	62.6	112.0	457.3	330.7	126.6
Finland	4,986	338,127	26,040	16,990	60	1,940	274	389.1	553.9	−164.8	54.9	111.7	−56.9	443.9	655.7	−211.8

Sources: (1) Urbanization and GNP data are from UN Center for Human Settlements and the World Bank, "The Housing Indicators Program, Volume II: Indicator Tables," October, 1993.

(1) The Penn World Table (Mark 5) per capita GDP, measured in 1990 current year international prices; the data for Tanzania, Ghana, Jamaica and South Korea are estimated using annual growth rate calculated from their available CGDP data for most recent years

(2) Motor vehicle data are obtained from United Nations, "Statistical Yearbook, 38th Issue." Those with asterisk are estimated using growth rate for the available previous year data. Data for China are obtained from "Statistical Yearbook of China, 1992."

(3) Country population and land area data are from United Nations, "Statistical Yearbook, 38th Issue."

Table A-3. *Population, GNP, and Car Ownership for Selected Cities: 1980*

City	*Data Source [1]*	*Total Population ('000)*	*Metropolitan Area (sq. km.)*	*Populatioon Density (Persons sq. km.)*	*GNP per Capita (US$)*	*PWT5 GNP per Capita [2] (US$)*	*Total Pasenger Cars ('000)*	*Cars per 1000 persons*	*Estimated Cars per 1000 persons*	*Difference Actual vs. Estimated*
1 Abidjan	AW	1,715	261	6,571	1,150	1,200	85	50	33	17
2 Accra	AW	1,447	1,390	1,041	420	735	27	19	29	−10
3 Amman	AW	1,125	36	31,250	1,420	1,921	81	72	39	33
4 Ankara	AW	1,900	237	8,017	1,470	2,210	65	34	60	−26
5 Bangkok	AW	5,154	1,569	3,285	670	1,705	367	71	55	16
6 Bogota	AW	4,254	1,518	2,802	1,180	2,293	180	42	77	−35
7 Bombay	AW	8,500	438	19,406	240	598	180	21	13	8
8 Buenos Aries	AW	10,100	210	48,095	2,390	3,759	537	53	71	−18
9 Cairo	AW	7,464	233	32,034	580	1,248	239	32	25	7
10 Calcutta	AW	9,500	1,414	6,719	240	598	95	10	16	−6
11 Harare	AW	670	223	3,000	630	917	107	160	30	130
12 Hong Kong	AW	5,067	1,060	4,780	4,240	6,746	200	39	207	−168
13 Jakarta	AW	6,700	650	10,308	430	992	222	39	25	14
14 Karachi	AW	5,200	1,346	3,863	300	855	184	35	26	9
15 Kuala Lumpur	AW	977	244	4,004	1,620	3,042	37	38	95	−57
16 Lagos	AW	1,321	665	1,986	1,010	917	62	47	32	15
17 Lima	AW	4,415	2,664	1,657	930	2,324	333	75	87	−12
18 Manila	AW	5,925	636	9,316	690	1,465	266	45	38	7
19 Medellin	AW	2,078	1,152	1,804	1,180	2,293	91	44	84	−40
20 Mexico City	AW	15,056	1,479	10,180	2,090	4,558	1,577	105	119	−14
21 Nairobi	AW	1,275	690	1,848	420	713	60	47	25	22
22 Rio de Janeiro	AW	9,200	6,464	1,423	2,050	3,347	857	104	130	−26
23 Santiago, 1990	HU	4,768	467	10,201	1,940	3,509	318	67	91	−24
24 Santiago, 1980	HU	3,615	467	7,734	1,794	3,139	216	60	86	−26
25 Sao Paulo	AW	12,800	1,493	8,573	2,050	3,347	1,935	151	90	61
26 Seoul	AW	8,366	627	13,343	1,520	2,420	127	15	59	−44
27 Singapore	AW	2,413	618	3,905	4,430	5,290	164	68	169	−101
28 Tunis	AW	1,230	115	10,696	1,310	1,941	38	31	49	−18
29 Adelaide	NK	932	722	1,291	10,470	10,041	457	490	407	83
30 Amsterdam	NK	717	141	5,077	12,010	8,832	235	328	269	58
31 Boston	NK	2,763	1,237	2,234	11,360	11,794	1,286	465	429	36
32 Brisbane	NK	1,029	1,007	1,021	10,470	10,041	515	501	428	73

Table A-3. *Continued*

33 Brussels	NK	997	148	6,739	12,140	8,976	360	361	258	103
34 Chicago	NK	7,104	3,880	1,831	11,360	11,794	3,161	445	447	−2
35 Copenhagen	NK	1,207	318	3,793	13,130	8,900	274	227	288	−61
36 Dallas	NK	2,974	8,326	357	11,360	11,794	2,528	850	626	224
37 Denver	NK	1,593	1,136	1,402	11,360	11,794	1,062	666	472	194
38 Detroit	NK	4,044	2,703	1,496	11,360	11,794	2,401	594	466	128
39 Frankfurt	NK	631	117	5,396	13,270	9,562	244	387	289	98
40 Hamberg	NK	1,645	394	4,172	13,270	9,562	567	344	304	40
41 Houston	NK	2,905	6,752	430	11,360	11,794	1,751	603	602	0
42 London	AW	6,851	1,579	4,339	7,920	7,985	1,932	282	251	31
43 Los Angeles	NK	7,477	4,070	1,837	11,360	11,794	4,049	542	446	95
44 Melbourne	NK	2,723	1,660	1,641	10,470	10,041	1,214	446	388	58
45 Moscow	NK	8,015	578	13,857	3,250	3,335	160	20	81	−61
46 Munich	NK	1,299	228	5,687	13,270	9,562	467	360	286	74
47 New York	AW	7,086	759	20,541	11,360	11,794	1,545	218	271	−53
48 Paris	AW	8,800	454	19,383	11,730	9,280	3,240	368	215	153
49 Perth	NK	899	836	1,076	10,470	10,041	427	475	423	52
50 Phoenix	NK	1,509	166	9,092	11,360	11,794	753	499	321	178
51 San Francisco	NK	3,251	2,060	1,578	11,360	11,794	1,766	543	461	83
52 Stockholm	AW	1,528	6,489	235	13,520	9,691	391	256	558	−302
53 Stutigart	AW	581	207	2,807	13,590	9,562	199	343	330	13
54 Sydney	NK	3,205	183	17,550	10,470	10,041	1,319	412	238	174
55 Tokyo	AW	8,352	592	14,108	9,890	8,100	2,219	266	200	66
56 Toronto	NK	2,137	540	3,960	10,600	11,360	989	462	367	96
57 Vienna	NK	1,531	212	7,210	9,990	8,293	477	311	235	76
58 Washington	NK	2,988	2,089	1,430	11,360	11,794	1,677	561	470	91
59 Wellington	AW	135	266	508	7,090	8,050	61	452	394	58
60 West Berlin	NK	2,001	315	6,354	13,270	9,562	538	269	279	−10
61 Zurich	NK	781	145	5,368	13,270	11,123	292	375	337	37
Average		3,966	1,290	7,240	6,671	6,488	774	251	225	26

Sources: (1) A. Armstrong-Wright, "Urban Transit Systems: Guidelines for Examining Options," Table II.1, The World Bank, 1986. (2) P. Newman and J. Kenworthy, "Cities and Automobile Dependence," Gower Publishing Company, 1989. (3) Per capita GNP for cities that are not included in Armstrong-Wright (1986) are obtained from "The World Tables, 1992. (4) Per capita GNP for Moscow uses the same statistic from Yugoslavia. (5) Population density for Harare is estimated by rule of thumb.
Notes: [1] AW—Armstrong-Wright (1986); NK—Newman and Kenworthy (1989); HU—Harvard University. [2] The Penn World Table (Mark 5) per capita GDP, meaured in 1980 current year international prices.

Table A-4. *Economic Evaluations of Road Investments for the Second Chilean Road Sector Reconstruction Project*

		Economic Cost (US$ million)		*Average Daily Traffic*		*Economic Rate of Return*	
Subproject	*Length (km.)*	*Appraisal*	*Actual*	*Appraisal*	*Actual*	*Appraisal*	*Actual*
A. Road Reconstruction	578 a/	88.93 a/	47.29 a/	766 b/	753 b/	34 b/c/	34
Longitudinal Road							
P. de Valdivia-Carmen Alto	44	5.65	2.83	359	293	23	15
Carmen Alto-Mantos Blancos	53	7.6	4.02	832	793	44	39
Mantos Blancos-Uribe	29	4.56	2.13	1121	981	48	42
Uribe-La Negra	22	3.82	1.42	247	218	38	39
Rosario-Los Vientos	68	8.82	5.59	432	220	20	16
Los Vientos-Of. Alemania	47	7.38	3.32	432	197	21	17
Of. Alemania-Agua Verde	37	5.82	3.6	432	382	20	21
Altamira-Las Bombas	11	1.32	1.46	581	653	40	20
Travesia-Q. Algarroal	65	10.56	5.34	971	712	28	57
Tongoy-Penablanca	72	11.35	6.38	998	1063	36	29
Transversal Roads							
Carmen Alto-Calama	110	17.16	7.24	548	879	36	42
Uribe-Planta de Filtros	5	0.68	0.58	992	861	48	26
Colcura-Laraquete	11	3.46	2.48	1466	1627	31	30
Corampagne-Ramadillos	4	0.75	0.9	1310	1474	59	35
B. Bridges and Accesses	320 a/	4.67 a/	5.08 a/	305 b/	453 b/	32 b/d/	>71
Santa Cruz-Lolol	35	0.75	0.76	362	626	29	>100
Ranco-Hualano	63	0.31	0.26	225	266	38	44
Cauquenes-Constitucion	108	0.51	1.19	527	397	26	50
Constitucion-Empedrado	44	0.71	0.81	318	832	21	>100
Chillan-Pemuco	44	1.65	0.66	417	473	35	35
Tucapel-Canteras	15	0.49	0.41	97	196	33	>100
Quillion-Nueva Aldea	11	0.25	0.99	186	382	39	91

Source: Adapted from The World Bank, "Staff Appraisal Report: Chile Second Road Sector Project," August 23, 1989.
a/ Total values. b/ Mean values. c/ Overall traffic increase rates estimated at 5%. d/ Overall traffic increase rates estimated at 4%.
e/ Individual traffic rate increase estimated for each road, averaging 5% for light vehicles; 0% for two-axle trucks; 7.5% for heavy trucks; and 3.5% for buses. f/ As in "e" averaging 4% for light vehicles, 0% for two-axle trucks; 8% for heavy trucks; and 7% for buses. g/ Length of rehabilitated road section 97 km instead of 65km.

Table A-5. *Economic Evaluations of Road Investment for the Second Chilean Road Sector Project*

Item	*Length (Km.)*	*Expenditure (in Millions of US Dollars)*	*NPV (in Millions of US Dollars)*	*IRR (%)*
Bituminous Paved and Unpaved Road Network (HDM Analysis including part of IDB Program)	75,661	434	494	44
Paved Roads	6,853	72	91	31
Asphalt Concrete	5,182	51	56	30
Surface Treatment	1,671	21	35	33
Unpaved Roads	68,808	362	403	48
Gravel	32,681	321	328	42
Natural and Earth Gravel	36,127	41	75	>100
Cement Concrete Roads (estimated)	3,470	60	60	>50
Dual Carriage Roadways and Bridges	156	120	628	70
Other Bank Joint Cofinanced Program Components (Bridges, Drainage Structures and Equipments) plus Administration	—	77	60	>50
Subtotal Bank Joint Financed Program	79,131	691	1,242	55
Subtotal IDB Financed Program not in HDM analysis	( ) a/	126 b/	120	30
Total Project	79,131	817	1,362	+/−50

Source: Adapted from The World Bank, "Staff Appraisal Report: Chile Second Road Sector Project," August 23, 1989. a/ Corresponds mostly to road sections and intersections within city limits, not included in MOP road network. b/ Some US$ 7.2 million included in the HDM analysis.

Table A-6. *Santiago Metropolitan Density Gradient Estimates*

Variable	OLS Estimate and (Standard Error)			
	Gross Household Density	*Net Household Density*	*Gross Population Density*	*Net Population Density*
Using Airline Distance to *Downtown Santiago*				
LN (Density at center)	9.09	8.70	10.45	10.06
	(0.01)	(0.13)	(0.41)	(0.13)
Density Gradiant	−0.08	−0.03	−0.08	−0.02
	(0.01)	(0.005)	(0.01)	(0.47)
R-squared	0.46	0.50	0.55	0.46
Using Average Travel *Time by Private Mode*				
LN (Density at center)	10.32	9.32	11.62	10.61
	(1.05)	(0.32)	(1.04)	(0.31)
Density Gradiant	−0.10	−0.04	−0.10	−0.04
	(0.03)	(0.01)	(0.03)	(0.01)
R-squared	0.25	0.36	0.23	0.31
Using Average Travel *Time by Public Mode*				
LN (Density at center)	9.83	8.98	11.04	10.19
	(1.03)	(0.34)	(1.03)	(0.34)
Density Gradiant	−0.06	−0.02	−0.06	−0.02
	(0.02)	(0.01)	(0.02)	(0.01)
R-squared	0.19	0.22	0.17	0.14

Table A-7. *Socioeconomic and Travel Data by* Comunas *in Santiago*

		Total Population		Gross Population Density (Persons/Sq. Km.)			1991 Santiago O&D Survey										
													AM Worktrip			AM Peak Trip Time to CBD (min.)	
Comunas	Area (Sq. Km.)	1982	1992	1982	1992	% Chg	Number of Persons	Number of Vehicles	Number of Households	Avg. Hsehd. Income ('000 CH$)	Vehicle per Hsehd.	Persons per Hsehd.	Destinations	Origins	Worktrip Org./Dest.	Private	Public
Santiago	22.3	232,667	202,010	10,433	9,059	−13.2	202,368	19,735	63,401	126.70	0.311	3.2	264,233	38,456	6.9	20.9	25.314
Providencia	14.2	115,449	110,954	8,130	7,814	−3.9	132,922	36,706	38,776	355.14	0.947	3.4	86,205	23,616	3.7	28.1	30.825
San Miguel	9.5	88,764	82,461	9,344	8,680	−7.1	74,645	7,446	17,843	118.97	0.417	4.2	27,630	15,559	1.8	30.5	36.91
Independencia	7.4	86,724	77,539	11,719	10,478	−10.6	81,527	6,143	21,009	92.74	0.292	3.9	24,415	16,966	1.4	25.5	30.917
Las Condes	98.5	175,735	197,417	1,784	2,004	12.3	222,971	65,469	51,700	419.60	1.266	4.3	53,141	40,497	1.3	35.6	41.118
Nunoa	16.3	168,919	165,536	10,363	10,156	−2.0	184,329	32,272	45,738	222.09	0.706	4.0	43,701	36,400	1.2	28.0	37.115
Vitacura	28.6	72,038	78,010	2,519	2,728	8.3	94,006	33,957	19,849	589.70	1.711	4.7	17,756	14,819	1.2	34.0	45.721
San Joaquin	9.9	123,904	112,535	12,516	11,367	−9.2	102,531	5,726	23,510	103.14	0.244	4.4	24,822	22,165	1.1	27.6	40.24
Recoleta	15	164,292	162,964	10,953	10,864	−0.8	167,082	7,778	39,128	74.66	0.199	4.3	29,492	28,767	1.0	26.8	39.912
Cerrillos	20.8	67,013	72,137	3,222	3,468	7.6	83,186	5,439	18,267	93.83	0.298	4.6	14,937	14,771	1.0	36.5	46.68
Quinta Normal	12.3	128,989	115,964	10,487	9,428	−10.1	122,282	7,183	29,830	82.72	0.241	4.1	22,217	22,665	1.0	26.3	38.07
Estacion Central	13.8	147,918	142,099	10,719	10,297	−3.9	138,137	8,246	32,058	79.14	0.257	4.3	23,970	26,200	0.9	27.5	34.226
La Cisterna	10	95,863	94,732	9,586	9,473	−1.2	82,012	8,627	19,700	112.00	0.438	4.2	13,801	15,262	0.9	31.8	41.831
Macul	12.3	113,100	123,535	9,195	10,043	9.2	126,444	14,587	28,733	147.51	0.508	4.4	24,451	27,540	0.9	35.6	45.916
Lo Barnechea	1029.5	24,258	48,615	24	47	100.4	31,589	7,138	6,821	426.96	1.046	4.6	4,463	5,280	0.8	42.1	55.16
Quilicura	56.6	22,605	40,625	399	718	79.7	36,794	1,829	7,974	80.80	0.229	4.6	4,970	7,571	0.7	29.9	48.619
La Reina	23.3	80,452	88132	3,453	3,782	9.5	88,738	20,744	20,748	300.87	1.000	4.3	11,093	17,884	0.6	36.2	48.230
San Bernardo	154.8	129,127	188,580	834	1,218	46.0	160,791	6,491	34,737	65.61	0.187	4.6	12,266	24,781	0.5	40.0	54.234
Puente Alto	87.8	113,211	254,534	1,289	2,899	124.8	226,358	11,372	51,180	81.17	0.222	4.4	17,117	42,639	0.4	48.5	71.05
Renca	22.8	93,928	129,173	4,120	5,665	37.5	130,654	3,680	28,901	68.37	0.127	4.5	9,570	24,282	0.4	25.9	39.12
Conchali	10.6	157,884	153,089	14,895	14,442	−3.0	135,950	5,416	30,295	73.28	0.179	4.5	10,161	26,612	0.4	24.3	39.533
La Florida	70.2	191,883	334,366	2,733	4,763	74.3	338,942	27,140	77,576	106.49	0.350	4.4	26,121	69,267	0.4	39.9	57.613
Maipu	131.2	114,117	257,426	870	1,962	125.6	194,470	14,753	44,447	105.26	0.332	4.4	13,019	35,358	0.4	33.5	49.724

Table A-7. Continued

							1991 Santiago O&D Survey										
		Total Population		Gross Population Density (Persons/Sq. Km.)									AM Worktrip			AM Peak Trip Time to CBD (min.)	
Comunas	Area (Sq. Km.)	1982	1992	1982	1992	% Chg	Number of Persons	Number of Vehicles	Number of Households	Avg. Hsehd. Income ('000 CH$)	Vehicle per Hsehd.	Persons per Hsehd.	Destinations	Origins	Worktrip Org./Dest.	Private	Public
San Ramon	6.6	99,410	101,119	15,062	15,321	1.7	94,935	3,830	20,387	55.02	0.188	4.7	5,248	17,256	0.3	23.8	52.129
Lo Espejo	7.1	124,462	119,899	17,530	16,887	−3.7	107,015	3,109	22,278	51.91	0.140	4.8	6,271	20,939	0.3	31.3	44.727
El Bosque	13.9	143,717	172,338	10,339	12,398	19.9	173,276	6,796	37,773	67.61	0.180	4.6	9,080	32,691	0.3	36.7	52.210
Pudahuel	196.8	97,578	136,642	496	694	40.0	114,183	3,256	25,120	60.85	0.130	4.5	5,509	21,274	0.3	34.2	42.932
Penalolen	54.9	137,298	178,728	2,501	3,256	30.2	149,636	6,423	32,893	71.67	0.195	4.5	7,107	27,992	0.3	44.9	50.022
La Garnja	10	109,168	126,038	10,917	12,604	15.5	123,537	5,750	27,367	62.16	0.210	4.5	5,708	23,737	0.2	34.4	51.69
Lo Prado	6.6	103,575	110,883	15,693	16,800	7.1	106,477	5,412	24,474	77.55	0.221	4.4	4,338	19,699	0.2	31.0	37.023
La Pintana	30.3	73,932	153,586	2,440	5,069	107.7	153,541	1,667	32,884	39.73	0.051	4.7	6,320	33,240	0.2	38.5	62.111
Cerro Navia	11	137,777	154,973	12,525	14,088	12.5	150,177	4,145	32,948	51.52	0.126	4.6	4,808	27,396	0.2	32.6	44.43
Huechuraba	44.3	56,313	61,341	1,271	1,385	8.9	56,476	1,165	12,099	59.75	0.096	4.7	1,785	11,636	0.2	26.4	50.128
Pedro Aquirre Cerda	9.8	145207	128342	14,817	13,096	−11.6	127,878	5,339	28,171	71.04	0.190	4.5	4,357	29,359	0.1	26.1	42.2
Total	2,259	3,792,070	4,547,980	1,679	2,013	19.9	4,387,981	399,430	1,020,444	126.78	0.391	4.3	835,725	833,217	1.0	#N/A	#N/A

Sources: Pontificia Universidad Catolica de Chile, Facultad de Ingenieria (1992), "Encuesta Origen-Destino de Viajes Del Gran Santiago 1991, Informe Final."

Table A-8. *City Population, Density, Income, and Journey to Work Travel Time, Selected Cities, 1990*

					Journey to Work Travel Time (Minutes)		
Country	*City*	*City Population*	*Urban Density (persons per ha.)*	*City Median Income ($)*	*Actual*	*Estimated*	*Difference A–E*
1 Tanzania	Dar es Salaam	1,556,290	35	763	50	46	4
2 Malawi	Lilongwe	378,867	82	692	60	34	26
3 Bangladesh	Dhaka	5,225,000	290	1,352	45	48	-3
4 Madagascar	Antananarivo	852,500	#N/A	747	60	#N/A	#N/A
5 Nigeria	Ibadan	5,668,978	#N/A	1,331	26	#N/A	#N/A
6 India	New Delhi	8,427,083	193	1,084	59	56	3
7 Kenya	Nairobi	1,413,300	20*	1,500	24	42	-18
8 China	Beijing	6,984,000	87*	1,079	25	56	−31
9 Pakistan	Karachi	8,160,000	61*	1,622	#N/A	55	#N/A
10 Ghana	Accra	1,387,873	58	1,241	35	41	−6
11 Indonesia	Jakarta	8,222,515	124	1,975	40	52	−12
12 Egypt	Cairo	6,068,695	260*	1,345	40	50	−10
13 Zimbabwe	Harare	1474500	66*	2,538	56	37	19
14 Senegal	Dakar	1,630,000	63	2,714	35	38	−3
15 Philippines	Manila	7,928,867	138	3,058	30	48	−18
16 Cote d'Ivoire	Abidjan	1,934,398	74*	3,418	38	37	1
17 Morocco	Rabat	1,050,700	#N/A	4,158	25	#N/A	#N/A
18 Ecuador	Quito	5,345,900	#N/A	2,843	56	#N/A	#N/A
19 Jordan	Amman	1,300,000	361*	4,511	30	31	−1
20 Colombia	Bogota	4,907,600	32*	3,252	90	47	43
21 Thailand	Bangkok	6,019,055	47	4,132	91	46	45
22 Tunisia	Tunis	1,631,000	142*	3,327	37	35	2
23 Jamaica	Kingston	587,798	#N/A	3,696	60	#N/A	#N/A
24 Turkey	Istanbul	7,309,190	#N/A	3,576	40	#N/A	#N/A
25 Poland	Warsaw	1,655,700	#N/A	2,265	45	#N/A	#N/A
26 Chile	Santiago	4,767,638	102	3,433	51	44	7
27 Algeria	Algiers	1,826,617	66	7,335	30	33	−3
28 Malaysia	Kuala Lumpur	1,232,900	69	6,539	34	31	3
29 Mexico	Monterrey	2,532,349	63	4,810	25	38	−13
30 South Africa	Johannesburg	8,740,700	39	9,201	59	45	14
31 Venezuela	Caracas	3,775,897	44	5,123	39	41	−2
32 Brazil	Rio de Janeiro	6,009,397	51	5,204	107	45	62
33 Hungary	Budapest	2,016,774	38	5,173	34	37	−3
34 Czechoslovakia	Bratislava	441,000	#N/A	3,677	40	#N/A	#N/A
35 South Korea	Seoul	10,618,500	175	19,400	37	39	−2
36 Greece	Athens	3,075,000	104	14,229	40	33	7
37 Israel	Tel Aviv	1,318,000	171	16,680	32	27	5
38 Spain	Madrid	4,845,851	#N/A	23,118	33	#N/A	#N/A
39 Singapore	Singapore	2,690,100	86	12,860	30	33	−3
40 Hong Kong	Hong Kong	5,800,600	397	15,077	45	35	10
41 UK	London	6,760,000	57*	18,764	30	38	−8
42 Australia	Melbourne	3,035,758	18*	26,080	25	33	−8
43 Netherlands	Amsterdam	695,221	35	14,494	18	26	−8

Table A-8. *Continued*

Country	City	City Population	Urban Density (persons per ha.)	City Median Income ($)	Journey to Work Travel Time (Minutes) Actual	Estimated	Difference A–E
44 Austria	Vienna	1,503,194	71*	22,537	25	27	−2
45 France	Paris	10,650,600	46	32,319	40	39	1
46 Canada	Toronto	3,838,744	71*	44,702	26	30	−4
47 USA	Washington	3,923,574	16	49,667	29	32	−3
48 Germany	Munich	1,277,576	41	35,764	25	26	−1
49 Norway	Oslo	462,000	30	34,375	20	22	−2
50 Sweden	Stockholm	647,214	51*	41,000	33	22	11
51 Japan	Tokyo	8,163,573	170	38,229	40	34	6
52 Finland	Helsinki	830,600	119	35,770	21	22	−1

Sources:
(1) The UN Center for Human Settlements and The World Bank, "The Housing Indicators Program, Volume II: Indicator Tables."
(2) Urban density data for cities with asterisks are estimated using metropolitan land area data from Armstrong-Wright (1986) or urbanized area data from Newman and Kenworthy (1989).

Table A-9. *Evolution of Santiago Public Transport Fares ($ of May 1, 1992)*

Date	Bus	Taxibus	Metro	Relative Fares Metro/Bus	Metro/Taxibus
Dec. 1976	44.7	74.1	45.4	1.02	0.61
Dec. 1977	46.9	62.2	55.5	1.18	0.89
Dec. 1978	46.9	62.9	49.7	1.06	0.79
Dec. 1979	51.3	70.8	51.3	1.00	0.72
Dec. 1980	53.8	71.7	62.4	1.16	0.87
Dec. 1981	61.3	78.1	70.2	1.15	0.90
Dec. 1982	83.6	102.6	74.8	0.89	0.73
Dec. 1983	91.5	96.9	60.4	0.66	0.62
Dec. 1984	112.3	106.0	66.6	0.59	0.63
Dec. 1985	117.7	122.4	70.0	0.59	0.57
Dec. 1986	112.3	116.7	83.7	0.75	0.72
Dec. 1987	103.6	116.6	87.5	0.84	0.75
Dec. 1988	107.4	113.7	78.9	0.73	0.69
Jun. 1989	112.9	112.9	75.5	0.67	0.67
Dec. 1989	123.7	123.7	74.5	0.60	0.60
Jun. 1990	125.2	125.2	89.8	0.72	0.72
Dec. 1990	120.0	120.0	82.1	0.68	0.68
Jun. 1991	112.3	112.3	87.7	0.78	0.78
Dec. 1991	101.8	101.8	88.6	0.87	0.87
Jun. 1992 (1)	98.1	98.1	85.4	0.87	0.87
Aug. 1992 (2)	88.7	88.7	82.7	0.93	0.93

Notes:
(1) This is the figure of May 1992, as delivered by the National Institute of Statistics, as an estimation for the value of june.

Table A-10. Number of Public Transport Vehicles in Santiago, 1978–91

Year	Month	Amount		
		Buses	Taxibuses	Total
1978		3,877 (1)	1,558	5,435
1979		3,925 (3)	2,065	#N/A
1980		3,972 (2)	2,115	6,087
1981		4,197	2,222	6,419
1982		4,437	2,142	6,579
1983		4,828	2,590	7,418
1984		5,548	2,703	8,251
1985		5,648	2,700	8,348
1986		5,323	2,917	8,240
1987		6,884	3,378	10,262
1988		7,482	4,145	11,627
1990	May	6,545	4,577	11,122
1990	Dec.	7,131	4,710	11,841
1991	Jan.	5,271	4,322	9,593
1991	Dec.	5,559	5,343	10,902

Notes: (1) Includes 710 buses of the ETC (State Public Transport Company); (2) Includes 44 buses of the ETC; and (3) Estimated.

6

The Spatial Implications of Housing Policy in Chile

JEAN CUMMINGS AND DENISE DIPASQUALE*

Introduction

In many countries throughout the world, housing and land markets are significantly influenced by government policy. Chile has a long history of government involvement in housing policy, having passed its first housing law in 1906, and today there continues to be extensive intervention in the housing market by the national government. While virtually all residential construction is done by the private sector, in the 1980s and early 1990s, over 40% of residential construction had direct public subsidy. If mortgage subsidies and housing vouchers[1] are considered as well, the government is involved in a much larger portion of the housing market.

Government intervention in housing and land markets can have profound implications for the spatial distribution of economic activity by influencing the location decisions of both households and firms. In this paper, we consider two levels of spatial distortions: interregional and intraregional. In the interregional case, we examine the extent to which government policy influ-

*We would like to thank Juan Braun, Jr., Ed Glaeser, Matthew Kahn, John Kain, Suzi Kerr, Sergio Leon, and John Meyer for useful comments on a previous draft of this paper. We would also like to thank Francisca Morales and Raj Shourie for expert research assistance. A special thanks goes to Ana Maria Pavez for her excellent research, comments, and guidance. The findings and conclusions of this research are solely the responsibility of the authors.

1. Throughout this paper, we translate *subsidios habitacionales* as "vouchers," to differentiate from subsidies provided by the government through mortgage assistance programs or the basic, progressive, and special unit production programs of the Ministry of Housing and Urban Affairs (MINVU).

ences the location decisions of households among the thirteen regions of the country. We measure this regional influence on household location in four ways: We compare 1) the regional distribution of government subsidized housing units and vouchers to regional shares of the population; 2) the regional distribution of subsidy dollars to shares of the population; 3) the distribution of subsidies relative to poverty levels; and 4) the regional distribution of subsidized units to government estimates of the housing need in each region. For the distribution of publicly subsidized units and expenditures on these units, we find that there are some disparities across regions; resources tend to be reallocated towards the more remote areas of the country to the north and south and to Region Metropolitana (R.M.), one of Chile's thirteen regions and the one that includes Santiago. Regional disparities are more apparent in the distribution of vouchers and voucher expenditures. In particular, R.M. receives a notably higher share of both vouchers and voucher expenditures, and Regions V (Valparaiso) and VIII (Bio-Bio with Concepcion) significantly lower shares, than expected from their shares of the country's population, households, poor households, and the housing deficit.

Chile is highly urbanized; in 1992 over 62% of the country's population lived in one of its three main cities. As in many large cities throughout the world, publicly subsidized housing in Greater Santiago tends to be located at the fringe of the city. Housing policy makers in Chile generally consider only land and construction costs in siting public housing. Given that many residents of this housing commute to the center of Santiago for work, there can be substantial additional costs to siting housing at the fringe in terms of travel time, increased congestion, and pollution. We attempt to quantify these nonland, nonconstruction costs associated with locating subsidized housing at the fringe of the city. We present crude estimates of what the magnitude of these other costs must be in order to justify the higher land costs associated with more central locations for subsidized units. We find that in many cases inclusion of these other costs makes central locations more attractive. While we only provide analysis of Santiago in this paper, similar analyses could be done for Chile's two other major urban centers, Valparaiso and Concepcion.

In the next section of this paper we highlight some of the salient characteristics of Chile's housing market and put them into an international context. Next, we briefly describe Chile's recent housing programs, emphasizing the goals and strategies of the government's housing policies. Throughout, our focus is on potential impacts on locational choice and mobility. Then we present an analysis of interregional distortions based on the current distribution of economic activity. In the following section, we examine the spatial distribution of population and jobs in Greater Santiago, followed by our estimates of the nonhousing costs of locating the poor at the fringe. We conclude with some policy recommendations.

The Chilean Housing Market: International Context

Few countries have as high a homeownership rate as Chile. The World Bank has assembled cross-national data on homeownership rates, based on the homeownership rate in the main city (usually the largest) in each country. As shown in Table 6-1, Chile's homeownership rate is 80%. Only Singapore (90%), Mexico (83%) and Pakistan (83%) have higher rates than Chile (World Bank 1993). The preference for homeownership in Chile is reflected in the government housing programs. In 1994, all government housing programs were for homeownership; there were no rental assistance or rental production programs.

As also shown in Table 6-1, the house price-to-income ratio for Chile is quite low at 2.10 compared to other countries, which means that buying a house in Chile is relatively affordable. The average for Latin American countries in this study is 3.92. The rent-to-income ratio for Chile is quite high at 0.28. Only Korea (0.35), Mexico (0.36) and Singapore (0.38) have higher rent-to-income ratios. In fact, Chile's ratio is high even compared to other Latin American countries, which average 0.20 in the World Bank data. This high rent-to-income ratio may be related to the fact that Chile has a very small formal rental market. As we discuss below, this weak rental market may be due to problems with clearly defining property rights. There seems to be evidence that while the formal rental market is small there is a larger informal market. The World Bank data in Table 6-1 may not adequately reflect the informal rental market.

In Table 6-2, we present simple correlations between cross-country homeownership rates and several other variables. The correlations between homeownership and both the national GNP and the average household income of the country's main city are positive but weak. The homeownership rate is positively correlated with the level of urbanization, although in many countries (e.g., U.S.), homeownership rates tend to be higher in rural than in urban areas. Finally, the house price-to-income ratio is negatively correlated with homeownership while there is a strong positive correlation between the rent-to-income ratio and homeownership.[2]

2. Identifying a causal relationship between homeownership and rents and prices is difficult since homeownership rates, rents, and house prices are all market outcomes. As a result, we do not include rent-to-income and price-to-income ratios as explanatory variables in the regression models examining the determinants of cross-country homeownership rates in Table 6-3.

Table 6-1. *Cross-Country Comparisons: 1990*

COUNTRY	Major City	GNP per Capita	Population (millions)	Urban Population (% of Total)	Homeownership Rate (Main City)	Annual Income (US$s)	House Price to Income Ratio	Rent to Income Ratio
ALGERIA	Algiers	2060	25.1	0.52	0.45	7335	11.70	0.05
AUSTRALIA	Melbourne	17000	17.1	0.86	0.73	26080	3.90	0.16
AUSTRIA	Vienna	19060	7.7	0.58	0.17	22537	4.70	0.13
BANGLADESH	Dhaka	210	106.7	0.16	0.30	1352	6.30	0.12
BRAZIL	Rio de Janeiro	2680	150.4	0.75	0.62	5204	2.30	0.14
CANADA	Toronto	20470	26.5	0.77	0.60	44702	4.20	0.18
CHILE	Santiago	1940	13.2	0.86	0.80	3433	2.10	0.28
CHINA	Beijing	370	1133.7	0.56	0.08	1079	14.80	0.06
COLOMBIA	Bogota	1260	32.3	0.70	0.62	3252	6.50	0.20
CZECHOSLOVAKIA	Bratislava	3140	15.7	0.78	0.14	3677	6.50	0.03
ECUADOR	Quito	980	10.3	0.56	0.79	2843	2.40	0.19
EGYPT	Cairo	600	52.1	0.47	0.32	1345	6.70	0.06
FINLAND	Helsinki	26040	5.0	0.60	0.63	35770	3.70	0.19
FRANCE	Paris	19490	56.4	0.74	0.43	32319	4.20	0.21
GERMANY	Munich	22320	79.5	0.84	0.17	35764	9.60	0.18
GHANA	Accra	390	14.9	0.33	0.28	1241	2.50	0.06
GREECE	Athens	5990	10.1	0.63	0.55	14229	3.80	0.15
HONG KONG	Hong Kong	11490	5.8	0.94	0.43	15077	7.40	0.08
HUNGARY	Budapest	2780	10.6	0.61	0.45	5173	6.60	0.06
INDIA	New Delhi	350	849.5	0.27	0.48	1084	7.70	0.25
INDONESIA	Jakarta	570	178.2	0.31	0.56	1975	3.50	0.15
ISRAEL	Tel Aviv	10920	4.7	0.92	0.80	16680	5.00	0.23
IVORY COAST	Abidjan	750	11.9	0.40	0.21	3418	1.40	0.13
JAMAICA	Kingston	1500	2.4	0.52	0.41	3696	4.90	0.16
JAPAN	Tokyo	25430	123.5	0.77	0.40	38229	11.60	0.16

Table 6-1. *Continued*

COUNTRY	*Major City*	*GNP per Capita*	*Population (millions)*	*Urban Population (% of Total)*	*Homeownership Rate (Main City)*	*Annual Income (US$s)*	*House Price to Income Ratio*	*Rent to Income Ratio*
JORDAN	Amman	1240	3.2	0.61	0.75	4511	3.40	0.16
KENYA	Nairobi	370	24.2	0.24	0.29	1500	1.00	0.10
KOREA	Seoul	5400	42.8	0.72	0.40	19400	9.30	0.35
MADAGASCAR	Antananarivo	230	11.7	0.25	0.36	747	3.30	0.21
MALAWI	Lilongwe	200	8.5	0.12	0.33	692	0.70	0.10
MALAYSIA	Kuala Lumpur	2320	17.9	0.43	0.59	6539	5.00	0.26
MEXICO	Monterrey	2490	86.2	0.73	0.83	4810	3.70	0.36
MOROCCO	Rabat	950	25.1	0.48	0.46	4158	6.70	
NETHERLANDS	Amsterdam	17320	14.9	0.89	0.09	14494	4.80	0.18
NIGERIA	Ibadan	290	115.5	0.35	0.62	1331	3.60	0.07
NORWAY	Oslo	23120	4.2	0.75	0.74	34375	5.50	0.09
PAKISTAN	Karachi	380	112.4	0.32	0.83	1622	1.90	0.19
PHILLIPINES	Manila	730	61.5	0.43	0.48	3058	2.60	0.14
POLAND	Warsaw	1690	38.2	0.62	0.35	2265	10.80	0.06
SENEGAL	Dakar	710	7.4	0.38	0.57	2714	3.00	0.19
SINGAPORE	Singapore	11160	3.0	1.00	0.90	12860	2.80	0.38
SOUTH AFRICA	Johannesburg	2530	35.9	0.60	0.64	9201	1.70	0.05
SPAIN	Madrid	11020	39.0	0.78	0.74	23118	3.70	0.10
SWEDEN	Stockholm	23660	8.6	0.84	0.45	41000	4.60	0.11
TANZANIA	Dar es Salaam	110	24.5	0.33	0.27	763	1.90	0.03
THAILAND	Bangkok	1420	55.8	0.23	0.68	4132	4.10	0.20
TUNISIA	Tunis	1440	8.1	0.54	0.67	3327	6.10	0.21
TURKEY	Istanbul	1630	56.1	0.61	0.60	3576	5.00	0.25
UNITED KINGDOM	London	16100	57.4	0.89	0.58	18764	7.20	0.25
UNITED STATES	Washington, D.C.	21790	250.0	0.75	0.61	49667	3.90	0.25
VENEZUELA	Caracas	2560	19.7	0.84	0.65	5123	2.00	0.24
ZIMBABWE	Harare	640	9.8	0.28	0.45	2538	2.80	0.14
MEAN		6717	78.56	0.59	0.51	11611	4.91	0.16

Source: World Bank 1992, 1993.

Table 6-2. *Cross-Country Correlations*

Variable	*Home-ownership*	*GNP*	*Popu-lation*	*Urban-ization*	*Price to Income*	*Latin America*	*Income*
Homeownership	1.000						
1990 GNP	0.016	1.000					
1990 Population	−0.216	−0.121	1.000				
1990 Urbanization	0.251	0.613	−0.143	1.000			
House Price to Income Ratio	−0.360	0.171	0.464	0.225	1.000		
Latin American Dummy	0.321	−0.225	−0.069	0.213	−0.201	1.000	
1990 Income	0.079	0.948	−0.101	0.568	0.155	−0.222	1.000
(observations = 52)							
Rent to Income Ratio*	0.499	0.130	−0.023	0.294	−0.118	0.297	0.149

* Rent to Income ratio was only available for 51 countries.

Results from an attempt to explain cross-country differences in homeownership rates are presented in Table 6-3. The results in Regression 1 are somewhat surprising. Per capita GNP has a negative and statistically significant impact on homeownership in the main city, while the extent of urbanization in the country has a positive and significant impact. Both of these results are quite robust to changes in specification. While an increase in GNP would be expected to increase homeownership, in this model GNP may be working as a proxy for property rights. If so, an increase in the development

Table 6-3. *Cross-Country Homeownership Regressions*

Dependent Variable: 1990 Homeownership Rate

	Coefficients (St. Error)	
Independent Variables	*Regression #1*	*Regression #2*
Constant	0.3457	0.3729
	(0.0833)	(0.08375)
1990 GNP	−2.23E-05**	−1.9E-05*
	(0.000011)	(0.00001)
1990 Urbanization	0.3444**	0.225
	(0.1522)	(0.1678)
1990 Population	−0.000217	−0.0002
	(0.00014)	(0.00014)
1990 Income	0.000006*	0.000006*
Latin America Dummy		0.14326
		(0.0906)
Observations: 52	Adjusted R-square: 0.11	Adjusted R-square: 0.14

* Statistically significant at the 10% level.
** Statistically significant at the 5% level.

of property rights will decrease homeownership rates. Property rights must be well developed to have an active rental housing market so that in poorer countries, homeownership may be the dominant form of tenure because of the lack of well-established property rights. The positive impact of a country's level of urbanization also may be due to differences in property rights across countries. We have not been able to find a cross-country index of property rights in order to test this explanation. In Regression 2, the dummy variable for Latin American countries has a positive impact on homeownership, although not statistically significant.

Households in Chile do not relocate very often. Although the World Bank has no official statistics, it published a working paper on the Chilean housing market commenting on that country's very low housing mobility rate (Renaud 1988, 28). In 1982, only 8.6% of people five years and older that year had changed the *provincia* (a geographical subcategory of Chile's thirteen regions) in which they lived sometime during the previous five years. By comparison, in the U.S. in 1990, 19.0% of people five years and older had changed the county they lived in during the previous five years.[3] Our interviews suggest, though, that there may be more mobility than these data suggest. Across Chile, many families are "*allegados*"—often translated as "drop-ins"—people living with friends or relatives in extra rooms or makeshift additions in the yard. In 1990, the government estimated that of the 3.2 million households in the country, 42% were living in *allegado* situations (Mideplan CASEN 1992, 124). This does not imply that 42% of households have no homes of their own, but are families directly affected by doubling or tripling up. Over 80% of the *allegado*-affected households are in urban areas.

From discussions with officials and a review of newspaper classified advertisements, it is clear that the formal rental housing market in Chile is small and, in Santiago, is focused on the upper end of the income distribution. The widespread existence of *allegados* may mask a large informal rental market (a market that may be more rentals of rooms than of independent units), higher actual mobility rates, and homelessness.

Lack of a significant rental housing market for low-income households can have important implications. In the U.S. experience, homeowners tend to move far less often than renters. A strong rental market in the U.S. for low-income households allows individuals and families greater opportunity to move to where the jobs are and to exercise their tastes and preferences in the market because the transaction costs of a move for renters are less than they are for homeowners. The dominance of homeownership for the poor in Chile, including the focus on homeownership in government housing programs for

3. Authors calculations using the 5% Public Use Micro Sample of the 1990 U.S. Census.

the poor, may substantially reduce the mobility of these households and limit economic opportunities. As a result, poorer families, as well as younger people who are compelled to live with their parents until they can purchase a home of their own, may be considerably under-consuming housing.

Chilean Housing Policy: Coping with Needs

With varying degrees of dedication, the Chilean Governments of the twentieth century have assumed a role in meeting the housing needs of the country. The focus of their housing policy has been almost exclusively devoted to promoting homeownership. Current forms of government intervention in the housing market include vouchers to households for the purchase of a house, subsidized housing developments, and mortgage programs offered by the State Bank. The 1992 census records 3,101,356 occupied units in the housing stock, compared with a population of 13,231,803 and 3,293,779 households. The Chilean Government frames its housing policy goals, for better or for worse, as the need to address the housing shortage, called the "housing deficit." Its approach to measuring housing need in the country is to divide it into two components: 1) the number of units required to provide each household with a home of its own, and 2) the replacement of units deemed inadequate.

The Chilean Government tracks three different housing-related measures: homes (*viviendas*), households (*hogares*), and families. There are more households than housing units. Homes often have more than one household; a household, in turn, can have more than one family. In 1988, Chile had 1.10 families for every household. Some portion of these households and families may be deemed *allegados.* Traditionally, the Chilean Government measures the housing deficit as the difference between the number of households and the number of adequate units. Its goal is to replace the worst quality shelter and to alleviate the significant overcrowding across the country.

Table 6-4 shows calculations of the 1988 housing deficit, taken from a Chilean housing department working paper (MINVU Antecedentes 1989). Countrywide, estimates of the magnitude of the deficit ranged from 850,000 to 1.1 million units. The first columns show the distribution of the housing stock by geographical region and the share of each region's stock that has been determined inadequate. In 1988, the government identified 330,000 inadequate units. The middle section of the table, the "conservative" estimate, shows the housing deficit by region as traditionally calculated by the government: adding to the inadequate units the difference between the total number of households and the existing stock. By this estimate, the 1988 housing deficit was

Table 6-4 *Housing Deficit, 1988*

			HOUSING DEFICIT							
			Conservative Estimate				*Revised Estimate*			
Region	*Housing Stock*	*% of Inadeq.*	*House-holds*	*Quantity (Household-Stock)*	*Quality (Inadeq. Units)*	*Total*	*Families*	*Quantity (Families-Stock)*	*Quality (Inadeq. Units)*	*Total*
I	61,253	12.9%	78,692	17,439	7,877	25,316	86,168	24,915	7,877	32,792
II	75,221	7.3%	91,601	16,380	5,454	21,834	100,303	25,082	5,454	30,536
III	40,675	9.1%	48,671	7,996	3,693	11,689	53,295	12,620	3,693	16,313
IV	88,966	25.7%	105,260	16,294	22,820	39,114	115,260	26,294	22,820	49,114
V	268,027	10.0%	333,773	65,746	26,749	92,495	365,481	97,454	26,749	124,203
VI	99,347	15.3	145,584	46,237	15,210	61,447	159,414	60,067	15,210	75,277
VII	137,832	23.8%	173,891	36,059	32,763	68,822	190,411	52,579	32,763	85,342
VIII	306,918	16.9%	362,290	55,372	51,992	107,364	396,708	89,790	51,992	141,782
IX	141,097	21.1%	163,984	22,887	29,757	52,644	179,562	38,465	29,757	68,222
X	167,715	11.9%	200,725	33,010	19,891	52,901	219,794	52,079	19,891	71,970
XI	15,205	10.9%	17,914	2,709	1,653	4,361	19,616	4,411	1,653	6,064
XX	32,243	2.5%	36,240	3,997	819	4,816	39,683	7,440	819	8,259
RM	991,646	11.2%	1,194,381	202,735	111,263	313,998	1,307,847	316,201	111,263	427,464
Total	2,426,145	13.6%	2,953,006	526,861	329,956	856,817	3,233,542	807,397	329,956	1,137,353

Source: "Antecedentes Regionales de la Situacion Habitacional en Chile," Documentos de Trabajo, MINVU, September 1989.

over 800,000 units, representing 35% of the existing stock at the time. Government officials, however, argued that using household totals as an estimate for housing need undercounts the real deficit. A more appropriate measure, they suggest, would be the difference between families and units. Using this approach, they calculate the 1988 housing deficit at over 1,100,000, as shown in the last panel, or 47% of the existing stock.

The exact definition of each of these components changes over time and is difficult to measure precisely. Determining actual households and families in a country with a large number of *allegados*, or doubling-up, is difficult. The definition of inadequate units is also hard to pin down. The census housing stock figures include unauthorized housing, which are units that did not meet building codes. According to the Chilean housing agency, 13.6% of the housing stock across the nation was considered "inadequate" in 1988 (MINVU 1989). In 1980, that figure was less than 12% (Mideplan CASEN 1992, 94-95). For the 1992 census, 12% of occupied units were classified as tenement houses, one-room shacks with lean-tos, shacks with no floors, and slums (*callampas*).[4]

Using housing deficits as a basis for government housing policy can be problematic since these measures do not consider the underlying demand for and supply of housing. Mayo, Malpezzi, and Gross (1986) indicate that housing shortages often arise from rapid growth in demand or impediments to supply. They argue that governments rarely respond to excess demand more efficiently than the private market but that governments can remove impediments to private market activity. For this project, we did not have access to micro data on households with information on housing unit characteristics, housing prices, and rents. As a result, we could not directly estimate housing demand and supply. This type of analysis would be required to assess the underlying economics of the Chilean housing market and the extent to which the housing deficit estimates are a reasonable basis for policy.

Modern Housing Policy: MINVU Programs

In 1964 the modern agency charged with housing policy, the Ministry of Housing and Urban Affairs (MINVU), was created with the specific goals of

4. Measuring the number of inadequate units is just one example of the challenges of accessing housing data in Chile. In some cases, information was simply not available. In most cases, we collected data from a wide variety of sources. Often, different sources did not provide the same information even when it seemed that they addressed the same question. As a result, there are places in this chapter where data on a question diverge due to different sources. Throughout, we attempt to use the best data available and always identify the source.

1) diminishing the housing deficit (which at the time was estimated at 420,000 countrywide), and 2) increasing production through direct construction and stimulation of the private sector (Kusnetzoff 1993). MINVU also has responsibility for much of the country's infrastructure. The ministry's creation began a ten-year era emphasizing the state as a housing provider. From 1964 to 1973, 400,000 units were added to the stock, 62.5% of which were built by the public sector (Kusnetzoff 1993), compared to less than 120,000 units built in the period from 1906–1960 (Trivelli 1987, 23).

In 1973, with the incoming military government, public sector housing policy shifted to a focus on the marketplace with a relaxation of regulations and a de-emphasis on public sector construction (Kusnetzoff 1993). By the mid-1980s, the government stepped up its efforts to address the housing deficit and began expanding the state role with production programs similar to those from earlier governments (Kusnetzoff 1993).

Table 6-5 gives a summary of the subsidy programs administered through MINVU in the early 1990s. Between 1988 and 1992, MINVU's subsidy programs generated direct production of 173,719 units and provided an additional 156,667 subsidy vouchers for units. This compares to the government's conservative estimate of a housing need of 856,817 in 1988, as in Table 6-4.

In 1991, MINVU had a total budget of over US $390 million[5] (MINVU 1992). Of that, about 75% was directly invested in housing, infrastructure, and other projects. In 1991, 80% of MINVU's direct investments was devoted to housing programs.[6] These housing programs fell into two types of activity: 1) the provision of housing subsidies or vouchers which the recipient could apply to the purchase of existing homes or the construction or alteration of new ones, and 2) direct involvement in housing production. These programs were exclusively for homeownership. As of 1994, there were no rental assistance subsidy programs.[7]

Vouchers. Roughly 35% of MINVU's direct investment in housing programs was used for the voucher programs. The specifics of the subsidy programs were continually altered by legislation, but generally fell into two groups: unified and rural. The unified program was a broad one, covering primarily urban but also some rural areas and serving a wide income range including middle-income families. Between 1978 and 1992, 273,853 vouchers were distributed. Since their inception in 1988, the unified subsidies ac-

5. Throughout this paper, all U.S. currency figures are in 1992 dollars.

6. MINVU's 1990 budget shows a similar breakdown. (MINVU 1991).

7. The government launched a leasing program in 1994. However, this was not a rental program, it was a lease-to-own program, focused on increasing access to homeownership.

Table 6-5.

	UNITS			VOUCHERS	
	Progressive Housing	*Basic Housing*	*Special Prog. for Workers*	*Unified Subsidy*	*Rural Subsidy*
Recipients	People living in extremely marginal condition. Situation of "allegados" (families sharing the same house). Urban or rural areas.	Families with very low incomes, living in marginal conditions. Urban or rural areas.	Workers who can demonstrate income that permits them to fulfill the requirement of savings and the monthly payment.	National system for low and middle income families. Urban and rural areas.	National system for low income families in the rural areas.
Application	Individual or in groups (i.e., cooperatives). Permanent registration.	Individual or in groups. Permanent registration.	Organized groups, sponsored by public or private entities.	Individual through cooperatives with Housing Projects.	Individual or in groups.
Selection	By score.	By score.	Given by the organizational entity.	By score.	By score.
Housing Price	1st phase, construction: max 140 U.F. 2nd phase, add-ons: max 70 U.F.	An average of 215 U.F. with a maximum of 330 U.F. in the extreme zones of the country.	Maximum of 400 U.F.	400–2000 U.F. with differences in each of 3 sections of program.	Maximum 260 U.F.
Subsidy	1st phase, max 132 U.F. 2nd phase, max 35 U.F.	Max 75% of the housing price with a maxim. of 180 U.F.	80 U.F.	Different for each section of program.	Changeable: 110 - 130 - 150 U.F.
Saving	1st phase, min. 8 U.F. 2nd phase, min. 5 U.F.	10 U.F. minimum.	40 U.F. minimum.	Obligation. Amount determined by the user.	Optional (affects score).
Mortgage Credit from SERVIU (arm of MINVU)	1st phase, maximum 17 U.F. 2nd phase maximum 30 U.F. With a deadline of 5 or 8 years respectively minimum monthly payment 0.3 U.F..	Given by SERVIU with a deadline of 20 years and with interest of 8 % per year.	Given by the State Bank of Chile.	Optional.	Optional.
Administration	SERVIU or private; construction by private sector.	SERVIU	By SERVIU through organizational entity.	Lump Sum Voucher. individual free to choose; acquisition or construction.	Lumo Sum Voucher. Depends on individual voucher; SERVIU or individual.

counted for the bulk of vouchers—over 80%, measured in both units and value.

In 1991, MINVU paid out over 22,000 unified subsidies. The average house value for 1991 was just over US $10,000, and the average subsidy covered 30% of that value; the maximum house value under the program was 2,000 UF (or about US $45,000) for subsidized housing in the extreme north and extreme south where construction costs are high.[8] These certificates were only valid for eighteen months, and could be applied to existing housing only in the last six months. As a result, in 1991, 86% of the unified subsidies were applied to new units. In 1991, MINVU administered three rural programs which paid out nearly 5,000 rural subsidies, worth about US $2,200 and applied to new houses valued at about US $3,850—therefore covering over 50% of the house price.

Units. Restarted in 1988, directly administered production programs (as contrasted with indirect voucher subsidies) used about 65% of MINVU's expenditures on direct housing investment. The three production programs were Progressive Housing, for the very poorest, Basic Housing, and the Special Program for Workers (PET). Together, these programs provided 172,719 units from 1988 to 1992.

All construction was done by the private sector through a bidding process. Private developers chose the site. MINVU defined basic standards for each program and the contracts were awarded to the developers with the lowest costs. For the Progressive and Basic Housing programs, MINVU and/or SERVIU (an arm of MINVU) administered the contracts directly; the PET program was administered through workers cooperatives or other political/social organizations.

MINVU explicitly sought to build as many units as possible while minimizing the direct costs. As a result, these programs produced relatively cheap housing units, which generated some concern that units were not sufficiently durable. However, these units were certainly of higher quality than many of the units that they replaced and the additions that residents constructed themselves.

In awarding contracts, the primary considerations were land and construction costs. The production programs did not consider transportation or congestion costs, or the provision of significant infrastructure. For many projects,

8. The unified subsidy program was modified in 1993. Changes included lowering the maximum value of the houses from 2,000 UF to 1,500 UF, and reducing the value of the subsidy in order to increase the number of subsidies available for unit production programs directed at low-income groups. (Interview with Sergio Leon.)

the developer had to provide some minimal project infrastructure such as roads and pavement, but the costs of connections between the projects and local infrastructure were largely left out of the cost calculations.[9] As a result, the work often went undone. In practice, subsidized housing units in Chile were built as large projects on a single large tract of land rather than on smaller in-fill sites.

The Progressive Housing program, targeted at the very poor in both urban and rural areas, had two phases: the first was construction of the basic unit, and accounted for roughly 70% of the program's expenditures; the second phase was additions to the unit.[10] In 1992, MINVU produced 8,053 units under the first phase. The units produced were very basic: they averaged around 120 square feet, provided the minimal structure and sanitary installation, and had a maximum value of about US $3,100. Virtually the total cost of the home was subsidized; the recipient needed to provide a minimum of 3% of house value from savings, representing US $120, as shown in Table 6-5.

The Basic Housing program produced the most units and spent almost eight times as much as the Progressive Housing program (not including administrative and personnel costs). Over 22,000 Basic units were completed in 1992. The Basic units averaged close to 400 square feet; the average house value was close to US $4,700 with a maximum of about US $7,300 occurring only in remote areas where construction was more difficult and therefore more expensive. The subsidy covered up to 75% of the house value.

Finally, the Special Program for Workers (PET), begun in a new form in 1990, was organized primarily around worker cooperatives or "syndicates." In 1992, this program completed 13,300 units. As with the Progressive and Basic Housing programs, MINVU set the building codes and maximum costs, but the syndicates administered the design, construction, and disbursement. The PET program had a maximum house value of roughly US $8,900; the subsidy could cover up to a maximum of 20% of the house value.

Mortgages. Each MINVU housing program also came with an option of a mortgage. These mortgages had very favorable terms—twelve- to twenty-year

9. In 1994, many projects still were without improved infrastructure systems. The national government, through MINVU and through its social service agency, budgeted funds to provide road paving and some sanitary service connections. The provision of these services was not programmed until after construction was complete and the area's needs were assessed. The agencies then attempted to secure funds and put these projects in a pipeline for infrastructure construction and hook-up. In addition, MINVU issued grants to income-eligible families to help them pay their utilities.

10. Interview with Jaime Silva, Seremi de la Region Metropolitana, MINVU, 1994.

terms at 8% real interest rate.[11] Except for the small amount of savings required by each program, the homeowner could easily secure a mortgage to cover all remaining costs after the subsidies. In addition, the government made attractive loans available to many households outside the unit subsidy programs.

While a few private banks provided mortgages, most banks found that the mortgages were too small to be the basis of a viable business. The State Bank of Chile held the vast majority of the mortgages. Significantly, people both within and outside the government were quick to say that repayment of State Bank mortgages could be easily ignored. If there are few consequences to defaulting on state-provided mortgages, households can effectively increase their total housing subsidy by refusing to make mortgage payments. In interviews, various government officials quoted default rates that ranged from 30% to 60%. Melo (1993) reports that in December 1989, 66% of the SERVIU borrowers were behind four or more payments. By 1991 that number had decreased to 38%, but had risen to 62% by October 1992.

The high default rates are of concern to government officials and are drawing increased attention from Chile's financial markets. Clearly, there is a need to step up enforcement of mortgage contracts to limit the costs of state housing programs.

Common Elements of the Programs. Although they differed significantly, MINVU's two basic programs also shared some common elements:

- Each program required some savings contributions by the recipient. Both the amount of the savings and the length of time the recipient had been saving were important. MINVU was explicitly looking for evidence of a commitment to owning a home.
- MINVU's stated policy was to help the poorest of the poor. For all the programs, selection was largely based on a points system awarded for an extensive list of family characteristics, including family size and income.
- A long waiting list existed for the programs. For the largest program (the Basic Housing program), MINVU received six to seven applicants per unit and had a four- to five-year waiting list.
- Most of Chile's housing assistance programs applied primarily to newly constructed units rather than to existing units. Specifically, the government's major program for housing assistance subsidized the production of housing units to be purchased by eligible households. The government's other major programs provided housing subsidies (vouchers) for the purchase of a home; the recipient could purchase existing housing only during the last six months of the life

11. These terms are for the Basic and Special Workers programs. The Progressive program offered 8% loans at five to eight-year terms.

of the subsidy (eighteen-months total). As a result, in the early 1990s, less than 12% of the subsidies were used for existing housing. It appears that these programs, with their deep subsidies, were essentially one-time opportunities for homeownership granted by the government.

- While the government programs assisted homeowners in providing additions to their homes, these additions did not significantly add value to the home. Most recipients did the work on their homes themselves. While the quality of the interior construction often seemed sound, the quality of exterior additions seemed quite poor. (Interview with Jaime Silva, MINVU).

Spatial Implications of MINVU's Housing Programs

There are two ways in which MINVU programs could potentially lead to spatial distortions. First, they could alter the location decision of households since some of the subsidies were location-specific. Second, they might limit the mobility of households. While there is nothing inherently wrong with households choosing to stay in their home for a long time, housing programs that limit households' abilities to move may restrict them from pursuing economic opportunities. The potential impacts on household location are the following:

1. The unit-based programs required the households to move to the location of the unit. The units often were built on undeveloped, remote land, so households were always relocated from their previous neighborhood.
2. The criteria for selecting the private contractor for building the units included only land and construction costs and encouraged very large-scale development. If the total costs of the location were considered, would different locations have been chosen?
3. The programs encouraged the purchase of new units, which in cities often meant limiting choice to distant locations.

Although beneficiaries of the housing programs were technically required to live in their homes for only five years, MINVU programs may further limit mobility. The potential impacts on mobility are:

1. The nearly exclusive focus on homeownership can decrease mobility, since the transaction costs of moving are higher for homeowners than for renters.
2. The programs generally provided a one-time deep subsidy for the purchase of the home. This subsidy structure implies a permanent location for the household.
3. The focus on providing very low cost units for homeownership can result in

low-quality units that, over time, may have limited resale value, thus decreasing household mobility.

4. The priority given to the purchase of new vs. existing units may significantly limit the resale market, which again decreases household mobility. Interviews with housing officials and research in newspaper real estate pages support the notion that the resale market for existing lower priced homes is small.
5. The high mortgage default rate means that it is difficult for many households to sell their homes because the outstanding mortgage is a lien against the home.

Housing Subsidies: Are There Spatial Distortions?

While we do not have the data to analyze the spatial distribution of mortgage assistance, we can measure the regional distribution of vouchers and subsidized new construction. We can compare the distribution of these vouchers and new units to the regional shares of population, the housing deficit, and regional poverty rates. Specifically, possible spatial distortions at the regional level might be revealed through four comparisons:[12]

1. Regional shares of population and households to units constructed and vouchers distributed;
2. Regional shares of population and households to housing subsidy funds spent by the government;
3. Regional shares of households and regional poverty rates to housing subsidy units, vouchers, and funds spent by the government; and
4. Regional shares of publicly subsidized units constructed and regional shares of the number of vouchers paid to the shares of the housing deficit.

Population and Units. Since the government contracts with the private sector for the construction of subsidized units, virtually all housing construction in Chile is done by the private sector. Chart A tracks private residential construction for the country and R.M. for 1980–1992. (Also see Appendix A.) In 1992, over 105,000 housing units were built countrywide; over the thirteen-year period, an average of more than 60,000 housing units were built each year.

12. In comparing regional shares of population with units constructed and vouchers received, it is important to keep in mind that we are not saying anything about the direction of causality. Are people following subsidies or are subsidies following people? From the information we have, we cannot tell. For our purposes, we are simply using this comparison as a static indicator of whether or not the spatial distribution of subsidies matches the spatial distribution of need.

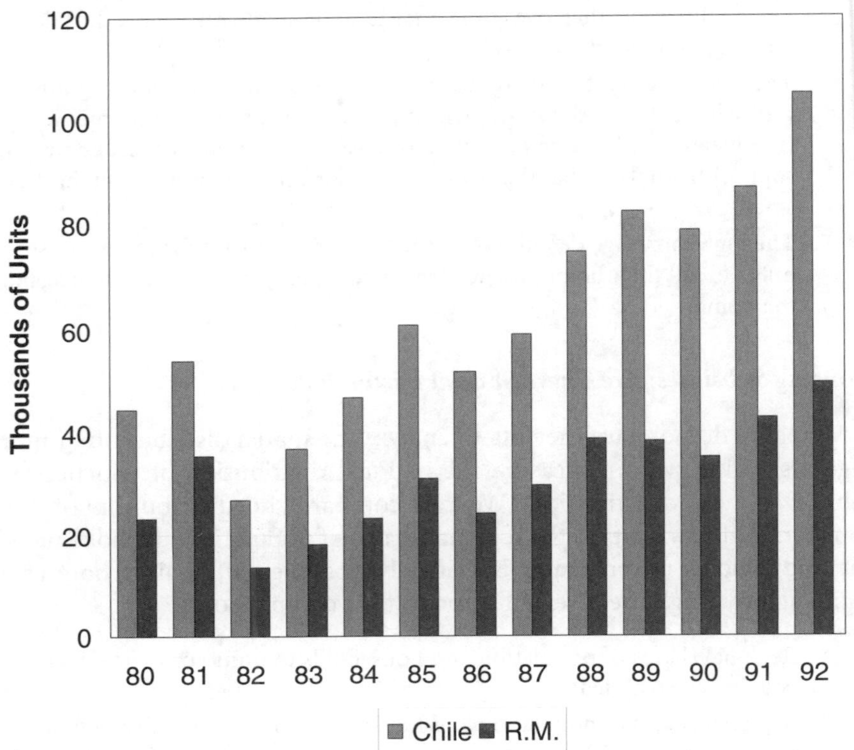

Chart A. Private Residential Construction for Chile and R.M., 1980–92.
Source: (INE 1993). See Appendix A.

As expected, the faster-growing regions in the country saw a good deal of construction as a percentage of their stock, although these regions are quite small and the absolute numbers of new units are modest. In the early 1990s, R.M. was the site of almost one-half of private construction. Despite that, though, the region's share of the 1992 housing stock was 37%, still short of its 1992 share of population.

Table 6-6 adds to this picture by comparing the distribution across regions of several indicators. The first section shows the regional shares of population, households, housing stock and construction. In addition, it lists the homeownership rates from the 1992 census; the census reports rates ranging from 60.3% to 72.2%. In 1990, 1,282,679 or 40.1% of the country's households were in R.M.

Table 6-6 also shows regional shares of publicly subsidized units, a subset of total private housing construction. These figures measure the units completed each year for the Progressive, Basic, and PET programs. Until 1990,

Table 6-6. *Regional Shares of Population, Housing Stock, Construction, Vouchers, and Regional Poverty Rates*

				Units							
	Population and Households			*Total—MINVU Production Programs*				*Vouchers*		*Poverty/Rate (Households)*	
Region	*1992 Population*	*1990 Households*	*1992 Homeownership Rate*	*1992 Housing Stock*	*Housing Construction 1988–92*	*Construction 1988–92*	*Value of Construction (MINVU Costs) 1988–91*	*Number of Vouchers Paid 1988–92*	*Value of Vouchers Paid 1988–91*	*1990 Poverty Rate*	*Distribution of Poverty*
I	2.6%	2.6%	63.9%	2.6%	2.5%	4.9%	5.8%	1.3%	1.4%	26.3%	2.0%
II	3.1%	2.9%	60.3%	3.0%	2.5%	4.4%	4.1%	2.4%	1.8%	28.0%	2.4%
III	1.7%	1.4%	63.4%	1.9%	1.8%	3.3%	3.5%	0.4%	0.4%	30.8%	1.3%
IV	3.8%	3.6%	69.2%	4.0%	4.5%	5.2%	4.5%	4.5%	3.8%	41.0%	4.3%
V	10.4%	11.1%	64.7%	12.3%	9.2%	7.0%	7.4%	7.2%	6.9%	36.8%	11.9%
VI	5.2%	4.9%	65.2%	5.2%	5.9%	4.9%	4.7%	8.7%	7.8%	36.9%	5.2%
VII	6.3%	6.5%	64.3%	6.4%	5.3%	4.5%	3.9%	8.9%	8.3%	42.7%	8.1%
VIII	13.1%	12.2%	68.2%	12.5%	9.4%	11.8%	11.7%	7.9%	7.3%	41.2%	14.6%
IX	5.9%	5.9%	72.2%	5.8%	5.5%	5.1%	5.0%	7.4%	5.5%	40.3%	6.9%
X	7.2%	6.8%	70.0%	7.1%	4.5%	6.0%	6.0%	3.7%	3.4%	37.6%	7.4%
XI	0.6%	0.6%	63.9%	0.7%	0.6%	1.1%	1.8%	0.2%	0.1%	27.2%	0.5%
XII	1.1%	1.2%	66.6%	1.3%	0.9%	1.6%	2.5%	0.1%	0.1%	25.0%	0.9%
R.M.	39.1%	40.1%	70.7%	37.3%	47.5%	40.1%	39.1%	47.2%	53.3%	29.9%	34.8%
TOTAL	13231803	3197429	68.3%	3260674	428277	172719	593129193	156667	351745747	34.5%	100.0%

UNITS: Housing Stock and Housing Construction include private and public sectors.
MINVU production programs represent Progressive, Basic, and PET programs.
VOUCHERS: Represent unified and rural subsidies paid.
Sources: Census 1992; INECON 1993; MINVU 1992, 1993a, 1993b; Mideplan CASEN 1992.

MINVU allocated its housing subsidies through a centralized program without consideration of the differences among regions. Beginning in 1990, however, each region's share of units was based on population.[13] The MINVU housing production column in Table 6-6 indicates that over the five-year period the shares did not reflect population shares. While R.M. received 40.1% of the publicly subsidized new units over the period, its share steadily declined over the period from 50.6% in 1989 to 36.5% in 1992. Over the 1988 to 1992 period, Regions V and VIII received a smaller share of public units than their shares of population or households would indicate. Their shares of public units have not been growing much over time: in 1992, Region V received 8% of the public units and Region VIII had 11.5%, well below their population shares. The faster-growing, more remote regions to the far north, on the other hand, received a larger share of the units than their share of population.

A somewhat similar story emerges from the regional distribution of vouchers presented in Table 6-6. R.M. received 47.2% of the vouchers over the 1988 to 1992 period compared to its 40.1% share of the households in 1990, but R.M. dropped from 50% of total vouchers in 1988 to 39.9% in 1992. Both Regions V and VIII received a smaller share of vouchers than their shares of the population. The regions to the extreme north and south also received relatively small shares of the vouchers. As with the distribution of units, though, there has been some correction. For example, in 1992 Regions V and VIII received 8.4% and 10.2%, respectively, of the country's vouchers, up from previous levels.

Population and Subsidy Dollars. The story is quite similar when expenditures on subsidies are considered, as also illustrated in Table 6-6.[14] The three exceptions are in Regions I, XI, and XII, where the share of subsidy dollars significantly exceeded the share of subsidized units. In 1991, the average subsidy per unit in these regions ranged from US $5,000 to US $8,000, while the average construction subsidy per unit nationally was US $4,730. While we have no data on regional variations in housing costs, the larger per unit subsidies in these regions may reflect higher construction costs in these areas due to their climate, terrain, and remoteness. In addition, several government officials point to a national defense strategy to create a solid population presence in the extreme north and south regions.

For expenditures on vouchers, regional disparities are more apparent. From 1988 to 1991, over 53% of the voucher expenditures went to R.M. with

13. Interview with Jaime Silva, MINVU.

14. The budget figures cover only 1988 through 1991.

a gradual increase throughout the period. In 1989, R.M. received 50.5% of voucher subsidy dollars but by 1991 the share was 53.9%. The average voucher per unit in R.M. in 1991 was US $5,929, more than twice the national average of US $2,890. Part of this discrepancy was due to the fact that virtually all (97%) of the vouchers going to R.M. were under the unified program, which generally provides larger subsidies than the rural program. In addition, the higher voucher values in R.M. may reflect higher construction costs and land costs in the city of Santiago.

Housing Subsidies and Poverty Rates. Although MINVU has primarily based the availability of subsidies across regions on regional shares of population, it is instructive to look at the levels of poor households in each region. The last section of Table 6-6 gives the census poverty rates for each region.[15] The figures are quite high. Nationally, 40.1% of the population and 34.5% of households live in poverty. The household poverty rate ranges from 25% in Region XII to 42.7% in Region VII. The column displaying the distribution of poor households across regions compares relatively proportionately to the distribution of population and households in general. With the exception of R.M., the regions in the middle section of the country, particularly the other urban Regions V and VIII (with Valparaiso and Concepcion), have higher shares of poor households relative to their shares of households and population.

In comparing the poverty distribution across regions to the regional shares of MINVU's subsidies, as shown in the middle section of the table, it is clear that as of 1992 the extreme north and south regions and R.M. had received a higher share of subsidies than their poverty levels might suggest: R.M. had 34.8% of the poor households, but received 41.8% of the total subsidies. Much of the middle section of the country, notably Regions V and VIII, received significantly less of the share of subsidies given their high poverty shares. Region V, for example, has 11.9% of the poor households but from 1988–1992 received only 7.0% of MINVU's units and 6.9% of the expenditures on vouchers. These facts seem to support the comments we heard repeatedly in interviews that households in R.M. could get subsidies more easily.

Using data in the 1990 CASEN study, we were also able to examine the allocation of MINVU subsidies across income quintiles.[16] For the nation as a

15. The poverty level is defined as per-capita income twice the value of the basic nutritional basket, as defined by the United Nations at a 1990 Regional Conference on Poverty in Latin America and the Caribbean (Mideplan CASEN 1992, 368–372).

16. In these figures, MINVU subsidies included all subsidies *used* by households during the 1989–90 survey period, not those issued 1988–1992.

whole, 43% of housing subsidies were for the poorest households in the first and second quintiles; another 23.5% went to households in the third quintile; the fourth and fifth quintiles received 33.5% of the subsidies. Of total households in the poorest quintile, 8.7% received a housing subsidy. The second, third, fourth, and fifth quintile received 9.7%, 10.6%, 8.7% and 5.7%, respectively. This pattern of distribution across quintiles was similar across all of the regions: the second and third quintiles tended to have the highest levels of access to subsidies, with the lowest share represented by the fifth quintile.

How is it that such significant portions of MINVU's subsidies were distributed to the third, fourth, and fifth income quintiles? First, even the programs targeted at the very poor require a down payment and a steady income stream and so are out of reach of the poorest households. Second, although we cannot distinguish the individual MINVU programs in these figures, the unified voucher program was specifically targeted at the middle income, and the PET production program was for working low-and middle-income families. In addition, the census statistics show that there are a lot of very poor people in Chile. With 34.5% of its population below the poverty rate, all the households in the first quintile and most in the second are poor by census definitions. Households in the third quintile are still quite poor, just over the poverty line. However, the fact that 33.5% of subsidies went to households in the fourth and fifth quintiles while only 8.7% of households in the lowest quintile receive subsidies suggests that there is insufficient targeting of housing subsidies.

Publicly Subsidized Units and the Housing Deficit. Chart B compares the regional share of directly subsidized units (from the Progressive, Basic, and PET programs) to the share of the 1988 housing deficit, as calculated conservatively by MINVU (using household figures rather than families). Regions V, VI, and VII were somewhat underserved and R.M. had somewhat more than its share of subsidized units over the five-year period. The extreme regions to the north and south also received considerable attention from MINVU relative to their shares of the housing deficit, although the absolute numbers are small.

Comparing the regional shares of vouchers distributed with regional shares of the housing deficit generates conclusions similar to the comparisons of the distribution of vouchers with regional population and poverty shares. Overall, though, the spatial distortions due to the regional distribution of subsidized units seem relatively modest. From 1988 to 1992, R.M. and the regions in the extreme north and south did get somewhat more than would be predicted based on population or the government's estimate of the housing deficit, while the more central regions (other than R.M.) got somewhat less.

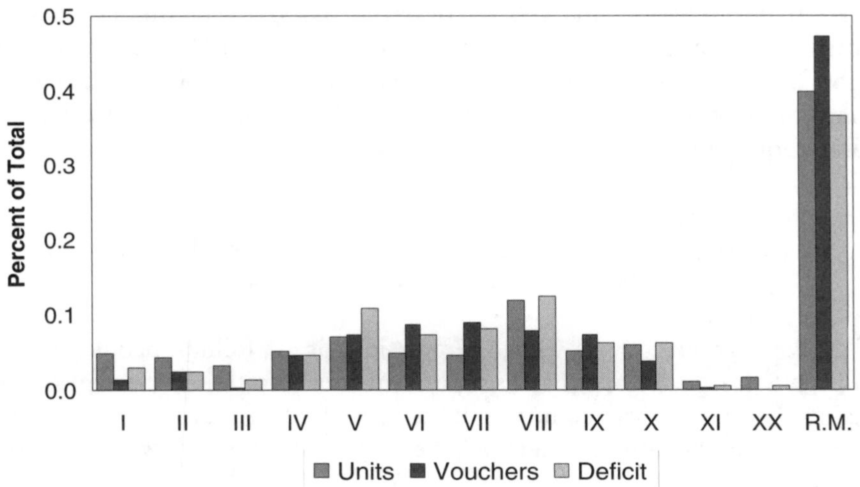

Chart B. Regional Share of Subsidized Units and Vouchers (1988–92) and 1988 Housing Deficit.
Source: (MINVU 1989–1993). See Tables 6-4 and 6-6.

R.M.'s portion of subsidized units in 1993 and 1994 is more in line with its population share. Similarly, the spatial distortions due to the regional distribution of subsidy expenditures seem small.

The voucher programs seem more distorted. What is most striking is what is happening in the middle section of the country. R.M. is clearly receiving a larger share of vouchers and a considerably larger share of voucher subsidy expenditures than its population share or its share of poor households and the national housing deficit would suggest. At the same time, Regions V and VIII are underserved, clearly receiving fewer vouchers and lower value per voucher than expected given their population shares and shares of the poor and the housing deficit. It seems clear that the population and housing deficit data do not explain the interregional distribution of vouchers and voucher expenditures. Perhaps vouchers are a more appropriate form of subsidy in some regional markets than in others. For example, there may be more opportunities to use a voucher in the Greater Santiago housing market than in some of the smaller markets in other regions of the country.

If the goal of housing subsidy programs is to increase supply, government unit production programs do produce units, although the standard question raised by government production programs is to what extent do they simply replace private sector activity. Vouchers are demand-side subsidies that are expected to stimulate supply. We would need detailed information on the operation of individual markets in order to assess the appropriateness of voucher subsidies versus construction subsidies. It would be useful to have more detailed information on who is being served by each of the housing programs in order to assess to what extent each of the programs is reaching their target populations.

Intraregional Distribution of Housing Subsidies: The Case of Greater Santiago

In 1992, about 39% of Chile's population, or 4.7 million people, lived in Greater Santiago. Because of this significant concentration in the capital, typical for Latin American countries, it seems useful to evaluate possible spatial distortions at the intraregional level. We begin with an overview of the metropolitan area.

Greater Santiago had 1.1 million housing units in 1992, representing on average 4.3 people per unit (compared to a countrywide "household size" of 4.1 in 1990). (Mideplan CASEN 1992, 24 and 94). Map A shows the distribution of the city's 1992 population over the thirty-four *comunas* that make up Greater Santiago.[17] (See Appendix B for population figures for each *comuna.*) The downtown Santiago *comuna* is among the largest, accounting for 4.3% of Greater Santiago population or 202,010 people. However, three *comunas* at the outskirts of the city are larger; Puente Alto and La Florida to the south and Maipu to the southwest are home to 18% of the total population. Other *comunas* at the northern fringe, despite their large land area, have the smallest share of total inhabitants: Quilicura, Huechuraba and Lo Barnechea each has about 1% of the population. Finally, a few areas have small portions of the population despite their central location and good access to downtown, notably Independencia, Vitacura, San Miguel and Cerrillos (each housing below 1.9% of the city's population).

Population Distribution and Dispersion

The population of Santiago has become more dispersed over time. Map B shows the population density by *comuna* for 1992. (See Appendix B for detail.) The relationship between population density and distance from the cen-

17. In the maps used here, the outside borders of the fringe *comunas* are rough estimates. Typically, borders for agricultural land at the fringe are not exact and often change. To give the reader a sense of scale, the distance from the center of Maipu to the center of Las Condes is about 26 kilometers. The distance from roughly the center of Puente Alto to the center of the Santiago *comuna* is about 19 kilometers. One centimeter on the maps represents roughly 0.32 kilometers.

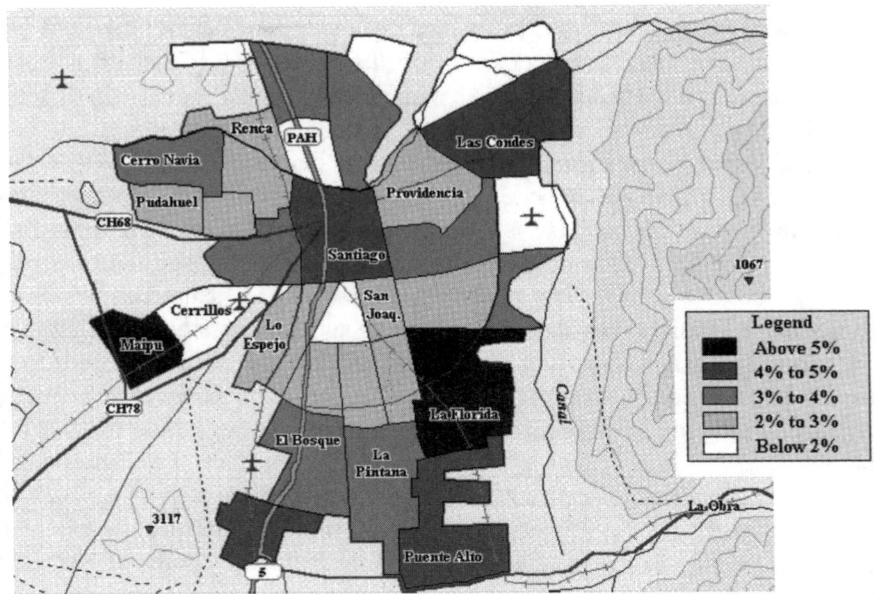

Map A. 1992 Population Distribution by Comuna *in Percent*

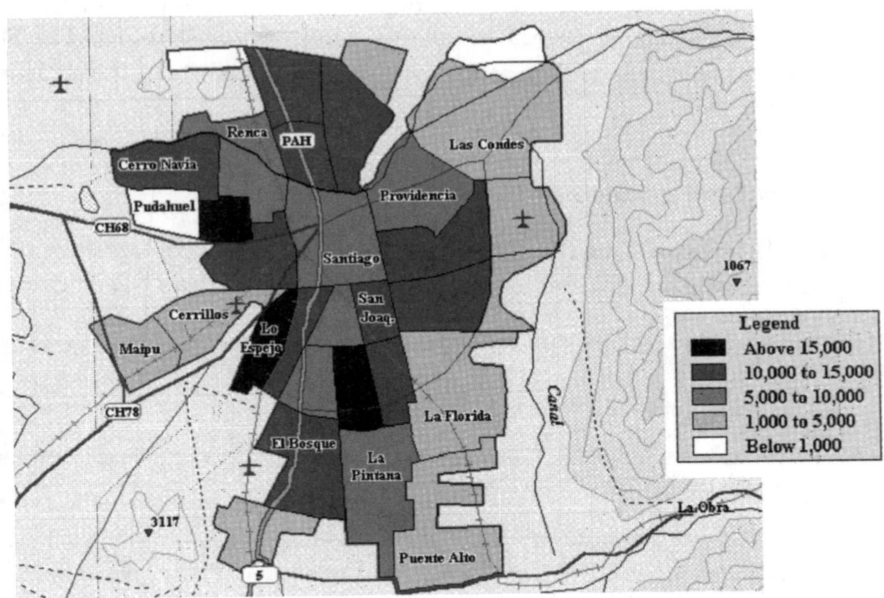

Map B. Population Density (per square kilometer) for 1992

ter of the city can be analyzed by estimating a standard density gradient (see Table 6-7).[18] For 1992, the coefficient on distance is −0.07, which suggests that population density decreases 7% with each kilometer increase in distance from Santiago.

Map C shows population growth by *comuna* between 1982 and 1992. (See Appendix B.) During that time, the population of Greater Santiago grew 18.8%, more than the country as a whole, but somewhat less than the growth rate for the Region Metropolitana. At the same time the population of the Santiago *comuna* in the center of the metropolitan area decreased by 13.2%. The density gradient has flattened over the ten-year period from 1982 to 1992, indicating the location of more of the population at more distant locations.[19] It is immediately apparent from the map that, along with Santiago, several *comunas* near the center of the city experienced negative growth, while the *comunas* at the fringe grew dramatically. In fact, La Pintana, Lo Barnechea, Maipu, and Puente Alto each more than doubled in population.

These density calculations may actually be underestimating the extent to which the population is moving further away from the center of Santiago, since implicit in them is the assumption that the population is uniformly distributed within the *comunas*. Instead, many of the more remote *comunas*—such as La Pintana, Puente Alto, Maipu, and several others—are characterized by pockets of relatively dense settlement next to vast tracts of vacant undeveloped land (INECON 1993). Therefore, population density measures for the fringe *comunas*, based on the total population of the *comuna* compared to the *comuna's* total land area, will underestimate the actual density of the areas in which people live.

Employment and Commuting Patterns

The 1991 Origin-Destination Study of Greater Santiago provides information on employment distribution across the city (Mideplan O-D Encuesta

---

18. To estimate the simple population density gradient, we use the standard negative exponential form:

$$D(u) = Ae^{-bu}$$

In order to transform this equation into a linear expression which can be estimated statistically, we take the natural log of both sides, which yields:

$$\text{Log } D(u) = \log(A) - bu$$

where the dependent variable D(u) is the log of gross population density by *comuna*, and the independent variable is distance u from the center of each *comuna* to the center of the Santiago *comuna;* A and b are parameters to be estimated from the data.

19. Estimating similar population density gradients for Boston and Los Angeles for 1990 yields coefficients on distance of −0.08 and −0.04, respectively.

Table 6-7. *Population and Employment Density Gradients*

	Population		*Employment*
	1992	*1982*	*1991*
Constant	5.7	6.04	9.91
	(0.39)	(0.41)	(0.98)
Distance	−0.07	−0.09	−0.111
	(0.014)	(0.015)	(0.015)
Adjusted R Squared	0.42	0.52	0.64
Observations	34	34	34

1992). Using the study's information on the number of daily work trips to each *comuna*, we can estimate the portion of city jobs located in each comuna. Map D illustrates the spatial distribution of these jobs.[20]

The northeastern corridor of Santiago, Providencia and Las Condes clearly dominates the employment picture. Santiago *comuna* has by far the largest share of employment with 31.5% followed by Providencia with over 10% and Las Condes at 6.3%. Together, these *comunas* employ 882,311 of the region's total 1.8 million employees. Nunoa, on the eastern border of Santiago and the southern border of Providencia, is the fourth largest employer in the Greater Santiago area, with just over 5% of the area's jobs.

As shown in Table 6-7, estimating an employment density gradient by *comuna* yields a distance coefficient of −0.11—a one-kilometer increase in distance from Santiago decreases employment density by 11%.[21] Distance explains 64% of the variance in employment densities across *comunas*. Map E presents employment density by *comuna* and again shows the dominance of Santiago and Providencia. Again, these density figures can be somewhat misleading because the more distant *comunas* have very large land areas, some of which are not urbanized.

A closer look at the Origin-Destination Study reinforces important work-related commuting patterns. For residents in thirty-two of the thirty-four *comunas*, Santiago was the most common workplace (for Quilicura and Lo Barnechea to the north, the dominant workplace was their home *comuna*). For these thirty-two *comunas*, the portion of employees traveling to Santiago for work ranged from 18% in Penalolen to 42% in Nunoa.

20. We applied the Origin-Destination Study distribution of A.M. peak hour work trip destinations across *comunas* for the entire region to the October-December 1991 INE employment figures for the R.M. to estimate the distribution of actual jobs. Unfortunately, we do not have the data to examine changes over time in spatial distribution of employment because the *comuna* boundaries were substantially redefined since the previous Origin-Destination Study in 1977.

21. Estimating an employment density gradient for Boston for 1990 results in a very similar distance coefficient of −0.09.

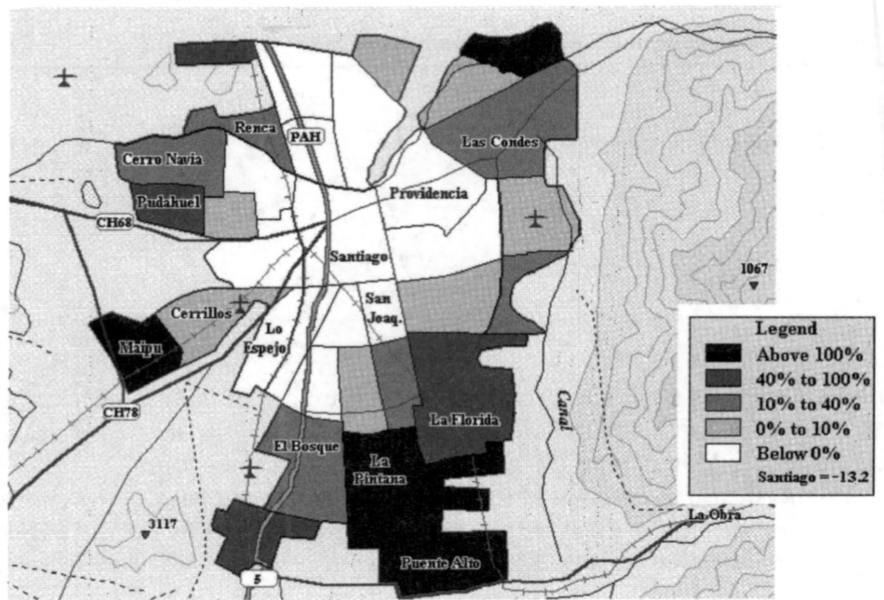

Map C. Population Growth from 1982 to 1992 by Comuna

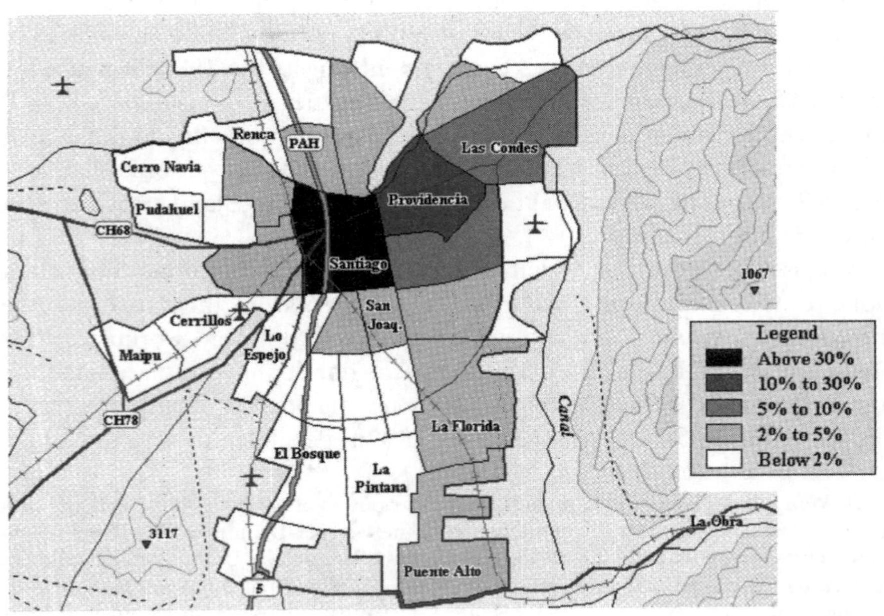

Map D. 1991 Comuna *Share of Employment*

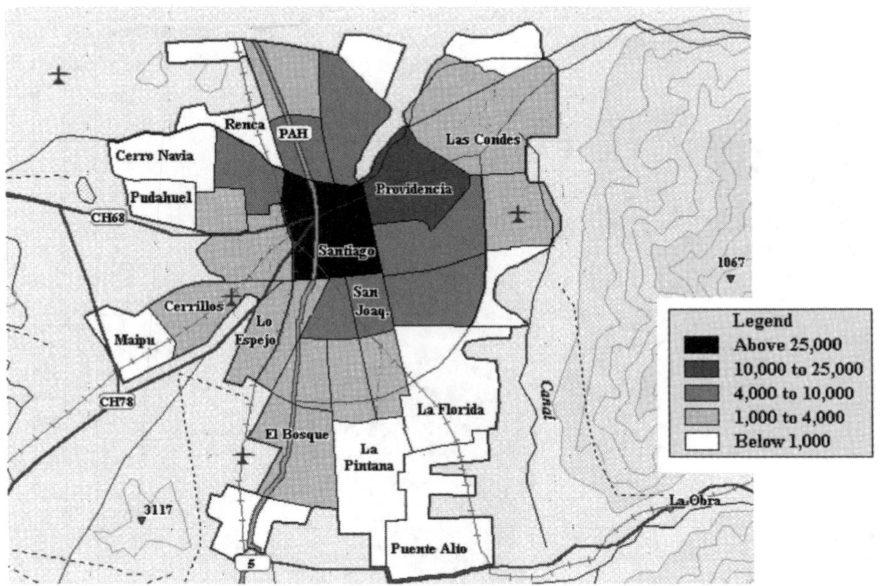

Map E. Employment Density (per square km) for 1991

The home *comuna* was the second largest employer for residents. For those *comunas* identified as having the fastest growing population in the 1980s—Maipu, Lo Barnechea, La Pintana, and Puente Alto—27% commuted to Santiago, 5% commuted within their own *comuna*, and 17% commuted to Providencia and Las Condes.

Income and Poverty

Despite the strong economic growth in Chile in the late 1980s, much of the population lived in poverty. Map F shows the 1990 poverty rates for select *comunas* as reported in the CASEN survey, using the previously reported poverty definitions. (See also Appendix B.) The average poverty rate for the twenty-five reported *comunas* was 34%.[22] As is the case in urban areas in many developing countries, the poor in Greater Santiago tended to be concentrated at the fringe of the city. There are significant concentrations of poor households in the south and east of the city. Five *comunas*—Cerro Navia, La Pintana, Penalolen, Quilicura and Renca—have poverty rates near or above 50%.

While data on income by *comuna* is scarce, the 1991 Origin-Destination

22. Poverty rates are not available for all *comunas*.

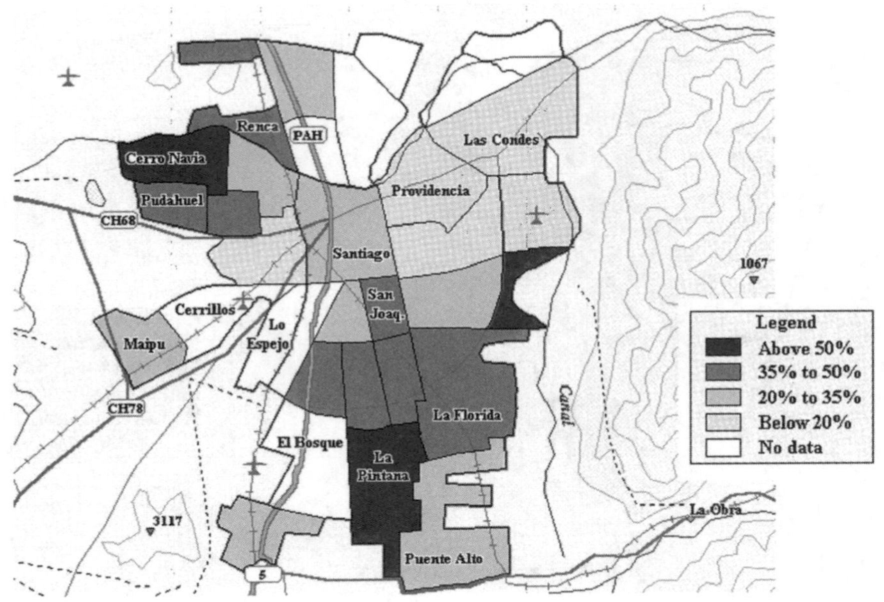

Map F. 1990 Casen Poverty Rates

Study reported distribution of households by income level. They divided income levels into eight categories, so there is not much detail. Map G shows the median income category for each *comuna* (Appendix B). Even with these somewhat crude data, it is clear that households are segregated by income level in Santiago. Particularly noticeable is the high income northeast corridor of the city. Not apparent from the map is the fact that in nearly all of the *comunas*, well over 50% of each *comuna*'s population is clustered within two or three adjoining income categories.

The Housing Market in Greater Santiago

As noted, one of the distinguishing features of the Chilean housing market is the primacy of homeownership. As can be seen in Map H, there is considerable variation in homeownership across *comunas*, ranging from a high of 90.3% in La Pintana to a low of 56.3% in the Santiago comuna (see Appendix B.)[23] Contrary to experience in the U.S. (where the national homeownership rate is 64%), homeownership seems inversely related to in-

23. In these data, the overall homeownership rate is 76.6%. The discrepancy between this homeownership rate and the 80% in Table 6-1 may be in part due to a difference in geographic definitions.

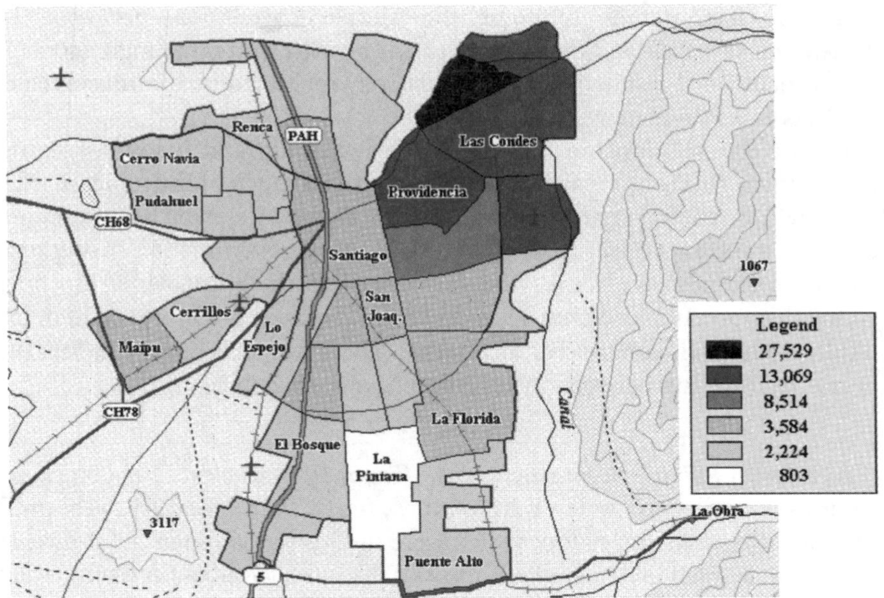

Map G. 1991 Median Annual Income (1992 US$s)

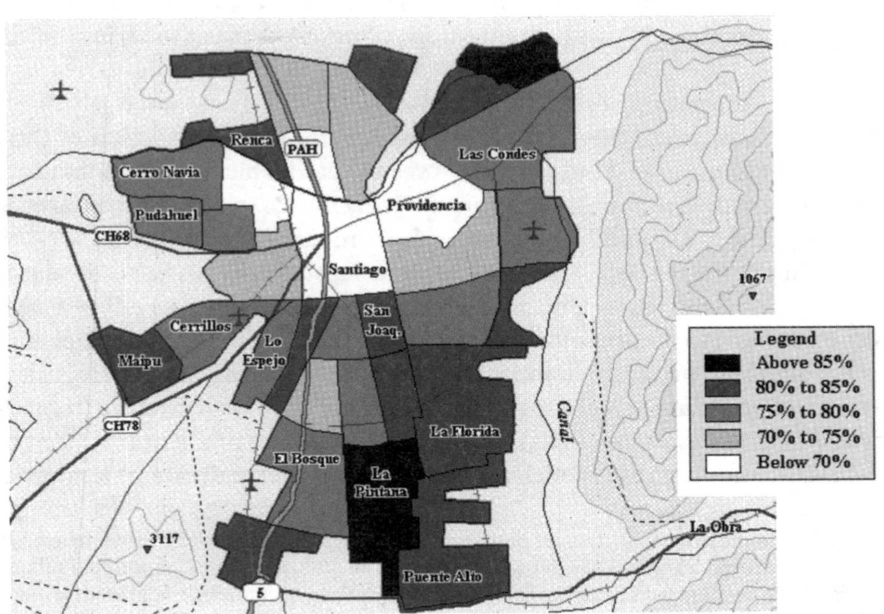

Map H. 1991 Homeownership Rates

come. In fact, across *comunas* the simple correlation between the homeownership rate and the poverty rate is positive and quite high at 0.47.[24] The homeownership rate is lowest in relatively high income *comunas* such as Santiago and Providencia.

The inverse relationship between homeownership and income is counter-intuitive. This result may be due to the fact that much of the rental market for poor households is an informal market that may not be accurately reflected in the data. However, the exclusive focus of government housing programs for the poor on homeownership drives up the homeownership rates among the poor. It is also clear the formal rental market is concentrated in the middle- to high-income end of the market. These two facts could produce the inverse relationship between income and homeownership.

Location of Publicly Subsidized Units. From 1988 to 1992, 203,000 housing units were constructed in R.M. Of these units, 70,000, or 40%, were publicly subsidized, virtually all of which were in Greater Santiago. As shown in Map I and detailed in Appendix C, most of the publicly subsidized units were located at the fringe of the metropolitan area with very large concentrations of this housing in *comunas* to the far south. La Pintana, Puente Alto, and La Florida contained over 40% of the publicly subsidized units produced in the city from 1988 to 1992. Many of these subsidized units were built in very large developments consisting of 350 or more units. As a result, the housing programs developed large concentrations of poor people at the fringe of the city.

This concentration of subsidized housing at the fringe seems largely due to the lower land prices there. MINVU contracts for the construction of these units went to the lowest bid per unit. It seems reasonable to assume that construction costs were roughly constant across *comunas* in Greater Santiago. As a result, land costs would be the major determinant of location.

As illustrated in Map J, land prices were substantially lower to the south and west of Santiago where most of the subsidized units have been constructed. (See Appendix B for details.) While there are some anomalies such as the high land prices in Vitacura, at the northeast fringe of the metropolitan area, land prices in Greater Santiago generally declined with distance from the center (the Santiago *comuna*), following the land price gradient predicted by the classic monocentric model of an urban area. Our estimate of land price

24. The homeownership rates are based on national surveys that include inadequate units, such as shacks and lean-tos, though undoubtedly not all of this housing is captured. Probably the rates also are clouded somewhat by unreported doubling up, although significant levels of *allegados* are included in census results.

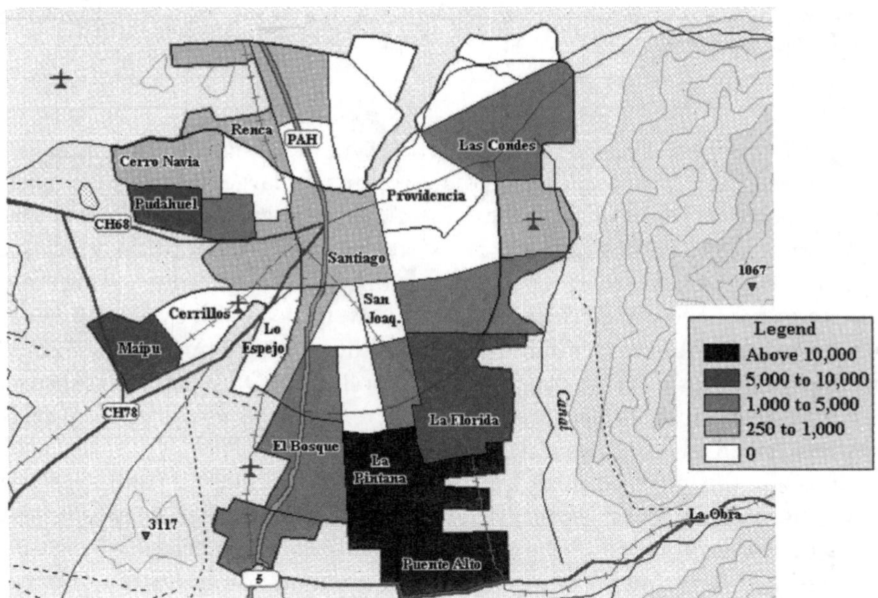

Map I. Total Number of Subsidized Housing Units Added from 1988 to 1992

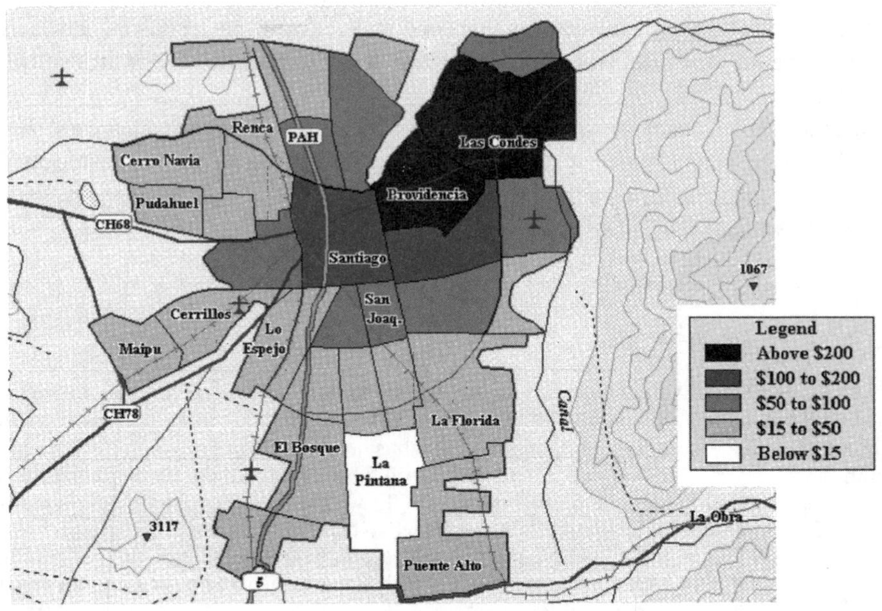

Map J. 1992 Land Prices per Square Meter (1992 US$s)

gradients indicates that land prices fell 8.2% with a one-kilometer increase in distance from the center.[25]

Are There Spatial Distortions? Potentially, there are significant spatial distortions resulting from locating subsidized units on large, inexpensive tracts of land. For many households, these locations were far away from employment opportunities. For example, for La Pintana and San Bernardo residents, Santiago was the dominant work destination; the average commuting time per trip to Santiago was 62.1 and 54.2 minutes, respectively, by public transportation, mostly buses (see Table 6-8). In addition to the time costs of commuting, these trips increase congestion and pollution. Other substantial costs may have been incurred because families were forced to move far from relatives and friends to get their unit.

Although the poverty rates and income data of Maps F and G show greater numbers of poor people living at the *comunas* farther away from the center of Santiago, locating the subsidized housing at the fringe of the city often resulted in recipients being forced to leave their communities. The implementation of MINVU's programs overwhelmingly resulted in very large projects, often built on entirely undeveloped land. By definition, this meant moving to the farthest edge of existing developments. In addition, MINVU's projects do not include razing existing housing. These modern programs, unlike some Chilean programs earlier in the century, revolved entirely around newly built developments, not the redevelopment of existing settlements.[26]

Finally, considerable anecdotal and documented evidence suggests that MINVU's current programs cause significant relocation of the new residents.

---

25. The estimated land price gradient is:

$$\log(\text{Price}) = \underset{(0.84)}{4.63} - \underset{(0.03)}{0.082u}$$

$$R^2 = 0.16 \qquad N = 34$$

26. As early as 1906, the Chilean government began demolishing units because of poor quality and sanitation problems (9000 units in Santiago between 1906 and 1925) (Trivelli 1987, 12). Until 1980 the dominant mechanism for establishing low-income housing was through political seizures of land by the poor. This land, all on the periphery of the city, supported unregulated makeshift campgrounds and shacks, tacitly accepted by the government. Literally hundreds of thousands of unregulated units were set up between 1930 and 1980 (Trivelli 1987, Kusnetzoff 1993). Beginning in 1980, government housing policy began explicitly addressing these *campamentos*, and the dominant activity in public lower-income housing was the regularization and relocation of these squatter towns (Trivelli 1987, 13–14 and 161; Kusnetzoff 1993).

Table 6-8. *Land Costs and Commuting Data*

All lots average land prices

	Land Costs							*Work Trips**				
	1992 Average Cost	*Total Lot Cost*		*Annual Cost at 12%*								
				10 years		*20 years*		*% to*	*% in home*	*Total*	*Work Trips to*	*Time to Santiago*
	(US$/SM)	*100 SM*	*60 SM*	*100 SM*	*60 SM*	*100 SM*	*60 SM*	*Santiago*	*Comuna*	*Work Trips*	*Santiago*	*(minutes)*
FRINGE COMUNAS												
La Pintana	8.03	803	482	142	85	108	65	30.8%	7.0%	70,775	21,799	62.1
Puente Alto	15.96	1,596	958	282	169	214	128	23.4%	22.3%	90,787	21,244	71.0
San Bernardo	23.20	2,320	1,392	411	246	311	186	26.3%	23.9%	52,764	13,877	54.2
TARGET COMUNAS												
Cerrillos	21.65	2,165	1,299	383	230	290	174	32.4%	19.6%	31,450	10,190	46.6
Cerro Navia	19.25	1,925	1,155	341	204	258	155	25.3%	8.4%	58,332	14,758	44.4
Lo Espejo	33.39	3,339	2,003	591	355	447	268	27.2%	10.5%	44,583	12,127	44.7
Pedro Aguirre Cerda	23.77	2,377	1,426	421	252	318	191	37.4%	2.8%	62,511	23,379	42.2
Renca	39.17	3,917	2,350	693	416	524	315	27.3%	17.6%	51,701	14,114	39.1
AVERAGE FOR 34 COMMUNAS	73.92	7,392	4,435	1308	785	990	594	30.6%	14.96%	1,836,600	562,000	NA

Sources: Land costs: Mercado 1993.
Work trips and travel time: Mideplan Origin-Destination Study 1992.
Employment data: INE 1993.
*Work trips were calculated by using total number of trips by *comuna* for all transportation modes, for the purpose of work, for morning rush hour (7:00–8:30 a.m.). These data gave the percentages of work trips to Santiago and within each *comuna*. Distribution of total morning rush hour trips was then applied to total employment figures for Greater Santiago, taken from the 1993 INE, to estimate total daily work trips.

A 1985 private study of residents in new projects reported that 47.5% of the displaced population at that time said they would immediately return to their previous location and living conditions if allowed to do so, even given the poorer conditions they previously lived in.[27] Among the reasons cited were removal from the city proper and less access to urban opportunities; smaller size units; lack of public space, urban amenities and important neighborhood infrastructure such as health and education facilities; higher transportation costs; destruction of previous neighborhoods and social networks; and job loss. In this study, 14.3% claimed that they lost their jobs due to relocation. Still, poor families in Chile who want to consume higher quality housing often rely on the units provided by MINVU's programs. The choice of unit under these programs is very limited since the waiting lists for units are long (often many years) and if a household does not take the first unit offered it moves to the bottom of the list.

Would these fringe locations have been chosen for subsidized units if housing policymakers considered the total costs of these locations rather than just the land and construction costs? In the standard monocentric urban models of Alonso (1964), Muth (1969) and Mills (1972), consumers trade off land costs against commuting costs. Land prices are in equilibrium when any benefit from moving farther from the center that takes the form of lower land prices is exactly offset by the increase in commuting costs. No household is better off by changing location. In other words, land prices are lower at more distant locations precisely because of increases in commuting costs. It is clear that the presence of location-specific subsidies alters the household's tradeoff between land costs and commuting costs. In addition, the standard monocentric model does not consider externalities such as congestion and pollution.

Estimating the Magnitudes of Spatial Distortion. The question we try to answer is: Where would subsidized housing for the poor in Santiago be located if the total costs of that location were considered rather than just construction and land cost? Measuring the total cost of locating subsidized housing at a particular site is a difficult task. A wide variety of costs beyond land and construction costs should be considered in any such calculation. These costs include commuting costs (including out-of-pocket, time, and congestion costs), pollution costs from traveling greater distances, lost opportunities due to locations far from employment prospects, and the costs associ-

27. From "Estudio de Evaluacion el Programa de Erraicacion de Campamentos en la Region Metropolitana," Santiago, CEPA Consultores, 1985 (Trivelli 1987, 161).

ated with moving far from family, friends, and services.[28] In addition, there also may be costs imposed on the surrounding community when publicly subsidized units are built nearby. To the extent that wealthier households prefer not to live near poor households, the existence of subsidized units may decrease property values in the area. If increases in the number of low-income households are correlated with crime, the community may be viewed as more dangerous with more subsidized units. Clearly, the measurement of some of these costs is straightforward while the measurement of others is virtually impossible.

For the purposes of this paper, we sought to obtain some estimate of the magnitude of the costs and benefits of more central locations, closer to the employment center of Santiago and more accessible to important services and infrastructure than the more remote areas where the majority of subsidized housing is being built. Current subsidized housing programs in Chile tend to generate very big sites with a large number of units. The priority given to large developments may limit the opportunities to build subsidized housing projects in more central locations. While very large tracts of vacant land may be hard to find in more central *comunas*, there is vacant land available, providing opportunities for building subsidized units. In Santiago, for example, 18% of the central *comuna*'s land was undeveloped, according to a recent study by Catholic University. (Pontificia Universidad Catolica de Chile 1988).

Our calculations are done on a per unit basis ignoring the possible costs and benefits of large-scale development. While there may be efficiency gains associated with large-scale developments, there also may be substantial increases in infrastructure costs if large-scale development requires more remote sites.[29] Unfortunately, we cannot measure these benefits and costs. Assuming that the cost of constructing a subsidized housing unit is roughly the same throughout the metropolitan area, the increase in land cost is the major extra cost of constructing a unit in a more central *comuna*.

Therefore, we begin by estimating the additional land costs that would

---

28. Other costs of such policies arise from the social problems resulting from large concentrations of poor. In the United States there has been extensive experience with large-scale housing projects that tend to isolate the poor in marginal neighborhoods. See William Julius Wilson's (1987, pp. 25–39, 56–62) discussion of social isolation and concentration effects in ghetto and inner city public housing projects in the United States. In addition, evidence suggests that the quality of neighborhoods has significant impact on education as well as on future success in the labor market for young people.

29. We expect that infrastructure costs may vary across locations as well. While we do not have any explicit measures of these costs, we expect that access to roads and water and sanitation systems may well be less expensive in more developed *comunas* than at fringe locations.

arise from building a publicly subsidized unit in more centrally located *comunas.* We then compare those costs to some of the benefits of moving the household to these closer *comunas.* As with costs, many of the benefits of more central locations are difficult to quantify. If the subsidized housing unit were located in the more central *comuna,* the household would realize a decrease in commuting time, which would decrease commuting costs. In addition, if the commuter were traveling by bus, and fares were based on distance, there would be an out-of-pocket savings as well. If the commuter were traveling by car there would be out-of-pocket savings in terms of operating expenses due to the shorter commute. A shorter commute also should have an impact on air quality in Greater Santiago.[30] The benefits of being closer to employment opportunities as well as family and friends are clearly important but far more difficult to measure. In our calculations, we use a rather crude measurement of some of the benefits of a shorter commute as a way to begin thinking about the benefits to be weighed against the increased land costs of moving units in from the fringe. We find that simply by including estimates of benefits from shorter commutes and decreased pollution impacts, it is immediately apparent that there are several locations closer to the center of the city where the increased benefits outweigh the additional land costs.

We evaluated moving subsidized units from three *comunas*—La Pintana, Puente Alto, and San Bernardo, all in the south—which house 37% of the publicly subsidized units constructed between 1988 and 1992 to target *comunas* that are closer to Santiago. La Pintana and Puente Alto have consistently been popular sites for significant numbers of publicly subsidized units. San Bernardo, while accounting for a smaller portion of units, seems to have attracted more subsidized units in recent years. While San Bernardo attracted 3% of 1990's units and 4% of 1991's units; it doubled to 8% of the units in 1992.

The target *comunas* considered are Cerrillos, Cerro Navia, Lo Espejo, Pedro Aguirre Cerda and Renca, all closer to the center of the city. Table 6-8 shows the average 1992 land costs per square meter in the fringe *comunas* and the target *comunas.* The land values are the average across all lots sold in the comuna across four quarters of 1992 (Mercado 1993). Even these crude average land costs vary considerably across these *comunas,* from $8.03/square meter in La Pintana to $39.17 in Renca. If we were to consider more central

30. We should also note that the Chilean Government made a very large investment in a subway system with plans for expansion. Even with the expansion, the system will only go as far south as La Granja. The system is currently underutilized. While we leave the analysis of the wisdom of building the system to others, the system exists, and there may be considerable benefits to locating subsidized housing units near this system in terms of reducing congestion and pollution from commuting.

comunas such as Santiago and Providencia where land prices are considerably higher, the variation would be much greater.[31]

When examining the land cost differentials, it should be remembered that the land prices are based on average land prices for all lot sizes by *comuna*. There may be considerable variation in land prices within a *comuna* and price will vary with the size of the lot (e.g., some parcels in San Bernardo may be less expensive than some parcels in the target *comunas*, while other parcels may be more expensive). However, average land prices do still provide a useful starting point for illustrating the impact of choosing different locations. It also should be noted that while average land prices by *comuna* generally fall with distance from Santiago, this is not always the case. In Table 6-8, the average land price in San Bernardo is higher than those in the target *comunas* of Cerrillos and Cerro Navia.

Current regulations suggest that the minimum lot size for a house in Greater Santiago is 100 square meters. However, subsidized units are often constructed with considerably less land per unit. In this analysis, we consider lot sizes of 60 and 100 square meters. As can be derived from Table 6-8, a 100 square meter lot in Renca, on average, is $3,117 more than a 100 square meter lot in La Pintana. Moving a unit from San Bernardo to Cerro Navia, however, could result in a $395 savings in land costs. These changes in land costs are substantial, given that house prices are typically between $5,000 and $10,000.

Given that households in Santiago tend not to move very often, we assume that households stay in their units for ten or twenty years. We calculate the annual cost of the increase in land prices by assuming a 12% discount rate for both a ten-year and twenty-year tenure for the two lot sizes.[32] The last four columns of the Land Costs section in Table 6-8 show these annual costs. The largest annual land cost differential occurs when moving from La Pintana to Renca at $551 for each of ten years for a 100 square meter lot, and $331 a year for a 60 square meter lot. Relocating a unit on a 100 square meter lot from Puente Alto to Cerrillos or Cerro Navia would only cost $101 and $59 per year, respectively (based on a ten-year term).

To calculate commuter savings, we assume, for simplicity's sake, that each household has one commuter, who works in the Santiago *comuna* and uses public buses.[33] Although we simplify here, we do not believe we risk overstat-

31. The average 1992 land value across the 34 *comunas* was $74. The lowest value was $8.03 per square meter in La Pintana, and Providencia had the highest at $442.38. The central *comuna*, Santiago, had an average value of $190.35.

32. The Chilean Government used a 12% discount rate to evaluate transportation investments (Kain and Liu, Chapter 5).

33. The 1991 Origin-Destination Study reported that 85% of morning rush hour trips from our three fringe *comunas* to downtown Santiago were by bus.

ing commuter savings. First, although not everyone works in the Santiago *comuna*, Map D and Appendix B illustrate the dominance of Santiago as a work destination. Providencia, Las Condes, Vitacura, and Recoleta *comunas* are also major employment centers for workers living in our three fringe *comunas* (La Pintana, Puente Alto, and San Bernardo), and they are further north (that is, farther away than these southern fringe *comunas*). In addition, on average Greater Santiago had 1.4 outside-the-home workers per household in 1991. By assuming one worker, we err on the side of underestimating commuter savings. In Table 6-8, commuting times to Santiago for each *comuna* are shown. The time saved by moving from each fringe *comuna* to the target *comunas* ranges from 32 minutes by moving from Puente Alto to Renca to 7.6 minutes by moving from San Bernardo to Cerrillos. To convert to annual time saved, we assume two work trips a day and 250 workdays a year.

The value of time is estimated by taking one half the hourly wage times the hours saved per year (which is a standard calculation in the transportation literature). We use the average wage according to the AFP, Chile's private pension system.[34] In effect, this exercise represents taking a household with a single wage earner working in the Santiago *comuna* who earns the average AFP wage and examining the costs and benefits of moving that household to different locations.

Estimates of the annual value of time savings associated with moving from the fringe *comunas* to each of the target *comunas* are presented in the Time Savings rows of Table 6-9. The annual household benefits from commuting time savings range from $66.70 by moving from San Bernardo to Cerrillos, to $280 by moving from Puente Alto to Renca. Clearly, these savings estimates are dependent on our assumptions about household wages. Lower income households have a lower value of time and therefore would realize less savings from the move. On the other hand, the time savings calculations could increase substantially with more than one worker per household.

In Santiago, bus fares do not vary with distance so we do not consider a change in out-of-pocket travel costs in these calculations. This implies, though, that if bus fares were restructured to match costs better, the additional out-of-pocket savings from moving the commuter closer to the center of the city would be added to the benefit calculations in Table 6-9, increasing the attractiveness of moving households from fringe to target *comunas*.

Comparing the values of time savings to the land premiums provides little evidence that land cost differentials simply reflect the costs of longer com-

---

34. All employees must make contributions to the AFP pension system. The Superintendencia de AFP records wage rates and publishes average wages on a monthly basis. The average wage for March 1993 was $136,926 Chilean pesos, which converts to $4,212 annually in 1992 U.S. dollars.

Table 6-9 *Comparing Measured Costs and Benefits of Different Locations (in 1992 $s)*

Assuming 100 Square Meters per Unit

	Target Comuna				
Fringe Comuna	*Cerrillos*	*Cerro Navia*	*Lo Espejo*	*Pedro Aguirre Cerda*	*Renca*
La Pintana					
Land Premium*	241.05	198.58	448.83	278.57	551.13
− Time Savings	136.03	155.34	152.70	174.64	201.85
− Pollution Savings	5.43	6.20	6.09	6.97	8.05
= Total Cost	99.60	37.05	290.04	96.97	341.23
Puente Alto					
Land Premium	100.70	58.23	308.48	138.22	410.78
− Time Savings	214.14	233.44	230.81	252.75	279.96
− Pollution Savings	8.54	9.31	9.21	10.08	11.17
= Total Cost	**−121.98**	**−184.52**	68.47	**−124.61**	119.66
San Bernardo					
Land Premium	−27.43	−69.91	180.35	10.09	282.64
− Time Savings	66.70	86.01	83.37	105.31	132.52
− Pollution Savings	2.66	3.43	3.33	4.20	5.29
= Total Cost	**−96.79**	**−159.35**	93.66	**−99.42**	144.84

Assuming 60 Square Meters per Unit

	Target Comuna				
Fringe Comuna	*Cerrillos*	*Cerro Navia*	*Lo Espejo*	*Pedro Aguire Cerda*	*Renca*
La Pintana					
Land Premium	144.63	119.15	269.30	167.14	330.68
− Time Savings	136.03	155.34	152.70	174.64	201.85
− Pollution Savings	5.43	6.20	6.09	6.97	8.05
= Total Cost	3.18	**−42.39**	110.51	**−14.47**	120.78
Puente Alto					
Land Premium	60.42	34.94	185.09	82.93	246.47
− Time Savings	214.14	233.44	230.81	252.75	279.96
− Pollution Savings	8.54	9.31	9.21	10.08	11.17
= Total Cost	**−162.26**	**−207.81**	**−54.93**	**−179.90**	**−44.66**
San Bernardo					
Land Premium	−16.46	−41.95	108.21	6.05	169.59
− Time Savings	66.70	86.01	83.37	105.31	132.52
− Pollution Savings	2.66	3.43	3.33	4.20	5.29
= Total Cost	**−85.82**	**−131.39**	21.52	**−103.46**	31.78

*Land Premium is annual differential cost of land assuming a 10-year term at 12%.

mutes, as suggested by the simple monocentric model. In some cases, the value of time savings is considerably higher than the price differentials while in other cases the opposite in true. For example, the time savings from moving from a 100 square meter lot in Puente Alto to a similar lot in three of the five target *comunas* are considerably higher than the land costs differentials.

Longer commuting trips also contribute to the pollution problem in Greater Santiago. In their paper on pollution (Chapter 3), Kahn and Kerr estimate pollution costs per bus trip minute per person per year at approximately $0.35. This estimate is conservative in that it only measures the health effects of particulates and ozone damage from buses. It does not include damage from other pollutants, agricultural damage, or decreases in visibility. Using this conservative estimate, we calculate the value of the pollution savings per year for each move. These savings are presented in Table 6-9.

In Table 6-9, the land price differentials are compared with the value of the benefits from reduced commuting time and pollution savings. The results clearly show that in most cases there are more central *comunas* that are feasible for subsidized construction. Moving households, for example, from 100 square meter lots in San Bernardo to Cerrillos could save nearly $100 annually. (Calculations in Table 6-9 assume a ten-year term; assumption of a twenty-year term would further increase the attractiveness of moving from fringe to central *comunas* because the annual land premium would drop.) Moving households from Puente Alto to Cerrillos, Cerro Navia, or Pedro Aguirre Cerda would result in significant savings. If the lots of land were 60 square meters, moves from fringe to target *comunas* become even more attractive. In most of the cases, the time and pollution savings far exceed the increased land costs. Even moving from a 60 square meter lot in La Pintana to one in Cerrillos would only cost $3.18; moving from San Bernardo to Lo Espejo would cost $21.52. It may well be that the benefits not measured here from the more central location would be larger than this cost, making the move worthwhile. The calculations for San Bernardo are less clear. In our data, San Bernardo has higher average land costs than Cerrillos and Cerro Navia.

These calculations are crude. Many of the costs and benefits listed in the beginning of this section are not included in the calculations. In addition, the data used must be viewed as, at best, rough approximations. The calculations provided here, however, are likely conservative estimates given that they tend to understate the apparent benefits.

Even with these crude calculations it is clear that consideration of costs beyond land could result in a different location pattern for subsidized units. Given the extraordinary concentration of subsidized housing construction at the fringe of Santiago and the crude calculations that we present in this section, more attention should be given to measuring accurately the total costs and benefits of alternative locations.

Policy Recommendations

Current housing policy in Chile contributes to spatial distortions, either by limiting household mobility or by explicitly altering household location by the provision of housing units. The evidence also suggests that the formal rental housing market is limited to the upper end of the income distribution. It is virtually impossible to measure the extent of the informal market. However, the focus of government programs on homeownership results in relatively large subsidies being provided to some households with others receiving no subsidies. More households could be served through rental subsidies. In addition, the focus of government programs on homeownership may limit household mobility since the moving costs are considerably higher for owners than for renters. The subsidy structure, which encourages the purchase of new rather than existing structures, may limit the future marketability of these subsidized units.

In our work, the spatial distortions in the provision of units across regions were found to be relatively modest, with the extreme south and north regions and R.M. favored. The distribution of vouchers has favored R.M., which has received a higher share of both vouchers and voucher expenditures than would be indicated by its share of the country's population or housing deficit.

The regional distribution of vouchers and voucher expenditures is difficult to explain on the basis of the population and housing deficit data provided in this chapter. While it may be that vouchers are a more appropriate form of housing subsidies in some regional housing markets than in others, we have no basis from which to make an assessment for Chile's regional markets. In fact, we would need to understand how the various markets respond to vouchers versus construction subsidies.

The largest spatial distortions resulting from government-subsidized housing construction identified in this paper were in Greater Santiago. The location of these units in areas far from the center of the region imposes significant costs on residents of these units, as well as on all residents of the region. Locating units on the basis of only construction and land costs ignores significant costs such as pollution, congestion, and social isolation. While our calculations include only the costs and benefits that we could easily estimate, this work clearly suggests that a different spatial distribution of these units could result if total costs of locations were considered. While we did not examine the spatial distortions in other cities in Chile, it is clear that in the building of any subsidized housing units, the total costs and benefits should be considered, regardless of the region of the country.

In order to consider the total costs and benefits of different locations, there is a need to have more information. Our crude calculations are based on available data on the costs associated with land, transport, and pollution. It would be useful to have better information on house prices and rents by geographic unit (i.e., by *comuna* in Greater Santiago and by the appropriate geographic unit in other major cities and regions in the rest of the country). The pollution costs in our calculations also are very rough estimates focused only on the health effects of particulates and ozone damage from buses. A different approach to estimating the costs of pollution from the buses would be to estimate hedonic regressions of house values where the direct impact of pollution on house values is estimated. This approach would require data on house values, housing and neighborhood characteristics and measures of the spatial variation in air quality.

The results presented in this paper on spatial distortions created by publicly constructed housing in Santiago suggest that modifications to current housing policy may be warranted. To the extent that government continues to construct housing units, consideration should be given to moving away from very large projects to smaller, scattered sites. The large-scale projects may limit opportunities for more central locations. In addition, there may be substantial social costs to isolating the poor in very large developments at the fringe of the city. Perhaps the government should consider moving away from a public construction program and expanding the voucher programs. Households with vouchers would certainly consider commuting costs in their location decision and private developers would consider differences in land costs. However, neither households nor private developers would consider pollution costs. The government could solve this problem by imposing a tax on travel that would cover this external cost of travel. It is clear, though, that the recent policies of government construction of large developments of low-income resident-owned housing at the fringe of the city are generating significant additional costs to individuals and to society.

References

Alonso, William. 1964. *Location and Land Use.* Harvard University Press: Cambridge, Massachusetts.

Fischel, William A. 1990. "Introduction: Four Maxims for Research on Land-Use

Controls." *Land Economics.* Vol. 66, No. 3. Madison, Wisconsin: University of Wisconsin Press.

Glaeser, Edward L. 1993. *The Political Economy of Urban Development.*

INE. 1991. INE Compendio Estadicstico. Instituto Nacional de Estadicsticas.

INECON. 1993. "Analisis Sobre el Desarrollo de la Infraestructura en la Regiones V, VI y Metropolitana." Comite Interministerial de Infraestructura. Chile.

Kain, John F. and J. Meyer. "Lessons and Summary: The Public/Private Frontier in Urban Development." Chapter 5 of this volume.

Kahn, Matthew E. and Suzi C. Kerr. 1994. *The Environmental Consequences of Growth in Santiago.* Chapter 4.

Kusnetzoff, Fernando. 1993. "Urban Housing Under Chile's Military Dictatorship, 1973–1985" in *Latin American Perspectives.* Series No. 11. London: Latin American Bureau.

Stephen Mayo, Stephen Malpezzi, and David Gross. "Shelter Strategies for the Urban Poor in Developing Countries," in *World Bank Research Observer,* Vol. 1, No. 2, July, 1986, pp. 183-203.

Melo Z., Pedro. 1993. *Lecciones de la Generacion y Gestion de Carteras Hipotecarias Estatales: El Caso del Ministerio de Vivienda Chileno.* Primer Seminario Internacional Sobre la Experiencia Chilena en Financiamiento Habitacional. CIEDESS; Santiago, Chile.

Mercado de Suelo Urbano en El Area Metropolitana de Santiago. July 1993. Boletin No 44. Second Quarter.

Mideplan. 1992. CASEN 1990: Poblacion, Educacion, Vivienda, Salud, Empleo y Pobreza. Santiago, Chile.

Mideplan. 1992. *Encuesta Origen-Destino de Viajes del Gran Santiago 1991,* Volumes III and IV. Santiago, Chile.

Mills, Edwin S. 1972. *Studies in the Structure of the Urban Economy.* Johns Hopkins: Baltimore.

MINVU. 1989. "Antecedentes Regionales de la Situacion Habitacional en Chile. Documentos de Trabajo." September.

MINVU. 1989. Ministerio de Vivienda y Urbanismo—Chile: Memoria Annual. Santiago, Chile.

MINVU. 1990. Ministerio de Vivienda y Urbanismo—Chile: Memoria Anual. Santiago, Chile.

MINVU. 1991. Ministerio de Vivienda y Urbanismo—Chile: Memoria Anual. Santiago, Chile.

MINVU. 1992. Ministerio de Vivienda y Urbanismo—Chile: Memoria Anual. Santiago, Chile.

MINVU. 1993a. Ministerio de Vivienda y Urbanismo—Chile: Memoria Anual. Santiago, Chile.

MINVU. 1993b. Inforrne de Regiones, Tables for years 1991 and 1992. Santiago, Chile.

Muth, Richard. 1969. *Cities and Housing.* University of Chicago Press: Chicago.

Pontificia Universidad Catolica de Chile. 1988. *Investigaciones de Alternativas de Sistemas Habitacionales Resumen Y Conclusiones.* Santiago, Chile.

Renaud, Bertrand. 1988. "Housing Under Economic and Structural Adjustment in Chile: An Innovative Approach to Finance and Production." INURD Working Paper. The World Bank: Washington, D.C.

Trivelli, Oyarzun and Pablo Arturo. 1987. "Intra-Urban Socio-Economic Settlement Patterns, Public Intervention, and the Determination of the Spatial Structure of the Urban Land Market in Greater Santiago, Chile: A Thesis in Partial Fulfillment of the Requirements for the Degree of Doctor of Philosophy." Cornell University: Ithaca, New York.

Wilson, William Julius. 1987. *The Truly Disadvantaged: The Inner City, the Underclass, and Public Policy.* University of Chicago Press: Chicago.

The World Bank. 1992. "World Development Report 1992: Development and the Environment." Washington, D.C.

The World Bank. 1993. "The Housing Indicators Program, Volume II: Indicator Tables." Washington, D.C.

Appendix A
Private Residential Construction for Chile and R.M., 1980–1992*

	Chile	*R.M.*
1980	44,438	23,125
1981	53,961	35,176
1982	26,900	13,652
1983	36,860	18,218
1984	46,493	23,002
1985	60,884	30,908
1986	51,404	23,952
1987	58,924	29,255
1988	74,880	38,477
1989	82,520	38,106
1990	78,621	34,927
1991	86,990	42,595
1992	105,266	49,437

*See Chart B.
Source: INE 1993.

Appendix B: Greater Santiago Comunas (1992 US$)

Comuna	Estimated Distance to Center (kms)	POPULATION 1982 Population	1992 Population Map A)	Population Growth 1982–92 (Map C)	1982 Density	1992 Density (Map B)
CERRILLOS	7.98	67,013	72,137	7.65%	3,221.8	3,468.1
CERRO NAVIA	9.12	137,777	154,973	12.48%	12,525.2	14,088.5
CONCHALI	8.36	157,884	153,089	–3.04%	14,894.7	14,442.4
EL BOSQUE	13.49	143,717	172,338	19.91%	10,339.4	12,398.4
ESTACION CENTRAL	4.75	147,918	142,099	–3.93	10,718.7	10,297.0
HUECHURABA	10.64	56,313	61,341	8.93%	1,271.2	1,384.7
INDEPENDENCIA	4.56	86,724	77,539	–10.59%	11,719.5	10,478.2
LA CISTERNA	9.5	95,863	94,732	–1.18%	9,586.3	9,473.2
LA FLORIDA	12.54	191,883	334,366	74.26%	2,733.4	4,763.0
LA GRANJA	10.83	109,168	126,038	15.45%	10,916.8	12,603.8
LA PINTANA	15.96	73,932	153,586	107.74%	2,440.0	5,068.8
LA REINA	12.54	80,452	88,132	9.55%	3,452.9	3,782.5
LAS CONDES	12.54	175,735	197,417	12.34%	1,784.1	2,004.2
LO BARNECHEA	20.9	24,258	48,615	100.41%	23.6	47.2
LO ESPEJO	7.6	124,462	119,899	–3.67%	17,529.9	16,887.2
LO PRADO	6.84	103,575	110,883	7.06%	15,693.2	16,800.5
MACUL	7.6	113,100	123,535	9.23%	9,195.1	10,043.5
MAIPU	13.3	114,117	257,426	125.58%	869.8	1,962.1
NUNOA	5.89	168,919	165,536	–2.00%	10,363.1	10,155.6
PEDRO AGUIRRE CERDA	6.46	145,207	128,342	–11.61%	14,817.0	13,096.1
PENALOLEN	12.92	137,298	178,728	30.18%	2,500.9	3,255.5
PROVIDENCIA	5.32	115,449	110,954	–3.89	8,130.2	7,813.7
PUDAHUEL	10.26	97,578	136,642	40.03%	495.8	694.3
PUENTE ALTO*	19	113,211	254,534	124.83%	1,289.4	2,899.0
QUILICURA	12.54	22,605	40,659	79.87%	399.4	718.4
QUINTA NORMAL	5.32	128,989	115,964	–10.10%	10,486.9	9,428.0
RECOLETA	5.89	164,292	162,964	-0.81%	10,952.8	10,864.3
RENCA	8.36	93,928	129,173	37.52%	4,119.6	5,665.5
SAN BERNARDO*	16.72	129,127	188,580	46.04%	834.2	1,218.2
SAN JOAQUIN	6.27	123,904	112,353	–9.32%	12,515.6	11,348.8
SAN MIGUEL	5.7	88,764	82,461	–7.10%	9,343.6	8,680.1
SAN RAMON	10.64	99,410	101,119	1.72%	15,062.1	15,321.1
SANTIAGO	0	232,667	202,010	–13.18%	10,433.5	9,058.7
VICATURA	12.16	72,038	78,010	8.29%	2,518.8	2,727.6
FOR ALL COMUNAS	9.78	3,937,277	4,676,174	18.77%	1,737.5	2,063.5

Sources and Notes: Distance to Center estimated as straight-line map distance from center of comuna to center of Santiago comuna.
Population and density data from 1982 and 1992 Census.
Work trip, commuting time, and share of employment (from share of work trips) data from Origin-Destination Study, 1991.
"Redistributed Employment" and "Employment Density" calculated using 1993 total employment for Region Metropolitana of 1,836,600, from INE, 1993.
Unemployment and Poverty rates from Casen 1990.
Income and Homeownership data from Origin-Destination Study, 1991.
Land prices from Land Bulletin, July 1993.

APPENDIX B: CONTINUED

EMPLOYMENT

1991 A.M. Rush Hour Work Trips to Comuna	*Redistributed Employment*	*1991 Share of Employment (Map D)*	*Employment Density (Map E)*	*1990 Unemployment Rate*
14,937	32,655	1.8%	1,551.33	
4,808	10,511	0.6%	952.9757	14.2%
10,161	22,214	1.2%	2,032.4	6.5%
9,080	19,851	1.1%	1,390.114	
23,970	52,404	2.9%	3,579.479	7.0%
1,785	3,902	0.2%	86.06956	
24,415	53,376	2.9%	7,203.299	
13,801	30,172	1.6%	3,017.196	13.4%
26,121	57,106	3.1%	705.0139	10.5%
5,708	12,479	0.7%	1,247.892	13.2%
6,320	13,817	0.8%	455.1014	14.9%
11,093	24,252	1.3%	1,054.421	3.2%
53,141	116,178	6.3%	1,205.663	3.3%
4,463	9,757	0.5%	9.512975	
6,271	13,710	0.7%	1,713.719	
4,338	9,484	0.5%	1,450.123	10.7%
24,451	53,455	2.9%	4,205.755	5.7%
13,019	28,462	1.5%	216.2463	6.3%
43,701	95,540	5.2%	5,686.892	3.8%
4,357	9,525	0.5%	1,101.195	
7,107	15,537	0.8%	303.7027	9.1%
86,205	188,463	10.3%	13,509.87	5.0%
5,509	12,044	0.7%	61.12703	9.4%
17,117	37,421	2.0%	428.31	5.3%
4,970	10,865	0.6%	200.5813	9.2%
22,217	48,571	2.6%	4,067.935	6.5%
29,492	64,476	3.5%	4,029.741	
9,570	20,922	1.1%	883.907	7.9%
12,266	26,816	1.5%	179.9256	13.3%
24,822	54,266	3.0%	5,448.417	5.6%
27,630	60,405	3.3%	6,305.337	3.4%
5,248	11,473	0.6%	1,818.266	7.8%
264,233	577,670	31.5%	25,225.77	5.6%
17,756	38,818	2.1%	1,404.938	
840,082	1,836,600	100.0%	810.5	NA

Appendix B: Continued

	INCOME		LAND COSTS	OTHER	
Comuna	1990 Poverty Rate (Map F)	1991 Median Annual Income (US$s) (Map G)	1992 Average Cost (all lot sizes) (US$s/SM) (Map J)	1991 Homeownership Rate (Map H)	Public Transit Time to Santiago (minutes)
CERRILLOS		2,224	21.65	79.8%	46.6
CERRO NAVIA	58.6%	2,224	19.25	78.6%	44.4
CONCHALI	32.0%	2,224	27.70	74.5%	39.5
EL BOSQUE		2,224	25.00	79.8%	52.2
ESTACION CENTRAL	12.5%	2,224	62.26	73.7%	34.2
HUECHURABA		2,224	36.87	82.9%	50.1
INDEPENDENCIA		3,584	92.83	67.7%	30.9
LA CISTERNA	40.0%	3,584	45.52	71.2%	41.8
LA FLORIDA	38.8%	3,584	24.55	81.4%	57.6
LA GRANJA	46.1%	2,224	18.75	80.7%	51.6
LA PINTANA	55.2%	803	8.03	90.3%	62.1
LA REINA	13.8%	13,069	84.09	77.6%	48.2
LAS CONDES	5.0%	13,069	281.02	77.3%	41.1
LA BARNECHEA		13,069	55.15	86.9%	55.1
LO ESPEJO		2,224	33.39	76.7%	44.7
LO PRADO	42.7%	2,224	36.58	79.8%	37.0
MACUL	21.4%	3,584	63.31	75.9%	45.9
MAIPU	28.2%	3,584	35.72	82.0%	49.7
NUNOA	10.7%	8,514	184.78	71.0%	37.1
PEDRO AGUIRRE CERDA		2,224	23.77	80.0%	42.2
PENALOLEN	50.2%	2,224	36.25	81.5%	50.0
PROVIDENCIA	7.9%	13,069	442.38	64.4%	30.8
PUDAHUEL	42.3%	2,224	28.01	79.7%	42.9
PUENTE ALTO*	29.5%	2,224	15.96	82.6%	71.0
QUILICURA	46.5%	2,224	22.81	81.2%	48.6
QUINTA NORMAL	29.2%	2,224	43.05	66.4%	38.0
RECOLETA		2,224	51.03	71.8%	39.9
RENCA	46.7%	2,224	39.17	81.5%	39.1
SAN BERNARDO*	27.1%	2,224	23.20	82.0%	54.2
SAN JOAQUIN	37.0%	3,584	59.15	80.0%	40.2
SAN MIGUEL	31.7%	3,584	73.04	75.2%	36.9
SAN RAMON	41.8%	2,224	24.84	79.8%	52.1
SANTIAGO	31.7%	3,584	190.35	56.3%	25.3
VITACURA		27,529	383.67	81.9%	45.7
FOR ALL COMUNAS	33.8%	3,584	73.92	76.6%	NA

Sources and Notes: Distance to Center estimated as straight-line map distance from center of comuna to center of Santiago comuna.
Population and density data from 1982 and 1992 Census.
Work trip, commuting time, and share of employment (from share of work trips) data from Origin-Destination Study, 1991.
"Redistributed Employment" and "Employment Density" calculated using 1993 total employment for Region Metropolitana of 1,836,600, from INE, 1993.
Unemployment and Poverty rates from Casen 1990.
Income and Homeownership data from Origin-Destination Study, 1991.
Land prices from Land Bulletin, July 1993.

Appendix C: Greater Santiago *Comunas* MINVU Housing Production (Map I)

	1988			*1989*		
Comuna	*Basic*	*Special*	*Total*	*Basic*	*Special*	*Total*
CERRILLOS			0			0
CERRO NAVIA	796		796			0
CONCHALI		512	512			0
EL BOSQUE			0			0
ESTACION CENTRAL		512	512			0
HUECHURABA			0			0
INDEPENDENCIA			0			0
LA CISTERNA			0	1,003		1,003
LA FLORIDA		1,508	1,508	3,055	226	3,281
LA GRANJA			0	1,367	102	1,469
LA PINTANA	1662		1,662	4,392		4,392
LA REINA		263	263			0
LAS CONDES	420		420	1,250		1,250
LO BARNECHEA			0			0
LO ESPEJO			0			0
LO PRADO		472	472		890	890
MACUL		495	495		572	572
MAIPU	1191		1,191	738	363	1,101
NUNOA			0			0
PEDRO AGUIRRE CERDA			0			0
PENALOLEN			0	134		134
PROVIDENCIA			0			0
PUDAHUEL			0		740	740
PUENTE ALTO*	1144		1,144	776		776
QUILICURA			0		155	155
QUINTA NORMAL			0			0
RECOLETA			0			0
RENCA			0		550	550
SAN BERNARDO*	686		686		320	320
SAN JOAQUIN			0			0
SAN MIGUEL			0			0
SAN RAMON			0			0
SANTIAGO			0			0
VITACURA			0			0
TOTAL	5899	3,762	9,661	12,715	3,918	16,633

Source: MINVU 1989–1993a and 1993b.

Appendix C: Continued

	1990				1991			
Comuna	*Basic*	*Special*	*Progressive*	*Total*	*Basic*	*Special*	*Progressive*	*Total*
CERRILLOS				0				0
CERRO NAVIA		140		140				0
CONCHALI				0	285			285
EL BOSQUE				0	1,168			1,168
ESTACION CENTRAL				0	136			136
HUECHURABA				0				0
INDEPENDENCIA				0				0
LA CISTERNA				0	1,080			1,080
LA FLORIDA		110		110		640		640
LA GRANJA		795		795	237	1,139		1,376
LA PINTANA	4,392			3,129	1,711	74	689	2,474
LA REINA		19		19				0
LAS CONDES	1,250			1,250				0
LO BARNECHEA				0				0
LO ESPEJO				0				0
LO PRADO		150		150		250		250
MACUL		144		144				0
MAIPU	1,915	363		2,278		1,352		1,352
NUNOA				0				0
PEDRO AGUIRRE CERDA				0	588			588
PENALOLEN	350	200		550	1,489			1,489
PROVIDENCIA				0				0
PUDAHUEL				0	1,830	609		2,439
PUENTE ALTO*		2,565		2,565	1,881	1,538	203	3,622
QUILICURA		516		516				0
QUINTA NORMAL				0				0
RECOLETA				0				0
RENCA				0				0
SAN BERNARDO*		372		372	682			682
SAN JOAQUIN				0				0
SAN MIGUEL				0				0
SAN RAMON				0				0
SANTIAGO				0				0
VITACURA				0				0
TOTAL	6,644	5,374	0	12,018	11,087	5,602	892	17,581

Source: MINVU 1989–1993a and 1993b.

APPENDIX C: CONTINUED

1992				1988–92	
Basic	*Special*	*Progressive*	*Total*	*Total*	*% of Total*
			0	0	0.0%
			0	936	1.3%
144			144	941	1.4%
708			708	1,876	2.7%
			0	648	0.9%
			0	0	0.0%
			0	0	0.0%
360			360	2,443	3.5%
300	376		676	6,215	8.9%
	563		563	4,203	6.0%
		488	488	12,145	17.4%
			0	282	0.4%
			0	2,920	4.2%
			0	0	0.0%
			0	0	0.0%
114			114	1,876	2.7%
			0	1,211	1.7%
240	957		1,197	7,119	10.2%
			0	0	0.0%
264			264	852	1.2%
1,416			1,416	3,589	5.2%
			0	0	0.0%
2,918	1,026		3,944	7,123	10.2%
741	1,371	296	2,408	10,515	15.1%
			0	671	1.0%
			0	0	0.0%
			0	0	0.0%
100			100	650	0.9%
660	431		1,091	3,151	4.5%
			0	0	0.0%
			0	0	0.0%
			0	0	0.0%
	256		256	256	0.4%
			0	0	0
7,965	4,980	784	13,729	69,622	100.0%

7

Spatial Distortions in the Provision of Social Services

EDWARD L. GLAESER

Introduction

When considering the locational implications of the provision of social services, there are two primary policy goals: (1) optimal service provision (where everyone consumes up to the point where the social benefit of his service consumption equals the social cost of that provision) and (2) spatial neutrality. The goal of spatial neutrality is to ensure that when locations decisions are made actors weigh social costs against social benefits.

Government services frequently violate spatial neutrality in two primary ways: (1) the prices of the services do not equal the cost of the services and (2) the service levels are set incorrectly in some locations. Both distortions occur when a particular government service is unpriced and available only in one location. For example, higher education was unpriced in Chile in the 1960s and available disproportionately in the capital; as a result there was a bias that may have induced migration to Santiago.

Other examples also exist. A service may be provided equally across space, and the charge for this service is equal across space (an example might be certain health expenditures). However, when a service costs different amounts in different locations, then uniform pricing suggests a probable subsidization of the high-cost location and, in fact, a spatial distortion.

The second major violation of spatial neutrality in government services comes when the wrong level of services is provided in one area relative to another. A classic example is when the same level of irrigation is provided across the country, and the same amount is charged in taxes for this quantity of irrigation. This level of water supply might be completely appropriate for one region of the country but entirely inappropriate for another.

Evidence on Social Welfare

Health and schooling are primary suspects for creating spatial distortions. A wide range of anecdotal evidence suggests that these services significantly effect the migration decision in many countries. For example, observers of migration to Mexico City or Lagos emphasize the differences in the quality and quantity of schooling and health care that can be received in these cities as compared to other cities or rural areas. In the United States, Glaeser, Scheinkman, and Shleifer (1995) document a strong connection between the number of educated persons in a city and migration to that city. This evidence is indirect, since a large number of educated persons may not necessarily reflect strong local provision of educational services. Nevertheless, the evidence is quite suggestive. The importance of education and health services makes it quite plausible that these services will affect migration. Less critical government services are less likely to create strong incentives for people to migrate in pursuit of the benefits that they provide.

Those individuals who value the future most will be more likely to respond to health and schooling provision (which, after all, pay off in the future) and also will be likely to migrate. The fixed costs of migration also will seem less relevant to these people relative to the future gains from migration.

Primary and Secondary Schooling

Chilean primary and secondary schooling has undergone significant changes over the past thirty-five years. There are two major periods of reform. The first period occurred from 1960–1973 when schooling budgets were expanded significantly. The second occurred from 1973 onwards. Within the later period, a more detailed study would focus on pre-1980 reforms and post-1980 reforms. The post-1980 reforms, in fact, directly shaped the form of modern Chilean education.

The First Transformation, 1960 to 1973

The reforms of the 1960s rapidly increased the scale of public education in Chile. In 1960, 9% of government expenditures went to education. By 1971, over 18% of government expenditures were so allocated. Over the same period, the government's share of GDP rose from 13.6% to 20.9% (measured in revenues). Accordingly, over the 1959–1973 period, the schooling share of GDP rose by more than 150%—a massive expansion of the educational sector.

Over the 1959–1973 period, government schooling expenditures were heavily targeted towards higher education. Before 1973, less than 40% of government educational expenditures were earmarked towards secondary and primary schools. At the same time, the eight major Chilean universities received a massive infusion of government funding. Indeed, the University of Chile was required, as per the General Budget Law of 1971, to receive at least 3.5% of the national budget. The differences between rural and urban schooling have always been striking in Chile. In 1960, 40% of the rural population was illiterate. By contrast, the urban illiteracy rate was only 14%. This gap had been lessened by the early 1970s, but the differences were still striking.

The Second Transformation, 1973 to Today

Post-1973, educational policy had several immediate effects on educational spending. Spending was reduced far more rapidly for higher education than for primary and secondary schooling. This change (which had its analogues in health care) was meant to be a means of concentrating government funding on early childhood education. At that time, focusing on primary schooling was widely thought to be a more efficient way of allocating educational expenditures in developing countries. This change also substantially altered the quantity of funding available to national universities. The overall reduction in funding was fairly temporary (the low point being 1976). By 1980, funding for Chilean education had almost returned to its 1973 levels. The changes of the 1970s also included a massive reorganization of teachers.

For the purposes of spatial policy, the most interesting changes in Chilean education came after the educational reform of 1980. These changes included (1) a massive decentralization of power in favor of localities; (2) an encouragement for private sector involvement in the provision of education; (3) the creation of new private universities; and (4) new wage provisions for teachers that gave municipalities the option of paying teachers based on negotiations rather than on the public sector pay scale. These changes were implemented extremely quickly and education was soon in the hands of municipalities and private entrepreneurs.

Unfortunately for advocates of local control, while the reforms nominally transferred control to local authorities many of the schools remained wards of the central government. Regulations issued by the central authorities closely tied the hands of local authorities and limited the extent to which schooling services could satisfy the demands of local constituents. So while the introduction of private schools (subsidized by vouchers) and local control represented major changes in the nature of Chilean education, a major gap persisted between reality and the decentralized/private system envisioned in the 1980 reforms.

The Situation circa 1990

The differences in the quality of education provided across regions in Chile have persisted during the 1990s. The most striking difference is the prevalence of subsidized private schools in the greater Santiago area. In 1988, 46% of primary school students and 57% of secondary school students in Greater Santiago were in subsidized private schools. The comparable national averages for all types of private schools were 38% and 46% respectively.[1]

These variations may create major differences in outcomes because private subsidized schools do seem to provide better education than their public counterparts. Test score differences between the two types of education are often greater than 10% in mathematics scores and over 15% in Spanish language scores. Of course, this may reflect differences in initial intellectual endowments, family support, and other factors as well as differences in school quality. Nevertheless, the differences in availability of private subsidized schools between Greater Santiago and elsewhere may alter significantly the quality of education being received in the different regions. Table 7-1 shows how enrollment is distributed among different types of schools in different regions. The Metropolitan Region of Santiago has by far the highest share of students enrolled in private subsidized schools (46%), and the lowest percentage in municipal schools.

Even within the public school sector, substantial differences are observable in test scores across regions. However, these data do not suggest that Greater Santiago has a particular advantage in test scores for its schools. The highest public school scores by region are often in the extreme north and south of the country (which may relate to a selection bias where the number of years completed is lowest in those regions).

Research on other outcomes by region indicates that while differences do exist in outcomes they are not overwhelming. Relative to a national average of 86.1%, Region IX achieves the lowest approval rate of 81.95%, while the highest rate of 91.14% is attained by the southernmost region of Magallanes and Antarctica. The evidence on the differences in years completed between Santiago and elsewhere in Chile is more worrying. Children in Santiago receive more than one year of schooling beyond the national average. Overall, the data suggest some important differences in the education being received in Santiago versus the rest of Chile.

1. Numbers from Compendio Estadistico 1991 and World Bank Report.

Table 7-1. *Private and public enrollment by region for level* basica regular, *1989*

Region		*Total*	*% Public*	*% Private*
I	Tarapacá	51,641	79.1	20.9
II	Antofagasta	64,442	78.5	21.5
III	Atacama	36,222	77.8	22.2
IV	Coquimbo	79,471	77.9	22.1
V	Valparaíso	203,339	59.9	40.1
VI	Gral. Bernado O'Higgins	107,968	76.9	23.1
VII	Maule	136,226	82.4	17.6
VIII	Biobío	278,408	75.9	24.1
IX	La Araucanía	134,729	60.7	39.3
X	Los Lagos	154,265	77.3	22.7
XI	Gral. Carlos Ibáñez del Campo	13,542	78.7	21.3
XII	Magallanes and Antarctica	20,251	73.9	26.1
	Greater Santiago	725,375	43.2	56.8
	TOTAL	2,005,879	62.3	37.7

Source: Compendio Estadistico, 1991

Before interpreting different educational outcomes by region as evidence of spatial distortions, at least two other factors need to be considered. First, differences in outcomes may come about because different regions have different costs associated with providing education. In that case, migration from low education regions might be efficient. Second, low educational outcomes may be the result of other factors, such as family inputs, and intellectually poorer families might not necessarily improve their outcomes by migrating.

Our studies on the different spending levels indicate there is apparently no government favoritism towards the Santiago region. If anything, Santiago is mildly penalized by having to subsidize schooling in most other regions. The net conclusion must therefore be that schooling outcome differences reflect one of three possible factors: (1) omitted forms of government spending in education; (2) differences between students of different regions (i.e. differences in the demand for human capital); and (3) differences in the costs of providing education. Only the first effect would suggest the existence of spatial distortions created by public policy.

Forms of spending omitted from this study could include a variety of hidden government expenditures that may go to schools in the Santiago area, ranging from subsidization of transport to school to easier access to government approval for private schools. Some forms of this type of hidden subsidization may exist, but it seems unlikely that it is a large and important enough part of overall spending to reverse the basic conclusion that there is little distortion attributable to the dispersion of government educational funds.

The second effect (differences between students) surely does exist. The needs and demands of rural students are surely different from those in Santiago. The government also may have a mandate to try and eliminate those differences. However, the focus should be on overall inequality not the inequality between the regions. Regional cross-subsidization (e.g. penalizing more able pupils in Santiago in favor of less able students elsewhere) would only add spatial distortions to the system.

There are also surely differences in the cost of providing education. The massive differences in private subsidized education between Santiago and elsewhere clearly suggest that these cost differences do exist. The presence of smaller class sizes (due to lower population densities) outside Santiago suggests that the inability to spread fixed costs over a large number of students may be one source of these higher costs. However, the fact that it is easier to provide education in Santiago is not an inefficiency. These cost differences should be experienced if migrants are to take into account the costs of providing them with education.

Our research also documents one major difference in primary and secondary education observable across regions, the provision of private subsidized vs. municipal schools. Santiago offers much more private subsidized education than municipal schooling. To determine that this represents any strong spatial distortion, further research would be needed. Again, if the difference occurs because of the lower costs of setting up private subsidized schools in Santiago, the difference in outcomes may not necessarily represent a spatial distortion.

College Education

The University of Chile is one of the most prestigious universities in all of Latin America (some might say it is the most prestigious). The Universidad Catolica has also had a remarkable history of excellence in both teaching and research. Public support for these two universities (and other smaller universities) has been massive. As mentioned previously, in the early 1970s the University of Chile was allocated more than 3.5% of the total national budget by law.

During the 1980s and early 1990s, new institutions of higher education sprung up throughout Chile. Smaller private colleges have flourished as the demand for higher levels of schooling has risen. Forces behind these colleges seem to include both heightened demand and a general governmental friendliness towards academic entrepreneurship. As a result, the number of students enrolled in universities, professional institutes, and technical training centers increased by about 31% between 1983 and 1989.

Table 7-2 shows the differences in higher education across regions. Santiago has a disproportionate number of the students in higher education. If this

Table 7-2. *Higher education by region, 1989*

Region		*Pop. (thou.)*	*% of total pop.*	*Enrollment in higher education (thou.)*	*% of total enrollment in higher education*
I	Tarapacá	363.4	2.7	6.8	3.0
II	Antofagasta	391.7	2.9	7.5	3.3
III	Atacama	201.5	1.5	1.9	0.8
IV	Coquimbo	489.4	3.7	6.7	2.9
V	Valparaíso	1,415.6	10.6	28.0	12.2
VI	Gral. Bernado O'Higgins	655.9	4.9	2.3	1.0
VII	Maule	857.4	6.4	7.5	3.3
VIII	Biobío	1,692.4	12.6	30.9	13.5
IX	La Araucanía	798.4	6.0	8.9	3.9
X	Los Lagos	934.6	7.0	12.4	5.4
XI	Gral. Carlos Ibáñez del Campo	80.8	0.6	0.1	0.0
XII	Magallanes and Antarctica	161.8	1.2	1.5	0.7
	Greater Santiago	5,342.9	39.9	115.1	50.1
	TOTAL	13,385.8	100.0	229.5	100.0

Source: Compendio Estadistico, 1991

is the outcome of differential federal funding, a sizeable spatial distortion may exist. If adjusted for the quality of higher education, the overrepresentation of Santiago would be even bigger. This spatial distortion becomes more important if there are positive externalities or spillovers connected with universities.

Santiago has Chile's two most important universities and also many of its less important ones. These educational institutions are massively subsidized by the government (more than 50% of their budgets are provided by governmental sources). Higher education and university enrollments are heavily centered in Santiago (with 49% and 45% of enrollments, respectively), as are government financial transfers to universities. The number of higher learning institutions is also concentrated in Santiago: more than 40% of the universities and 35% of higher education institutions are located there.

Of course, Santiago also has a disproportionate share of Chile's population, just under 40 percent. Furthermore, any spatial distortion created by Santiago's large shares of education may be efficient. If money spent in the hinterland would create less productive higher education than spending on the Santiago universities, then a cost in lost efficiency would be created by eliminating spatial distortions. In short, there probably is a spatial distortion created by public pending on higher education, but eliminating subsidies to the major universities may be a very costly way to eliminate this distortion.

Alternatively, greater subsidies might be given to schools outside Santiago to offset this possible distortion.

Health Programs in Chile—History

The history of government health policies in Chile has, like that of the history of schooling, displayed dramatic changes and stages. A period of reforms in the 1960s had a substantial impact on infant mortality rates, which fell from 119.6 per 1000 live births in 1960 to 70.5 per 1,000 live births in 1970. However the share of public health in total government expenditures did not rise over that period. By 1970, the life expectancy at birth had reached 65 years. However good this change was, these figures still suggested major health problems in Chile.

The reforms of the post 1973 regime substantially improved infant mortality figures. By the early 1990s, Chile's infant mortality rate has dropped to 18.5 per 1000 live births. In general, Chile's health improvements were quite striking in the 1960s, 1970s, and 1980s.

Like education, public health has undergone a transition away from extreme centralization. From 1952, when the National Health Service was established, to 1973, health provision was extremely centralized. Only with the post-1973 reforms was there an attempt to decentralize decision-making about health choices.

As in education, some attempt was made to give individuals choices between private and public health care. However, nowhere in health services are there institutions as pervasive as the private subsidized schools that provide such a large portion of education in certain areas of Chile. Within health care, decentralization mainly meant decentralization to regional provision away from central provision. Throughout the reforms the ministry of health retained its essential policy making control.

In no real sense can it be argued that regions competed among each other for patients or that regions were able to experiment independently or create innovative health care provisions. Some of the benefits of decentralization may have occurred as the central bureaucracy's direct role in provision was lessened but in many respects Chilean health care remained centralized.

Spatial Distortions

With health programs, as with education, there are two questions involved in determining the existence of spatial distortions: (1) are the outcomes uneven across regions? and (2) is government spending unequal across regions? As in the case of education, the answer to the first question is a tentative yes and the answer to the second question is no.

Table 7-3 provides data on health care by region. Individuals in Santiago are much likelier to have a doctor present when they give birth to a child. A vast variety of other measures suggest that the rural areas receive vastly different levels of health care from Santiago (or Valparaiso). It seems that the cities do enjoy better health care in some respects.

However, Table 7-3 suggests that the Santiago region is not an overwhelmingly healthier place to live. The particular advantages of living in the capital seem to be only in certain limited forms of health care and are confined to certain regions within the metropolitan area.

It is also clear that government spending is fairly equal across regions and that, if anything, interregional transfers favor the outlying regions over Santiago. For 1990, health subsidies per capita are much higher in the north and south of Chile than they are in Santiago. The cross-municipality transfers make up a much higher share of expenditures in those other regions. To the extent to which cash distributions are creating spatial distortions, these distortions are favoring certain outlying areas, not Santiago.

It seems that those regions with lower health-related outcomes must either have residents who are simply more likely to suffer from ill health or they have higher costs of providing health care. A variety of evidence suggests that both effects take place. There is extensive discussion in the literature of the difficulties in providing basic health care to rural areas and of the difficulties in inducing physicians to serve in distant regions. It is clearly cheaper and more ef-

Table 7-3. *National Health Services hospital beds by region, 1990*

Region		*Hospital beds*	*Persons per hospital bed*
I	Tarapacá	829	432
II	Antofagasta	977	399
III	Atacama	451	439
IV	Coquimbo	1,030	472
V	Valparaíso	4,395	314
VI	Gral. Bernado O'Higgins	1,490	436
VII	Maule	2,345	358
VIII	Biobío	4,470	375
IX	La Araucanía	2,306	345
X	Los Lagos	2,842	324
XI	Gral. Carlos Ibáñez del Campo	288	279
XII	Magallanes and Antarctica	439	364
	Greater Santiago	11,069	473
	TOTAL	32,931	400

Source: Compendio Estadistico, 1991

ficient to provide health care to 10,000 people concentrated over a few city blocks than to 10,000 people spread over thousands of square miles of hinterland.

Again, these differences in costs may make it appear that there is a spatial distortion. However, since the government is not over-allocating funds towards Santiago (and seems in fact to be allocating funds away from that city), government health expenditures are probably not providing distortions that induce individuals to come to the central city.

Other Social Welfare Programs

Chile has a variety of other social welfare programs. The largest of these is the pension plan, but smaller social insurance programs also exist. A preliminary investigation does not suggest the presence of much spatial distortion. The Santiago region has a high number of paid pensions per capita, but controlling for GNP, this advantage lessens. Still, there is enough spatial inequality in pensions that a possibility of some inequality merits further research.

The other programs are spatially related in many ways. One possibility is that access to government offices that are administering these programs differs across locations; but as long as expenditures on offices are equalized, these differences could represent a cost of provision difference and not a true distortion.

The Net Flow of Social Service Funds

A central empirical issue concerns whether there are some areas in Chile that receive more or fewer services than they are paying for. The first step is to establish whether government funding is equal (in a per capita sense) across regions. The inequality or equality of government spending is not, however, enough to confirm or deny the presence of spatial distortions. We must also ask whether there are differences in tax payments and individual characteristics across regions that are responsible for the differences in spending.

This decomposition is fully outlined in the appendix. The basic idea is that spatial distortions coming from spatial redistribution of income occur only when individuals receive more than they pay and this extra receipt is based on where they live. If the extra government spending on individuals arises because these individuals pay more taxes or because they are poor people who receive more from welfare programs, then this spending will not create spatial distortions. Only when this spending is based on location alone will spatial distortions emerge.

Conclusion

The overall conclusion is that there seem to be no major spatial distortions favoring Santiago in primary schooling, secondary schooling, or in public health provision. Any pro-Santiago spatial distortion that does exist seems to be a result of the concentration of higher learning within the capital city. This concentration may indeed bring about spatial distortions, but solutions to this problem are not obvious. Funding other institutions is not an obvious answer, since the funding of alternative universities may well be less productive than the funding of Catolica and the University of Chile. Furthermore, government spending differences actually favor outlying regions more than Santiago.

Reference

Glaeser, Edward L., Jose A. Scheinkman, and Andrei Shleifer. 1995. "Economic Growth in a Cross-Section of Cities." *Journal of Monetary Economics*, Volume 36, (August), pp. 117–144.

Appendix A:
Spatial Distortions of Government: Inputs vs. Outputs

The correct way of going from data on governmental actions to deducing whether or not that governmental action produces a spatial distortion is sometimes not obvious. This appendix presents a simple model that, hopefully, clarifies some of the issues. The model is not completely general, but much of its central points generalize fairly easily.

The model assumes a two-region world, where regions will be indexed by 1 and 2. Individuals have perfect mobility between the two regions. They also receive a wage premium or loss in moving to the first region; this premium (loss) will be noted W (i), where i is an index measuring the degree of desire to be in the first region. I assume that i is distributed uniformly on the unit interval, that the total population is 1 and that $W'(i)^{3}0$. All of these assumptions actually involve no significant loss of generality.

Individuals maximize wages plus government services minus tax levels. I will denote per capita expenditures on government services, El, where l = 1 or 2 depending on location. The actual amount of government services provided per person can be denoted Gl(El). I assume no public good aspects to this service nor any congestion (across people) in providing this service. Note that the production function for the goods differs by location. I also assume tax levels T1 and T2, which are assumed to be lump sum taxes. For the marginal migrant (noted i*):

(1) $W(i^*) + G1(E1) - T1 = G2(E2) - T2$, or

(1′) $i^*(E1, E2, T1, T2) = W-1(G2(E2) - T2 - G1(E1) + T1)$.

From the assumption on the distribution of i, i* in fact measures the size of the second region and 1−i* measures the population of the first region. I also assume a benevolent state that is interested in maximizing:

(2) $\circ\, i^*(E1, E2, T1, T2)1W(i)\, di + (1-i^*(E1, E2, T1, T2))\,(G1(E1) - T1) + i^*(E1, E2, T1, T2)(G2(E2) - T2)$,
subject to $(1-i^*)\, E1 + i^*E2^{2}\, (1-i^*)\, T1 + i^*T2$

The intuition of this is that the government sums up the total wage benefits being received by the recipients of Region I and the total government service benefits of the individuals in both regions, and subtracts the total tax bill. The government then just maximizes this subject to taxes equaling expenditures in equilibrium—no international borrowing is assumed here. Here (1) indicates that i* is a function of taxes and expenditures in the regions. When the government can choose both tax rates and expenditure levels, it is trivial to show that the first best is reached with $G1'(E1) = 1$ for both regions. When taxes are not allowed to differ, or by assumption do not differ, the governments optimization problem becomes more difficult. The first order conditions from taking the derivative with respect to the two expenditure levels and simplifying are as follows:

(3) $-G1'(E1)(E1 - E2)/W'(i^*) + (1 - i^*)(G1'(E1) - 1) = 0$, and

(4) $-G2'(E2)(E1 - E2)/W'(i^*) + i^*(G2'(E2) - 1) = 0$,

The first and most important result from these equations is that if the production functions differ in a way that effects average but not marginal costs of the public service then the government should equalize expenditures, i.e. when:

(5) $G1(E1) = G2(E2) + X$,

so that there is simply more of a public good in Region I, then the first order conditions (3) and (4) are satisfied when the government sets E1 equal to E2 equal to $G2'^{-1}(1)$ not when the government sets G1(E1) equal to G2(E2).

More generally, when the difference in the production function changes the marginal as well as the average cost, then things do become more complex. However, the basic result is not lost. In fact, usually the optimal difference in levels between communities becomes larger not smaller as the changes effect marginal as well as average service costs.

The intuition of these results is quite clear. It is not always a distortion to have different service levels across areas when tax levels are constant. In fact, it is much more of a distortion to equalize service levels. Such forced equalization eliminates the incentive for individuals to move where government services are cheapest, and eliminating that incentive is a major distortion.

Appendix B: Decomposing Regional Expenditures

The correct theoretical framework for thinking about regional expenditures is critical for both evaluating and operating spatial policy. This framework allows us to think about the size of current spatial distortions in the provision of public services and transfers. The particular innovation introduced here is looking at the degree to which we would expect regional spending to change based on the characteristics of individuals in the region. If government spending is meant to differ across agents (i.e. poorer people should get more unemployment support per capita) then since different regions have different agents, we would expect those different regions to have different regional expenditures. Looking at the net spatial distortions requires correcting for the different expenditures that should exist as a result of different levels of characteristics.

While this framework is useful in evaluating the current level of services, it is also critical in carrying out government policy. As argued extensively previously, the government will want to have a centralized transfer policy that is designed to redistribute income to different individuals. This transfer policy will result in having different levels of expenditures across regions. However, the non-transfer aspects of government services should not have different levels of spending across space. In order to evaluate whether the government is following this requirement, it is critical to separate out the amount of spending that is redistributional and the amount that is based on a return for taxes paid. This decomposition allows us to separate out those different forms of government spending.

The following decomposition gives a method of separating out the spatial aspects of government expenditures from other types of government expenditures.

$$
\begin{aligned}
(1)\quad & Ej(I, X)=T(I, X)({}^{\circ}\,{}^{\circ}Ej(I, X)dIdX/{}^{\circ\circ}T(I, X)dIdX) + \\
& (({}^{\circ}\,Ej(I, X)dI/{}^{\circ}\,P(I, X)dX) - \\
& (({}^{\circ}\,{}^{\circ}Ej(I, X)dIdX/{}^{\circ\circ}T(I, X)dIdX)({}^{\circ}T(I, X)dI/{}^{\circ}P(I, X)dI)) \\
& + (T(I,X) - {}^{\circ}T(I, X)dI/{}^{\circ}P(I, X)dI)))({}^{\circ}\,{}^{\circ}Ej(I, X)dIdX/{}^{\circ\circ}T \\
& (I, X)dIdX)((Ej(I, X) - ({}^{\circ}\,Ej(I, X)dI/{}^{\circ}\,P(I, X)dX))
\end{aligned}
$$

where Ej(I, X) is the amount spent on good j, a person with characteristics X in Region I, T(I, X) is the amount of taxes paid by individual I with characteristics X, and P (I, X) is the population of individuals with characteristics X in Region I. The interpretation of this decomposition is quite simple. The first portion:

$$
(2)\quad T(I, X)({}^{\circ}\,Ej(I, X)dIdX/{}^{\circ\circ}T(I, X)dIdX)
$$

is the baseline expenditures. It multiplies the share of total expenditures in the country on this good times the taxes paid by this individual. This is a baseline quantity of spending. It is supposed to reflect how much an individual would be expected to receive of expenditure on a commodity as a function of his tax revenues.

The second portion of the decomposition:

(3) $$((^{\circ} Ej(I, X)dI/^{\circ} P(I, X)dX) - (^{\circ}\,^{\circ}Ej(I, X)dIdX/^{\circ}T(I, X)dIdX))$$
$$(^{\circ}T(I, X)dI/^{\circ}P(I, X)dI))$$

represents the amount that the individual receives as a result of income transfers. The first term is simply the average expenditures on an individual with characteristics across the country. The second term is the total expenditures divided by total taxes in the country multiplied by total taxes in the country paid by individuals with characteristic X. This term lets us correct regional expenditures by the characteristics of the individual in the region.

The third part of the decomposition:

(4) $$(T(I,X) - {}^{\circ}T(I, X)dI/^{\circ}P(I, X)dI))\ )(^{\circ}\,^{\circ}Ej(I, X)dIdX/^{\circ\circ}T(I, X)dIdX)$$

represents the extra tax burden paid the individual in location one when compared to individuals with similar characteristics across the country (this is assumed to be zero in our estimates since we do not have location specific taxes).

The final portion of the decomposition:

(5) $$(Ej(I, X) - (^{\circ} Ej(I, X)dI/^{\circ} P(I, X)dX))$$

represents the extra amount individuals with characteristics X are receiving in that region over and above the national average. This term reflects the added spatial transfer to individuals in that region.

In order to perform this decomposition for regional aggregates, we can integrate equation (1) over X characteristics in each region (although this loses much of the point of these decompositions). This methodology, which is performed in the tables for current data, is useful and gives us an idea of the size of current total distortions. However, aggregating up masks potential distortions that exist for subgroups of the population. For example, if one region subsidizes the poor and another subsidizes the rich, then the aggregate spatial distortion may be zero. However, the total number of spatial distortions in the population might be quite large.

8

Lessons and Summary: The Public/Private Frontier in Urban Development

EDWARD L. GLAESER AND JOHN R. MEYER

This study was deliberately given an expansive title: "The Political Economy of Urban Development." The subtitle was at least a bit more modest: "Lessons derived from the Chilean Experience." In summing up, it seems best to proceed in reverse order, starting with the Chilean experience and proceeding to more general conclusions.

Of course, as noted in the very first chapter of this study, the possibility of developing more general conclusions from the Chilean experience depends to a considerable extent on how typical that experience might have been. This is particularly true for Santiago that accounts for so much of urban Chile and so much of the analyses reported here.

Every city has its unique physical and, usually, cultural characteristics. Santiago is no exception. For example, because of its physical location in a basin surrounded on one side by the towering and beautiful Andes and on another by a low-lying but not insignificant coastal range, Santiago's vulnerability to air pollution is matched by only a few other cities in the world.

The city's exposure to poor air and other sources of pollution has been intensified by Chile's rapid economic development. The country enjoyed almost two decades of rapid development in the late twentieth century, with remarkably few interruptions, though some of these interruptions were quite traumatic. Certainly, by the standards of Latin America, Chile's economic performance has been outstanding, probably the best in its region by most measures. Superior or equivalent rates of economic development in the past two or three decades of the twentieth century mostly are found only on the other edge of the Pacific Rim.

Significantly, Chile's economic transformation was apparently built on long-term structural reforms, rather than short-term expedients achieved by temporarily manipulating price-wage or other nominal monetary relationships. A leader in the privatization of state enterprises, Chile was among a small number of countries to explore and experiment with private sector provision of public infrastructures. Also, its highly successful pension reforms implemented in the 1980s are far reaching and have been widely studied and copied by both industrialized and developing countries. Chile may be the world's best case study of how, and possibly how not, to make the transition from a highly protected to an open economy. The distinctions made in Chilean public policy between foreign direct and portfolio investments may be instructive elsewhere as well. Finally, and perhaps most important, Chilean public policy almost invariably has emphasized the importance of competitive markets, even though that emphasis has sometimes led to temporarily perverse results as in the case of Santiago's buses (see Chapter 5).

Chile's economic successes in the last two decades might be described as an economic restoration rather than as economic development. Like its neighbor Argentina, Chile in the early part of the twentieth century enjoyed one of the world's highest standards of living. This is evidenced by its aging, but often still functional, infrastructure and the presence of a relatively well-developed and vital educational system. Not surprisingly therefore, Chile's stock of human capital seems relatively deep and broad, especially for a so-called less developed country.

In short, in many ways Chilean urban development has occurred in an unusual environment. In addition to rapid economic development, the country has enjoyed openness to structural reforms, at least in the general economy if not always at the local level. Competitive markets have been sought and emphasized. The physical environment of the nation's largest city might be described as fragile, being vulnerable to considerable air pollution. Finally, the legacy of infrastructure and human capital is remarkably rich.

Nevertheless, Chilean urban development also seems quite conventional in many ways. As noted in Chapter 1, the largest city, Santiago, accounts for a remarkably high percentage of the total national population, as is the case in the rest of Latin America and much of the third world. As in many countries, both developed and developing, urban development in Chile has been little guided by market forces; rather, primary reliance was placed on bureaucratic directives. In several of the sectors researched in this volume, this failure to use market signals was identified as a major source of problems. To the extent the Chilean experience was different, the question arises of why this happened in an economy that otherwise seemed dedicated to finding market solutions to public policy problems.

Apparently in Chile, as elsewhere, urban development has long been considered an activity characterized by many spillovers or externalities. Since people live at high densities in cities, the activities and decisions of different individuals are likely to have a substantial impact on others. Proceeding from this observation, central governments have commonly taken over the major responsibilities for urban development and planning, often responsibilities that in other sectors would be bequeathed to the private sector or to markets. As the World Bank's policy report on Urban Policy and Economic Development summarizes the situation:

> The urban development model of the post-war period in most countries has relied on central government finance and the technical capacity of public agencies. . . . Control of public investment even in large countries such as India and Indonesia was highly centralized. Urban planning tended to mirror state economic planning, with public control over most urban activity. Policy focused on public investment. It paid little regard to other critical responsibilities of local institutions, such as operation and maintenance of infrastructure, and establishing incentives required for private economic activities.[1]

As the World Bank report suggests, urban development could be characterized as one of the last remaining refuges of the command and control approach to economic decision making, especially since that approach has disappeared so substantially in so many other sectors. Accordingly, the central issue of the political economy of urban development is much the same as it is in so many other sectors: determining to what extent a transition from a command to a market economy is desirable and then how to do it. More precisely, it means determining what is best done by markets and the private sector and what is best retained as a public sector responsibility.

A common theme or presumption for most command to market transitions is that less government will be needed. While that may be so, some government activity and responsibilities will remain. Even though the government role in a market economy may be less than under central planning, some role is still necessary and it may need to be substantial. This may be true particularly for urban planning and development. As the discussion in the preceding chapters robustly suggests, internalizing all the many externalities of urban development so that the market can properly perform its functions, may be difficult or even impossible unless government intervenes. As a consequence, for better or worse, a government role in implementing urban devel-

1. International Bank for Reconstruction Development; Washington, D.C: 1991.

opment reforms and policies is almost unavoidable, perhaps even essential. The difficult question, as the Chilean experience amply illustrates, is defining exactly how much government involvement is needed and where. Indeed, the specific findings and attendant policy prescriptions for urban development in Chile almost all involve "fine tuning" the relationship between market solutions and government policies.

To illustrate, the principal findings (starting with Chapter 3 on the environment and proceeding through Chapter 7 on welfare policies), might be summarized as follows:

- Failure to price environmental damage leads to too much of certain high-polluting activities. Unless vigorously abated by government policies, these activities could pose very serious threats to Santiago's development and represent a substantial liability in a very few years.
- A more careful calibration of incremental benefits to incremental costs of different levels and types of infrastructure investments (e.g., sewage treatment) would probably yield much higher returns on given levels of investment than decisions dictated by arbitrary performance specifications (e.g., certain levels of water purity or air cleanup).
- The determination of urban transportation investments by hurdle rates rather than net present values, has led to over-investment in rail relative to highway modes so that capital for development of transportation infrastructures has not always been well allocated. In essence, urban transportation investments in Chile may have achieved the targeted rate of return for public infrastructure investments, but because of capital shortages (at the targeted rate) more could have been achieved by a more selective allocation of the available investment funds.
- The partial application of congestion pricing principles to urban buses (via franchise bidding) has greatly improved traffic flows in downtown Santiago and suggests that the extension of congestion pricing to all Santiago's central area traffic would yield even larger benefits
- The failure to account fully for extra commuting, environmental, and social costs in public housing location choices has led to inefficient peripheral locations for such housing in Chilean cities, particularly within Santiago.
- Regional development location distortions created by government policies exist in Chile but are probably not too great, especially when netted against one another.
- To the extent that interregional redistributions exist in Chile, the apparent winners are the extreme northern and southern provinces and, to a lesser extent, the Santiago metropolitan district. The provinces associated with the second and third largest cities, Valparaiso and Concepcion, seem to be the losers. These results may reflect the deliberate intent of public policy as motivated by considerations of nation building or national defense.

Obviously, these findings are not necessarily all that unique to Chile. Similar or parallel problems might be identified in almost any similar survey of urban development problems almost anywhere in the world. A crucial general point, though, does emerge from the specific sectoral findings: much could be achieved by better matching of the economic margins, that is of benefits and costs (including all costs, social as well as private). This brings us back to the basic economic welfare theorems, enunciated in Chapter 2. As a corollary to this general point, incentive or principal agent control problems often exist within government bureaucracies, moving them well off production frontiers where best productive practices are achieved. Finally, one other conclusion strongly emerges from the Chilean experience as well as from casual and analytical observations elsewhere: urban development patterns are easily distorted, diminishing or subverting the achievement of various public policy goals, both social and economic. The law of unintended side effects can sometimes hold with a vengeance, as is apparently the case with housing policy in Chile.

In many ways the current political economy of urban development, both in Chile and elsewhere, might be seen as a historical legacy. Marginal cost pricing for the use of urban facilities was beyond technical capability when most cities were founded. Given the extensive externalities involved in urban living, a command and control approach may have been the only feasible way to proceed. Furthermore, cost and benefit measures were often crude at best. Political centralization and over-reliance on government only made the situation worse, as noted in the World Bank report.

The historical tendency, therefore, was to use quantitative controls, such as zoning or building restrictions or "purity" standards, rather than prices or market mechanisms. Implementing user charges, especially those varying by congestion or intensity of use, could have been highly costly economically or administratively as well as politically. Meters were costly (or in some cases not yet invented), so flat rates often were used even where metering otherwise might be deemed sensible (e.g., to charge out water usage). Charging by the length of a transit trip, let alone by the time of day of the trip, requires a very honest and responsible citizenry or extensive enforcement costs. Indeed, only recently have electric and other utilities devised administratively feasible means to differentiate charges for use of their facilities at different times of day. In general, the technologies for better incorporating marginal costs into prices have only emerged during the last two decades or so of the twentieth century. An arbitrary flat rate user charge or a command control approach (financed by broad-based general taxes) was therefore often unavoidable, even if the will had existed to do otherwise (which in most cases it probably did not).

Furthermore, flat rates, unrelated to marginal costs, often had great political appeal. Flat rates may have appeared more egalitarian, though perhaps falsely so. They were certainly simpler to explain and administer than the available alternatives. Flat rates also were sometimes seen as a vehicle for building community identity and fostering development (as in the famous case of the nickel fare for the New York subway).

The obvious question then is to how to best undo this historical legacy: How should the transition from a command to a market economy be made? How can society avail itself of the burgeoning opportunities to better match marginal benefits, costs, and incentives, while still meeting broader equity or social policy goals? It should always be remembered that efficiency goals are not necessarily incompatible with other goals, especially environmental.

A natural place to look for answers is obviously at other efforts for dismantling command-control systems. Because of the break up of the Soviet Union and the widespread experimentations with privatizations elsewhere, a plethora of potentially cogent experiences is available. The relevant sample, though, is hardly so limited. Deregulations, denationalizations, decentralizations, and deconglomerations—all popular in many market economies over the past two decades—might be viewed as exercises in dismantling command-control systems or substituting market choices for administrative decisions.

In short, both the public and private sectors in both socialist and market economies have been experimenting, sometimes quite extensively and intensively, with different organizational structures for large-scale economic organizations. For the most part, these experiments often have moved away from broad social or political control to more localized or individualistic structures. Many seemingly unrelated processes—from privatization to corporate governance reforms to deregulation—are related: they all deal with defining the division of responsibility in a society between private individuals and the general body politic for control of large-scale economic activities.

Certain standard approaches to effectuating these repositionings or restructurings have emerged.[2] Each of these tends to make rather different demands on government, as well as having different degrees of applicability to particular urban development problems.

Perhaps the most widely advocated reform for improving the response of government to local urban problems and needs is decentralization, that is as-

---

2. Much of the discussion of corporatization and privatization in the remainder of this chapter is adapted from John S. Strong and J.R. Meyer, *Moving to Market: Restructuring Transport in the former Soviet Union* (Cambridge, Mass.: Harvard University Press, 1995) and José A. Gomez-Ibanez and J.R. Meyer, *Going Private: The International Experience with Transport Privatization* (Washington, D.C.: Brookings Institution, 1994).

signing more responsibility to local levels of government. The case for localization of authority is strong in general, but not universal. For example, the determination of the levels of social welfare may be better done centrally. Nevertheless, as noted in several of the preceding chapters, achieving the correct balance of local autonomy is critical for long-term elimination of spatial distortions.

The first major argument for a decentralized urban federalism stems from Tiebout, who argued that a large number of local governments allow voters to choose among a variety of service levels.[3] These options accommodate the variety of tastes in the population and allow all people to have the level of services that they want. Some districts exist with high taxes and excellent local services; others with low taxes and few services. Those individuals who desire high levels of services migrate to the more expensive communities and those individuals with a preference for fewer services move to the cheaper communities.

This system has the obvious advantage of allowing more tastes to be accommodated than in the fully centralized bureaucracy with a fixed level of services. It also has an advantage of allowing migration to signal to the government how much service is desired. For example, if a region is charging high taxes and providing extremely good education, and many people stream into that region, then other regions (and possibly the centralized government) will realize that there is more demand for higher levels of education.

The benefits of local provision can be mimicked by the centralized government and possibly even improved upon by the private sector (as discussed below). The centralized government can create separate spatial authorities that provide different levels of services in different spaces. However, this artificial localization of authority is never as effective, since the central government officials are not fully beholden to the local voters and do not face the discipline that comes from local elections. At the same time, private sector provision of these services might provide as much variety and good incentives as possible.

As long as citizens and firms have the ability to leave localities, their migration should punish government incompetence, depriving ill-governed localities of both prestige and tax base. Hence, emigration serves as a disciplinary device that limits the degree of governmental inability. By contrast, migration will not create many incentives for the national government since intercountry migration is generally quite restricted. Highly localized authority also creates incentives for voters to be better informed on local elections. Indeed, U.S. history suggests that an increasing share of government control at the Federal level has been accompanied by a decrease of attention to local elections.

3. Tiebout (circa 1956), *Journal of Political Economy.*

In the case of a completely benevolent and responsive government, localization of authority also helps by simply increasing the flows of information between voters and politicians. For example, ministers in Santiago can try to learn about localized needs but their knowledge is limited by their physical distance from the locality and by their extensive areas of responsibility. Smaller authorities are able to have closer connections to the needs and desires of their voters.

Of course, this benefit is most important in government services where knowledge of consumer desires is particularly important. Schooling and health are likely candidates for these benefits. In contrast, defense or high level research are not activities where the tastes of consumers are likely to be well informed so there may be fewer gains from gathering accurate information about those tastes. The decree to which this benefit operates is also a function of the political system. The more the political system is designed to accumulate knowledge about voter preferences (i.e. the more democratic the system), the higher will be the benefits accruing from localization.

Government, like industry, also grows through its knowledge and is benefited by innovations. As in industry, a large single government is not ideal for the spreading of innovation (see Glaeser et al. (1992) for empirical evidence). Smaller units lead to a faster rate of growth in governmental innovations.

This effect comes from two forces. The first is that more competition creates stronger incentives to innovate. A second force connecting innovation with smaller units is that multiple units allow for a greater range of evidence on how innovations work. When there are many small firms each attempting different modes of production, many more innovations will occur and much more evidence will be produced on which innovations succeed. Likewise in governments, when there are many units, each of which is free to experiment, then there will be much more evidence on what type of government policy is successful.

Another, generally less important, benefit of local authorities is that they can serve as a check on national governments. Localities compete among themselves (as discussed above) but they also compete with national authorities. Frequently government services can be provided either at the local or the national level (funding for higher education in the United States often comes from all levels of jurisdiction). This type of competition can provide better incentives for the central government. Also, if localities are able to evade national regulation, this ability puts a natural ceiling on the level of national regulation. Through local evasion, any exceptionally stringent national regulation is limited. This, in effect, means that any regulation requires both local and national support to be implemented.

Centralization, though, also has its advantages. The most ancient, and perhaps important, gain from centralized authority is that cross-regional spillovers can be internalized. Regional areas are obviously only going to care about the welfare of their own community. When the actions of their inhabitants affect other areas, then local governments may not be efficient. The cross-regional externalities will not be internalized.

An obvious example of this is pollution regulation. Frequently, smog travels across borders and the failure of one community to regulate its industries may affect other communities. Local governments will only consider the benefits to themselves of limiting the amount of pollution in their own community. They will not consider the benefits received by or costs imposed on other communities. The net result is that too little pollution control is enacted.

The general solution to this effect is that the government or other regulatory body should be influential enough that these externalities are internalized within the relevant jurisdiction. This suggests that jurisdictions should be tailored to the geographic unit containing all of the effects of an action. Actions with particularly large spillovers may need to be centrally provided.

Provision of public goods also should be carried out by jurisdictions large enough to internalize all (or at least most) of the benefits of those public goods being provided. A classic example of a public good that needs to be provided nationally is defense. The benefits of defense apply to everyone equally and the right decisions about the level of defense must be made by the entire effected population. Other examples exist of semipublic goods that seem to merit national provision (perhaps some parks), but these seem relatively rare. Certain regulations, especially those creating uniform networks (highways, telecommunications, public health, and the legal system) are government services (or more precisely standards set by the government) that resemble public goods that are often best done on a national level.

Certain actions of government also may display physical (or other) returns to scale. If the government actually produces goods for public consumption (like nationalized industries) then the production of those goods often will benefit from centralized production. Large factories will enable production to spread fixed costs over a wider number of goods. Examples of scale economies include activities in health and schooling, such as large hospitals and universities. Scale economies, though, may be rarer than they seem to be. Costs from overly large production also abound. But to the extent that returns to scale exist, they may justify government provision of a service or government regulation of that service.

Highly skilled or knowledgeable government agents are also a type of fixed cost that can be shared over multiple jurisdictions. If a particular disease is rare in the country, then only a handful of experts in that disease will be needed and not an expert for every region. Likewise, if a certain governmental problem comes up only rarely, then a country may need only a single administrator to handle that problem.

Another version of this same effect comes with rare services and learning-by-doing. Learning-by-doing just means that specific skills are developed by experience. One becomes a better pianist by playing the piano repeatedly. Likewise, one becomes better at deciding intricate patent decisions by handling multiple patent problems.

The handling of a government service by a single national agency ensures that the members of that agency quickly will gain experience in the provision of that service. This centralization also ensures that the skills acquired in this learning process will be applied as often as possible to the service in question. The costs should be minimized as government agents use the benefits of their previous experience.

Quite strikingly, many of the advantages of centralization might just as easily, and perhaps more efficiently, be achieved by the selective privatization of some local government activities, particularly scale economies and learning–by-doing. This would happen, for example, if just a few private suppliers emerged for particular activities or services. Internalizing externalities and the provision of public goods, on the other hand, almost certainly require some centralization of government responsibilities.

Although much discussed, privatization has been little used in strictly urban contexts. Clues about its applicability to urban problems must be sought elsewhere.

Privatizations are generally of three basic types: (1) transfer of state-owned enterprises (SOEs) to private ownership; (2) operation and construction by the private sector (under concession or franchise) of infrastructures; and (3) contracting out by government of routine traditional functions (e.g., equipment maintenance, catering, etc.) previously performed within government. The third of these forms is by far the most common in urban applications.

The motives and considerations behind these different forms of privatization usually differ. The privatization of an SOE is usually motivated by a desire to achieve greater efficiency in the enterprise's activities or to realize a cash windfall or revenues that would not otherwise be available to government. Privatization of SOEs can also often have an ideological element, such as broadening capitalistic ownership in a society. In the urban context, as the Chilean experience illustrates, the usual state-owned enterprises available for privatization are transit operations, housing, land development, and various construction activities. The list can vary widely from one situation to another, but the essentials are usually much the same.

Government franchising of infrastructure maintenance and development is usually undertaken so as to expand the resources—financial, managerial, technical—available for such purposes. Efficiency gains are also often expected but are usually not so central as with privatization of an SOE. Privatization of infrastructures also may be seen as a way of finessing certain environmental, distributional, or locational issues that often complicate new urban development undertakings; for example, the private enterprise is often able to pursue buyouts or other accommodations that are not always available to government agencies.

Commonly cited possibilities for private franchising of urban infrastructure development include transit and highways (particularly very expensive bridges or tunnels). Private franchises or private concessions also are increasingly suggested for maintenance or development of high performance urban highways. Water and sewage systems have long been developed privately, in some countries representing the dominant form of organization. Some airports have been privately developed. In the United States, private development of what is essentially public housing has sometimes been encouraged through use of tax incentives. Local area telephone networks often have been privately developed; furthermore, where they were not, they have increasingly been privatized. Cable and wireless local telecom networks have been widely developed by the private sector. Even some fire departments and prisons have been developed privately. While not all of these efforts could be classified as successful, they do illustrate the breadth of possibilities.[4]

The contracting out of routine activities mainly represents an attempt to achieve economies through efficiency gains (e.g. via scale economies or learning by doing) or factor cost reductions. Such privatizations are often seen as a means of avoiding civil service and other government restrictions and tend to be relatively simple in concept and execution. For the most part, they involve fairly straightforward contracts between a government agency and a private supplier of products or services. The contracts usually can be done efficiently for relatively short periods, like a year or two. Unlike the private provision of infrastructures, large commitments of specialized capital normally are not required nor are there normally large uncertainties about the probable costs. As a consequence, complex contractual or regulatory arrangements for dealing with unexpected cost overruns, inflation, or other such contingencies are rarely needed.

Some procurement of supplies or services from outside sources will be needed by almost any government. Substituting contractual procurement from outside for in-house provision largely represents extending already existing practices, though possibly on a greatly enhanced scale. Contracting out

4. John D. Donahue, *The Privatization Decision: Public Ends, Private Means.* New York: Basic Books, 1989.

is only privatization when private contractors truly replace government provisions, not when private contractors are really acting just to increase the overall scope of government. A politically active trade union of the relevant government workers also will help draw attention. Accordingly, proposals to contract out local government responsibilities for operating schools or prisons or for performing law enforcement or fire protection usually will attract public interest and be identified as "privatizations." On the other hand, contracting out food services, mailrooms, and similar such routine activities, widely done in the private as well as the public sector, probably will not attract much attention. The provision of hospital care, rubbish removal, and other such services widely associated with public duties or needs but often done by private as well as by public vendors, will fall somewhere between.

Whatever the type of privatization or its motive, privatization almost always involves a shift in government orientation away from operating responsibilities and toward monitoring. Privatization also often requires that some sort of contract between the government and the private sector be established. These contracts can be very simple, as in the case of contracting out for procurement of standard products or services, or quite complex, as in the private provision of infrastructures. Contracts with privatized SOEs can vary widely, with the complexity commonly depending on the degree to which government is concerned about regulating the activities of the newly privatized enterprise.

Whether simple or complex, such contracts require, in turn, that property and other legal rights be defined.[5] These legal arrangements, in most instances, will be more a responsibility of national than local government. Accordingly, local government's possibilities of substituting private for public undertakings will depend on the larger societal milieu. Local options will sometimes be limited.

Corporatization represents something of a hybrid or compromise between privatization and continued government operation. With corporatization an activity is typically spun off from a government ministry or civil service and established as a separate corporate operating entity. As a freestanding entity, a corporatized enterprise is expected to be better able to tap into private capital markets and to have better defined and focused managerial responsibilities than a typical government ministry or civil service. In the urban context, corporatizations are commonly found in the form of toll authorities or port authorities established for the development and operation of particular facili-

5. See R. Coase, *The Firm and the Market in the Law* (Chicago: Chicago University Press, 1988); Douglas North, *Institutions, Institutional Change and Economic Performance* (Cambridge: Cambridge University Press, 1990)

ties. Their application, therefore, is much like that of privatization for the development of infrastructure facilities. In the United States, corporatizations are more local government phenomena than national.

By retaining government as a major owner, corporatization may attenuate the need for the economic regulation of prices, service offerings, etc. Corporatization also seems to eliminate some of the principal agent problems encountered with privatization and regulation, since government is both owner and regulator. Corporatization also may finesse financing, legal, and property rights problems that almost inevitably arise with privatization.

Unfortunately, if badly done, corporatization can combine some of the worst of both government ownership and regulation. The history of corporatized special authorities (for ports, airports, toll bridges, toll ways, etc.) in U.S. urban areas is replete with political maneuvering of an almost mythical scale and is perhaps most richly reflected in the life and times of Robert Moses (who headed many such special authorities in and around greater New York City.)[6] Furthermore, the government still remains the owner with all that implies about various politically sensitive responsibilities. With government ownership, the corporatized enterprise may still look upon the government as a financial source of last resort. So may also many client or associated stakeholder groups. A conduit thus might be established for private suppliers and other stakeholders to "feed at the public trough" more subtly and less obviously than otherwise.

In urban applications, corporatization is often viewed as a device for achieving a closer tie between the source of funding for a public project and the actual expenditure. The earmarked public trust fund (e.g., for highway or airport development) financed by user fees is obviously an alternative route to much the same goal. Although almost universally deplored by economists,[7] the earmarked trust fund does seem to have advantages in terms of political acceptability. That is, people seem more willing to accept additional taxes when applied as user fees to finance specific and visible improvements.[8] An efficiency loss, of course, is created because a trust fund is restricted in its use, thereby attenuating some of the mutability advantages of unrestricted funding. In short, trust funds for the development of particular facilities often involve a tradeoff between efficiency and political acceptability. Corpora-

---

6. Robert A. Law, *The Power Broker Robert Moses and the Fall of New York* (New York: Vintage Books, Division of Random House, 1974)

7. Jose A. Gomez-Ibanez, "The Political Economy of Highway Tolls and Congestion Pricing," *Transportation Quarterly*, vol. 46, no.3, July 1992, pp.343–360.

8. Jose A. Gomez-Ibanez and John R. Meyer, "Alternatives for Urban Bus Services: An International Perspective on the British Reforms," *Transportation Reviews*, 1997, vol.17, no.1, pp. 17–29.

tization in the form of a toll (see earlier question) or port authority not only may sublimate some of these public finance issues, but also bring about some improvements in managerial efficiency (i.e., improvements in the technical efficiency with which the enterprise is conducted).

However, privatization or corporatization may not be needed to achieve a better match between prices, costs, and incentives. An alternative would be simply to improve government policies and performance. As noted, decentralization of government responsibilities is one possible route to such improvements. In more ambitious formulations, this is sometimes described as "re-engineering" or "re-inventing" government. Like decentralization, privatized or corporatized activities can provide useful yardsticks or role models for such efforts. This suggests a mixed strategy in which some selected decentralizations, privatizations, and corporatizations provide feedback to improve public sector performance.

Intriguingly, the highly important technical efficiency gains that have motivated so many privatizations and corporatizations not only seem to have been widely achieved but also to have spilled over into the public sectors "left behind."[9] For example, when urban bus services in Great Britain were deregulated and privatized everywhere except in London, London services achieved approximately the same technical efficiency gains as those realized elsewhere in the country. London buses were forced by the Thatcher Government to contract out a larger percentage of their activities than previously but were exempted from deregulation and privatization. A key element for achieving efficiency gains in many cases seems to be change almost for its own sake and suggests the wisdom of the old business motto "If in doubt reorganize." If the reorganization also intensifies competition, or at least produces some organizational rivalries (as it certainly did in the British bus case), better performance seems likely.

Many of the specific findings of the Chilean study, in fact, lead to suggestions about how public policies and government operations could be improved by relatively modest or marginal adaptations: e.g., by eliminating unintended incentives for housing programs to move to peripheral areas (perhaps by the greater use of vouchers and private markets for achieving public housing goals); by more use of congestion charges for allowing access to central business areas of cities (through the use of auctions or other special licensing schemes as is already done for buses in Santiago); by eliminating unintended tax advantages or other subsidies for downtown parking; establish-

9. Peter R. White, "Three Years Experience of Bus Service Deregulation in Britain," paper presented at the International Conference in Privatization and Regulation in Passenger Transportation, Tampere, Finland, June 1991.

ng investment priorities for urban infrastructures by maximizing net present values rather than simply exceeding a hurdle rate; and by shifting to marginal calculations of benefits relative to costs to determine investments in environmental improvements.

While it can be argued that all these policy improvements might be effectuated without the massive restructurings of widespread decentralization, privatization, or corporatization, it might nevertheless be easier to do so if some such restructurings take place. As already mentioned, decentralization, privatization, and corporatization can provide yardstick and rivalry benefits not otherwise readily available. Evidence also suggests that private organizations tend to be more innovative and receptive to new technologies than government operations. Due to the discipline of the profit motive, private organizations may think more instinctively in terms of marginal trade-offs than government agencies.

All this suggests the crucial questions of how to define and identify appropriate government structures. There are two major areas in which an optimal government structure can be judged: (1) to what extent does it represent the goals of the people and (2) what kind of incentives does it give to government agents for carrying out those goals. In a sense these can be broken into an ideological area of government, i.e. goals, and a competence area of government, i.e. incentives. These two areas certainly overlap. They also are often complementary; good goals are useless without sufficient incentives for competence.

Voting is the primary political mechanism in most modern democracies. It serves as a means of connecting governance with voter preferences. Democracy acts to reveal those preferences and assigns a set of weights to the different views within the community. It also can discipline bad governments and create incentives.

If local government officials like to manage as much as possible, they will act in a way that maximizes their revenues (following Brennan and Buchanan).[10] This suggests that taxes should be designed so that local governments can affect the amount of revenues that they raise. Pooling revenues from multiple locations and then redistributing those revenues across municipalities directly works against these incentives. The more that local government revenues are directly tied to the local tax base, the more likely that revenues will provide an incentive for efficiency.

This view suggests that optimal taxes are those that tax activities which are a good indicator of government competence. For example if property values reflect governmental competence more than local earnings, then local prop-

10. Brennan and Buchanan, 1979

erty taxes will create better incentives than local income taxes. Taxes based on various commercial activities also will provide strong incentives for local government if those commercial activities are highly reliant on local government action.

Local government officials thus have the natural incentive of elections and the less natural incentive of tax revenues. Lobbyists also can provide a series of incentives for local government officials. Some of these incentives may be desirable for society, while others may not. Still other incentives may be created by the reputable concerns or larger ambitions of government officials.

Incentives also can be created if higher levels of government have the ability to reward or punish the actions of lower levels of government. Examples of these institutions are national grants to local governments or appointment to national positions for previously local officials. However, one problem with giving the national government the ability to make interjurisdictional transfers is that local officials may spend much of their time lobbying for a larger share of these funds. The national leaders must be trusted to a very high degree for this to be a sensible policy.

A final critical issue in urban political economy is determining the optimal relationship between levels of government. Close coordination between levels and branches of government has obvious benefits. For example, some connection between local and national government may allow the national government to influence the local government into internalizing the externalities of its actions. Close coordination also may allow units of government to share the fixed costs of public goods. Informational coordination between levels of government may allow knowledge to be dispersed adequately. Finally, coordination may be a way that local risks (either to the community or to the government) are shared.

There can be costs, though, to overly strong coordination between levels of government or across jurisdictions. As already noted, one of the great advantages of multiple jurisdictions is competition. When coordination is easy, then it is likely that the competition between governments will slacken. Perfect coordination means that cartel-like behavior is likely, with governments maximizing their joint surplus. The optimal structure of government should balance these costs of coordination with the benefits of internalizing cross-jurisdiction externalities.

A final crucial issue is that of intergovernmental transfers. One of the most common arguments made by members of the central government against granting authority to local governments is that those local governments have not reached standards of competence high enough to trust them with autonomy. While it is certainly true that there are dangers involved in giving authority to incompetent local governments, it is also true that a rational procedure or test must be designed in order to determine local governments' competence. In Chile, as in most countries, funds are given to the local authority from the national government. While occasionally this has value and allows the national government to correct for externalities or equalize social transfers over space, there also can be large costs attached to this type of policy. A tendency may be created for localities to be supplicants who do what the national government wants (or lose funding), which eliminates healthy competition between branches of government.

In general, the gains from local autonomy are likely to be largest when combined with reforms that strengthen the incentives facing local officials. The more institutions that are put in place to limit the negative externalities that one region can impose on another, the more likely that the switch to local autonomy will be effective. The move to local autonomy should, therefore, probably proceed at several levels simultaneously.

A final issue to consider in the transition to local authority is the interaction between jurisdictions. A spatial distortion is created when one locality is reformed and efficient but a neighboring locality is kept totally subservient to the central government and is less adequate. Individuals will migrate from the less autonomous region to the more autonomous to receive better government. This suggests simultaneity in reforming areas that are likely to provide migrants to each other.

To summarize, the urban development problem often represents a special case of the general class of transitions from command to market systems. As in other such transitions, the role of government does not disappear, but the nature or character of the government role does change. For example, the transition is often aided by a decentralization of government responsibilities. Furthermore, with a greater use of markets, the government's roles as auditor, regulator, contractor, jurist, overseer, rule-maker, and monitor all seem to increase. On the other hand, government should become less involved in the management and operation of many activities.

This change in role is important. It means that central government in particular, and local government to a lesser extent, focus on creating a general milieu conducive to efficient urban development, rather than being concerned with micro management of such development. Broad oversight is substituted for detailed planning and operational management. People with legal and accounting skills are recruited to government rather than people with a managerial bent. Managerial and entrepreneurial types are left to pursue their self-interest in the private sector, subject to the general rules and regulations established by government and the legal system. To the extent that government remains involved in operational details, this is likely to be done better at the local than the national level.

Indeed, one of the most important policy conclusions from this study, at least in Chile, is that there are many services with strong benefits from localized authority and these services are not always determined locally. Services that might best be provided locally are those (1) where tastes differ over space, or (2) when eliciting tastes is difficult. Also, those services where there are not strong returns to scale or cross-jurisdiction externalities should be decentralized so that localities can offer differentiated products and compete with one another. Furthermore, privatization and corporatization are alternative, and often complimentary, devices for achieving these same goals.

In essence, the critical distinction is not so much how much government there is but rather what kind of government should be established. This means better defining the frontier between the public and private sectors. In many ways the quintessential role of government when pursuing a market approach is to create an environment where determinations of which sector or level of government does what best can be done efficiently. It seems difficult to imagine how, without central government involvement, many of the larger externalities of pollution, aesthetic, and environmental considerations can be properly internalized.

A large remaining question is whether society will like the "brave new world" of a more market-determined and decentralized urban development with marginal benefits and user charges more closely associated with marginal costs.[11] We really do not know what that world might be. The urban settlements that emerge from a more market-determined equilibrium might be more dispersed—or more crowded. Different individuals also may evaluate these developments quite differently. Processing and politically adjudicating these differences ultimately may be the most important chores of government. Certainly, such adjudications are likely to generate some very large issues of urban political economy.

References

Brennan, G., and Buchanan, J. 1979. "The Logic of Tax Limits: Alternative Constitutional Constraints on the Power to Tax." *National Tax Journal* 32 (2): 11–22.

Coase, Ronald H. 1988. *The Firm, the Market and the Law.* Chicago: University of Chicago Press.

Donahue, John D. 1989. *The Privatization Decision: Public Ends, Private Means.* New York, NY: Basic Books.

---

11. Some thoughts on these possibilities, (not necessarily fully intended or advocated), might be found in Joel Garreau, *Edge City* (New York: Doubleday (Anchor Books), 1988).

Garreau, Joel. 1988. *Edge City.* New York: Doubleday (Anchor Books).

Glaeser, Edward L.; Kallal, Hedi D.; Scheinkman, Jose A.; and Andrei Shleifer. 1992. "Growth in Cities." *Journal of Political Economy* 100(6): 1126–1152.

Gomez-Ibanez, Jose A. 1992. "The Political Economy of Highway Tolls and Congestion Pricing." *Transportation Quarterly* 46(3), July 1992, p. 343–360.

Gomez-Ibanez, Jose A. and John R. Meyer. 1997. "Alternatives for Urban Bus Services: An International Perspective on the British Reforms." *Transportation Reviews* 17(1): 17–29.

Gomez-Ibanez, Jose A. and J.R. Meyer. 1994. *Going Private: The International Experience with Transport Privatization.* Washington, DC: Brookings Institution.

Law, Robert A. 1974. *The Power Broker: Robert Moses and the Fall of New York.* New York, NY: Vintage Books, Division of Random House.

North, Douglas. 1990. *Institutions, Institutional Change and Economic Performance.* Cambridge: Cambridge University Press.

Strong, John S. and J. R. Meyer. 1995. *Moving to Market: Restructuring Transport in the Former Soviet Union.* Cambridge, MA: Harvard University Press.

Tiebout, C. 1958. "A Pure Theory of Local Expenditures." *Journal of Political Economy* 64: 416–424.

White, Peter R. 1991. "Three Years Experience of Bus Service Deregulation in Britain." paper presented at the International Conference in Privatization and Regulation in Passenger Transportation, Tampere, Finland, (June).